P9-CFU-817

INTERNET MARKETING FOR YOUR TOURISM BUSINESS

Other Titles of Interest From Maximum Press

For more information, visit our Web site at
www.maxpress.com
or e-mail us at *moreinfo@maxpress.com*

INTERNET MARKETING FOR YOUR TOURISM BUSINESS

Proven Techniques for Promoting
Tourist-based Businesses Over the Internet

Susan Sweeney, C.A.

MAXIMUM PRESS
605 Silverthorn Road
Gulf Breeze, FL 32561
(850) 934-0819
www.maxpress.com

Publisher: Jim Hoskins

Manager of Finance/Administration: Donna Tryon

Production Manager: ReNae Grant

Cover Design: Lauren Smith Designs

Compositor: PageCrafters Inc.

Copyeditor: Andrew Potter

Proofreader: Kim Stefansson

Indexer: Susan Olason

Printer: P.A. Hutchison

This publication is designed to provide accurate and authoritative information in regard to the subject matter covered. It is sold with the understanding that the publisher is not engaged in rendering professional services. If legal, accounting, medical, psychological, or any other expert assistance is required, the services of a competent professional person should be sought. ADAPTED FROM A DECLARATION OF PRINCIPLES OF A JOINT COMMITTEE OF THE AMERICAN BAR ASSOCIATION AND PUBLISHERS.

Copyright 2000 by Maximum Press.

All rights reserved. Published simultaneously in Canada.

Reproduction or translation of any part of this work beyond that permitted by Section 107 or 108 of the 1976 United States Copyright Act without the permission of the copyright owner is unlawful. Requests for permission or further information should be addressed to the Permissions Department, Maximum Press.

Recognizing the importance of preserving what has been written, it is a policy of Maximum Press to have books of enduring value published in the United States printed on acid-free paper, and we exert our best efforts to that end.

Library of Congress Cataloging-in-Publication Data

Sweeney, Susan, 1956-

   Internet marketing for your tourism business: proven techniques for promoting tourist-based businesses over the Internet / Susan Sweeney.

      p. cm.

   Includes index.

   ISBN 1-885068-47-6 (pbk: acid-free paper)

   1. Internet marketing. 2. Tourism--Marketing. I. Title.

HF5415.1265 .S934 2000

338.4'0688--dc21

                                                            00-009769

Acknowledgements

Thanks so much to my dynamite team at Connex Network—Ed Dorey, Andy MacLellan, Raland Kinley, and Lynn Wilson. Your constant enthusiasm and tireless effort on this book and for our varied Internet marketing projects is much appreciated. Never a dull moment around our office!

I would also like to extend gratitude and appreciation to Stefan Gashus, CA for his valuable contribution to the e-commerce section of this book.

Thanks to Jim Hoskins and Donna Tryon at Maximum Press for making this a reality and being such great people to deal with.

Thanks to Brooke O'Donnell at Independent Publishers Group for the great job on distribution.

Thanks to ReNae Grant at PageCrafters for her patience and guidance and making everything look great.

Special thanks to my husband Miles and our three wonderful children Kaitlyn, Kara, and Andrew for their love, encouragement, and support. Love you more than the last number!

Special thanks to my mom and dad, Olga and Leonard Dooley, for always being there and for instilling in me the confidence to know that I can do anything I set my mind to. It's amazing what can be done when you "know you can."

And very special recognition to my "Nanny," the greatest in the world, who was always such a great role model.

Disclaimer

The purchase of computer software or hardware is an important and costly business decision. While the author and publisher of this book have made reasonable efforts to ensure the accuracy and timeliness of the information contained herein, the author and publisher assume no liability with respect to loss or damage caused or alleged to be caused by reliance on any information contained herein and disclaim any and all warranties, expressed or implied, as to the accuracy or reliability of said information.

This book is not intended to replace the manufacturer's product documentation or personnel in determining the specifications and capabilities of the products mentioned in this book. The manufacturer's product documentation should always be consulted, as the specifications and capabilities of computer hardware and software products are subject to frequent modification. The reader is solely responsible for the choice of computer hardware and software. All configurations and applications of computer hardware and software should be reviewed with the manufacturer's representatives prior to choosing or using any computer hardware and software.

Trademarks

The words contained in this text which are believed to be trademarked, service marked, or otherwise to hold proprietary rights have been designated as such by use of initial capitalization. No attempt has been made to designate as trademarked or service marked any personal computer words or terms in which proprietary rights might exist. Inclusion, exclusion, or definition of a word or term is not intended to affect, or to express judgment upon, the validity of legal status of any proprietary right which may be claimed for a specific word or term.

Table of Contents

Chapter 3:
Designing Your Site for Search Engine Prominence 41

Chapter 4:
Search Engine and Directory Submission Strategies 64

Chapter 5:
Using Tourism Newsgroups
to Reach Your Target Market   **122**

Chapter 6:
Utilizing Signature Files
To Increase Web Site Traffic   144

Chapter 7:
The E-mail Advantage   154

Chapter 8:
Mailing Lists—Reach Out to Your Visitors　　　　175

Chapter 9:
Grand Opening Tips for You
Web Site Virtual Launch   203

Chapter 10:
Develop a Dynamite Links Strategy   207

Chapter 11:
Winning Awards/Cool Sites and More   226

Chapter 12:
Maximizing Promotion with Meta-Indexes   240

Chapter 13:
Online Advertising   259

Chapter 14:
Associate and Affiliate Programs 292

Chapter 15:
The Cybermall Advantage   312

Chapter 16:
E-commerce—Accept Online Reservations   **331**

Chapter 17:
Keep 'Em Coming Back   356

Chapter 18:
Maximizing Media Relations   380

Chapter 19:
Online Publications   402

Chapter 20:
Web Rings as a Promotion Tool   421

Chapter 21:
Effective Offline Promotion   437

Introduction

"We are crossing a technology threshold that will forever change the way we learn, work, socialize, and shop. It will affect all of us, and businesses of every type, in ways far more pervasive than most people realize."

Bill Gates
Comdex 1994

Over the course of the last year I have given many seminars and participated in a number of industry specific conferences always speaking on my favorite topic—Internet marketing. People always like to see information and examples relevant to their particular industry. I've also received lots of feedback from individuals who have read and enjoyed *101 Ways to Promote Your Web Site*. Often included in their remarks were comments like "I wish there was a book like this specific to our industry."

This is the first book in a series of industry-specific Internet marketing books. Each book will encompass the in-depth material presented in *101 Ways to Promote Your Web Site*, reworked to contain comprehensive information and examples specific to the industry being discussed.

So, why did I choose to do tourism first? Internet marketing seems to be a natural for this industry. According to the Travel Industry Association of America (*http://www.tia.org*)

"the number of online travelers has grown 190 percent from 29 million in 1996 to 85 million in 1999."

They also state that the

"correlation between the online population and travel is so strong that almost all Internet users are also travelers with 93 percent of Internet users (91 million U.S. adults) responding that they took at least one trip of 100 miles or more, one-way, away from home in 1999." The growth of

the tourism industry online continues to expand at a rapid pace."

The phenomenal boom in web site creation and the explosive growth of online traffic has intensified the battle for the consumer's time and attention. The secondary component or required follow-on to web site design and development involves developing comprehensive online marketing strategies to capture online market share. The need for information and advice on developing Internet marketing strategies is tremendous.

Building a web site is just the first step. Driving targeted traffic to your site takes knowledge, planning, time and effort. If you are intent on maintaining a competitive advantage, then you need to build the traffic to your site by implementing an effective Internet marketing strategy.

This book is meant to be a guide in marketing your tourism operation online. It offers comprehensive, hands-on, step-by-step advice for building web site traffic using hundreds of proven tips, tools, techniques, and industry specific examples to achieve optimal results. You will find out how to:

- Make your site unique, attract new visitors and keep them coming back

- Prepare and submit to hundreds of search engines and directories to be listed in the top search results

- Maximize your web site promotion using meta-indexes

- Pull traffic to your site by implementing a personalized, targeted e-mail campaign

- Develop an effective banner ad campaign to draw the right customer to your site

- Use Newsgroups and mailing lists to communicate with your target market and build your reputation

- Hype your operation in the media for increased exposure through interactive press releases

- Increase awareness of your operation and brand with Webcasting (rich media)

- Use one of the most effective Internet marketing tools—links

- Find and use free promotion tools available on the Internet

- Keep visitors coming back to your site

- How to develop your own Affiliate or Associate Program

You will be provided with a wealth of information on how to use proven promotion, marketing, and advertising strategies to increase the traffic to your site. Also, comprehensive lists of resources are provided at the end of each chapter to assist you in locating additional marketing media to effectively promote your tourism operation online.

Your "Members Only" Web Site

The Internet world changes every day. That's why there is a companion web site associated with this book. On this site you will find updates to the book and other Web site promotion resources of interest. However, you have to be a member of the *Internet Marketing Success for Your Tourism Business* "Insiders Club" to gain access to this site.

When you purchased this book, you automatically became a member (in fact, that's the only way to join), so you now have full privileges. To get into the "Members Only" section of the companion web site, go to the Maximum Press web site located at *http://www.maxpress.com* and follow the links to the "Internet Marketing For Your Tourism Business" area. From there you will see a link to the "Internet Marketing for Your Tourism Business Insiders Club" section. When you try to enter, you will be asked for a user ID and password. Type in the following:

- For your user ID enter: *imtourism*

- For you password enter: *edge*

You will then be granted full access to the "Members Only" area. Visit the site often and enjoy the updates and resources with our compliments—and thanks again for buying the book. We ask that you not share the user ID and password for this site with anyone else.

1

Marketing Principles

Some areas are much more conducive to research online. Areas that facilitate and encourage travel/vacation planning are high on the list. As a tourism operator you are provided with a great opportunity to reach vast numbers of your target market quickly, easily, and at very little cost. The geographic reach that the Internet provides is phenomenal.

With millions of web sites competing for viewers how do you get the results you're looking for? When asked if they are marketing on the Internet, many tourism operators say, "Yes, we have a web site." However, having a web site and Internet marketing are very different things. Yes, usually you need a web site to market on the Internet, but a web site is simply a collection of documents, images, and other electronic files that are publicly accessible across the Internet.

Your site should be designed to meet your online objectives and should be developed with your target market in mind. Meanwhile, Internet marketing encompasses all the steps you take to reach your target market online, attract visitors to your tourism web site, encourage them to purchase your products or services, and make them want to come back for more.

Having a web site is great, but it is meaningless if nobody knows about it. Likewise, having a brilliantly designed brochure does your tourism operation little good if it sits in the bottom drawer of your desk. It is the goal of this book to help you take your tourism operation's web site "out of the desk drawer," into the spotlight and into the hands of your target market. You will learn how to formulate an Internet marketing strategy and match it with your objectives, your products or services, and your target market. In this chapter, you are provided with an overview of this book and introduced to the importance of:

- Defining your online objectives

- Defining your target market

- Developing an Internet marketing strategy that is appropriate for your tourism operation

- Developing your web site with your target market in mind

Objectives

Before you start to create your tourism web site, you must clearly define your online objectives. What is the purpose of your web site? Brainstorm. Generate a list of primary and secondary objectives. Every element of your site should relate back to your objectives. When you decide to update, add, or change any elements on your web site, examine how these changes relate to the primary and secondary objectives you have identified. If there is not a clear match between your objectives and your intended changes, you might want to reconsider the changes. It's amazing how many web sites have been developed without adequate planning or tie-in with the corporate objectives.

Some of the most common primary and secondary online objectives for a tourism operation might include:

- Taking reservations online

- Promoting your tourism operation

- Selling products or services

- Creating and establishing your operation's identity or brand awareness

- Providing customer service and product support

- Generating repeat traffic

- Advertising an event, product or service

Taking Reservations Online

Your online objectives might include increasing the number of reservations at your tourism operation or increasing the number of bookings made through your travel agency. What better way to do so than online? You want people to visit your site, learn about your offerings, and be enticed enough to make a reservation on the spot. By incorporating an online reservation system, you're facilitating your efforts to increase reservations because you're providing customers with what they want—the means to make a reservation now, when they're ready and willing to. If you do not have an online reservation system, (even a simple e-mail reservation will do) then your potential customers will probably find another site online offering what they are looking for where they can and will complete the transaction and you've lost a potential customer. Chapter 16 discusses the benefits and applications of being able to take online reservations as well as other important information surrounding e-commerce.

Promoting Your Tourism Operation

Some tourism operations simply wish to provide information on their operation, their products, or their services to a particular target market. These types of sites usually have a Frequently Asked Questions (FAQ) section where they provide useful and pertinent information on their operation, products, or services. If the organization courts the media, they might include a Media Center, which could include all of their press releases, a backgrounder on the operation, information on key personnel, articles that have been written about the operation, and a gallery of relevant pictures that the media can use, as well as a direct link to the company's media person.

Selling Products or Services

Do you intend to sell a tourism related product or service that people can order directly from your site? If so, your web site may need to be on a secure server. You will require an order form and perhaps a shopping cart and an e-commerce payment system. Chapter 16 outlines how you might implement an e-commerce system and security for your web site.

People do not just visit a web site to fill out the order form. You will need to provide detailed information about your products or services, as well as your shipping options, return policies, guarantees, and so on. You will also have to help people find your web site easily and encourage them to keep coming back. This book includes numerous techniques you can use to build traffic to your site and give visitors reasons to return.

Creating and Establishing Your
Operation's Identity or Brand Awareness

Another objective might be to create and establish your tourism operation's corporate identity or brand awareness. To "brand" your product, a memorable name and an eye-appealing product logo are necessities. The graphics developed for your web site must be top-notch. A catchy slogan will further promote brand identity. The same branding techniques are also applicable to establishing corporate identity. If building and reinforcing corporate and brand identity are important to you, your web site must have a consistent look and feel. Likewise, all offline promotional campaigns and materials must be consistent with your online presence.

Based on the success of companies such as Travelocity, America Online, Yahoo, Netscape, Amazon, Priceline, Infoseek, and Excite, it is apparent that branding a company or product on the web can occur swiftly. It is amazing how quickly these relative newcomers to the business world have achieved megabrand status. Although they all had significant financial resources, each company used a combination of online and offline advertising to meet their objectives. Their web sites reflect their branding. Each of their sites features a prominent logo, consistent imagery, and a consistent color scheme. Check out the sites of these upstarts who have become big online players if branding is your goal. There is a lot we can learn from them.

Providing Customer Service and Product Support

From time to time, customers will require assistance with the products or services they have purchased or wish to purchase. For instance, Dell *(http://www.dell.com)* sells a lot of personal computers. People will surely come to them for after-sales service if problems arise with their hardware or if they need help setting up their system.

Therefore, Dell created a support and service web site *(http://support.dell.com)* for their customers. The site includes a Frequently Asked Questions (FAQ) database that customers can reference to help solve common problems. Your site might simply require a single page. Other ideas (chat rooms, newsgroups, etc.) presented in the following chapters will also be very applicable to you if your online objective is to provide postsale support.

Most tourism related sites need not have the level of product support that Dell has, but it is important to have customer service representatives available to help people book or verify their accommodations, flight schedules, and so forth. Travelocity *(http://www.travelocity.com/)* and other major travel sites such as Expedia *(http://www.expedia.com/)* provide 24-hour telephone customer service support. Make customer satisfaction your tourism operation's number one objective. After all, it's cheaper and more profitable in the long run to build on customer loyalty to encourage repeat sales than it is to constantly battle for new customers.

Generating Repeat Traffic

Attracting new and repeat traffic to your site is a key factor in establishing an online clientele and increasing sales. How do you encourage repeat visits to your web site? You must provide content that is current and interesting. A system for changing and updating the content on your web site must be established. You must also have strategies for submitting to search engines, acquiring links from other sites, developing a mailing list, and having the kinds of features on your site that help form an online community. Offering a virtual tour of your tourism operation would be one example. This book will demonstrate these and many other ideas you can implement to generate repeat traffic to your web site.

Advertising an Event, Product, or Service

The objective of some sites is simply to advertise or promote their tourism operation rather than to directly sell accommodation space, events, products, or services. For instance, well in advance of the release of a new film, Hollywood movie studios often establish information sites that include advance multimedia clips from the movie, background information, and details about the actors and actresses. The studios will also issue interactive press releases to the entertainment media. This helps generate interest in the film, and the hope is that people will then want to pay to see the film when it appears in theaters. You could do the same thing before the grand opening of a new golf course. The following chapters will teach you how to legitimately (i.e., using proper Netiquette) disseminate information quickly across the Internet and build traffic to your site.

Whatever your objectives may be, you must carefully consider how best to incorporate elements in your web site and your Internet marketing strategy to help you achieve them. Successful marketing on the web is not a simple undertaking. Before you begin to brainstorm over the objectives of your tourism site, be certain you have read and studied all information that is pertinent to your target market as it relates to their Internet preferences. Read everything you can get your hands on, and examine the findings of tourism industry experts.

After you have designed, created, and presented your web site for the world to see, test your site on a small group of individuals in your target market. Then, after analyzing their feedback, you can tweak your site before engaging a larger audience. For instance, let's say you have a travel agency and accept online reservations. The people visiting your site may be very interested in your vacation packages, but perhaps they have commented that the registration form requires too much information and takes too long to complete. You might want to tweak the form before you promote your travel agency's site to a larger audience. Reducing the amount of information that people must submit might be the key to obtaining more reservations.

Another example would be if your home page utilized a lot of Macromedia Flash or other multimedia effects and the majority of visitors to your web site did not have the browsers or plug-ins to be able to view these elements installed on their systems. Given this situation, you might consider simplifying your home page by removing some of the multimedia effects or creating a second version of your home page for people who are not able to use the latest Internet technologies. Thus, everyone who comes to your web site will have the opportunity to enjoy your web site, read your message, gather information about your product or service, and so on. You will have to keep in mind your target market and the configuration they are likely to be using. Most people will do their vacation planning at home, where their computer may not have the latest version of the browser. The home user may not be apt to download the latest versions of the browsers as they are released, and some may even have the same browser that was installed on that old 486 when they bought it!

Once you have tested your site with your test market, do not stop there. Continue testing and tweaking your online marketing strategy until you find the methods, tools, and techniques that work best. Whenever you add an element to your web site or your online strategy, ask yourself, "Is it consistent with my online objectives, my product or service, and my target market?"

In Chapter 2, web site essentials are discussed in detail to assist you with developing or renovating your tourism operation's site. You will learn which elements to include on your web site and how to effectively implement these elements in conjunction with your strategic objectives.

Product or Service

Web sites and Internet marketing strategies will differ depending on the product or service you are selling. For instance, when they are promoting their vacation packages, Disney knows that children have a major influence on their family vacation destination. Given this target market for their vacation packages, Disney will have to develop a fun and interactive web site that is attractive to children. The web site will then have to give children a way to tell their friends about the web site as well as a reason to return to the site. Disney might wish to have a contest of interest to children or offer an electronic postcard service whereby children can send a colorful and musical message to their friends to tell them about the site.

When promoting their merchandise, Disney might want to provide a "wish list" service. Children could visit the Disney store online, adding items they like to their wish list with the click of a button. This wish list could then be sent to the parents via e-mail. With a few strategic clicks and the input of credit card information, the parents could then make and finalize their purchasing decisions. The parents know the children will enjoy their gift, and the children will certainly become loyal to the Disney site. Likewise, some companies offer reminder services that send an e-mail message to visitors who have registered and completed the appropriate questionnaire to remind them of a child's birthday and offer suggestions for gift ideas. Once again, this promotes sales and repeat traffic, and increases customer loyalty.

A travel agency's web site might include features such as an opt-in mailing list to send people information on weekly vacation deals or simply have a page on the site detailing the latest specials. They might also want to include downloadable or streaming video tours of vacation resorts to entice visitors to buy resort vacation packages. Another idea would be to have a system in place to help customers book vacations, rent cars, and check for available flights. The travel agency might also want to store customer profiles so that they can track of where particular customers like to sit on the plane, the type of hotel room they usually book, the type of car they like to rent, and any other travel preferences. They may also gather their credit card information and travel-related membership information to make bookings more efficient for the customer and the agency.

If you are marketing a travel service online, it can be difficult to visually depict what your service is all about. Visitors to your site need some reassurance that the service you are selling them is legitimate and valuable, and that you are the best company for them to do business with. Therefore, you might wish to include a page on your site that lists testimonials from current and past customers with contact information if possible. This will give prospective customers more confidence about purchasing your service.

The bottom line is that the tourism-related product or service you are selling will determine the direction of your web site development process and the features that will be included. Remember to think of your online objectives first, then storyboard the site on a sheet (or several sheets) of paper. Once you are satisfied that you have included elements in your site to meet all of your online objectives, given your product or service and your target market (which we will speak of next), you can proceed with the coding of your site.

Target Market

This is your target audience—the people to whom you are trying to market your tourism-related product or service. Ask yourself who makes the buying decision for your products or services and also who influences that buying decision. Look at this from a geographic, demographic, and psychographic perspective. You may have several target markets. Once you have determined your target markets, you will want to ascertain why each of them decides to buy your product or service. What is it that influences their buying decision? Is it price? Is it location? Is it the package? Is it product quality? Is it availability? Is it your company's reputation? Or is it post sale service and guarantees that make people buy from you? These factors will directly determine the tone and content of your site.

Once again, if you intend to market travel services geared toward children, your web site will be colorful and the text simple and easy to understand, in keeping with what appeals to your target market. Chances are, fun-looking graphics will be used intensely on your site to draw children further into it (see Figure 1.1). If you market business travel services, your web site will require a more professional approach. The graphics will convey a clean appearance, and the text will be informative and written in a businesslike fashion (see Figure 1.2). As this example demonstrates, the content and tone of your site must be tailored to your target market. After all, this is the best way to attract the attention of the people who are interested in purchasing your product or service.

Another aspect of the design of your web site to consider with regard to your target market, as mentioned earlier, is their propensity to utilize the latest technologies and the configuration they are likely

Figure 1.1 Disney *(http://www.disney.com/)* uses a Web site design that is appealing to children to promote their Disney vacations.

to be using. An online business that sells streaming multimedia presentations of tourism resorts on CD-ROM would expect its clientele to be technically inclined. Their clients are more likely to have the latest software, web browser technologies, and faster machines.

On the other hand, clients of a tourism operator who promotes a bed and breakfast (B&B) online may have the technology savvy and also those less likely to have fully embraced the latest technologies in their target markets. Some of these people planning their vacation or trip will be connecting from home rather than from their workplace. They may have a slow dialup connection to the Internet, slower machines, and outdated software. They might still be using the web browser that was originally installed on their system simply because they are uncomfortable downloading the latest version of the browser, they are unaware of the more recent version, or they are uninterested in downloading a large file. If your target market includes this demo-

Figure 1.2.   Meanwhile, Trip.com *(http://www.trip.com/)* must cater to both business and vacation travelers alike. Thus, their site emphasizes information over graphical content.

graphic, you will have to be careful with your use of Java, Macromedia Flash, and large graphic files.

What does this mean for developing and designing your tourism site? Well, a streaming multimedia developer could design a web site with more graphics and multimedia effects because their clients expect to be impressed with the use of technology when they visit the developer's site. If the B&B operator designed a site similarly, many of their potential clients could be alienated because the site would be too slow to load. They might take their business elsewhere. The B&B operator's site will require a more basic design: less concentration on large slow-loading graphics and multimedia effects, and more focus on presenting information and optimally sized graphics which are quick to load. You must know the demographics of the people who are interested in your product, service, or information and develop your web site to appeal to this target market.

This book will describe how you can use a variety of Internet tools and resources to promote your tourism web site. You will learn how to design your site to achieve higher search engine rankings and how to submit your web site to major search engines, web directories, and meta-indexes.

E-mail is an important communication method. Chapter 7 steps you through proper e-mail etiquette and explains the concept of conducting an e-mail marketing campaign to help you reach your target market.

You will also learn about using newsgroups, mailing lists, interactive press releases, affiliate programs, banner ads, online and offline publications, and webcasting (rich media) to promote your web site to thousands of potential customers. Once you have absorbed the content of this book and developed an Internet marketing strategy that is focused on your objectives, products, or services and your target market, your tourism-related business will reap the benefits of Internet marketing.

Marketing your tourism site can be a full-time occupation. Some organizations have a team of Internet marketing specialists to build, maintain and promote their site. For others, their online business is a part-time endeavor and they only have an hour or two each week to spend promoting and developing their web site. Whatever your situation, the better informed your are about Internet marketing, the better chance your online business will have to succeed. Ensure that your site is user-friendly and designed with your target market, your products or services and objectives in mind. The more you put into the development and implementation of your Internet marketing strategy, the greater the return will be to your online tourism operation.

Internet Resources

WilsonWeb
http://wilsonweb.com
One of the greatest sites on the Internet for anything you want to know about Internet marketing.

The Top Banana Chat Room for Marketing @ About.com
http://marketing.about.com/business/business/marketing/mpchat.htm
Get your marketing questions answered or chat with others.

Network Marketing Weekly Online Newsletter
http://www.he.net/~image/nwm/imin.html
Archive of network marketing newsletters.

Bplans.com
http://www.bplans.com
Business planning resource center.

ConsultHQ
http://www.consulthq.com
Free marketing resources for professionals.

Business Planning Center
http://www.businessplans.org
Business and marketing planning, and business strategy information, advice, and software.

Tilburg University
http://marketing.kub.nl/links.htm
An exhaustive list of marketing-related links.

Marketing Resources, Ltd.
http://www.mrlweb.com
Business to business marketing solutions, marketing tips, and a marketing newsletter.

2

Essentials of Web Site Design

Site design, appearance, functionality, and features are all-important aspects to consider before you think about promoting your tourism operation's site. If the site is designed to achieve your marketing objectives, if it looks good, and if the layout is easy to follow, you are ready to open your online doors. There are many key factors to consider that may be overlooked in the initial design stages. A great domain name should be chosen, and whenever possible the operation's name should be used. Appropriate titles should be located on each page to identify the name of your tourism operation and the page content. In this chapter we cover:

- How and why Meta tags should be prepared for each page of your site

- The importance of each page's title, description, and keywords

- Web site features and design guidelines

- Checking out the competition

- The use of graphics

- Top-rated sites

- Encouraging repeat visits

- Incentives for increasing visitors

- Corporate identity and your web site

- Guiding the search engines to you

- Ensuring your site works with different web browsers

Building Traffic to Your Tourism Site

The phrase "if you build it, they will come" worked in the movies, but it does not work with your web site. Building a web site is just the first step. Driving traffic to your site takes knowledge, planning, time, and effort. This book's focus is on increasing traffic to your tourism operation's web site.

To achieve the maximum marketing potential of your site, we cover several topics that relate to your web site content and design. We recommend that the following Internet marketing tips, tools, and techniques be used in conjunction with your overall web site design.

Consider Your Web Site Objectives First

As discussed in Chapter 1, it is imperative to determine your online objectives before you plan your online strategy, and certainly before you start construction of your site. What do you want your web site to accomplish? Do you want to increase your reservations? Do you want to increase non–peak season sales? Do you want to sell tourism-oriented products or services directly to your customers? Do you want your site to provide information? Do you want to promote tourism products or services (e.g., travel packages) on behalf of another tourism operator?

Determine the objectives of your web site or online presence before you begin to build the site. Some common objectives include:

- Advertising tourism-related products or services

- Selling products or services (golf supplies, vacation packages, airline tickets, etc.)

- Providing tourist service or support

- Providing useful information on booking reservations, air fares, etc.

- Reinforcing your tourism operation's brand image

- Providing tourism information cost effectively (the Web is free, full-color brochures are not)

Know your objectives and build your site around them. This will ensure satisfaction at the end of the process.

Presenting Your Operation's Web Site Message Clearly

Most visitors to your web site need to know and understand your message instantly from the very first page. If not, visitors can leave your site just as quickly as they could press a button on their TV remote control. Your site must load quickly and immediately direct your visitors toward your message. Do you want them to make a reservation? Browse? Provide feedback? Order? In traditional advertisements you need to attract the attention of your audience immediately. This is also the case with your Internet audience. However, unlike traditional advertising, you can deliver more information over the Internet than you can in a 30-second commercial or a half-page print ad. However, you must avoid overloading visitors with information. Too much information on the opening page of your tourism site can make it appear cluttered and unorganized. As a general rule, keep your message simple and to the point.

Using Competitor Sites to Your Advantage

Keeping up with the CyberJoneses is very important. Visit tourism-related sites for some ideas. Also visit sites that are listed on hot sites pages. Look at the design of these sites to get a better idea of what you should (and should not) include in yours. Examine the colors and backgrounds used, see how the information is organized, and look at the features provided. Some sites with lots of links to travel-related sites to visit for ideas are:

- BedandBreakfast.com: *http://www.bedandbreakfast.com/*

- Biztravel: *http://www.biztravel.com*

- Travelocity: *http://www.travelocity.com*

- Expedia: *http://www.expedia.com*

Realizing the Potential of Your Domain Name

One of the most important things from an online marketing perspective, often overlooked when developing your web presence, is your **domain name.** Your Internet domain name is your exclusive web address, which you can purchase through several domain name registration sites online, one of which is Network Solutions *(www.networksolutions.com)*, an online organization in charge of domain name registration. Having your own domain name provides you with many benefits:

Domain name
The unique name that identifies an Internet site, *www.site name.com.*

- The name itself can increase traffic to your site.

- Having your own domain name builds credibility for your operation.

- Your presence is mobile when you own your domain name.

- Internet marketing efforts travel with the domain name.

Your domain name should be easy to remember and relate to your online presence. Your operation's name is usually the best choice, and should be used whenever possible.

People will generally try *www.youroperationsname.com* first when they know you operation's name. If customers or potential customers know your operation exists, they will find your web site quickly and easily if your domain name is your operation's name. If your operation's name is not well known, you may choose to use a catchy descriptive phrase or the subject of your web site as its domain name. For example, imagine that you were searching for information on tropical vacation packages and one of your search engine results is a site with a **URL** named *www.tropicalvacations.com* with accompanying text, "The best rates and selection for tropical vacation packages." What are the chances that you would click through to that site? Pretty good. Keep your domain name simple, easy to remember, and related to the subject of your site.

URL
Uniform Resource Locator: an address on the web.

You can register multiple domain names with Network Solutions. You might choose this option if there are several keywords you believe potential customers would be inclined to search for. For instance, you might register a domain name for your operation's name and a separate domain name for each of the tourism products and services you are selling. You can have several domain names, all pointing to the same web site. One of the reasons you might consider doing this is that some of the search engines will give your site higher ranking if the keyword being searched is found in your domain name. For example, if your bed and breakfast is located next to Yellowstone National Park and is called The Sunshine Inn, you might want to register *www.sunshineinn.com* and *www.innatyellowstone.com*. Basically, you can consider registering a domain name for any keyword or phrase you think most people would use to try to find your type of tourism operation.

Of course, registering a domain name costs money. Besides the registration fee, you may also be paying another company to host each of your domain names, and it requires a lot of time to register multiple domain names with the search engines. Therefore, do not get carried away with registering too many domain names for your tourism operation unless you can afford the time and money. Perhaps the best suggestion would be to register one domain for your company name and one domain name for the most important keyword. With the keyword included in the domain name, your site will rank higher in the search engines and web site traffic will increase.

Having your own domain name projects a professional image for your operation. One of the benefits of the Internet is that it creates a level playing field for small and medium-sized companies. Having your own domain name projects the image of an established business operating online in a professional manner.

Businesses that develop an online presence without registering their own domain name generally use the domain name of the **ISP** or company that is hosting their site. Your site address would generally have the following address: *http:// www.yourISP.com/yoursitename*. This type of address is not mobile, meaning you can't take it with you should you ever want to move your web site to another host. If you own your own domain name, it is yours as long as you keep your registration fees current with Network Solutions *(http://www.network solutions.com)* or the domain name registration company you are dealing with. You then have the option of moving your site to another host without losing your web address. You can change the host of your site at any time and take your domain name with you.

ISP
Internet
Service
Provider

If you allow your ISP or any other party to take care of the domain name registration process, make sure that you are listed as the actual owner of the domain so that you don't run into problems if you decide to move your site. You want to make sure you are listed as the administrative contact as it is the administrative contact that controls the domain name and can request any changes. You might also want to be identified as the billing contact as well. This way, Network Solutions (see Figure 2.1), or the domain registration service of your choice, will send the invoice directly to you so you will never have to worry about the annual fee being unpaid and losing your domain name. In the long run, listing yourself as the administrative and billing contact will help you skirt any potential complications.

It takes a great deal of time and effort to promote your site online. Getting listed in all the search engines and directories, developing links to your site, and getting listed in meta-indexes, all are time-consuming tasks. These listings and links all automatically link the viewer to your site address. If you don't own your address, you can't take it with you if you want to move your site to another ISP or host. If you move you would lose most, if not all, of the momentum gained by your previous online marketing activities. Having your own domain name gives you the option to move your site at any time without having a negative impact on your previous marketing efforts.

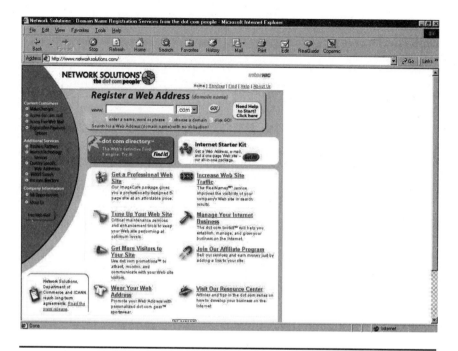

Figure 2.1. Network Solutions offers domain name registration services.

When conducting business in an international environment you need the most common top-level domain name, ending in *.com,* which is used around the world. Canadian sites can use *.ca*. However, to be globally recognized you should use the *.com* designation. As mentioned earlier, when a person knows of your operation and wants to visit your web site the first inclination is to check *www.youroperationsname.com*.

Your domain name must be registered with a domain name registration service like Network Solutions for the top-level domains: *.com, .net, .org,* and *.edu*. Registering a domain name with Network Solutions can be done through your ISP, or you can do it yourself through the Network Solutions web site at *www.networksolutions.com*. You can do a search at the Network Solutions web site to determine whether or not your preferred domain name is available.

The fee for registering your domain name is $70 US for the first two years, and there is a $35 US renewal fee for every year thereafter. Network Solutions' registration fee covers the cost of processing the initial registration and maintaining the domain name record. The renewal fee covers one year of maintenance for the domain name record and is assessed each year on the anniversary of the original registration.

The registration process begins once you have submitted your complete and correctly formatted agreement. Your registration request is processed immediately, and you will be notified via e-mail when processing is finished. The complete process generally takes less than 24 hours, with some requests processed in as little as 10 minutes. Network Solutions will mail your invoice to you within a few days. The invoice will name you as the rightful owner and administrative contact for the domain name.

The Essentials of Your Web Site Design

These web site design tips are relevant to all web sites:

- Your online and offline image should be consistent.

- Your site should be easy to read.

- Your site should be easy to navigate (include a site map and/or a search engine tool).

- Your web pages should have a consistent layout.

- Your web pages should be no larger than 50K.

- Have a What's New section to let visitors know what has changed on the site.

- Do not overuse **image maps.**

- Avoid Under Construction pages on your site. These usually look tacky (see Figure 2.2) and are of no value to the visitor. When you have information, post it. Until then, don't mention it.

- Your web site should steer clear of scrolling marquee text. Scrolling marquees are difficult to read and are

Image maps Large single images with clickable "hot spots," commonly used for site navigation.

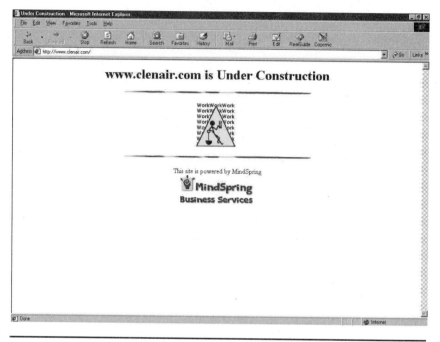

Figure 2.2. "Under Construction."

not compatible with all browsers. Simply post text directly on your pages if you have something important to say.

- Design for various screen widths. Try to accommodate visitors regardless of the screen resolution they use. Twenty percent of web users still run their systems at 640 pixels wide by 480 pixels high. Keep your image sizes small enough to be fully viewable at this resolution, and use percentage widths in your tables so that your pages are flexible to any screen resolution.

- Use thumbnail graphics where applicable. When you have a page with a lot of large images (i.e., an online photo collection), create small "thumbnail" versions of each image, and give visitors the option of clicking through to the larger version of each image. This is far superior than making your visitors wait for a series of large images to load.

- Include contact information on every page. This includes your address, phone and fax numbers, and especially your e-mail address or a contact form. Make it easy for people to get in touch with you.

- Security information. Explain to your customers when transactions or exchanges of information on your web site are secure. This is important if your site will be accepting credit card orders.

- Privacy policy. Tell people how their personal information (their name, e-mail address, etc.) will and will not be used. This will make visitors more comfortable submitting inquiries to your site.

- Minimize the use of background sounds and autoplay sounds. Some people surf the web from their office at work and wish to discreetly go from one site to the next. Background sounds and sounds that load automatically can compromise their discreetness. Give your visitors the option to listen to you audio, but do not force it upon them. If you do, you could lose visitors forever.

The tone of your text and the design of your graphics will convey your intended image. For example, if your target audience comprises mostly business-minded travelers, you will want to keep things straight to the point. Minimize the graphics, and use just enough text to get your point across and heighten the interest of your audience. On the other hand, a theme park for children might prefer a more graphic-oriented site with some multimedia effects such as Macromedia Flash. Keep your online image consistent with your offline image. Be consistent with the use of logo, corporate colors, and any other marketing collateral associated with your company.

When determining the text content of your site, be mindful of the fact that your own biases may preclude you from placing information on your site that is second nature to you but important data for your visitors. Review all text content on your site to ensure you have not omitted anything crucial. People planning their vacation will be looking for as much information as possible. What other tourism destinations are in close proximity? How do you get there? What are the seasonal temperatures? What amenities are provided? Test your site with your target market and ask for feedback on what is missing.

Also, keep text brief. Almost 80 percent of web users scan text online as opposed to actually reading it. Therefore, make your key points quickly and succinctly, and use lots of bulleted lists, headers, and horizontal rules to create visual "breaks" in the content. This will keep visitors interested enough to read the information on your site. If they are faced with huge blocks of text, many visitors will be overwhelmed by the quantity of the information and too intimidated to read your message.

Choose your background and font colors carefully. Using backgrounds that are too busy will obscure your text and will not provide a pleasant viewing experience for your visitor. Only some colors will show up properly on certain backgrounds. A light background with dark text is easiest on the eyes.

White text displays best on black backgrounds, and black text is most readable on white backgrounds. Of course, you can use other color schemes, but choose your scheme carefully. Nothing is more annoying than a web site that is virtually unreadable. Also, be mindful that some people might wish to print pages from your site. If you incorporate a lot of your text into the actual graphics on your site, the text might be difficult to read when printed. Also, graphic-intensive sites load more slowly. If you have to incorporate text content into your graphics, ensure that it is sensible to do so.

Don't set your text size too small, because this is too hard to read. Don't set it too large, because this looks like you are shouting!! Also, avoid using ALL CAPS, WHICH ALSO COMES ACROSS AS SHOUTING!

Use the default colors for links whenever possible. Blue text usually indicates an unvisited link. Purple, maroon, or darker blue usually represents a link which has been visited, and red is the color of an active link. It should not be difficult for visitors to identify your links. If you decide not to use the default colors, your links should be emphasized in a consistent manner through font size, font style, or underlines.

Ease of navigation is very important to your site. Provide a navigation bar at a consistent location on every page that links to all of the major pages of your site. Make it easy to get from one page to any other. Search engines can index any page of your site, so your home page might not be the first page visitors come to, and you want your visitor to be able to navigate your site no matter where they enter your site.

Never have dead ends, where viewers scroll down a page or two of information only to find that they must scroll all the way back up to the top to move on (because you have no links at the bottom of the page). A consistent-looking and well-positioned navigation bar with functioning links is the key to efficient site navigation.

Also avoid dead links. These are links that don't go anywhere and the viewer usually receives a 404—File not found error message (see Figure 2.3) from the web server after clicking on a dead link. Verify periodically that all your links are still active.

Your visitors should be able to get anywhere they want to go on your site in two to three clicks. Developing an effective navigation bar as previously described and, if your site is large, having an up-to-date site map (which will be explained later in this chapter) allows visitors to quickly find the information they are seeking on your site.

Keep the design of your site consistent. Font types, headers, footers, navigational bars, buttons, bullets, colors, and so on should be consistent throughout the site to maintain a polished professional look.

Your **home page** should be 50K or less, and your home page should be displayed on one or two screens maximum. Studies have shown that visitors will rarely wait beyond 15 seconds to download a site. Test the download time of your site with a 14.4 modem to ensure that it is reasonable for all users.

Home page
The main page of a web site.

Keeping Web Site Graphics in Perspective

Graphics can be an extremely important element on a tourism-related web site. A picture is worth a thousand words—particularly in this industry. However, many of the people in your target market

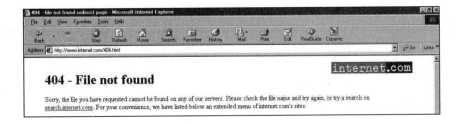

Figure 2.3. Broken links result in a 404—File not found error message.

will be accessing your site from their home computers. Some will have slower machines, older modems, and dial-up connections. Be discriminating with the file size of your graphics as you add them to your site. Graphics that are too time-consuming to download may cause visitors to leave your site before they get a chance to see it. Remember that a lot of Internet users are still using 14.4, 28.8 and 56k modems. The combined size of your text and graphics for each of your web pages should not exceed 50K.

Some people turn graphics off in their browsers to save time, so you should provide all of your information in text as well as graphics. For each graphic you use you should develop descriptive Alt attributes in your image tags. The Alt text will load in place of the images when the graphic cannot be shown for any reason. This way, visitors who choose to browse with graphics turned off will have an easier time navigating your site. Also, Alt text is spidered and indexed by a lot of the major search engines. Using your most important keywords in your Alt text and in your image tags will improve your ranking in search engines and provide a description of the images in the event they are not loaded. If you use any large files for graphics, audio, or video, warn your visitors by providing some text stating the size of the files.

You should be careful with your use of image maps as well. Image maps (see Figure 2.4) are large graphics with clickable "hot spots." Image maps are typically used for navigation. They are useful if your web site contains 5 or more major sections. If you do use an image map, make it obvious what portions of the image are clickable and where each link will lead.

Very often, when a large graphic is used for an image map, visitors must wait for the entire image to load before it is apparent where they must click to begin navigating your site. Instead of using a large image map, break the image into smaller images so that the visitor will receive faster feedback from your site without having to wait for a huge graphic to load. Also, always provide an alternate text link navigation system to assist people who surf with their graphics turned off.

Provide Ease of Navigation with User-Friendly Site Maps

For very large sites (i.e., those sites consisting of more than 8 to 10 major sections) it is a good idea to include a site map that users can access from any page in your site. Site maps, as shown in Figures 2.5

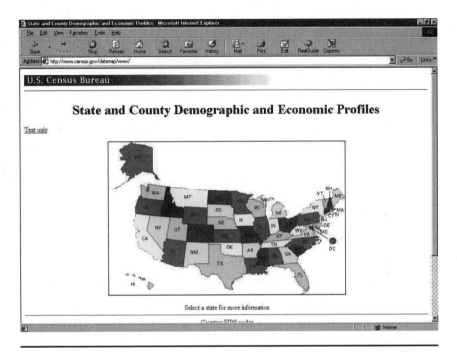

Figure 2.4. A good use of an image map. There are lots of links, and the hot spots are well defined. Each state can be clicked on to obtain more information.

and 2.6, are usually text-based or graphic-based lists that name and provide links to all of the site's pages and their content. Site maps make it easy for users to access the information they are looking for without causing them much frustration. Include a link from your main navigation bar to the site map for the easiest possible reference.

Identify Your Site with Page Titles

Each of the pages in your web site should be given a title. The title is inserted between the title tags in the header of an HTML document. Title tag information identifies and describes your pages. Titles can tell readers where the information contained on a page originated.

Figure 2.5. Most site maps are provided in a tree structure and provide the user with an easy way to navigate a large site.

Browsers
Software
programs
that let you
"surf" the
Internet.

Most web **browsers,** such as Netscape, display a document's title in the top line of the screen. When users print a page from your web site the title usually appears at the top of the page at the left. When people bookmark your site, the title appears as the description in their bookmark file. These are all reasons why it is important that a page's title reflects an accurate description of the page.

Go through each and every page of your Web site, bookmark each one, and check that your titles represent each page clearly without being lengthy. Try to include relevant keywords in your page titles because some of the search engines will give your site a higher ranking when this is done. Longer page titles can dilute the relevancy of your keywords. Keeping your page titles brief (5 to 10 words or fewer) will increase the potency of your keywords and earn your pages higher search engine rankings. The titles should always identify your company. Examples of appropriate titles are:

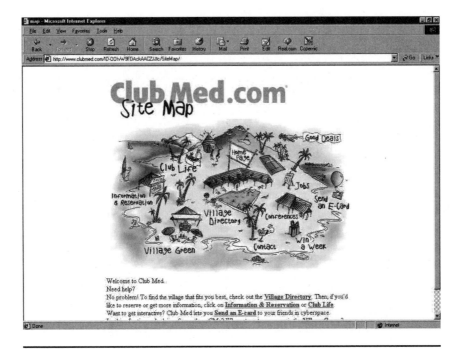

Figure 2.6. ClubMed (http://www.xlubmed.com) provides an excellent example of a graphical site map.

- "TravelWeb – The Online Travel Specialists"

- "TravelWeb – Plan Your Next Vacation"

Inappropriate titles are:

- "The Best Travel Page on the Web"

- "The Tourism Home Page"

- "Order Form"

Match the keywords you use in your Meta tags with the keywords you use in your page titles. Search engines check page titles, Metatags, and page content for keywords. Your pages will be more relevant, and therefore place higher in the search engines, for certain keywords if these keywords appear in each of these three sections. Position your keywords near the beginning of your page titles to increase your keyword relevancy.

Viewing Your Site Through Browser Eyes

Check your site using different browsers. What viewers see when your site is downloaded depends on what browser they are using. Different browsers will display the same web site differently. Before you post your site online, check your site with the most popular browsers:

- Netscape Navigator 4.7

- Netscape Navigator 3.0

- Microsoft Internet Explorer 5.0

- Microsoft Internet Explorer 4.0

- Microsoft Internet Explorer 3.0

- America Online 5.0

It is obvious that there are a lot of browsers to consider when designing your web site. Some people may also be using very old browsers like Netscape 2.0, Mosaic, or a text-only browser. When designing your site, consider your target audience. What browsers will your visitors most likely use? Your target audience will likely be a home user planning a vacation. With this demographic in mind, you are best advised to design for the lowest common denominator. Design for Netscape 3.0 and Internet Explorer 3.0 browsers or higher. Few people continue to use really old browsers, so unless you know your target audience will be using Netscape 2.0 or Mosaic, the 3.0 browser versions are the most appropriate to design for.

America Online bases its browser on either Netscape or Internet Explorer (depending on who they are currently affiliated with-- Netscape or Microsoft). Therefore, if your web site displays properly in Netscape and Internet Explorer, you can safely assume that AOL users will have no trouble viewing your web site.

If your audience is more likely to be technically inclined, you can safely design for the latest browser editions. In this case, you might wish to use HTML 4.0, Java applets, Active X, or Flash media to make your web site more attractive to your visitors.

Generally speaking, given your target audience, you should design your pages using HTML 3.2 and minimize the number of slow-loading multimedia elements. This will allow everyone to enjoy your site without having to wait too long for each page to load.

Choosing Web Site Features To Meet Marketing Objectives

There are many features that can be incorporated into your web site. It is important to look at each feature from both marketing and administrative views before deciding to incorporate it into your site. A **chat room** might seem like a nifty feature to have at first blush, but you have to ask the questions, What is the marketing value to our tourism operation in having this on our web site? Will it increase targeted traffic to our site? Will it encourage repeat visits from our customers and potential customers? Will it result in increased sales?

> **Chat room**
> A site where you can chat, in real time, with others.

Assuming that you can justify a chat room on your site from a marketing perspective, then you must look at the feature from a financial perspective. What will this feature cost to develop? What will be the ongoing costs of operating this feature in technical resources as well as in human resources? What is our budget? Can these resources provide a better return on investment if spent elsewhere? Would we achieve our objectives more effectively if we put these financial resources into banner advertising or other online marketing activities?

Customer-Enticing Traffic Builders

The following traffic builders are used to attract and invite visitors to your site:

Free Offers

People love to get something for nothing. Offering something for free is a good way to get lots of traffic to your site. This is great if your objectives include generating lots of general-user traffic to your site. Free offers also provide you the opportunity to be linked from the many **meta-indexes** related to freebies and giveaways. If you are giving something away, you might consider tying it into a registration for your newsletter or mailing list. You should relate giveaways to your company, your products, or your services. Perhaps your freebie could be a weekly or monthly drawing for a weekend for two if you have a tourism accommodation operation, or a downloadable golf screen saver if you have a golf course.

Meta-indexes
Collections of URLs for related Internet resources.

Coupons

Coupons are an effective way to increase traffic to your site. If your coupons are valuable and you change them daily or weekly, you will encourage visitors to return frequently. Dineaid.com *(http://www.dineaid.com)*, a promotional site for restaurants located in Atlantic Canada, allows partner restaurants to provide coupons on its site. Customers print the coupons and redeem them at the respective restaurants. This is a great marketing technique for the restaurant because their customers are encouraged to visit the web site and the physical storefront as well. A closer bond is created between the featured restaurant and their customers, and sales increase as a result. Ask your visitors if they would like to be notified when you update your coupons. This gives you permission to add them to your mail list and send them e-mail on a regular basis as you update the coupons.

Contests

Contests are very popular online, particularly when prizes are involved. To encourage repeat visits you should change the contest regularly or design it in such a way that your visitors can enter often. To get some information about the people who are visiting your site, and to help you with your marketing efforts, include a few pertinent questions on the entry form—one of them being "At which e-mail address would you like to be notified of the winner?" This again gives you permission to send them an e-mail.

Once the winning candidate is selected, you can send a message to all contest participants to announce the winner. Thank them for their participation and invite them to return to your site. Enticing them with a special offer or a discount on all purchases might be good way to increase traffic to your site. By sending the contestants a message like this, you may generate sales from people who might not have purchased from you otherwise. The more often you get your target market to visit your site, the more likely they are to buy from you.

Interactive Tours

Interactive tours take your visitors on a virtual tour of your bed and breakfast resort, golf course, restaurant, ski hill, or web site. Visitors can acquire an understanding of what your venue looks like and how your tourism operation works. This is a great way to provide information on the quality of your facility.

You can make your interactive tour more interesting by incorporating a contest with the tour. For the purpose of the contest, ask your visitors detailed questions about the tour. They will be more attentive, and they will absorb your message and the information on your site more clearly. If you can make them understand your message, this can lead to sales.

Guiding the Search Engines with Meta-Information

A common problem faced by tourism operators marketing on the Internet is how to influence search engines to index their site appropriately and how to ensure that their site appears when people use relevant search criteria. Many of the interesting and creative sites on the Internet are impossible to find because they are not indexed with the major search engines. The majority (85%) of Internet users planning their vacation employ search engines or directories to conduct their research. This research is performed by typing in a keyword or phrase that represents what they are looking for.

Retaining a certain measure of control over how search engines deal with your web sites is a major concern. Often web sites do not take advantage of the techniques available to them to influence search engine listings. Many search engines evaluate the Meta-HTML tags in conjunction with other variables to decide where to index web pages based on particular keyword queries.

The Web Developer's Virtual Library defines a Meta-HTML tag as follows:

> *An HTML tag used in the Head area of a document to specify further information about the document, either for the local server, or for a remote browser. The Meta element is used within the Head element to embed document Meta information not defined by other HTML elements. Such information can be extracted by servers/clients for use in identifying, indexing, and cataloging specialized document Meta information. In addition, HTTP servers can read the contents of the document head to generate response headers corresponding to any elements defining a value for the attribute HTTP-EQUIV. This provides document authors with a mechanism for identifying information that should be included in the response headers of an HTTP request.*

To summarize this lengthy definition, Meta information can be used in identifying, indexing, and cataloging. This means you can use these tags to guide the search engines in displaying your site as the result of a query.

Meta and Header Elements

A header without Meta information will look like this:

<html>

<head>

<title>Travel Nation—National TravelSpecialists</title></head>

If you want your site to be displayed properly in search engines, you should create a header as follows:

<HTML>

<HEAD>

Document Title Here</TITLE>

<META NAME="keywords" CONTENT="keyword1, keyword2, keyword3">

<META NAME="description" CONTENT="200-character site description goes here">

<META NAME="robots" CONTENT="index, follow">

<!--Comments Tag, repeat description here?>

<HEAD> indicates the beginning of the header, and the ending of the header is marked by </HEAD>

<TITLE> indicates the title of the page. The end of the title is marked by </TITLE> which is called the closing tag.

<META NAME= "keywords" CONTENT= "..."> tells search engines under which keywords to index your site under. When a user types one of the words you listed here, your site should be displayed as a result. A space must be used to separate the words. Do not repeat any of the words more than five times (a lot of the bots will not recognize repeat words). You should list the most important words first because some bots only read the first 200 characters. You should create a keywords tag for each page of your site listing appropriate keywords for each separate page.

<META NAME= "description" CONTENT= "..."> this should be added to every page of your site. It is used to provide an accurate description of the page to which it is attached. Keep the description under 200 characters, or it may be cut off when displayed by the search engines.

<META NAME="robots" CONTENT=" "> tells certain bots to follow or not follow hypertext links. The W3 Consortium white paper on spidering (spiders are defined below) offers the following definition and discussion:

<META NAME="ROBOTS" CONTENT="ALL | NONE | NOINDEX | NOFOLLOW">

default = empty = "ALL" "NONE" = "NOINDEX, NOFOLLOW"

The filler is a comma-separated list of terms:

ALL, NONE, INDEX, NOINDEX, FOLLOW, NOFOLLOW.

Note: This tag is meant to provide users who cannot control the *robots.txt* file at their sites. It provides a last chance to keep their content out of search services. It was decided not to add syntax to allow robot specific permissions within the Meta tag.

INDEX means that robots are welcome to include this page in search services. FOLLOW means that robots are welcome to follow links from this page to find other pages. A value of NOFOLLOW allows the page to be indexed, but no links from the page are explored (this may be useful if the page is a free entry point into pay-per-view content, for example. A value of NONE tells the robot to ignore the page.

The values of INDEX and FOLLOW should be added to every page unless there is a specific reason why you do not want your page to be indexed. This may be the case if the page is only temporary.

<!--Comments Tag, repeat description here?--!> is a tag that is read by the Excite and Magellan spiders. A spider is an artificial intelligence agent that reads all of the information on a page and develops a "page description." The comments tag can be used to encourage a spider to display an accurate description of your pages. The description that a spider creates without this tag is often not pleasing, and usually doesn't depict what your pages are actually about.

The Future of Meta Tags

XML
eXtensible Markup Language: an emerging tag-based language.

New technologies are constantly replacing existing technologies. The introduction of **XML** may signal the end of the Meta tags and Meta-oriented search engines. XML is a markup language for structured data that allows you to specify both the tags you use and the semantics of these tags. In HTML, both the tag set and the semantics of the tags are fixed.

XML uses a **DTD** to define its tags. Search tools are being developed that search for DTDs when a particular keyword is sought. For instance, if you search for "whale watching," the XML search engine will seek all DTDs related to "whale watching." The result is that fewer pages are returned, but the search results are more focused.

A similar search for "whale watching" in an HTML search engine will return thousands of results barely related to the intended topic. XML search tools will focus on structured data and are more efficient than HTML search tools. HTML Meta tags can be misleading, and search criteria varies from engine to engine. This is why Meta-based search engines may eventually be replaced by their XML counterparts as XML becomes a more commonly accepted technology for web development.

DTD
Document Type Declaration: specifies the organization that issued the language specification.

Internet Resources

Review Your Site

Web Site Garage
http://www.websitegarage.com
This is a one-stop shop for servicing your web site. Here, you can run critical performance diagnostics on your entire web site and ensure browser compatibility by seeing your site in 18 different browsers, platforms, and screen sizes. This speeds up your site by optimizing your images and drives traffic to your web site. Provided is a comprehensive registration with up to 400 search engines, directories, and award sites. With this tool you can announce news through a Business Wire press release. You can target your industry, an Internet population, and analyze your web site traffic with a customizable tracking tool. This site will allow you to run a number of diagnostics on your site for free, including spellcheck, browser compatibility, load time, link popularity, and HTML design.

Net Mechanic
http://www.netmechanic.com
This site will check your web site to find broken links, perform HTML validation to make sure the format is compatible with the most common browsers, optimize your images for quicker loading, and monitor your server's performance for speed checking with different modem speeds. NetMechanic is a free online service.

Northern Webs
http://www.northernwebs.com
Northern Webs' Engine Tutorial is one of the recognized leaders in exposing the nuances of the various search engines and explaining what makes them tick. See if your site can stand the test of their exclusive Meta Medic!

Interactive Tools
http://www.arrowweb.com/graphics/tools.html
This site includes Interactive tools for webmasters and site designers. Use these tools to submit and promote your web site or to find problems. Utilities are included, such as an encyclopedia, a dictionary, a complete reference, and search tools.

Reviews of Relevant Web Site Performance Books
http://www.connectingonline.com/bookmark/books-15.html
If you are serious about maintaining an efficiently operating and easy to navigate web site, there is a link to a few books on the subject.

How To Build Lame Web Sites
http://www.webdevelopersjournal.com/columns/perpend1.html
A tongue-in-cheek article describing the methods you can utilize to achieve a poorly designed web site. Don't follow these methods, and your site will be fine.

Meta Tags

Meta Tags & Search Engines
http://www.webdigger.com/meta_tags.htm
Need to improve your search engine standings? Here are a few ideas to get you started: Meta tags as well as search engine and web site design tips.

Meta Tag Analyzer
http://www.scrubtheweb.com/abs/meta-check.html
This will check your Meta tags and your HTML code to help you achieve better placement in search engine results. Let their free Meta Tag Analyzer Program check your Meta tags and help analyze your HTML syntax online.

GoTo.com Search Suggestions
http://inventory.go2.com/inventory/Search_Suggestion.jhtml
Enter a keyword into the GoTo.com engine, and it will tell you how many people searched for that keyword. It also generates a list of other related keywords.

Meta Tag Generator
http://www.siteup.com/meta.html
The Meta Tag Generator will automatically generate Meta tags used by search engines to index your pages. SiteUp Internet Promotions offers a free download of the Windows 95 Meta TagGenerator.

Dr Clue's HTML Guide – Meta Tags
http://www.drclue.net/F1.cgi/HTML/META/META.html
Includes a short tutorial on Meta tags in addition to the keywords and description tags. It includes the Meta-Maker.

How To Use Meta Tags Tutorial
http://searchenginewatch.com/webmasters/meta.html

World of Design
http://www.globalserve.net/~iwb/search_engine/killer.html
This is a tutorial for writing Meta tags for higher search engine placement and good descriptions.

References

Web Developers Virtual Library
http://www.stars.com\ul
A comprehensive illustrated encyclopedia of web technology, the WDVL is for web masters and Internet developers. It's a well-organized gold mine of tutorials, demos, and links to great resources.

The World Wide Web Consortium
http://www.w3c.org
Find out everything you need to know about the past, present, and future of the World Wide Web. This web site has specifications for every web-related language. It's a valuable resource for all web developers.

Whatis.com
http://www.whatis.com
Whatis.com is "definition" paradise. It defines any computer-related word you ever wondered about.

WWW Meta Indexes and Search Tools
http://www.fys.ruu.nl/~kruis/h3.html
This is a Library of Congress Internet Resource Page.

Argus Clearinghouse
http://www.clearinghouse.net
The premier Internet research library or meta-index to locate everything you need to find on the web.

A Dictionary of HTML Meta Tags
http://vancouver-webpages.com/META

Graphics

The Gif Wizard
http://www.gifwizard.com
You can reduce all your graphics using the Gif Wizard Site Scan Monitor, a free service from Raspberry Hill Publishing.

3

Designing Your Site for Search Engine Prominence

Let's assume your tourism site is built and you feel you are now ready to submit to search engines and directories, where it must be found easily by your customers and prospective clients. You need to be listed in as many search engines as possible. Who knows which is the preferred directory or search engine of your potential visitor? When people conduct Internet searches they rarely go beyond the first few pages of results. You need to appear in the top 20 search results to be noticed. Before you submit to the search engines, you have to be sure your site is search engine friendly. In this chapter we cover:

- The key do's of web site design to accommodate search engines

- The major don'ts of web site design pertaining to search engines

- Using your competition and industry leaders as guidance

- The importance of keywords in all aspects of your web site

Increasing Your Web Site's Exposure on the Internet

A variety of search tools (search engines, directories, spiders, etc.) are currently used to navigate the World Wide Web. Due to the unprecedented growth of the information available on the Internet, there has been an unqualified demand for simplifying this information. As a result, the creation of search tools has catapulted. To maintain a competitive edge, it is absolutely imperative that your tourism web site be registered with as many search tools as possible. You never know which one is being used by your potential clients when they are planning their vacation. You want to make sure you are included in as many of them as possible and that you rank highly.

A Georgia Tech survey found that people find web sites using the following methods:

- Links from other sites, 88%

- Search engines, 85%

- Friends, 65%

- Printed media, 63%

- Directories, 58%

- Signature files, 36%

- Television, 32%

- Usenet, 30%

- Other, 29%

- Books, 28%

Search Engines and Their Indexing Methods

The most common search tool is the search engine. Search engines use programs or intelligent agents, called bots, to actually search the Internet for pages, which they index and include in their database using specific parameters as they read the content. The agent will read the information on every page of your site and then follow the links. For example, AltaVista's spider continually crawls the Web looking for sites to index and, of course, indexes sites upon their submission. Infoseek uses a spider as well, but their spider does not scour the web for sites to index. You must submit your site to Infoseek or it will never be listed. Inktomi also uses a spider; however, a user cannot access Inktomi's information directly to search. Instead a user will use other search engines and directories who use Inktomi's search engine technology, such as HotBot, Lycos, and Yahoo. Inktomi is very important in the search engine community, so be sure your site is easily accessible to its spider.

To register with search engines you simply visit their Web site and submit your URL on their submission form. This will be discussed in greater detail in the following chapter. The following sections discuss what to do and what not to do during web site design and development to best accommodate the search engines.

Use of Image Maps

An image map is a single graphic or image that has multiple hot links to different pages or resources. Some sites have only an image map on their home page—no text or navigation other than that found in the image map. Most search engines cannot read text that is embedded within a graphic or follow links embedded in a graphic. These image maps can actually prevent search engines from getting inside your site—you're basically locking the door on many of the search engines. This may result in some of the pages on your site not being indexed, or none of your site being indexed at all.

If you do use image maps, make sure that your site includes text as well as **hyperlinks** to other pages in your site.

Hyperlinks
Automatic links that connect a word, phrase, or picture on one web page to another web page.

Site map
A site map is a web page that provides links to all major sections of a web site.

This will ensure that search engines will find all of your pages and index them. You might consider developing a **site map** that has text links to all relevant pages within your web site. Once you have created your site map submit it to the major search engines. This will help the search engines find and index all the major pages within your site. Figure 3.1 shows an example of a site map.

Don't Spam the Search Engines

Some Internet marketers are trying various techniques to try to trick the search engines into positioning them higher in search results. The search engines are becoming more intelligent these days so I advise you stay away from the spam techniques. If it is discovered that you are trying to dupe the search engines, some may not list you at all. They have been programmed to detect some of these techniques, and

Figure 3.1. An example of a well-done, text-only site map.

you will be penalized in some way if you are discovered. Here are a few techniques that may be considered spam by some of the search engines:

- Repeating hidden keywords over and over again in your HTML and Meta tags.

- Repeating keywords over and over again by displaying them at the bottom of your document after a number of line breaks.

- Hiding keywords by displaying them in your document using a very small font.

- Repeating keywords in your document by making the text color the same as the background color.

- Making frequent and regular title changes so that the bots think your site is a new site and they list you again and again.

- Changing the name of your site to have a space, exclamation mark (!), or A as the first character so that you come up first in alphabetical lists.

Anytime you make significant changes to your site you should resubmit your site to the search engines. Search engines normally revisit on a regular schedule. However, these search engines are growing smarter every day—some monitor how often the site is updated and adjust their "revisit" schedule accordingly.

Meta Refresh

Have you ever visited a site and then been automatically transported to another page within the site? This is the result of a **Meta refresh tag.** A Meta refresh tag is an HTML document that is designed to automatically replace itself with another, after a certain specified period of time. Now that I've mentioned this, don't use them. Search engines generally do not like Meta refresh tags. Infoseek will not add sites that use a

Meta refresh tag
A tag used to automatically reload or load a new page

fast Meta refresh. If you do use a Meta refresh tag to redirect users, you should set a delay of at least 7 seconds and provide a link on the new page back to the page they were taken from. Some people use meta refresh tags to redirect users from a page that is obsolete or no longer there. People may also use meta refresh tags if they want to give an automated slideshow. Here's an example of what the HTML code for a meta refresh tag with a 30-second delay looks like:

```
<META HTTP-EQUIV="Refresh"
Content= "30;
URL=http://yourdomain.com/directory/refresh.html">
```

Search Engines and Frames

Frames
Divisions of a browser's display area into two or more independent areas.

From a marketing perspective you should avoid **frames** when developing your web site. See Figure 3.2 for an example of a Web page using frames. Frames may result in search engines being unable to index pages within your site or in improper pages being indexed.

What I mean by improper pages being indexed is that content pages will be indexed and when users are directed to these content pages by the search engines, they will likely not be able to navigate your site because the navigation frame probably will not be visible. To prevent this, one technique you can use is a Robots Meta tag in the head section of your HTML that does not allow bots to proceed beyond your home page. As a result, you can really only submit your home page to the search engine for indexing, which means you have less of a chance of receiving the high rankings you need on the major search engines. If you do use frames you should include textual links to all major sections within your site to make site navigation possible for those users who enter your site on a page other than a home page, and to assist the search engines with indexing your site.

Most search engines can only read information between the <NOFRAMES> tags within your master frame. The master frame identifies the other frames. I've found that all too often the individuals who apply frames ignore the <NOFRAMES> tags, which is a BIG no-no. If you do not have any text between the <NOFRAMES> tags, the search engines that reference your site for information will have nothing to look at. This will result in your site being listed with little

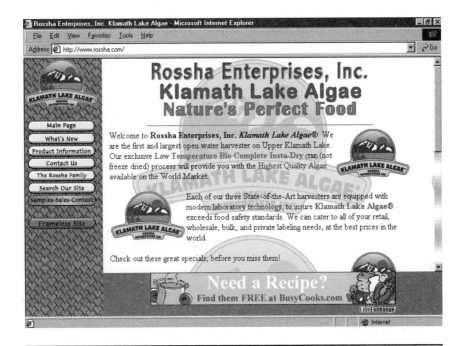

Figure 3.2.   An example using frames to split a page into three sections.

or no information in their indexes or so far down in the rankings that no one will ever find you anyway. To remedy this situation insert textual information that contains your most important descriptive keywords between the <NOFRAMES> tags. This will give the search engines something they can see, and it also helps those users who are browsing with non-frames-compatible browsers. Now that the search engines have found you, you still have a problem. They can't go anywhere. Create a link within your <NOFRAMES> tags to allow search engines and users with non-frames-compatible browsers to get into your site.

Frames are a headache when you are trying to design your site to be search engine friendly, and there's plenty more that can be said other than what was covered earlier. For example, if you bookmark a page other than the home page within a framed site your browser will likely only bookmark the home page because it is reading from the main frame and the URL of the main frame does not change. To make your life easier and from a marketing perspective it's better to avoid frames altogether.

Effective Use of Splash Pages

A splash page is basically an opening page that leads into a site. Often splash pages consist of a Java or a Marcomedia Flash intro that can be slow to load for some users. If you'd like to see an example, view one of the many feature film sites out there, they usually have a Flash intro to assist in the promotion of their movie.

Some people use splash screens that consist of an eye-pleasing image and an invitation to enter the site. Many splash pages implement techniques that automatically send you to the home page once you've seen the splash page; others will invite you to "click to enter" in some form or another. Why do people use splash pages on their sites? For one, they usually look beautiful. Another reason is to provide the user with something to look at while images or content for the home page loads in the background. Individuals also use splash pages as a means of advertising. Splash pages are usually very attractive in appearance, but they often lack content relevant to search engines.

If you do use a splash page on your site, be sure you include the proper Meta tags within your HTML header. This is important so that search engines that use Meta tags can access this information. This ultimately affects your ranking and how your site is displayed to users in the search results. If possible, include a paragraph or statement on your splash page that pertains to your site's content. This can help boost your rankings on some of the major search engines that both use and do not use Meta tags. Some search engines will review your opening paragraph and use this information when developing a description for your site that is presented in their search results. Figure 3.3 provides an example of an attractive Splash page with an opening paragraph.

Dynamic Pages and Special Characters

CGI
Computer
Gateway
Interface

Don't bother submitting pages that consist of **CGI** content or question marks (?) in the URLs. Search engines simply won't index them. In addition, some search engines such as Lycos will not index pages on your site that have the ampersand (&) or percent sign (%) charac-

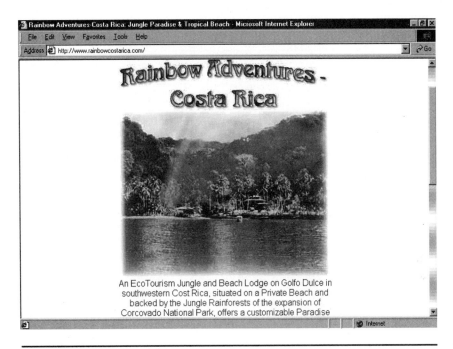

Figure 3.3. Here's an example of an attractive Splash page with an opening paragraph.

ters in the URL, for example, *http://www.yourdomain.com/ default.asp?bcr=1.*

Pointers To Remember When Using Tables

Tables can confuse some search engines, so be careful. Also, by using tables, you are potentially forcing the content you want search engines to see further down on your page. Because some search engines only look so far, you might be hurting your chances of receiving a high ranking. If you are using tables, place any important information pertaining to the page content above the table if possible to help prevent any potential problems. See Figure 3.4 for an example of a table.

Tables
Information arranged in columns and rows.

Here's an interesting problem some search engines suffer from. Assume you have a web site, the main color of the background is white, and you have a table on the page with a dark background. If you were to use white text in the table, some of the major search engines would pick this up as using white text on the white background and ignore your site's submission because it will be considered spam to them. Using tables is okay, many people do, just be careful with your choice of colors.

Maximizing Your Web Site's Visibility with Directories

Directories are often referred to as search engines. Unlike search engines, directories will not find your site if you do not tell them about it. Directories do not use bots or other intelligent agents to scour the Internet for new pages. Web sites must be submitted, and often the

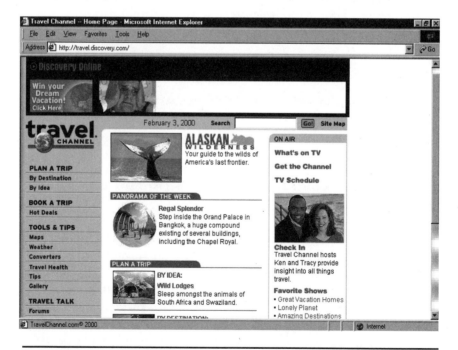

Figure 3.4. Often, tables are integrated seamlessly into a Web site.

submissions are monitored by human administrators. Some of the more popular directories are LookSmart, Snap, Yahoo (the most popular of all search engines and directories), and the DMOZ Open Directory Project. In general, directories do not have nearly as many sites indexed as do the search engines; however, the sites that are indexed are typically more appropriate content wise.

To be listed in a directory you need to submit or register your site information and URL address. This is best accomplished by visiting all the directories in which you want to be listed and filling out the required form. The registration forms are all quite similar and generally require information such as your URL, the name of your site, a description of your site, a list of keywords, your contact information, and other information depending on the particular directory. You must complete the form and click on the submit button to complete the registration process. More detail on submitting your site to a directory is covered in the next chapter.

Know your search engines and directories. Each one is different, using different criteria or algorithms to determine which sites rank highly. They also use different mechanisms to provide a description of your site and allow different lengths for a description. See Appendix C for details on popular search engines and directories. These are constantly changing, so to stay current you should follow up with a visit to the search engine and directory web sites and read their instructions and **FAQ** files.

Some directories automatically include the information you have submitted while others review and approve your site for inclusion. The latter can take up to a month.

FAQ
Frequently asked questions.

The Importance of Keywords

Keywords are an important aspect of every web page because the search engines use keywords in determining your site's ranking, and these are the words people are most likely to use when they're searching for your site. When you are creating your keyword list, don't just use nouns. Think of descriptive words that may be associated with benefits of your products or services. For example, if your site pertains to a bed and breakfast, then some of your keywords may be "bed and breakfast, lodging, travel, accommodations," and so on.

You can also add some keywords that describe advantages a person may receive from visiting your site.

When determining what your keywords will be, always keep your target visitors in mind. Try to think the way they would if they were to do a search for information on your topic. Don't just think about what people would do to find your site, think about what they would do if they didn't know your operation existed and were looking for the types of services you provide.

Here is an exercise to assist you in developing appropriate keywords for your site. Start by taking your brochures and all your other marketing materials, as well as a print copy of the site itself, and indiscriminately highlight any words that individuals might search on if they are looking for the services your tourism operation has to offer. Record these words in a text document in your word processing program.

Next, edit the list by deleting words that are too broad (for example, "Premier" or "Popular") or are not appropriate for keyword purposes. Review each word and ask yourself if someone would search using that word if they were looking for your products and services.

Always use the plural when forming your keywords where the plural is formed by adding an s. If you list "campground" as your keyword and someone uses "campgrounds" to do a search, then your site will not be found. If you include the word "campgrounds" in your keywords and someone requests information on the word "campground," your site will be found because "campground" is part of the word "campgrounds." Don't use both versions, because you're then running the risk of spamming the search engines, and you want to be able to use other keywords to increase your chances of achieving high rankings. The only time it is acceptable to use both the singular and the plural is if the plural does not include the singular in its entirety—for example, "ferry" and "ferries." In this case, you should list both the singular and the plural as part of your keyword list. It is also important to note that when most people perform their searches they will use the plural version. You're more likely to search for "beaches" than you are to search for "beach."

Now you have your master keyword list. For every page you want to submit to the search engines, take a photocopy of your master keyword list, eliminate and words that are not appropriate for the page you are submitting and then reorganize the remaining words in order of priority. By having the most important words first, no matter how many keywords the particular directory will allow, you are ready to submit. You can now simply Copy-Paste your keywords into your HTML for the keywords meta tag and also into the submission form for the directories that request a list of the appropriate keywords for the page you are submitting. Different directories allow for different numbers of keywords to be submitted. Because you have organized your list with the most important words first, you simply include as many of your keywords as the directory will allow. When a directory will allow multiple submissions for the same URL, you might consider submitting as many times as it takes to include all your keywords. You won't have to change your description or other information every time, just the keywords.

If you plan to submit every page of your site, your master list provides a valuable document. For each page that you are indexing, take a photocopy of the comprehensive list and delete words that are not appropriate for that particular page. Then re-prioritize the remaining keywords based on the content of the page you are indexing. This is then the keyword list for that page. Repeat this procedure for every page you will be indexing. If you make changes to your web pages, change the title and keywords contained in the title as well. This will allow you to be reindexed by search engines.

There is often the question of whether to include your competitors' names in your keywords. This follows the premise that if someone searches for them they will find you as well. There is, however, an ongoing debate as to whether this is useful. My position on this issue is *no*. Because several of the search engines allow for only 200 or fewer characters for keywords, you would be losing vital space to include keywords that describe or even name your products and/or services.

Your keyword list should be included in your submissions to directories and in a keyword Meta tag. However, to be listed in a higher position in search results you should include your most important keywords in other places as well, such as:

- Your page title

- Your description

- The first 200 to 250 characters of your page

- The beginning, middle, and end of your page text

- If frames are used, between the <noframes> tags

- In Alt tags

- In the keywords Meta tag

- In the descriptions Meta tag

- In comments tags

Include a comments tag in your HTML that has your keywords and your description in it. The comments tag is used by the Excite spider and if you include your most important keywords in it you may have your site rank a little higher in the search results for the keywords included.

Some search engines rank sites by how early the keyword appears on the site. The earlier a keyword is mentioned on your site, the higher your site may be positioned in search results. And remember the points made earlier, though you don't want to repeat a keyword hundreds of times (some search engines are on to this), you do want to repeat keywords a number of times on each page of your site. I recommend using keywords in conjunction with each other. AltaVista, Infoseek, and Webcrawler all like it when different keywords appear relatively close together in the page content.

Spiders and crawlers
Programs that visit web sites and read their pages to create entries for a search engine index.

Tips To Remember for Spider and Crawler Discoveries

Although **spiders and crawlers** can find your site whether or not you actually submitted it, I suggest you take the proactive approach. Check to see if they have already found your site, and if they haven't, submit your URL. Methods of checking whether or not your site is already in a search engine's database are discussed in the next chapter.

When a spider adds your page to its database, it uses the title found in the <TITLE> tag as the title of your page; hence, using good descriptive titles is very important. Different spiders use different methods to index a site. Some will index a portion of the page; some will index the entire page. Numerous keywords should be used on your home page to ensure that people who are looking for your type of operation will find you. For example, Lycos uses the first 200 characters in the description, yet indexes the 100 most important words on each page. Infoseek takes the first 250 characters of a site for its description.

For your site to be listed higher in search results, you must do a fair bit of research on ranking criteria and adjust your submission accordingly. WebCrawler, for example, will give your site a higher ranking if the word the user is employing as the keyword of the search (vacation, festivals, cruises, whatever) appears many times in the first paragraph or so of the page. Print your home page to get an idea of what may be listed for your site after you submit and your site is indexed. Check to ensure that this is an accurate portrayal of your site.

Because spiders will index pages other than your home page, you should go through this process for your entire site. Remember to have good navigational tools on every page of your site—you never know where your prospective customer is going to enter the site! With a good navigation bar, the users can get where they want to go on your site quickly and easily.

Study Competing Sites

Check out your competition. I use the term "competition" very loosely. I mean your industry leaders (whether or not you compete directly) and people who are selling noncompeting products to your target market, as well as your direct market. Search their names and see what they are using for descriptions and keywords. Next, search using some of your keywords and see what sites receive top ranking. This research will illustrate why they have received such a high ranking—and you can incorporate what you've learned into your web site. What do I mean? No one knows exactly how each search engine works, but by searching for your most important keywords and observing what the top ranking sites are using for their page content, title tags, description Meta tags, keywords Meta tags, and so on, you can formulate a good plan of attack. Remember that if you don't appear in the first two or three pages of search results, it is unlikely that prospective visitors will access your site through the search engine.

Check to see what your competitors have for Meta tags. Not only can you learn from the sites that catch your eye, you can also learn from your competitors' mistakes. After you have done a thorough job of this market research, you will be in a good position to develop a description that is catchy and adequately describes your site.

To check your competition's Meta tags in Microsoft Internet Explorer, you simply go to their site then click on "View" from your menu bar and in the drop-down menu select "Source." (See Figure 3.5) This will bring up the source code for that respective page in whatever your default text browser is. For most people this will be Notepad.

Looking for the same information in Netscape is just as easy. From the menu bar select "View," and then select "Page Source" from the drop-down menu. What you see is the HTML code for that page of the web site.

Figure 3.5(a). Look for the Source option under Internet Explorer's View menu.

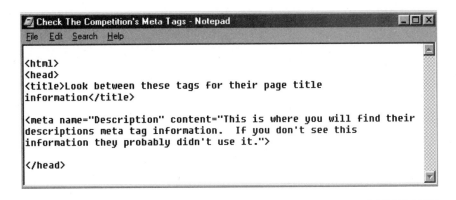

Figure 3.5(b). This is what you should look for in the source code of the site you're viewing.

The Benefits of Descriptive Page Titles

The <TITLE> tag is the first item a search agent reads, and many believe that next to site content, the title tag is the most important element used in determining your site's relevancy. Make sure every page in your site is titled properly for marketing purposes.

Don't just use your company name—use a descriptive title and make sure you include some keywords. Search engines will retrieve your page, look at your title, and then look at the rest of your page for keywords that match those found in the title. As mentioned before, many search engines use title tags in determining your ranking. Among the search engines that use page titles in their ranking criteria are AltaVista, Excite, Google, HotBot, Infoseek, NorthernLight, WebCrawler, and Yahoo. Pages that have keywords in the title are seen as more relevant than similar pages on the same subject that don't, and may be thus ranked in a higher position by the search engines. However, don't make your title a string of keywords like "Adventure Travel, Camping, Hiking, etc." because this will likely be considered spam by the search engines and you will end up worse off in the rankings or removed altogether. Also keep in mind that people will see that title in the search results and they're more likely to click on a site with a title that flows and is descriptive—not a list.

Keep in mind that when people bookmark your site or add it to their favorites, it is the page title that appears as the description. It is important that you keep your page titles under 50 characters in length if possible. Most search engines will not read past 50 characters, so you should concentrate on two or three keywords in your title tag.

The Importance of Meta Tags

Meta tags are an important part of reaching your goals online. AltaVista, Excite, Inktomi (e.g., HotBot), Infoseek, Lycos, WebCrawler, NorthernLight, and Google are all examples of search engines that use Meta tags in one form or another. Some search engines use your keywords Meta tags and description Meta tag in determining your ranking in their results. Some search engines also use this information as the source of description displayed to searchers out there looking for information. Detailed information on Meta tags can be found in Chapter 2, "Web Site Essentials."

As a general rule, keep your description and keywords Meta tags to under 200 characters in length. Some search engines allow for more, for example, Infoseek, which allows 1024 characters in the keywords Meta tags. I do not advise you use this many keywords unless you plan on creating a doorway page specifically for that search engine. When you use too many keywords you end up diluting the importance of each keyword, meaning potentially lower rankings in the search engines.

Another rule of thumb is to use lowercase letters when formulating your keywords Meta tags because most search engines are not case sensitive. Only AltaVista and Infoseek are truly case sensitive, and even then most people perform searches using only lowercase letters anyway.

It is important not to repeat a keyword more than five times within your keywords Meta tags. Doing so will be considered spam by some of the search engines, which means they'll likely ignore your submission—not something you want. Another tactic to prevent keyword spamming is to formulate keyword phrases. Instead of using the word "ski" over and over again, mix it up by creating phrases like ski resort, ski lessons, ski lodge. When you do this be sure to separate the phrases with commas, or it will simply look like "ski resort ski" which may be considered spam by some of the search engines.

As always with keywords, place the most important words first in your description and keywords Meta tags. This will help you in achieving higher rankings because most search engines consider the first few keywords the most important in their ranking criteria. Also, what if the search engine you're submitting to only looks at the first 30 or so characters? You're OK, because you placed the most important keywords first.

Why Bother With Alt Tags?

Some search engines will include information within Alt tags when they form the description for your site and in the ranking of your site. Alt tags appear after an image tag and contain a phrase that is associated with the image. Ensure that your Alt tags contain descriptive keywords. This gives your page a better chance of being ranked higher in the search engines' results, for example, <image src="logo.gif" alt="Tattingstone Country Inn Logo">

You do not want your Alt tags to look something like "Our Logo" because this does not include any keywords. Be sure you apply proper Alt tags to all images on your site to achieve best results. Keep in mind that users who browse with graphics disabled must be able to navigate your site, and proper use of Alt tags will assist them in doing so.

The Significance of Your URL

Where possible, apply keywords in your URL. Some search engines give higher rankings to sites that do.Make sure you own your own domain name. If your site is listed as a subdirectory on your ISP or web host's domain, the search engines will not give you as much credibility. For example, you don't want your site address to be *http:// www.yourhostsdomain/tourism/youroperation.html,* you want to be registered under your own domain such as *www.youroperation.com* or *www.keywordorkeywords.com.* Google prefers domain names that match the keyword being searched for. Try searching for "hotel" on Google. What are the results? The number one result and likely most of the other top results all include hotel in their domain name. Try a couple of other searches as well, maybe "trip" for example—I'll bet Trip.com's home page is the one that comes up first.

Try to use keywords in your subpages where possible. For example, if your site has a list of local golf courses, you may want to have a sub-page named *golf-courses.htm* or *golf_courses.htm*. An important item to remember here is that some of the search engines can't tell two keywords exist if you join the words together in your subpage like *golfcourses.htm*. Be sure you separate the keywords with either an underscore (_) or a dash (-). Using these little tips can go a long way in helping you achieve success among the search engines.

Another Look at Site Content and Additional Design Factors

To achieve optimum results, you should design your site content carefully. You want to apply the most important keywords near the beginning of your page because many search engines weigh the content near the start of a site as the most important.

Always have a descriptive paragraph at the top of your web page. Search engines that do not use Meta tags will use this as their source for a site description and keywords on your site. Also, search engines will use the content found within the opening paragraph in determining the ranking of your site among search results. Again, be sure to use the most important keywords first, preferably within the first two or three sentences. This is very important. Infoseek and AltaVista boost pages that use well-placed keywords near the top of the page content. Make sure that the keywords you use flow naturally within the content of the opening paragraph and relate to content/purpose of your site—you don't want the search engines to think you're trying to cram words in where they don't fit.

Use your HTML <H1>headers</H1> effectively to indicate the subject/content of a particular page. Most people only use them as a method of creating large fonts. Some search engines, including Google, use the content included within the header text in their relevancy scoring.

As you can tell, textual HTML content is extremely important to the search engines, which brings me to my next point. Never create a page that is excessive in graphical content. For example, don't display information that should be displayed in text as a graphic file. I've seen this done numerous times. A site may have the best opening statement in the world, but the search engines can't use it because the information is presented in the form of a graphic. No matter how great it looks, the search engines can't read your graphics for content.

Do not make your home page excessively lengthy. The longer your page is, the less relevant the information on the page becomes to the search engines. I recommend you keep your home page short and to the point. Of course, no technique is going to work all of the time —AltaVista seems to like pages that are somewhat longer in length.

Little things like how often you update your site can have an affect on how well your site places in search engine results. Spiders can determine how often a page is updated and will revisit your site accordingly. This may lead to higher rankings in some of the major search engines. Remember, you can also resubmit your site manually once you have made changes; however, I don't advise doing so if you already have a high ranking. If the criteria used for ranking a site has changed, you may actually end up worse off.

Before you submit your site, be sure the content on the page you're submitting is complete. Yahoo, for one, may ignore your submission if you have Under Construction or related signs on your page.

Internet Resources

Search Engine Watch
http://www.searchenginewatch.com
Search Engine Watch is a web site devoted to how search engines work, search engine news, search engine information, tips on using search engines, and more about search engines. More information than you can stand! Be sure to sign up for the Search Engine Report mailing list.

Search Engine World
http://www.searchengineworld.com
A great resource for everything surrounding search engines. Plenty of articles, tips, and information to help you achieve online success. This site also has in-depth information on the various search engine spiders.

PegasoWeb: Web Promotion Portal
http://www.pegasoweb.com/
Information on promoting your web site through search engines, e-zines, newsletters, and banner advertising. Tools, resources, and services both free and fee-based.

Search Engine Matrix
http://searchenginematrix.com/
Learn about search engines and search engine positioning to achieve greater positioning within any given search engine.

Search Engine Forums
http://searchengineforums.com/bin/Ultimate.cgi
Information pertaining to search engines and web site promotion presented in the form of a bulletin board.

Internet InfoScavenger
http://www.infoscavenger.com/engine.htm
Internet InfoScavenger is a monthly newsletter publication devoted to helping busy professionals market their products and services on the web. Invaluable help, techniques, and tips for top search engine placement.

WebReference.com
http://www.webreference.com/content/search
Search engines and examples, tips, and hints for getting the most out of your search engine, for people who work on the web.

Submit It! Search Engine Tips
http://www.submit-it.com/subopt.htm
The purpose of this document is to provide you with background information on search engine technology and some tips on how to get your web site to appear on the result pages of search engines and directories.

World of Design—Search Engine Secrets
http://www.globalserve.net/~iwb/search/
References to monitor, submit, and improve search engine placements and positions.

Bruce Clay—Search Engine Optimization Tools
http://www.bruceclay.com/web_rank.htm
Free search engine optimization, ranking, web site promotion, key-words advice, and placement material for designers.

Net Promote
http://www.netpromote.com/
Net Promote has Promotion 101, a web site marketing and promotion information center, where you can find all kinds of free articles, resources, tools, and links to help you promote your site. They also offer web site registration, web site consultation, press release distribution, site launch services, banner advertising, consulting, and more.

JimTools.com Webmaster's Toolkit Command Center
http://www.jimtools.com/
A number of tools are available on this site that you can use for free. There's information on the search engines and Meta tags, a link checker, and a link popularity tool.

LinkPopularity.com: The Free Link Popularity Service
http://www.linkpopularity.com/
A free service that queries AltaVista, Infoseek, and HotBot to check your link popularity.

Note: Resources found in the next chapter on search engine submissions are closely related to the information found in this chapter. I recommend reviewing the resources in the next chapter because many contain valuable information on designing your site to be search engine friendly.

4

Search Engine and Directory Submission Strategies

Maximizing Exposure with Search Tools

There are an estimated 1.5 billion web pages on the World Wide Web, so how can you increase the chances of your site being found? One method is submitting to the many search engines and directories. Once you've optimized your web site to be search engine friendly you are ready to face the challenge of submitting to the most important search engines. When I say search engines I'm referring to the combination of search engines and directories. You need to be within the first two pages of search results to ensure your best possible success online. This is no easy feat, and this chapter will provide you with the knowledge necessary to get on the road to success. This chapter covers:

- Search engines, directories, and their ranking criteria

- An in-depth look at Yahoo's submission process

- An in-depth look at AltaVista's submission process

- The submission tools available to you

- Search engine and directory submission pointers

Understanding Search Engines and Directories

The last chapter discussed how search engines and directories differ. In general, search engines have a much larger index and utilize spiders to add sites to their index. In contrast directories typically have a smaller index and are usually maintained by humans. When you're submitting to a site, you can usually tell the difference between a directory and a search engine by the information they request. A search engine typically asks for the URL you wish to submit and sometimes your e-mail address. A directory will usually ask for much more, including your URL, the category you wish to be added to, the title of your site, a description, appropriate keywords and your contact information.

When you do a search on the Internet, in seconds the search engine digests what you are looking for, searches the millions of pages it knows about, and responds to your request with appropriate sites ranked in order of importance. Amazing! How do they do it?

Search engines use spiders to index your site. Usually a search engine's spider will index or include the pages on your site once you have submitted the request to be added to their database, but sometimes they can't for a number of reasons. They may have problems with frames or image maps on a web site, they may simply miss a page, and so on. Even though a number of the spiders out there constantly crawl the web looking for sites and your site may be found and indexed without any effort on your part, I suggest you take the pro-active approach and submit all appropriate pages on your site to the search engines to guarantee that all your important pages are properly listed. Also, before you submit, check the search engine's submission document to be sure submitting more than one page is permitted, because you don't want your site to be rejected. A search engine may also have restrictions on the number of pages you can submit in a single day—perhaps they only allow 5 or 10 to be submitted.

Some of the search engines share technology; for example, MSN Search uses Inktomi's technology for some of their results. All search engines have different ranking criteria to determine who gets top placement. Some search engines look for how often a keyword appears on the web page. It is assumed that if a keyword is used more frequently on a page, then that page is more relevant than other pages with a lower usage of that keyword. Some search engines look for the keyword in the title of the web page and assume that if the keyword is in the title, then that page must be more relevant than those that don't have the keyword in their title. Some search engines determine where keywords are used and assume that pages with the keyword in headings and in the first couple of paragraphs are more relevant. Some search engines use the number of links pointing to a particular page as part of their ranking criteria. Some search engines use information contained in Meta tags; others don't look at the Meta tags at all.

To summarize, search engines all have different ranking criteria and this is why you receive different results when you search on the same keyword with different engines. For each of the major search engines you should learn as much as you can about their ranking system and adjust your submission or your site's content accordingly. One site that is particularly useful with this information is *http://searchenginewatch.com*.

Some of the more popular search engines (see Figures 4.1 to 4.8) include:

- AltaVista

- Excite

- Google

- HotBot

- Infoseek/Go

- Lycos

- NorthernLight

- WebCrawler

Figure 4.1. AltaVista's home page.

Figure 4.2. Excite's home page.

Figure 4.3. Google's home page.

Figure 4.4. HotBot's home page.

Figure 4.5. Infoseek/Go's home page.

Figure 4.6. Lycos' home page.

Figure 4.7. NorthernLight's home page.

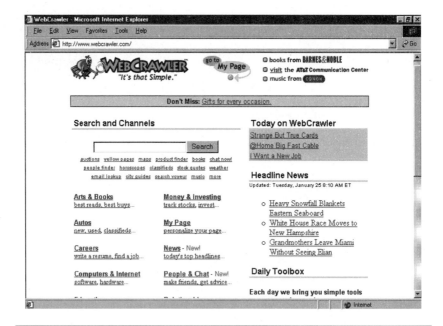

Figure 4.8. WebCrawler's home page.

Let's turn our attention to directories now. Because directories are usually maintained by human administrators you can expect to wait a longer period of time before seeing your page appear in their index. In general you can expect to wait between two and eight weeks. It takes longer because the human administrators review every page submitted before adding it to their database. Make sure your page is easy to use, visually appealing, and rich in content, because it is the administrators who decide if your page is worthwhile before they include it.

When you submit to a directory you will also have to take the time to find the best category for your site. Submitting your site to the wrong category could mean a minimal increase in traffic if no one thinks to look for you in the category you submitted to. Also, your site may not be added if you select an inappropriate category. LookSmart's Travel category contains subcategories including Activities, Destinations, Lodging, Transportation, and so on. These categories are then often broken down further into other categories within the subcategories. The deeper you go, the more specific the category becomes.

Unlike a search engine, your site's position in directories (see Figures 4.9 to 4.13) relies much less on web site design and more on the initial submission process itself, which is why it is important to review each directory's submission procedure and submission tips. You will be asked for a lot more information when submitting to a directory. The title, description, and any other information you give them during submission is what will be used to rank your site.

Here are some of the more popular directories:

- Argus Clearinghouse

- LookSmart

- Open Directory Project

- Snap

- Yahoo!

There are many travel and tourism search engines and directories on the web (see Figures 4.14 to 4.30) that you may want to investigate further. Here's a list of some of the travel- and tourism-related search engines and directories:

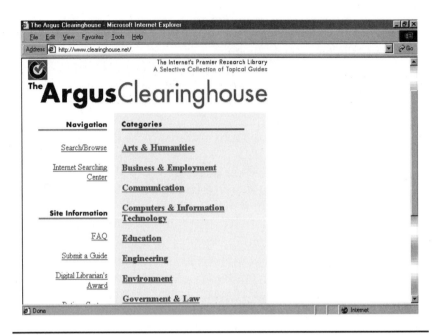

Figure 4.9. Argus Clearinghouse's home page.

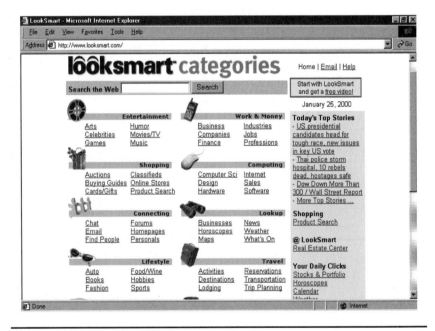

Figure 4.10. LookSmart's home page.

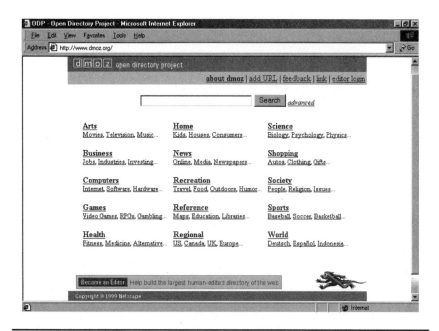

Figure 4.11. Open Directory Project's home page.

Figure 4.12. Snap's home page.

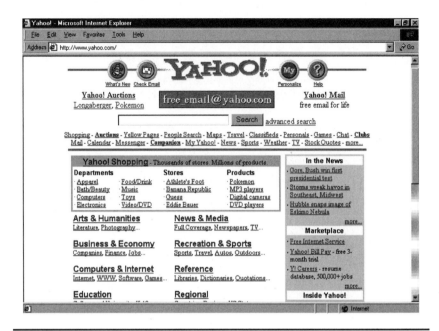

Figure 4.13. Yahoo's home page.

Figure 4.14. Accommodation Search Engine's home page.

Figure 4.15. Asiaco's home page.

Figure 4.16. Online City Guide's home page.

Figure 4.17. EuroSeek's home page.

Figure 4.18. EXES Travel Search's home page.

Figure 4.19. Guide 105's home page.

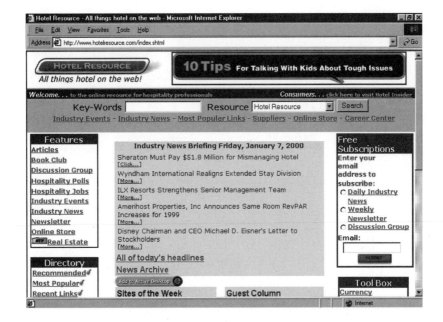

Figure 4.20. Hotel Resource's home page.

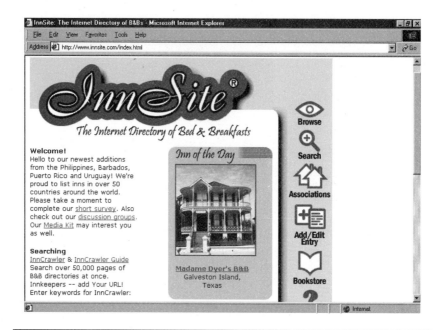

Figure 4.21. InnSite's home page.

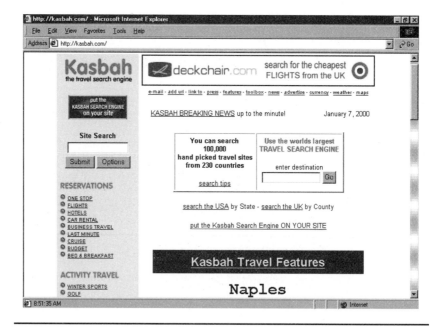

Figure 4.22. Kasbah's home page.

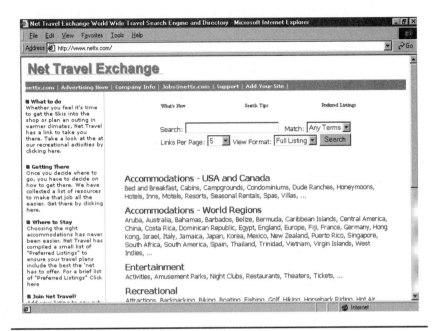

Figure 4.23. Net Travel Exchange's home page.

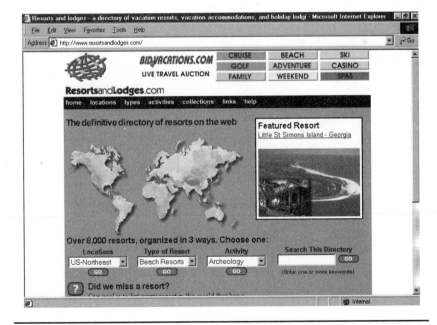

Figure 4.24. ResortsandLodges.com's home page.

Figure 4.25. SkiPages.com's home page.

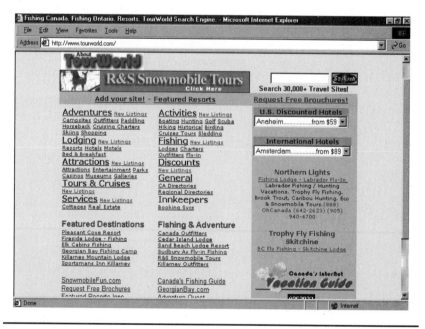

Figure 4.26. TourWorld's home page.

Figure 4.27. 111 Travel Directory's home page.

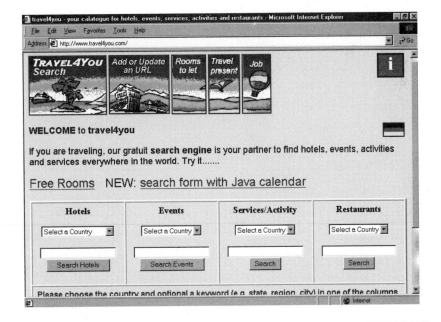

Figure 4.28. Travel4You's home page.

Figure 4.29. Travel-Finder's home page.

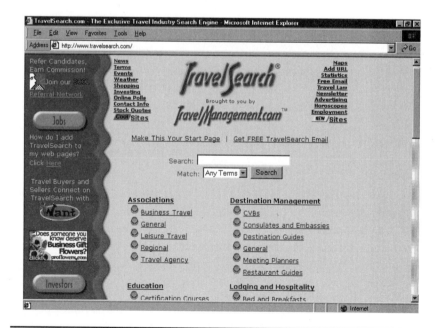

Figure 4.30. TravelSearch's home page.

- Accommodation Search Engine

- Asiaco

- Online City Guide: Your Link to America

- EuroSeek

- EXES Travel Search

- Guide 105

- Hotel Resource

- InnSite

- Kasbah: The Travel Search Engine

- Net Travel Exchange

- ResortsandLodges.com

- SkiPages.com

- TourWorld

- 111 Travel Directory

- Travel4You

- Travel-Finder

- TravelSearch

Maximizing Visibility with Submission Pointers

Submitting to the search engines and directories is a very time-consuming but extremely important task. Don't rush! Take your time, do your research, know the ranking strategy employed, and prepare your submission for optimal results. It's very difficult to change your entry once it has been submitted, and the last thing you want is a typo. If the time available for indexing is limited, start by focusing on the most popular search engines and directories for individual submissions and use a multiple submission site for the less important ones. Remember, 85% of all Internet users use search engines and directories to find what they are looking for.

When submitting to the search engines and directories, take the time up front to develop the submission material carefully. Organize the information in a logical order in a text file. Then when you go to submit you will be able to copy and paste the content to the appropriate fields on the submission form. Be sure to spell check, check, and recheck everything before you start. Spell-checkers won't pick up misspelled "works" if that word is also in the dictionary. The information prepared for each page on the site to be indexed should include:

- URL

- Page title

- 10-word, 25-word, 50-word and 100-word descriptions for the page (different engines allow different lengths of description)

- List of keywords for each page (see the Keyword section of this chapter for tips)

- Description of the ideal audience for the site

- Contact information:

  - Your operation's name

  - Contact name

  - E-mail address

  - Your operation's address

- Telephone and fax numbers

Print the submission forms (see Figures 4.31 to 4.36 for some examples) for the various search engines and directories, and examine them to determine that you have all the information required for submission.

When submitting forms to directories, be very careful to fill in every field on the form. Some of the search engines will reject your registration automatically if you have not filled in all the blanks.

When you have to choose categories, select them very carefully. It would be a shame to have a great product, a great price, and a great site, but be listed in a place where your potential customer would never think about looking for you.

Read the FAQ files or instructions first to ensure that you understand exactly what information they are requesting.

Proofread your submission at least twice before you hit the submit button. It isn't quick or easy to change listings if you make a mistake. Your listing may be wrong for quite awhile before it gets corrected.

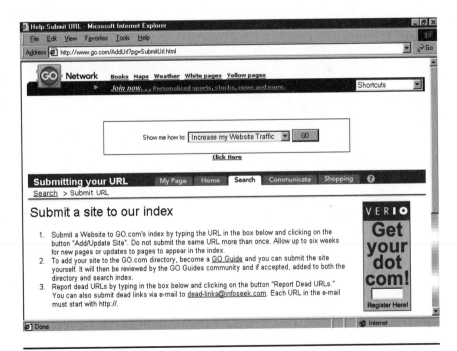

Figure 4.31. Infoseek's submission page.

Figure 4.32. NorthernLight's submission page.

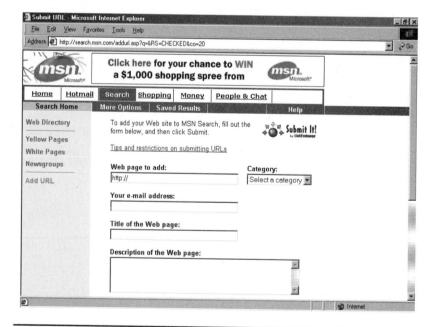

Figure 4.33. Submitting to MSN Search.

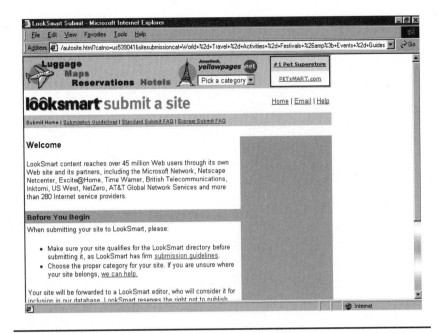

Figure 4.34. Submitting to LookSmart.

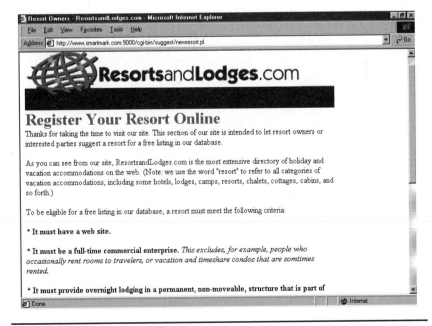

Figure 4.35. ResortsandLodges.com's resort registration page.

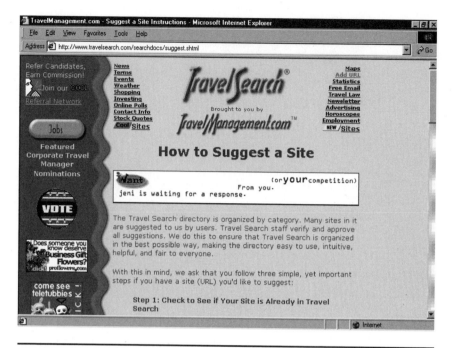

Figure 4.36. How to suggest a site on TravelSearch.

Coming to Terms with the Proper Use of Keywords

It's important to take another look at keywords. Keywords are the words used by your target customers when they do a search for your types of products and services in the search engines or directories. Your keywords will be used in everything you do and are the key determining factor in how you rank in the search results among many of the major search engines.

As a general rule you should ensure you use keywords where appropriate. Keywords should be applied in your page titles, headers, Alt tags, keywords Meta tags, description Meta tags, hyperlinks, textual content information, and so on. Another rule of thumb is to apply keywords naturally, so that they flow with the information. For example, a description that is just a list of keywords is likely to get you bumped down in search engine results or removed altogether because some search engines consider this spamming. Last, apply the most important keywords first. Many search engines place greater emphasis on keywords near the beginning of your keywords list, description, and so on.

Be sure to use different keywords and strings of keywords for different pages on your site. Each page is unique, with different content, so by using keywords specific to each page you're increasing your chances of being found by your target audience. If you have the same keywords on every page, you're limiting yourself to the exact same range of keywords.

Review the keywords section in the previous chapter. It discusses how to develop your master keywords list and how to apply it to the appropriate sections of your site. The keywords you want to use are the ones individuals are likely to use when performing a search.

When applying keywords, the most important places to remember are:

- Your page title

- Your page content—beginning, middle, and end of your page's text

- Your Meta tags—keywords and description

- Between your <noframes> tag if your site uses frames

- In Alt tags applied to your images

Great Descriptions Return Great Results

It is a good idea to create a number of different descriptions of varying lengths because the different search engines and directories allow different description sizes. Start off creating a description of 10 words, then 25, then 50, and then 100. Make sure that you use the right length description for each search engine because you don't want it to be truncated when displayed in search results.

Your description should be compelling. When you get your site to appear in the first 20 to 30 top results of a search, the description is what differentiates your site from the rest. It is the description that will entice the prospective visitor to click and visit—or pass and go to a more exciting site.

Always use keywords in your description. Apply the most important keywords first because keywords used further along in the description are generally given less weight by the major search engines. If possible use keywords in combination with other keywords, but make sure your description flows naturally.

Be sure to use a call to action in your description. It's amazing how many people do what they are told. Perhaps your description could have a line that says, "Visit us now and sign up for our free monthly newsletter."

Multiple Listings Do Help!

One way to get your site listed many times is to submit many times. Because each page on your site is a potential entry point for search engines and each page has a unique URL, you can submit each URL (each page) in the various search engines, directories, and so on. Each page of your site should be indexed to improve your chances of having your site listed in the top 10 search engine results. Because every page on your site is different, each page should have a different title, a different description, and different keywords. In doing so you're increasing your chances of being found by people searching for different criteria and keywords.

It is important to abide by Netiquette. In some search sites the previously discussed practice of submitting multiple times is acceptable and may even be encouraged. In others it is considered abuse and is discouraged. Use your judgment on this one!

Development of Doorway Pages

Due to the need to be ranked high in search engine results and the enormous competition between sites trying to get listed on search engines, doorway pages have become increasingly popular. Each search engine is different and has different elements in their ranking criteria. Developing doorway pages allows you to tailor a page specifically for each search engine before submitting to achieve optimal results. Be careful, though, some search engines frown upon doorway pages, so perform a background check before creating and submitting one.

Doorway pages, also known as gateway pages, are pages that lead to your site but are not considered part of your site. Do not include doorway pages on your site's site map! In fact, do not allow any pages within your site to link to the doorway pages you have created. If you do and a search engine spider finds these pages it will likely consider them spam and you will be removed from their directory or at minimum your current ranking will fall.

Doorway pages are focused pages that lead to your web site but are tuned to the specific requirements of the search engines. By having different doorway pages with different names (e.g., *indexa.html* for AltaVista or *indexi.html* for Infoseek) for each search engine, you can look back and see which page is bringing in the most traffic. Those pages that are not bringing in the traffic can then be edited and resubmitted until you get it right. Make sure that the doorway page you create represents the page it leads to.

The various criteria search engines use in determining their rankings are always changing as the fight for top spot as search engine king progresses; however, some general pointers always apply, and they revolve around keyword use and placement.

Apply keywords or a keyword phrase in your title tag as well as in your keywords Meta tag and description Meta tag. Many search engines consider your title tag when ranking sites. If you use a header tag, be sure you apply keywords or a keyword phrase here. Try to keep it a close match with what you use in your keywords Meta tag, descriptions Meta tag, and title tag. Stick with your keywords! Try to use the keywords you used in the preceding steps naturally near the start of the first paragraph on your doorway page. The further down the page the keywords appear, the less emphasis the search engines will place on them. If your doorway page is going to include a graphic or graphics, then be sure to use those ever-important descriptive keywords once more in your Alt tags. This provides users who browse with graphics disabled the ability to understand what graphic you wanted them to see.

Perhaps more important is the fact that a number of the large and popular search engines reference keywords they find in Alt tags when ranking your site. Ensure that you place keywords within your hyperlinks as well. This can also increase search engine rankings! Last, use descriptive keywords throughout the content portion of your doorway page with the most important keywords being applied first. The title and content of your doorway page are the two most important places, so take your time and do it right. For more details on what the major search engines use for ranking criteria, visit the URLs in the resource section of this chapter that relate to search engine feature charts. Also refer to Appendix C.

As one would expect, doorway pages have their drawbacks as well. Doorway pages are often easy to duplicate. You competition may use your doorway page as a template and tweak/modify it to suit their purposes. If you create a doorway page be sure not to use a fast Meta refresh as discussed in Chapter 3. In addition, if your competition copies and modifies your page to the search engine, it's likely that most of the content will remain very similar. If this is the case, the search engine may think you're trying to spam them by submitting duplicate sites and you'll both get removed.

Keywords are the important thing to remember here. When you develop a doorway page keep the tips that were mentioned earlier in mind. Place the most important keywords and keyword phrases first in your title tag, keyword Meta tags, description Meta tags, opening page paragraph, headers, hyperlinks, and so on.

An In-Depth Look at Yahoo

Yahoo, developed by David Filo and Jerry Yang around April of 1994, is the most popular directory among Internet users today. Millions of people use Yahoo every day, and it is definitely a location where you want your site listed.

Yahoo is not a search engine, it is a directory. Yahoo has approximately 150 human administrators who review every site submitted. By default Yahoo displays information contained within its own directory; however, Yahoo also allows you to perform searches outside its own database by referencing Inktomi's search technology. To view results returned by Inktomi's engine, click on "Web Pages" at the top or bottom of the page once you have performed your search.

Yahoo's directory is broken down into 14 major categories:

- Arts & Humanities

- Business & Economy

- Computers & Internet

- Education

- Entertainment

- Government

- Health

- News & Media

- Recreation & Sports

- Reference

- Regional

- Science

- Social Science

- Society & Culture

Each of Yahoo's 14 major categories is broken down into subcategories, which also contain sub-subcategories. The deeper you go into the categories the more content specific the directories become. Within the Recreation & Sports category you can select Travel, and from there you can select more specific categories such as Boating, Budget Travel, Business Travel, Ecotourism, Resorts, and so on. When you are looking for categories appropriate for your site, take your time, because you want to be listed in the best location. If you submit to a category that is not appropriate, your site users may not think to look for you there or Yahoo may not even add your site at all. Check out your competitors and perform some searches using keywords you feel people would use when looking for your products or services and observe the categories that are displayed. The category or categories you want to be listed in will likely be included in these. Pick the most relevant categories that apply to your page, but keep in mind that when searches are performed the categories are displayed in alphabetical order. Once you find a category you wish to submit, select "Submit a Site."

Before you go any further, is your site complete? Yahoo may not add your site if you have Under Construction signs on your pages. Yahoo likes sites that are complete, contain good and pertinent information, are aesthetically pleasing, and are easy to use. Also, check to see if you're already in their directory. You may not want or need to submit your site if you're where you want to be already. If you are in their directory but want to change the information displayed, then you can fill out a form located at *http://add.yahoo.com/fast/change* that is specifically used for changing information already listed in their directory.

Now that you are ready to submit, take your time to read all of their documentation on submitting. You want to follow their guide to the letter to ensure the best possible chance of being added to their directory. Yahoo administrators are overwhelmed with submissions and will not take the time to review a site that has not followed their submission directions. Open up your text document where you've saved all of that relevant submission information I mentioned before. It will come in handy here. Fill out their submission form fully and completely. Before proceeding with the submission process, make sure your information is correct and you have made no errors. *You do not want to make mistakes.*

Once you have submitted your information, be patient, it takes an average of six to eight weeks for a submission to be reviewed and added to the directory, if it's going to be added at all. If you feel you have done everything right and have been waiting for what seems an excessive length of time, and you have not been added to their directory, then resubmit. If you still aren't added, then send a polite e-mail to Yahoo discussing your situation and request assistance. As a side note, if you're a U.S. commercial operation then you can pay $199 US for express submission service. This service does not guarantee you'll be listed faster or even that you'll be listed at all, it just means they'll put a priority on reviewing your web site.

The following are some other tips to remember when submitting your site to Yahoo:

- Remember, your submission counts for almost everything here, so do it right. Yahoo is a directory, not a search engine. Designing your site to be search engine friendly means very little here.

- Make sure that what you submit is actually what your site is about. Yahoo's administrators will review your site, and if they feel the description you provided does not match up with your site, then you will not be added to their directory.

- Keep your description to 25 words or less and use descriptive keywords that flow naturally within the description. Yahoo reserves the right to modify your description if they see fit. You're the only one who knows what information is important to have included in your description, so you probably do not want Yahoo's administrators to modify your description, because you may lose an important part of your description, resulting in less traffic. Also remember that Yahoo does not like submissions that sound like an advertisement—they like concise, pertinent information.

- Submit a short, relevant title, not something like "The Best Adventure Travel Site on the Web." Also, be sure to use descriptive keywords in your title. When searches are performed, your page title will be referenced. In addition, when search results are displayed, they are displayed in alphabetical order. If possible, try to generate a title that starts with a letter near the beginning of the alphabet. If the title you submit is not appropriate, Yahoo may consider your submission spam and your page will be rejected. For example, don't title your site "AAA Adventure Travel," if that's not the name of your site, just to appear near the top of the rankings. Like the description, make sure your title flows naturally.

- When submitting, develop your page title and descriptions to try to use keywords in combination with others because this can also give you a boost. Check out your competitors to see who's on the top and what they're doing right.

- If you're looking for local traffic, then submitting to a Regional category may be appropriate for you.

- Don't fill out the submission form using all CAPITALS—they hate that. Use proper grammar and spelling. Before you submit, be sure to check and recheck your submission to ensure all is well.

- If your domain name contains keywords, you will benefit here. Keywords in your domain name can help you out when a user performs a search on a keyword that is in your domain name.

- Don't forget to fill out Yahoo's submission form (see Figure 4.37) exactly as requested! Read their help documentation and FAQ files, beginning with "How to Suggest Your Site," which can be found at *http://docs.yahoo.com/info/suggest/*.

An In-Depth Look at AltaVista

Originally launched near the end of 1995, AltaVista is the second most popular search tool after Yahoo and claims to have the largest index of catalogued web pages at 250 million.

AltaVista is a true search engine whose spider, Scooter, indexes web pages. Scooter is a "deep search" spider, meaning it will visit all pages on your web site as long as it is given the opportunity to. A fast Meta refresh or a dynamic page developed using CGI can cause problems for Scooter. I recommend reading Chapter 3, the search engine friendliness chapter, for more information, because it discusses web site design and its effects on how your site is indexed by the major search engines. AltaVista also uses the DMOZ open directory project for some of its results, so be sure to submit your site to the open directory project at *http://www.dmoz.org/*.

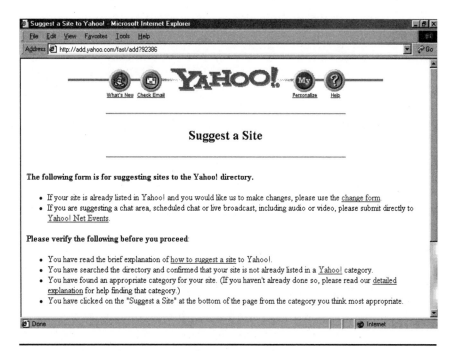

Figure 4.37. Submitting to Yahoo!

Before you submit, make sure your page is complete. AltaVista wants quality pages and does not like to index pages that are incomplete or inappropriate. Every search engine wants quality sites indexed, because if they list a lot of junk, then users will stop returning.

Submitting to AltaVista is a simple process. See Figure 4.38 for the submission form. All you have to do is click on "Add a URL" from their home page. This will take you to their submission page, where you enter your URL into the designated field. That's it, you're done—the rest relies on your site design.

It typically takes 24 to 48 hours before your site is added to AltaVista's index. Scooter will then periodically revisit your site, looking to add new and updated pages. If you feel you have done everything right but are not showing up in their index, then send them a polite e-mail asking if there's a problem and if anything can be done.

Figure 4.38.   Submitting to AltaVista.

It could be that your site is not optimized for AltaVista and that is why you're not appearing in the results.

AltaVista uses Meta tags. It will use your description Meta tag to formulate a description of your site, which is then presented to users when they perform a search. In addition, AltaVista uses your keywords Meta tag and your descriptions Meta tag as a factor in determining your site's ranking among its results. Keywords applied in your title also affect your page's position. If you do not have a description Meta tag, AltaVista will reference your site's content and formulate its own description based on this. If you do not have a title tag, AltaVista will display "No Title" in the search results, if you're ranked at all. Here are some tips to improve your ranking in Alta Vista:

- Your ranking on AltaVista is determined by your site's design, so be sure to make it easily accessible for AltaVista's spider Scooter.

- Use keywords in your title, Meta tags, Alt tags, and page content. Make sure the most important keywords are used first because more weight is given to the keywords that appear first. Also, try to use keywords in combination with other keywords because this can boost your ranking.

- AltaVista is a case-sensitive search engine. If any of your keywords are usually uppercase, you may want to include both the upper- and lowercase version of the word in your keyword Meta tag.

- Link popularity can influence your position. If possible increase the number of links pointing toward your site.

- Search Engine World *(http://www.searchengineworld.com/)* mentions that older pages tend to perform better in AltaVista's rankings, as do pages with a lot of content.

- Do not spam AltaVista, or your ranking will quickly drop— or your site may be removed altogether. For example, AltaVista does not like multiple doorways or pages that repeat the same keyword over and over again (e.g.,"Cruise, Cruise, Luxury Cruise, Cruise, Cruise").

Effective and Efficient Use of Submission Tools and Services

There are many multiple search engine submission services available on the Web that will submit your site to varying numbers of indexes, directories, and search engines. They will register your URL, description, and keywords. Check them to see how comprehensive they are before using these services. Here are a couple of sites for you to look at:

The Postmaster
http://www.netcreations.com/postmaster
This is one of the best URL submission services on the web.

Add-Me
http://www.addme.com
This site allows you to submit your page to 34 popular sites for free, using one form.

Submit It!
http://www.submit-it.com/
Submit-It (see Figure 4.39) is one of the oldest and most respected submission services.

Add Me Too
http://www.addmetoo.com/
Add Me Too is a free Web site promotion and search engine submittal service.

Figure 4.39.   You can use Submit It! to submit your page to 400 search engines and directories.

Although these services save a lot of time, it is essential that you be registered accurately in search engines and directories. For the best results, register individually in as many of the top search engines as you can before you resort to multiple submission sites. There aren't that many search engines or directories that have long submission forms, so submit manually to ensure the best results. If you have taken the time to do the work described earlier, submit to the major engines yourself. This way you can take full advantage of the legwork you have done targeting the differences between the engines.

To summarize, each search engine is different. Know the unique qualities of each before you submit and be sure to check out Appendix C, where details are provided on many of the popular search engines and directories.

Don't Submit Before You're Ready!

Before you submit to any of the search engines and directories, take the time to complete your site. Many of the major search engines and directories are not fond of receiving submissions from people who have pages that are not yet complete. You do not want to spend your time submitting your page only to find out it has not been added because it is "under construction." Also, be sure to validate your HTML before submitting. You want your site to be free of errors to ensure your success with submissions. A couple of tools you can use to validate your HTML are:

SiteInspector
http://www.siteinspector.com/

W3C HTML Validation Service
http://validator.w3.org/

NetMechanic
http://www.netmechanic.com/index.htm

Dr. Watson, v4.0
http://watson.addy.com/

Web Site Garage
http://websitegarage.netscape.com/

Are You Already Listed?

Before you submit or resubmit to a search engine, check to see if your page is already indexed. Perform a search using the most important keywords you think people will use to find your page. Also, perform a search using your company name. If your page is found and you're happy with the results, you will not need to submit or resubmit. In fact, if you do resubmit you could end up worse off, because you never know when a search engine is going to change its method of determining what pages receive a high ranking. If you are not listed or not happy with your listing, you can submit your page. If need be, you can edit your page and then resubmit to achieve a higher position. To see if your URL is indexed by AltaVista and Infoseek/Go, enter *url:yourdomain.com/directory/page.html* in the search field of each search engine. Check out the help files for each search engine for more information on how to verify that your URL is included in their index.

Observe Your Competition

Using the techniques just mentioned, you can check out your competitors' rankings as well. By looking at the top results you can see what they're doing right to achieve those top placements and learn from them to help you develop a successful submission strategy. You should look at your competition's keywords Meta tag, descriptions Meta tag, page content, page titles, and so on. They may have great keywords you missed. You might want to consider printing some of their pages or information so you can use it for reference later. Do not copy their information—you just want to use their information for guidance and reference about what has given their site the high ranking. The top results for your keywords and your competitors can also be analyzed for link popularity, which you can then research to find appropriate links you may be able to use to increase your link popularity. This is discussed in the next section.

Does Link Popularity Affect Rankings?

Now that you know who is appearing at the top of the search results, check out the number of links pointing to their site. Techniques for this are found in Chapter 10. Link popularity is becoming more and more important among the major search engines, including AltaVista. Google is another example of a search engine that uses link popularity in determining a page's position in its rankings. Perform a search using your most important keywords on Google to see who is appearing at the top of the results. Chances are the sites near the top contain the most incoming links. Look at the links leading to your competitors because they're likely appropriate links for you as well. If so, ask for a link, ask for a reciprocal link, or add yourself to their links if possible to build up your link popularity. This is a time-consuming task, but it will benefit you in the end. Keep in mind that link popularity is good, but link popularity from quality sites is better. Details on finding appropriate link sites, requesting links and having your link stand out are all covered in Chapter 10.

Other Effective Methods of Promotion

Some search engines, such as GoTo.com *(http://www.goto.com/)*, allow bidding for certain keywords. The higher you bid for the keyword or term, the higher your ranking on the search engine will be when someone searches for that keyword. On GoTo, if no one visits your site you are not charged; however, if someone does visit your site you are charged on a per click-through basis. As you can imagine, this can be a costly process to increase your site's traffic, but it's an option you may want to look at. Visit GoTo's site for more information.

If you're curious about what the going rate for your particular choice of keyword or keywords is on GoTo (see Figure 4.40), then perform a search for your word or words of interest. JimTools.com *(http://www.jimtools.com)* (see Figure 4.41) has a GoTo Keyword Wizard that will allow you to see how many searches were performed on a particular keyword over the last month, the current top bidding rates, and who is associated with those rates. If you're looking for a keyword like "Golf" then you can expect to see fairly high bidding rates because a large num-

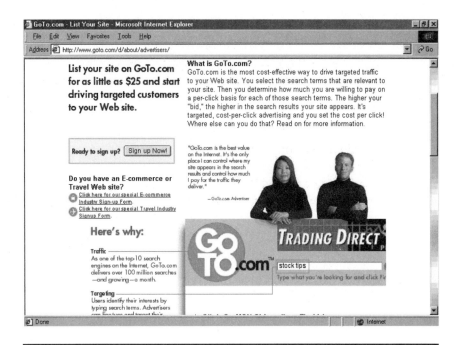

Figure 4.40. On GoTo.com you can bid on keywords.

GOTO**KEYWORD**WIZARD

#	Title	Domain	Cost/Click
1.	Baja Outpost - Refuge from Civilization	www.bajaoutpost.com	$0.21
5.	Alaska Yacht Adventures	www.alaskayachtcharters.com	$0.07
10.	Alaska Top Dog Charters	www.alaska.net	$0.01
15.			
20.			
30.			
40.			

whale watching 338 searches last month

Figure 4.41. You can use JimTools.com's Keyword Tool Kit to check out the going rate for your ideal keyword or keywords.

ber of sites are competing for this keyword. You'll also notice that the number of searches performed on this word each month is typically much higher than for a more concentrated keyword phrase. At the time this chapter was written the going rate for the top bidding position for "Golf" was $1.91 per click, and there were 24,201 searches on this word the preceding month. In contrast, the top bid for "Golf Game" was $0.27 per click. There were 1051 searches on this phrase over the last month. Similarly, the top bid for the terms "Whale Watching" was $0.21 per click-through, but only 338 searches were performed.

Another way of having your site displayed at the top of the search results is to purchase keywords from the search engines and directories. AltaVista (see Figure 4.42), Excite (see Figure 4.43), and Snap (see Figure 4.44) are all examples of search tools that offer this service. When you purchase a keyword or keywords your site will usually be displayed above the search results in the form of a banner

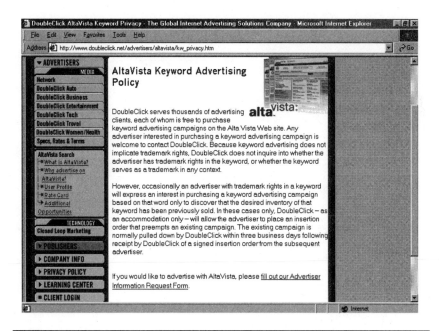

Figure 4.42. You can purchase keywords on AltaVista.

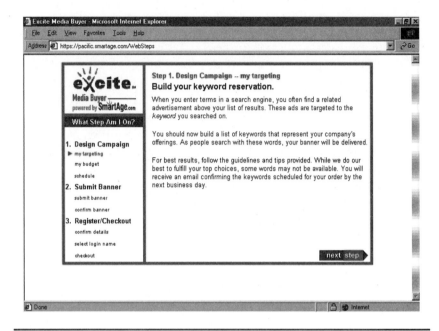

Figure 4.43. Excite also offers targeted keyword advertising.

Figure 4.44. You can purchase keyword advertising from Snap.

advertisement or a "select" link above the other links. A common cost for this service is $85 US CPM (cost per thousand).

Boosting Your Search Engine Rankings with RealNames

The RealNames Corporation *(http://www.realnames.com)* (see Figure 4.45) provides individuals, small businesses, and corporations the opportunity to skirt the search engine mind games and instantly achieve top rankings using Internet keywords. In exchange for an annual fee, you can register an Internet keyword that is relevant to your online business from RealNames. Relevant keywords would include your operation's name, product/service names, brand names or slogans.

The objective of RealNames' Internet keywords is to have the most deserving company's web site appear at the top of the search engine rankings when a user searches on that company's keyword.

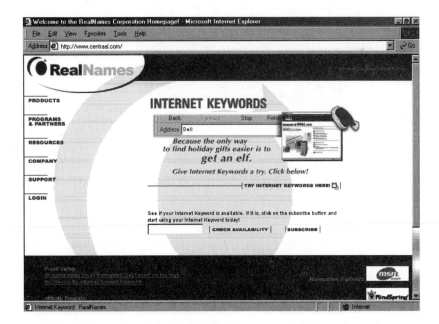

Figure 4.45. RealNames issues Internet keywords to deserving registrants.

For instance, if you search for "Holiday Inn" in AltaVista, the RealNames result for "Holiday Inn" is listed above the rest of the search results. See Figure 4.46 and 4.47. Clicking on the RealNames link takes you directly to Holiday Inn's home page *(http:// www2.basshotels.com/holiday-inn)*.

By registering an Internet keyword with RealNames Corporation, you can generate more traffic to your web site. As long as you maintain the registration for these keywords, you can have them forever. Keywords are also easier to remember and easier to type than a regular URL.

Individuals and small businesses can register a RealNames Internet keyword for $100 US per year. In exchange, RealNames will issue (pending approval) you a keyword within 72 hours and provide your site with up to 30,000 keyword-driven hits annually. RealNames will also provide you with keyword statistics and traffic reports.

Corporations must contact RealNames for subscription rates because RealNames customizes its services for larger business entities.

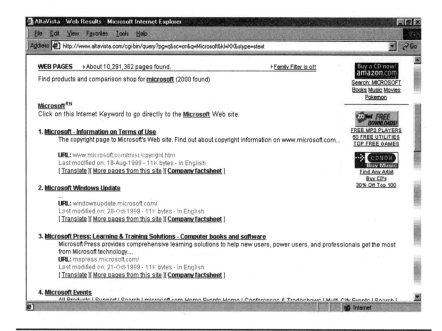

Figure 4.46.   You can get a RealName for your online business just as Holiday Inn did.

Figure 4.47. RealNames makes it easier for users to find a Web site among the clutter of search engine results.

RealNames will provide corporations with advanced keyword traffic analysis, marketing statistics, special RealNames promotions and account management services. Typically, the subscription rate for corporations is determined by a performance-based pricing scheme related to the number of visitors or sales the RealNames keyword generates.

Of course, the scope of the RealNames Internet keyword system is limited by the number of major search engines that support it. Currently, only sites such as AltaVista, LookSmart, GO Network, and MSN Search support the RealNames protocol (see Figure 4.48). Therefore, users of other major search engines such as Excite or Lycos will not see RealNames' results.

RealNames also has its own criteria and regulations for granting Internet keywords. They prefer that you use keywords that are specific to your company. If you do this, you are guaranteed the keyword(s). However, what if you want a keyword phrase such as "Theme Park"?

Figure 4.48. Some of RealNames' navigation partners.

"Theme Park" is a general search keyword phrase. Therefore, no single company, individual, or organization can have exclusive rights to it. However, RealNames will display a list of all web sites with RealNames closely related to a common search term. Figure 4.49 shows the first page of RealNames' results for "Theme Park." There are pages of other sites listed under "Theme Park," but some of these sites will earn a few more hits because their registered keyword phrase is closely related to "Theme Park."

RealNames is very selective about the Internet keywords they issue and to whom the keywords are issued. In order to maintain the value of the RealNames directory, RealNames can deny the issuance of a keyword if it suspects any of the following conditions exist:

- *Cybersquatting.* This is a common problem with domain name registration. A person will speculatively purchase a domain name (or keyword in the case of RealNames) in the hope

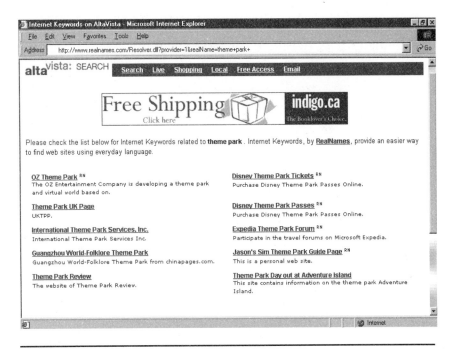

Figure 4.49. These sites share a common RealName.

of selling it at a considerable price to a more deserving company later.

- *Use of others' intellectual property.* RealNames will deny anyone but the rightful owner from buying the name of an actual company, brand name or slogan as an Internet keyword (i.e., you could not register "Disney" or "Westin" as a RealName keyword unless you were a representative from either one of these respective companies).

- *Misdirection.* This situation arises when a commonly known word or phrase is misrepresented and leads visitors to a site containing content that is other than what was expected.

RealNames represents a new use for search engines and allows you to reinforce your tourism operation and its identity. If there are keywords specific to your operation, strongly consider registering one, some, or all of these keywords with RealNames Corporation for increased exposure.

Don't Try to Trick the Search Engines'

If you want to achieve high rankings, then you should avoid spamming the search engines. A common name given to spamming the search engines is spamdexing. People often use these techniques to try and "cheat" their way to the top of the search engine rankings. See Figure 4.50 for AltaVista's stand on spam. What is considered spam?

- Keyword stuffing, which is repeating the same keyword or keywords over and over again hidden in your HTML and Meta tags.

- Repeating keywords over and over again by displaying them at the bottom of your document after a number of line breaks.

- Submitting multiple pages from the same domain during the same time frame is considered spamming by some search engines, so be sure to do your research and check how many submissions per day from a single domain they allow. Some search engines only want you to submit your home page and

> Sometimes sites submit a large number of pages to AltaVista hoping to have them show up often on our result pages. They submit pages with numerous keywords, or with keywords that are unrelated to the content of the pages. Some other people submit pages that present our spider with content that differs from what users will see. **We strongly discourage these practices.**
>
> Attempts to fill AltaVista's index with misleading or promotional pages lower the value of the index for everyone and render Web indices and your search experience worthless. **We do not allow URL submissions from customers who spam the index and will exclude all such pages from the index.**

Figure 4.50. AltaVista, like many other search engines, frowns upon spamming.

allow their spider to do the rest, others say it's okay to submit as much as you want.

- Submitting identical pages but using different page names will also get you removed if discovered.

- Hiding keywords, often called tiny text, is also considered spamming. This is when you place keywords on your page by displaying them in your document using a very small font.

- Repeating keywords in your document by making the text color the same as the background color is considered spam.

- Making frequent and regular title changes so that the bots think your site is a new site and they list you again and again.

- Using page redirects or a Meta refresh can result in your site being eliminated from a search engine's index.

- Using keywords that cannot be found on your page or are unrelated to your page.

- Altering the name of your site to have a space, exclamation mark (!) or A as the first character so that your site is displayed first in alphabetical lists.

Keep Note of Your Online Efforts

Keep a record of the directories and search engines to which you have submitted. The information recorded should include the following:

1. Date of the submission

2. URL of the page submitted

3. Name of the search engine or directory

4. Description used

5. Keywords used

6. Password used

7. Notes section for any other relevant information

8. Date listed

A Few Points of Interest

There are some important final pointers you should keep in mind. Always, always, always read the submission guidelines before submitting. Search engine and directories will also often provide a number of valuable tips that can help you to achieve better rankings.

Periodically review your rankings in the major search engines and directories. To make this manageable, I suggest you make a list of the search engines and directories to which you have submitted. Divide your list into four groups. Every week check your ranking with each of the search engines and directories in one group. If you have dropped in the ranking or don't appear in the first couple of pages of search results, then you want to resubmit to that particular search engine or directory. The next week you check your ranking with the next group. By doing so, you can set a regular schedule for yourself, keep organized, and determine the search engines and directories you need to resubmit to and those you do not. Sometimes your site may be removed from an index because the search engine has flushed their directory, or maybe it is just one of those things no one can explain—either way you will be on top of things. If you make any significant changes to your site, you may also want to resubmit. You want to ensure your content is fresh.

You may also want to consider submitting to country-specific search engines and directories. Country-specific search engines and directories will often give the user the option of searching for sites from a specific country, which may benefit you if you are only looking for an audience in your country. A couple of examples are Canada.com *(http://www.canada.com/)* (see Figure 4.51) and Yahoo! Sweden *(http://se.yahoo.com)* (see Figure 4.52).

Figure 4.51. Canada.com is a search engine that targets a Canadian audience.

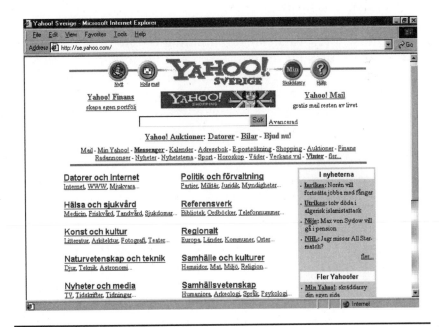

Figure 4.52. Sweden's Yahoo! Directory.

Internet Resources

Web Position Analyzer
http://www.webposition.com
Software that tells you where your site is positioned in search results of the 10 most popular search engines. Builds traffic by tracking your search engine positions and helping you improve your rankings.

Position-It
http://www.position-it.com
How to use Internet search engines and directories to "skyrocket" your web site traffic using search engine secrets for top positioning.

Position Agent
http://www.positionagent.com
This is a great utility that will automatically check your ranking on 10 top search engines for free.

Promotion World
http://www.promotionworld.com/
Lots of information surrounding online promotion, with some good information on search engine submission and preparing your site to be submitted to the search engines. This site also contains some tools you can use to generate Meta tags or check your position on search engines, and a free search engine submission service.

Search Engine Showdown
http://www.notess.com/search/
Detailed analysis of Internet search engines, their features, databases, and strategies.

Search Engine Tutorial for Web Designers
http://www.northernwebs.com/set/
Lots of valuable information on web site design and search engine ranking methods and policies.

The Web Developer's Journal
http://www.webdevelopersjournal.com/articles/search_engines.html
A good article on maximizing search engine positioning.

Browser News
http://www.upsdell.com/BrowserNews/stat_search.htm
A weekly web-based newsletter that provides a variety of browser news and search engine statistics.

Promotion 101—Web Site Marketing and Promotion Info Center
http://www.promotion101.com/
A good resource with a search engine placement guide, free tools, and promotion articles.

CNET features digital life—how do search engines work?
http://coverage.cnet.com/Content/Features/Dlife/Search/ss03.html
An article about how search engines operate.

Search Engine Search Features and Submission Charts

Search Engine Chart
http://www.advance-training.co.uk/free/chart.htm

Search Engine Features for Webmasters
http://www.searchenginewatch.com/webmasters/features.html

Search Engine Display Chart
http://www.searchenginewatch.com/webmasters/display.html

Search Engine Features for Searchers
http://www.searchenginewatch.com/facts/ataglance.html

Search Engine Comparison Chart
http://www.kcpl.lib.mo.us/search/chart.htm

Search Engine Feature Chart
http://home.sprintmail.com/~debflanagan/chart.html

Comparison of Search Capabilities of 6 Major Search Engines
http://www.cyward.com/chart1.htm

Submission Tools

World Submit
http://www.worldsubmit.com/
World Submit will submit your web site to 1550 of the World's search
engines directories including Yahoo, what's new sites, and award sites
in 90 categories.

SubmitPlus
http://submitplus.bc.ca/
SubmitPlus helps you promote your web site with two very effective
web site announcement programs. They offer free and pay services.
Before you register your site, make sure you check out their Free
Promotion Tools section for invaluable tips on how to make your
web site ready for the Internet!

The Broadcaster
http://www.broadcaster.co.uk/
Broadcaster search engine submission and announcement services covers
all aspects of web site marketing, promotion and search engine secrets.

MetaCrawlers Top Searches List
http://www.metaspy.com
Ever wonder what the rest of the world is searching for? Catch a
glimpse of some of the searches being performed on MetaCrawler at
this very moment!

WebStepTop 100
http://www.mmgco.com/4-star.html
This isn't a standard "link" site; it's much better than that. A listing
of hundreds of search engines.

SiteOwner.com
http://www.siteowner.com/
Tools to help individuals submit their site to search engines, develop
Meta tags, locate dead links, and so on.

AAA Internet Promotions
http://www.web-ignite.com
One of the first professional web site promotion services on the Internet, and certainly the most reputable. AAA Internet Promotions manually submits your web site to search engines and directories. AAA also offers a Partner Program for webmasters and web site owners. Over 10,000 clients are served, including Price Waterhouse, AT&T, Sony Music, and Warner Brothers.

Web Themes Internet Consultants
http://www.webthemes.com
One of the most active submission and promotion services on the Net. They take a very active role in generating traffic to your site. Web Themes Advertising, Marketing and Promotion, and Design, home of The Web Hitman, has been promoting new businesses on the web since 1995. They have experience and the resources to promote your Internet web site using a variety of tools to accomplish the task. Their web page promotion services start with your standard professional submission services and extend to extensive programs for increasing traffic on a daily basis.

Wilson Internet Services
http://www.wilsonweb.com/webmarket/
Dr. Wilson's Web Marketing Info Center is a "must visit" site. You'll find links to hundreds of online articles about effective Web marketing and resources for search engine and directory submission. From its beginning in August 1995, this site has become one of the most comprehensive Web marketing sites of its kind. It is a fantastic resource.

Jayde Online Directory
http://www.jayde.com/
The Jayde Online Directory offers a list of places to promote your site organized by type of directory. In addition, be sure to submit your site to the big site database maintained by Jayde.

Submit-It!
http://www.submit-it.com
A very popular Web site promotion tool. You can use Submit It! to register your URL with hundreds of search engines and directories.

Business@merica
http://web.idirect.com/~tormall/links.html
A long list of 2000 places to submit your site. With their Submission King, they will submit your URL to 900 search catalogs and directories for only 4 cents each. You get a full report on all those that post your info. Their list includes the top 100 catalogs such as AltaVista, Lycos, WebCrawler, Infoseek, Yahoo, and hundreds of others worldwide.

SOFTSEEK.COM—Search Engine Submission Tools
http://www.softseek.com/Internet/Web_Publishing_Tools/ Search_Engine_Submission_Tools/
A directory of freeware and shareware search engine submission tools.

AddMySite.com
http://www.addmysite.com/
A free web site search engine submission service.

Traffic Boost
http://www.inetexchange.com/unfair.htm
The Unfair Advantage submission service. Instantly submits your web site to 500 Internet search engines and directories.

Net Submitter Pro
http://www.promotion-expert.com/
Net Submitter Pro will guide you through the correct ways to prepare your web page information prior to submission and can submit that information to 500 search engines.

QuikLaunch Web Site Announcer
http://www.qwiklaunch.com/
A quick free way to get listed and launched in a number of popular search engines.

A1 Web Site Promotions
http://www.a1co.com//freeindex.html
Over 800 free WWW URL submission and search sites that will take your announcement.

SubmitWolf Pro
http://www.msw.com.au/swolf
With a database of over 2500 sites to promote your URL and hundreds of fully automated submission scripts, SubmitWolf can dramatically increase your site traffic. SubmitWolf is loaded with features. It provides detailed submission reports, and it can generate Meta tags to help search engines correctly index your site. It even enables you to add your own engines.

Dynamic Submission 2000 Version 4
http://www.submission2000.com/index1.html
This software program is a five-star award-winning web site promotion tool. It will submit your web site (or URL) to 800+ search engines with just a few button clicks. Enter your web site details and press a button. This program will automatically submit to hundreds of major search engines within minutes.

TotalHost Global Submissions
http://www.totalhost.com/
Submit your web site to over 1000 search engines, media outlets, registries, and directories.

Note: If you haven't already done so, be sure to review the resources for Chapter 3. The information contained in Chapters 3 and 4 is closely correlated, and their resources tie in well together.

5

Using Tourism Newsgroups to Reach Your Target Market

It is estimated that over 10 million people participate in discussions taking place in Usenet newsgroups, making them an ideal marketing vehicle for companies in tourism-related industries. The number of newsgroups is always increasing, with over 100,000 different topics now estimated. Of course, you will be most interested in newsgroups with topics related to your tourism operation. Using proper netiquette is important. To do this read the FAQ files and rules, "lurk" first, and stay on topic. In this chapter we cover:

- The benefits of using newsgroups in your tourism marketing plan

- Newsgroup Netiquette

- Reading the FAQ files, abiding by the rules, and lurking

- How to advertise if advertising is not allowed

- Developing your Usenet marketing strategy

- Identifying travel-related newsgroups

- Participating in this online community

- How to respond correctly to messages

- How to start your own newsgroup

- Cross-posting and spamming

- Using signature files

Newsgroups—An Ideal Marketing Vehicle

It is estimated that over 10 million people read **newsgroups.** Usenet newsgroups are hierarchical and are arranged by subject. Each newsgroup is dedicated to a discussion of a particular topic, such as travel, resorts, hiking, or golf vacations. Usenet has been defined as follows:

> *Usenet is the Internet's public forum, comprising thousands of newsgroups, each of which is devoted to the public discussion of a narrow, chartered topic such as microbrews, baseball cards, arthritis research, or traveling in Africa.*

News-groups
Discussion groups on the Internet that focus on specific subjects

Usenet facilitates the exchange of an abundance of information on every topic imaginable. Many newsgroups are tight-knit communities with very loyal residents. Each group's readers are interested in the newsgroup topic, so when you find a newsgroup related to your product or service, you have likely found members of your target market.

The number of newsgroups is steadily increasing. Currently it is estimated that there are more than 100,000 topics available. Different newsgroups have varying numbers of readers. Some are read by hundreds of thousands of readers a day; others see very little traffic.

The newsgroups you decide to participate in may be read by a relatively small number of people or have a large number of participants. Large isn't always better. A smaller group may provide you with a better chance of having your message read by your ideal target market. A larger group will provide you with better exposure by sheer volume. Whether you pick a large group or a small group depends on your objectives and also on your operation, product, or service. For example, even though a posting to *alt.politics* may be seen by 300,000 readers, if what you are trying to sell is honeymoon vacation packages in Aruba, it will not likely generate more potential business than a posting to a Usenet group such as *rec.travel.caribbean* with only 1000 readers. Not to mention that if you're posting to *alt.politics* is inappropriate for that group, you will have done more harm than good. Newsgroup readers do not appreciate messages unrelated to their topic posted to their newsgroup, especially if these are advertisements.

If you use an online service, you can still participate in newsgroups, because they have similar services. CompuServe has forums or special-interest groups, AOL has forums and clubs, and Prodigy has forums and bulletin boards. The same rules regarding participation, acceptable messages, and marketing activities generally apply. Not only are newsgroups helpful marketing tools, they can also help you identify competitors and trends in the tourism industry, help you find valuable information from experts in your field, and assist you in the performance of market research activities.

The Benefits of Newsgroups

There are many ways online marketers can benefit from participating in newsgroups:

- **Reaching prospective customers:** You can immediately reach thousands of your targeted potential customers with a single message.

- **Communicating with existing customers:** You can provide your loyal customers with valuable information.

- **Market research:** You can use newsgroups to find out the latest travel trends, customer needs, what people are looking for, and what they are talking about.

- **Reputation building:** By answering people's questions and helping to solve their problems, you will build your reputation as an expert in the tourism field.

- **Increased traffic:** You can direct people to your tourism web site if you do it in an informative way.

Thousands of Newsgroup Categories

Newsgroups are organized into different types of discussions or categories. Each of the major categories has lots of individual newsgroups in which you can participate. Major newsgroup categories include:

alt	Discussions on alternative topics
biz	Discussions on business topics. You may find groups that allow advertising here
comp	Discussions on computer-related topics
misc	Discussions of miscellaneous topics that don't have their own category
news	Discussions on Usenet news and administration
rec	Discussions on recreation, travel, and leisure topics
sci	Discussions on science
soc	Discussions on social issues
talk	Making conversation

Each of the major categories has a number of subgroups, and each subgroup has a number of sub-subgroups. For example under the rec major category you will find a subgroup *rec.travel*. Here the discussion revolves around all kinds of travel. Under the subgroup *rec.travel*, you will find sub-subgroups and sub-sub-subgroups. For example: *rec.travel, rec.travel.resorts, rec.travel.resorts.all-inclusive, rec.travel.resorts.all-inclusive.hawaii.*

As you can see, the longer the name, the narrower the discussion that is taking place. At the broadest level of conversation *(rec.travel)*, anything to do with travel would be an acceptable posting. However, as the newsgroup topic coverage narrows to "all-inclusive resorts in Hawaii," all postings must now have something to do with all-inclusive resorts in Hawaii. You would not be able to post a message referring to a great park you camped at in Connecticut.

Of course, *rec.travel* will discuss travel for recreational purposes. So if you are planning a vacation to Memphis, you might post questions you have about tourist attractions in Memphis here. Meanwhile, in the *biz.travel* category, all postings have to relate to business travel. Therefore, you would not discuss your vacation plans here, but you might ask the newsgroup a question such as "Where can I find a good hotel conference room in Toronto to hold our annual meeting?"

Finally, in the *alt.travel* category, you can discuss alternative forms of travel. For instance, you could post messages about cycling across the state of Missouri or ask where to find the best nature resorts in Canada.

Target Appropriate Newsgroups

With the large number of Usenet newsgroups that currently exist, and the additional groups that are being introduced every day, it is a formidable task to identify appropriate newsgroups for your tourism operation's Internet marketing activities. First, you need to determine which newsgroups your prospective customers frequent.

Look for a close fit between a newsgroup and the product or service you are offering. For example, if your company sells golf clubs and accessories, then one appropriate newsgroup for your business might be *rec.sport.golf*. Try finding newsgroups that your target market may enjoy reading, or ask your clients or customers which newsgroups they participate in or find particularly interesting. Find and make note of all appropriate newsgroups that might be of interest to your target customer.

There are many ways to find appropriate Usenet newsgroup listings: There are more than 54,000 mailing lists and newsgroups located at the Liszt Web Site, *http://www.liszt.com.* You can also do a search using the newsgroup functions of the two leading **browsers,** Netscape Navigator and Microsoft Internet Explorer. Check out Appendix B for more information on newsgroups.

Browser
The soft-
ware used
to view the
various
kinds of
Internet
resources.

Most newsreader programs have a search capability. Search the newsgroups for keywords that relate to your target market and your tourism product or service to identify possible appropriate newsgroups for your marketing effort.

Another good place to start is Deja.com at *http://www.deja.com.* At Deja.com you can conduct a keyword search of the Usenet newsgroups. The search results are displayed in chronological order, with the results at the top being the most recently used. You should choose keywords appropriate for your target customer or client. These methods will identify a fairly large list of potential newsgroups that may be included in your marketing activities. A benefit of the Deja.com web site is that you can post to the newsgroups directly from the site. You don't have to go through alternative software.

If your operation specializes in providing exotic vacations to Mexico, you may want to search Deja.com for keywords such as "Mexico, vacation, travel, tropical, resorts, beaches," and so on to find potential newsgroups for your marketing effort.

Very often, posting messages in newsgroups related to a particular geographic region can be appropriate for your tourism operation. If you have a bed and breakfast operation in Massachusetts, you could search Deja.com for the keyword "Massachusetts" and post your messages in newsgroups relevant to this state.

Once you have done your preliminary research and compiled a long list of what you think are the most appropriate newsgroups related to your target market, you are ready to investigate further and qualify your list.

The next step is to go to the Usenet Info Center Launch Pad at *http://sunsite.unc.edu/usenet-i/home.html.* There you can look up the newsgroups on your list. From this site you will be able to find out where the FAQ (frequently asked questions) files for each newsgroup are located. The FAQ files will usually provide information on the newsgroup's stance on advertising. Info Center Launch Pad will also provide you with details on the number of people participating in the group.

Following is a list of categorized newsgroups where you might find ones appropriate for your tourism operation.

Hotels/Motels/Accommodations

alt.business.hospitality
Caters to hotel, resort, tour. and restaurant businesses.

pdaxs.ads.hotels
Caters to hotels, motels, inns, and bed and breakfasts.

Bed and Breakfasts and Country Inns

fido7.su.dacha
Looking for information on summer cottages? Join this group (moderated).

pdaxs.ads.hotels
Find the perfect hotel, motel, inn,and bed and breakfast for your trip.

rec.travel.bed+breakfast
A forum for bed and breakfast guests (moderated).

Outdoor Recreation and Camping

alt.rec.hiking
The recreational hiking and outdoors newsgroup.

gov.us.topic.nat-resources.parks
Public land for recreation and tourism, museums (moderated).

phl.outdoors
Outdoor recreation—camping, hiking, parks.

rec.outdoors.national-parks
Discusses activities and politics in our national parks.

rec.outdoors.rv-travel
Discussions related to outdoor recreational vehicles.

rec.photo.technique.nature
Discussions of wildlife, landscapes, travel tips and so on.

rec.scuba.locations
Ask questions or post information about scuba travel and good locations for scuba diving.

rec.skiing.resorts.europe
All about skiing in Europe.

rec.skiing.resorts.misc
Discussions about skiing in locations other than Europe and North America.

rec.skiing.resorts.north-america
All about skiing in North America.

rec.travel.budget.backpack
If you like the outdoors, join the backpack travel discussion group.

ucb.org.hiking-club
The hiking club discussion group is perfect for all people who enjoy a good walk in the woods.

Cruises

rec.travel.cruises
Discussions about cruise ship travel, great deals, and great places to go.

Airline Travel

rec.travel.air
All about airline travel around the world.

airnews.alt.travel.air.airports.bicker
Discuss anything you like or don't like about airports, including bickering.

Travel Industry

bit.listserv.travel-1
Tourism and travel industry discussions.

Theme Parks

rec.arts.disney.parks
Find information on Disney parks, resorts, dining, attractions, and vacations.

rec.parks.theme
A general discussion about entertainment theme parks.

Travel Deals

rec.travel.marketplace
Tickets and accommodations wanted and for sale—find a great bargain.

General Travel

alt.travel.road-trip
Ever go to Montreal for pizza-from Albany? Tell the group about your last unplanned road trip.

clari.biz.industry.travel+leisure
Discussion about the travel and leisure industries (moderated).

clari.biz.industry.travel+leisure.releases
More travel and leisure discussions (moderated).

rec.gambling.misc
All gambling topics including travel discussions.

rec.travel.misc
Everything and anything about travel.

rec.travel.resorts.all-inclusive
Find information about all-inclusive resorts (moderated).

tnn.travel
Topics and discussions about traveling.

Geography Specific

alt.travel.canada
All about traveling to Canada.

can.travel.citc
Canadian travel industry forum.

rec.travel.africa
Discussions about traveling in Africa.

rec.travel.asia
Discussions about traveling in Asia.

rec.travel.australia+nz
Find travel information for Australia and New Zealand.

rec.travel.caribbean
Discussions about traveling to the islands of the Caribbean, sans pirates.

rec.travel.europe
Discussions about traveling in Europe.

rec.travel.latin-america
Discussions about traveling in Central and South America.

rec.travel.usa-canada
Discussions about traveling in the United States and Canada.

Read the FAQ Files and Abide by the Rules

Charter
Established
rules and
guidelines.

Read the FAQ files, **charter,** and rules about posting and advertising for each of your target newsgroups. It is very important that you abide by all the rules. If the FAQ files do not mention the group's stance on commercial advertising and announcements, then go back to Deja News. Conduct a search based on the group's name and charter. This will tell you where the newsgroup stands on commercial activity.

Lurking for Potential Customers

Lurking
Browsing
without
posting.

Once you have narrowed your potential newsgroup list, you will want to visit each and every one to determine if the participants of the newsgroup are, in fact, potential customers. Spend time **lurking.** Monitor the types of messages that are being posted. Is there likely to be an opportunity for you to contribute? Are the participants your target market? Research the newsgroup to ascertain if it will appeal to your customers. The name of the newsgroup may not reveal what the newsgroup is about, so take your time and make sure.

Tips on Posting Messages

After you have become familiar with the rules of your selected newsgroup, have spent some time lurking, and have decided that the newsgroup is one where your target market is participating, you may begin to post messages. Remember to abide by the rules! If the rules do not allow advertising, then do not blatantly post an ad. To take full advantage of the newsgroup, you have to gain the trust of its members. With one wrong message you could outrage all of the potential customers who participate in the newsgroup.

It is a good idea to run a test before you post a message to a newsgroup. Doing a test will show you how the posting works and prevent you from making a mistake when it comes to the real thing. For a test mechanism, go to the newsgroup *misc.test*.

Becoming a respected member in a newsgroup is a great way to promote yourself and your tourism operation. In time you may forget that you began reading the newsgroup to promote your business. You will find yourself reading newsgroups in order to participate in stimulating discussions. You will be discussing anything and everything about the newsgroup subject. Only mention your web site when you find an appropriate opportunity to bring your knowledge about the topic being discussed into the conversation.

Newsgroups exist for specific purposes. They can be designed for discussions, news announcements, postings related to particular topics, and even buying and selling goods.

Newsgroups may have hundreds of messages sorted and available for access at any point in time. Newsgroup participants will decide whether to open or pass your posted message based on the words in the subject area. Make your subject short and catchy so that your message will be read and not passed over. Try to put the most important words of the subject first. This is a very critical part to posting a message to a newsgroup. Some people adjust the screen to see only the first few words in the subject area. When deciding on the text for the subject area, think about what keywords someone would use to search for information on the content of your message. The worst thing that you can do is post a message to a newsgroup with no subject at all. This will definitely receive no attention and is basically a waste of your time, because nobody will read your message.

Start your message with a short description on how it relates to the group's main topic. People are looking for answers to specific questions, so it is rude to jump into the conversation with a topic that doesn't match the one in the subject line. You should attempt to get your message across right away. You should get to the point of your message in the first sentence. By doing so you will catch the readers' attention and ensure that they will read the entire message.

Messages should be short, no longer than 24 lines. Messages should briefly discuss main points and ask if readers would like to have more information. Once people show an interest in the information you are offering, your message can be as long as needed.

When responding to a message in a newsgroup, you have the option of responding to the individual who posted the message privately or responding to the newsgroup. Determine which is more appropriate under the given circumstances. If your message will be of value to the entire group or will appropriately promote your company's capabilities, then post the response to the newsgroup for all to see. If you think that your tourism operation has a solution for the individual and would like to provide details to the "target customer," but feel that it would not benefit the other members of the group, then deliver a private response. Sometimes you may choose to do both. Whichever approach you take, make sure that you respond as quickly as possible so that the first message is still fresh in the mind of the recipient.

Tips To Ensure Your Messages Will Be Well Received

Here are some basic rules to help you post messages that have the best opportunity of being well received:

Keep to the Newsgroup Topic

Make sure to always stay on the newsgroup topic of discussion. People participate in specific newsgroups because of that subject and don't appreciate off-topic postings.

Stay on the Thread

When responding to a message, use the Reply option to stay on the same thread (see Figure 5.1). When you reply without changing the subject line, your message will appear immediately below the message you are responding to in the Newsgroup. This makes it easy for others to follow the discussion.

@	↓	66	Subject	From	Sent
			Vacation villas near Disney World	ajhmba	12/11/99 10:29 PM
			NY trip	mstriumph1@my-deja.com	12/11/99 10:25 PM
			Re: NY trip	Ron Newman	12/12/99 12:28 AM
			Re: NY trip	mstriumph1@my-deja.com	12/12/99 3:07 AM
			Re: NY trip	Ron Newman	12/12/99 8:45 AM
			Re: NY trip	jean sterling	12/12/99 1:52 PM
			Re: NY trip	Me	12/12/99 7:32 AM
			Re: NY trip	Naomala	12/12/99 11:15 AM
			Webcam, maps, traveldescriptions	Morten Halvorsen	12/11/99 9:41 PM
			Free British Columbia screen saver, win a trip, save $200.0...	awebstar creations	12/11/99 8:36 PM
			Looking for accomodation in Rome??? http://www.romepo...	Marcus	12/11/99 7:49 PM
			Hotel in Quebec City	Anonymous	12/11/99 4:51 PM
			Re: Visit Canada from US and come back?	Harry	12/11/99 2:57 PM
			Re: Visit Canada from US and come back?	J. Harris	12/11/99 9:00 PM
			New York New Years Eve	ARKADYA	12/11/99 1:11 PM
			Re: New York New Years Eve	Rita	12/12/99 12:33 PM
			Travel Pictures	Jorge V. Geaga	12/11/99 12:25 PM
			Travel Pictures	Jorge V. Geaga	12/11/99 3:00 PM
			Florida Interest Website [New] Need your input	S & L	12/11/99 11:48 AM
			Re: Wanted To Buy -- All item types --	Harry	12/11/99 10:56 AM
			New Orleans	Melroy D'Souza	12/11/99 10:33 AM
			Re: New Orleans	Jane Dozier	12/11/99 2:29 PM

Figure 5.1.   It is very important to stay on thread. As you can see in this travel newsgroup, the NY trip messages are staying on thread.The messages have been replied to keeping the same subject line.

Make a Contribution

Informed quality responses to people's questions will give you credibility with the group and reflect well upon you and your company. If you post positive and informative information visitors will return to the newsgroups and look for your posts.

Don't Post Commercials

Advertising is not welcome in most newsgroups, and many charters specifically disallow the posting of ads. Read the FAQ files before posting a message. If the newsgroup does not allow commercial or ads don't post them.

You Don't Have To Have the Last Word

Don't post gratuitous responses in newsgroups. Never post a message with just a "Thanks" or "I like it" if you have nothing else to contribute. If you feel such a response is warranted or would like to discuss the issue privately, send a private e-mail to the person to convey your appreciation or opinion.

Signature Files as Your E-business Card

Signature file
An e-business card, usually attached to e-mail.

E-mail messages, usually text, sent from one person to another via computer

A **signature file**, or sig.file as it is commonly referred to, is your e-business card. It is a short message at the end of an **e-mail**. Most, if not all, e-mail programs allow for the use of a signature file. Sig.files can be attached at the end of your message when you post to a Usenet newsgroup or a mailing list, even if the group does not allow advertising.

You can use your sig.file in a number of clever ways. Sig.files can be simple—only listing phone numbers and addresses—or they can be a virtual ad for your company. They can be very useful in providing exposure for your operation. You can use your sig.file to offer some substantial information, like letting people know about a special event you are putting on at your location, informing people about an award or honor your operation has received, or promoting a specific product or service your operation has to offer.

You can design and use different sig.files for posting to different newsgroups. A particular sig.file may be appropriate for one newsgroup but not for another. Always ensure that the message in your sig.file is appropriate for its audience.

Keep your sig.file short. Usually four to eight lines is a good size. There is nothing more annoying than a sig.file that is longer than the text of your message to which it is attached, or one that resembles a brochure.

Sig.files should include the following:

- Contact name

- Business name

- URL

- Address

- E-mail address

- Telephone number

- Fax number

- A brief company tag line or a company slogan

This is an example of what a sig.file looks like:

Jane Doe, Marketing Assistant
jdoe@sunnyvale.com
Sunnyvale Tours
101 Main Street
Woodstock, NY, 10010
Toll Free Tel: (800) 555-1001
Fax: (800) 555-1000
Touch the sun. Visit our site @ http://www.suntours.com

For a complete discussion of sig.files and how to use them, see Chapter 6.

Newsgroup Advertising Hints

Newsgroups have been developed for different audiences and different topics. Some newsgroups are dedicated to posting advertisements. If advertising is appropriate for your company, the following newsgroup types might be included in your Internet marketing strategy. Most of the newsgroups that allow advertising are readily identifiable. The newsgroup name itself might include one of the following:

- biz

- classified

- for sale

- marketplace

Again, read the FAQ files and lurk to determine if the newsgroup is appropriate for your target market before you post. Use a short, catchy subject line with keywords at the beginning—the subject will determine whether your message warrants a read or a pass. Avoid all CAPITALS. This is equivalent to shouting on the Internet. Stay away from !!!!, ****, @@@@, and other such symbols as well.

When you have found a newsgroup whose participants include your target market but the newsgroup does not allow advertising, don't despair. By responding to queries or providing information that is of genuine interest to the newsgroup, you have the opportunity to attach your sig.file. A sig.file can be as effective as an ad if it is designed properly. Your message should offer substantial information to the discussion (a thinly veiled excuse to get your sig.file posted will not be appreciated). If your information is relevant and of value to the participants of the newsgroup, the fact that your sig.file is an advertisement will not matter—in fact it may add credibility to the information you have provided and enhance your company's reputation.

Cross-Posting and Spamming

Cross-posting is when someone posts identical messages to a number of relevant newsgroups. Doing this is considered to be inappropriate because of the number of common users in associated newsgroups. Spamming is when you post identical or nearly identical messages to irrelevant newsgroups without care or regard for the posting guidelines, the newsgroup topic, or the interests of the group. Cross-posting and spamming will annoy the readers of the newsgroup. Doing these things will reflect badly on you and your tourism operation, and prevent you from achieving your online marketing objectives.

Sometime in your online postings, no matter how careful you are, someone is bound to get upset. Accept this as fact and learn how to handle flames appropriately. Be sensitive to complaints. Learn from them, but do not worry unnecessarily. If someone posts a message that reflects badly on your company, you have three options: Defend your comments in the newsgroup, send the person a private e-mail, or do nothing. Responding to the person via e-mail is the most appropriate response, even though in most cases your message will be ignored.

If you disobey proper newsgroup etiquette by cross-posting or spamming, you may quickly learn what a flame is. A flame is a reply that may be posted into a newsgroup or sent to you by e-mail and contains extremely negative feedback. In the worst cases, people have been sent 100 e-mails, each with a copy of a 16 MB file, which could take your computer hours to download or even crash your server. Although these acts are very immature, you must remember to obey newsgroup etiquette to make sure that this does not happen.

Earning Respect with Newsgroup Netiquette

Following are ten rules for Netiquette. Incorporating them in your newsgroup posting will gain you respect by the other participants:

1. Don't use CAPITALS. CAPS are akin to shouting on the Internet.

2. Don't post ads where they are not welcome.

3. Do provide valuable, on-topic information for the newsgroup.

4. Don't be rude or sarcastic.

5. Don't include the entire message you are replying to in your response. Only quote relevant sections of the original message.

6. Do a thorough review of your message before you post. Check your spelling and grammar. Check your subject; it should be short and catchy with the keywords first.

7. Do provide an appropriate sig.file.

8. Don't post messages that are too lengthy. Online communication tends to be one screen or less.

9. Don't spam or cross-post.

10. Don't post replies that contribute nothing to the discussion ("I agree" or "Thanks").

Have Your Own Newsgroup

You can start your own newsgroup if you feel it is warranted and appropriate. All group creation requests must follow set guidelines and are first met with discussion. If you need help, you can always find a body of volunteers who are experienced in the newsgroup creation process at group—*mentors@acpub.duke.edu*. They assist people with the formation and submission of good newsgroup proposals.

The Discussion

A request for discussion on creation of a new newsgroup should be posted to *news.announce.newsgroups* and *news.groups*. If desired, the request can also be posted to other groups or mailing lists that are related to the proposed topic. The name and charter of the proposed group and whether it will be moderated or unmoderated should be determined during the discussion period.

The Vote

The Usenet Volunteer Vote Takers (UVT) is a group of neutral third-party vote takers who currently handle vote gathering and counting for all newsgroup proposals. There should be a minimal delay between the end of the discussion period and the issuing of a call for votes. The call for votes should include clear instructions on how to cast a vote. The voting period should last for at least 21 days and no more than 31 days. Only the votes that are mailed to the vote taker will be counted.

The Result

At the completion of the voting period, the vote taker must post the vote tally to the applicable groups and mailing lists. The e-mail addresses and names (if available) of the voters are posted along with the tally. There will be a five-day waiting period, beginning when the voting results actually appear. During the waiting period there will be a chance to correct any errors in the voter list or the voting procedure. For a proposal to pass, 100 more Yes/create votes must be received than No/do not create votes. Also, two thirds of the total number of votes must be in favor of creation. If a proposal fails to achieve two thirds of the vote, then the matter cannot be brought up for discussion until at least six months have passed from the close of the vote.

The following locations will help you should you wish to create your own newsgroup:

- How to Format and Submit a New Group Proposal: *news.announce.newgroups, news.groups*

- How to Write a Good Newsgroup Proposal: *news.announce. newgroups, news.groups*

- Usenet Newsgroup Creation Companion: *news.groups, news.announce.newusers, news.answers*

Internet Resources

Other Newsgroups
News.newusers.questions
News.announce.newusers
News.newusers
These provide information to new Usenet users on posting, finding appropriate newsgroups, Netiquette, and other frequently asked questions new users are faced with.

Reference.COM Search
http://www.reference.com
Reference.com has searchable directories of newsgroups and mailing lists. Newsgroups are archived, but mailing lists are only archived and searchable with the permission of the list owner.

Deja.com—The Source for Internet Newsgroups!
http://www.deja.com
The web site where you can read, search, participate in, and subscribe to more than 50,000 discussion forums, including Usenet

newsgroups. Deja.com is a resource for finding people, getting noticed, and getting answers to all sorts of questions. You can find discussion forums on any topic imaginable.

Liszt of Newsgroups
http://www.liszt.com/news
A complete listing of newsgroups organized by different categories. Has listed over 30,000 newsgroups and is the largest directory of newsgroups on the web.

How to Advertise on Newsgroups
http://www.nsmi.com/noflames.html
How to Advertise on Newsgroups shows step-by-step techniques to follow so you won't get blacklisted. Everything you need to know about how to advertise in newsgroups and mailing lists without getting flamed.

Creating Newsgroups
http://www.fairnet.org/fnvol/training/newsgrp.html
All you need to know about how to create your own newsgroup.

Public news servers
http://login.eunet.no/~kjetilm/news.htm
Free access to newsgroups/NNTP servers.

Open Newsserver Search
http://www.muenz.com/sdienst/html/sgroup_e.html
English/German search engine that finds open newsservers that carry newsgroups matching your search terms.

Newsgroups
http://www.engl.uvic.ca/OnlineGuide/News/newsGroupsWel.html
Introductory information called the Online Guide.

NIC—Master List
http://www.engl.uvic.ca/OnlineGuide/News/newsGroupsWel.html
See this master list for a description of newsgroups.

Downloading Free Agent
http://www.forteinc.com/getfa/getfa.htm

Free Agent furnishes newsreader software.

Talkway
http://www.talkway.com
This membership site attempts to provide a friendlier interface to the arcane structure of Usenet newsgroups.

6

Utilizing Signature Files To Increase Web Site Traffic

A signature file is a short memo at the end of your message. You can use your signature file in a number of clever ways, from just giving out phone numbers and addresses to offering some substantial information. Sig.files can be used to inform people about a special event or an award or honor your tourism business has received. In this chapter we cover:

- The appropriate size of sig.files

- Content and design of sig.files

- Creating sig.files to add statements to your messages

- The benefits of sig.files

Presenting Your E-business Card

A signature file, or sig.file as it is commonly referred to, is your e-business card. It should be attached at the end of all your e-mails, those that are sent to individuals and especially those that are sent to Usenet newsgroups and mail lists.

Most, if not all, e-mail programs allow you to automatically insert a preformatted signature file at the end of your messages. If yours doesn't, you should consider switching e-mail programs because sig.files can be very effective in drawing traffic to your web site when used appropriately.

You can use your sig.file in a number of different ways beyond providing the basic contact information such as phone, fax, e-mail, and URL. You should provide every way possible for the recipient to contact your tourism operation. It is each recipient's choice to call, e-mail or fax you. Some people also have a "click here" link in their sig.file that takes you directly to their web site. This is a nice idea, but you must also remember to type your full URL in the sig.file so that they will have it. Sometimes people will just print their e-mail to take home that night, and it can be really hard getting to a web site by trying to click on a piece of paper. Inform your readers about a current sales promotion, the location of your next trade show, a special event you are hosting, or an award your operation has received in your tag line in your signature file. Sig.files are readily accepted online and, when designed properly, comply with Netiquette.

Developing Your Signature File

In preparation for designing and developing your sig.file, you should decide what information you want to include and what you want your e-business card to look like. Create your sig.file using Windows Notepad or Simple Text and save it as a text file (that's with a .txt extension).

If you are using Netscape or Internet Explorer, the following are the steps to develop your sig.file:

- Microsoft Outlook Express 5

  1. On the menu bar click "tools."

  2. On the drop-down box click on "options."

3. Click on the "Signatures" tab.

4. Click on "New" to create you sig.file.

5. Click on "Add sig.file to all outgoing messages."

- Netscape Messenger:

    1. On the menu bar click "Edit."

    2. Click on "Preferences."

    3. Go to the folder named "News Groups Folder."

    4. Go to the folder named "Identity."

    5. Choose a file to create your sig.file in.

After you have developed your sig.file, send an e-mail message to yourself with the sig.file attached to see what it looks like. Make sure to check and double-check for typos, errors, or omissions.

One of the most important elements from a marketing perspective is the **tag line.** Does your tag line give the reader a real and compelling desire to visit your web site?

If you are using one of the online services, there are different ways to develop your sig.file:

Tag line
An advertising message, usually included in your signature file attached to e-mail.

- America Online

    1. Click on "Mail Center" on the toolbar.

    2. Click on "Set up Mail Signature."

    3. Click on "Create," type in the name of the sig.file, and create the sig.file using the different options available.

    4. Set the default to "On" so that your sig.file is added to your outgoing mail.

- CompuServe

  1. Click on "Mail Center" on the toolbar.

  2. Click on "Set up Mail Signature."

  3. Click on "Create," type in the name of the sig.file, and create the sig.file using the different options available.

  4. Set the default to "On" so that your sig.file is added to your outgoing mail.

- Prodigy

  1. Prodigy uses Microsoft Outlook for their e-mail service. Creating signature files with Outlook was discussed earlier in this chapter.

The Do's and Don'ts of Signature Files

It is a good idea to develop several signature files to use with different groups of recipients. You can use an appropriate sig.file for each group you are targeting. Update your sig.file often to reflect current marketing related information.

Some e-mail programs allow a maximum of 80 characters per line for sig.files. You should design your sig.file to fit well within the limits of all programs. Use no more than 70 characters per line to be assured that your sig.file will be viewed as you have designed it no matter what mail reader is being used.

Some people get really innovative in the design of their sig.files. They often include sketches, designs, or logos developed by combining keyboard numbers and punctuation.

Including graphics in your sig.file is not a good idea. This may look quite nice on your screen, but when you send it to other people using different e-mail programs or different screen resolutions, it could look quite different on their monitors. You should stay away from using icons or sketches in your signature files.

Check out sig.files included in messages you have received to determine what you like, what you don't, and what suits you best. Then build your signature file and test it with different e-mail programs and different screen resolutions.

The use of signature files offers a number of benefits to your tourism business. If you use sig.files appropriately, you will be able to promote your operation and your online presence in the following ways.

- The use of sig.files will increase your tourism operation's online exposure. By merely placing a sig.file at the end of a posting to a travel-oriented newsgroup, your tourism operation name may be seen by thousands of people. A great tag line with a call to action will encourage people to visit your site.

- Like any advertisement, the design and content of your sig.file can be used to position your business within the tourism industry or a particular geographic region and create or complement a professional image.

- Using your sig.file can enhance the reputation of your tourism operation. If your postings to newsgroups and mailing lists are helpful and continually appreciated, this knowledge and helpfulness will become associated with your business name.

- Using appropriate sig.files, as shown here, will signal to the online community that you are a member that respects proper netiquette.

Sig.file Do's	Sig.file Don'ts
List all appropriate contact information.	Don't list prices of any kind.
Keep it short, say 4 to 8 lines.	Don't use a sales pitch.
Keep it simple.	Don't use too many symbols.
Provide an appropriate and professional tag line.	Don't list the company's products or services.

Sig.files To Bring Traffic to Your Web Site

The major benefit of sig.files is that they can attract visitors to your web site. Use your signature file as a mini advertisement for your operation and its services. With sigvertising you can go beyond offering the basic contact information. Use your sig.file as a tool to bring traffic to your web site. Instead of simply listing your company phone number and URL, give the reader some insight into your tourism operation and a reason to visit your web site. Use some of the following tips to increase the traffic to your web site:

> *Announce a special offer.*   Briefly mention that your tourism business has a "honeymoon special" or "family reunion package." Inform people that there is a special offer available on your web site.

> *Offer something for free.*   Inform readers of free information or discounts that they can access if they visit your site. Everyone likes getting something for free.

> *Announce an event.*   If your operation is organizing or sponsoring a special event, inform people through your sig.file, and invite them to your site for more information.

> *Announce a contest.*   If your site is holding a contest, tell readers that they can enter by visiting your site.

> *Announce an award or honor.*   If your tourism operation or your web site has received special recognition, tell people about it through your sig.file.

Sig.files are accepted online in e-mail, newsgroups, mailing lists, and discussion groups. However, be cautious when developing your sig.files to ensure that they will be well received. Sig.files that look like billboards or are longer than the text in the message to which they are attached are to be avoided. Sig.files that are blatant advertisements will definitely not be appreciated. The online community reacts unfavorably to hard-sell advertising unless it is done in the proper forum.

Here is an example of a sig.file that may offend Internet users.

XXXXXXXXXXXXXXXXXXXXXXXXXXXXXXXXXXXXXXXXXXXXXXXXXXXXXXXXXXXX
Are you in need of a good night's sleep?
If you are, come visit Rancher's Valley Inn Resort!
We have the best prices in town and the cleanest rooms you will
ever stay in!
Money back guarantee!
Rooms start from $89.95 to $179.95
Talk to Jane Doe about reserving your room today!
101 Main Street, Nashville TN 00123
Tel: (800) 555-0000
Cell: (800) 555-1010
Fax: (800) 555-1020
www.ranch.com
XXXXXXXXXXXXXXXXXXXXXXXXXXXXXXXXXXXXXXXXXXXXXXXXXXXXXXXXXXXX

Another mistake that people make is that they try to make their sig.files too flashy or eye catching. Using a lot of large symbols may catch people's eye, but the impression it leaves will not be memorable. Here is an example of what not to do.

```
☻☺☺✉☺☺✉☺☺☺✉☺☺☺✉☺☺☺✉☺☺☺✉☺☺☺✉☺☺☺☻
☻  !Rancher's Inn Valley Resort !
☻  !Jane Doe, Owner/Operator !
☻  !jdoe@ranch.com !
☻  !101 Main Street !              ☏   (800) 555-0000
☻  !Nashville, TN !                🖷   !(800) 555-0002
☻              !"Clean Rooms @ www.Ranch.com" !
☻☺☺✉☺☺☺✉☺☺☺✉☺☺☺✉☺☺☺✉☺☺☺✉☺☺☺✉☺☺☺☻
```

Here are some examples of what sig.files should look like.

```
==========================================================
            Rancher's Inn Valley Resort
            Jane Doe, Owner/Operator
                jdoe@ranch.com
101 Main Street                     Tel: (800) 555-0000
Nashville, TN 00123                 Fax:(800) 555-0002
   "Reserve your room on our web site at www.ranch.com today!"
==========================================================
```

✉———————————————————————✉
Jane Doe, Owner/Operator * Sunnyvale Ranch
jdoe@ranch.com
101 Main Street   Tel: (800) 555-0000
Nashville, TN 00123   Fax: (800) 555-0001
Rated Best Outdoor Wilderness Ranch in 1999
Visit our site @ www.ranch.com
✉———————————————————————✉

Jane Doe, Owner/Operator
Jdoe@ranchersinn.com
Rancher's Inn Valley Resort
101 Main Street,
Nashville, TN 00123
Tel: (800) 555-0000
Fax: (800) 555-0101
Enter to win a free night's stay @ www.ranch.com

>>
Jane Doe, Owner/Operator
Rancher's Inn Valley Resort
101 Main Street   jdoe@ranch.com
Nashville, TN   Tel: (800) 555-0000
00123 USA   Fax: (800) 555-0001
URL: www.ranch.com
Check us out in this month's issue of Travel & Tourism
>>

✉🏠🏠🏠🏠🏠🏠🏠🏠🏠🏠🏠🏠🏠🏠🏠🏠🏠🏠🏠🏠🏠✉
Jane Doe, Owner/Operator   jdoe@ranch.com
Rancher's Inn Valley Resort
101 Main Street   Tel: (800) 500-1000
Nashville, TN   Fax: (800) 500-1002
00123 USA   URL: www.ranch.com
Make Your Reservation Today @ www.ranch.com
✉🏠🏠🏠🏠🏠🏠🏠🏠🏠🏠🏠🏠🏠🏠🏠🏠🏠🏠🏠🏠🏠✉

Internet Resources

123 Promote
http://www.123promote.com/workbook/plan1.htm
E-mail guide to e-mail styles, mail-merging, autoresponders, autoreminders, Netiquette, e-mail headers, signature files, announcements, press releases, business administration, free designs, mailing list announcements, newsgroup announcements, office automation, mass e-mailing, publicity, form letters, form folders, e-mailed databases, programs, and software.

Coolsig.com
http://coolsig.com
Over 72,432 people have shown their good taste by signing up to get coolsig delivered by e-mail. It comes once or twice a week, and like everything good in life, it's free.

Webnovice.com
www.webnovice.com/sig_files.htm
Everything you wanted to know about signature files but didn't know where to ask.

Using Signature Files
http://www.emtech.net/links/signaturefiles/sld001.htm
Using signature files—how to create them and what to include.

Internet Strategist
http://www.techdirect.com/strategy/sigfiles.html
What to do and not to do on sig.files and mailing lists. Learn how to create your personal sig.file and what the different types are used for.

SquareOne Technology: How To Create an E-mail Signature
http://www.squareonetech.com/signatur.html
How to create a sig.file with Notepad and import it to use with all your e-mail messages.

Signature Files
http://www.smithfam.com/news/n8.html

Signature files are an absolutely vital way of promoting your web site. Learn how to market your product on the Internet from the leading Internet marketing experts, and it is all free.

GFOFN Help: How To Make and Maintain a Signature File
http://www.gnofn.org/info/help/ppp/makesig.html
A tutorial on designing and developing your signature file.

Esther's Massive Signature File Collection
http://www.contrib.andrew.cmu.edu/~moose/sigs.html
A massive collection of sig.files to review—the good, the bad, and the ugly.

32bit.com
http://www.32bit.com/hyper95/get/internet/798.html
A tutorial on adding links in signature files in Netscape 3.x and 4.x.

Signature Museum
http://huizen.dds.nl/~mwpieter/sigs/
The Signature Museum is a gallery of signature files sorted by category. At this site you will also find a list of other sites that provide examples of lots and lots of signature files.

7

The E-mail Advantage

E-mail is rapidly becoming one of the most crucial forms of communication you have with your clients, potential customers, suppliers, and colleagues. E-mail is now a widely accessible and generally accepted form of communication. CyberAtlas *(http://cyberatlas. internet.com)* reported that there were 435 million active e-mail accounts in the world. There are enough e-mail addresses for each person in North America to have his or her own account.

In the online community e-mail is an extremely efficient way to build and maintain relationships. As a marketing tool, e-mail is one of the most cost-effective ways to maintain an ongoing dialogue with your audience. In this chapter we cover:

- Strategies for creating effective e-mail messages

- E-mail Netiquette

- Information access with autoresponders

- Customer service and e-mail

- E-mail marketing tips

- Sending HTML versus ASCII (text-based) e-mail messages

Making the Connection

E-mail is a communication medium, and, as with all forms of communication, you do not get a second chance to leave a first impression. E-mail must be used appropriately. People receive large amounts of e-mail each day, and the tips in this chapter will help to ensure that your e-mail is taken seriously.

One of the greatest benefits of e-mail is the speed with which you can communicate. E-mail takes seconds rather than weeks to send a message around the world. The cost of this form of communication is negligible compared to making a long distance phone call or sending a fax. The economies of scale are significant. One e-mail message can be sent to millions of people across the globe simultaneously. This type of mass mailing is done at a fraction of the cost and a fraction of the time (and internal resources) it would take with **snail mail.**

All kinds of files can be sent via e-mail—including sound, video, data, graphics, and text. With an **autoresponder,** information can be sent to your guests and potential guests 24 hours a day, 7 days a week, 365 days a year in response to their online requests. People are planning their vacations and need information quickly. With e-mail, you have an opportunity to promote your operation, answer questions from your target market, and provide other targeted information to encourage them to make your location their destination.

Snail mail Slang term for the regular postal service.

Autoresponder Program that automatically responds to incoming e-mail. An electronic fax-back system.

Effective E-mail Messages

Most people who use this medium get tons and tons of e-mail, including their share of junk e-mail. The following tips will increase the effectiveness of your e-mail communication.

The Importance of Your E-mail Subject Line

The subject line is equivalent to a headline in a newspaper in terms of attracting reader attention. It is the most important part of your e-mail message because this phrase alone will determine whether or not the reader will decide to open your e-mail or delete it.

When you receive e-mails, what do you use to determine which e-mail to read first or at all? The subject line of course! Never send an e-mail message without a subject line. Subject lines should be brief, with the keywords appearing first. The longer the subject line, the more likely it is that it will not be viewed in entirety.

Effective subject lines will:

- Be brief, yet capture the reader's interest

- Build business credibility

- Attract attention with action words

- Highlight the most important benefits

- Always be positive

- Put the most important words first

Effective headlines should grab the reader's attention, isolate and qualify your best prospects, and draw your reader into the subheadlines and the text itself. Remember to avoid SHOUTING! Using CAPITALS in your subject is the same as SHOUTING AT THE READER! DON'T DO IT!!

E-mail To and From Headings Allow You to Personalize

Use personal names in the To and From headings whenever possible because this creates a more personal relationship. Most e-mail programs allow you to attach your personal name to your e-mail address. If you don't know how to do this, look at the help file of the e-mail program you are using.

Blind Carbon Copy (BCC)

Did you ever receive an e-mail message in which the first screen or first several screens was a string of the other people's e-mail addresses to which the message had been sent? Didn't you feel special? Didn't you feel the message was meant just for you? This sort of bulk mailing is very unpersonalized, and often the recipient will delete the message without looking at it.

It is advisable to use the BCC feature when sending bulk or group e-mails; otherwise every person on the list will see that this e-mail was not sent just to him or her. The e-mail recipients will see the list of the other recipients first and not the intended message. They will be required to scroll down past the list of recipients to get to your message. This is not the best way to make friends and influence people. Make sure that you know how to use the blind carbon copy function in your e-mail program.

BCC
Blind
carbon
copy.

Even better than blind carbon copy is using a software application that can send personalized messages to each recipient in your database. E-mail applications like this are far more flexible than the blind carbon copy method because there is no limitation on the number of messages you can send and the field merge capabilities enable you to create a more personalized message. MailWorkz.com has a great program for this.

Before you send any "live" bulk e-mail, do a test with a number of your colleagues and friends to make sure you are using the program and features effectively and that all of their addresses do not appear by mistake in each message.

Effective E-mail Message Formatting

The content of the message should be focused on one topic. If you need to change the subject in the middle of a message, it is better to send a separate e-mail. Alternatively, if you wish to discuss more than one topic, make sure you begin your message stating "I have 3 questions" or "There are 4 issues I would like to discuss." People are busy, they read their e-mail quickly, and they assume you will cover your main points within the first few sentences of your message.

E-mail is similar to writing a business letter in that the spelling and grammar should be correct. This includes the proper use of upper- and lowercase lettering, which many people seem to ignore when sending e-mail. However, e-mail is unlike a business letter in that the tone can be completely different. E-mail correspondence is not as formal as business writing. The tone of e-mail is more similar to a polite conversation than a formal letter, which makes it conducive to relationship building.

In general, you should do the following:

- Keep your paragraphs relatively short—no more than seven lines.

- Make your point in the first paragraph.

- Be clear and concise.

- Give your reader a call to action.

- Avoid using fancy formatting such as graphics, different fonts, italics, and bold, since many e-mail programs cannot display those features.

- If your e-mail package doesn't have a spell check feature, you might want to consider composing your message first in your word processing program. Spell check it there and then Cut and Paste it into your e-mail package.

- Choose your words carefully. E-mail is a permanent record of your thoughts, and it can be easily forwarded to others.

- If you want to be really careful, test the e-mail in a number of the popular packages to ensure your message will be received in the intended format.

A Call to Action

When you give your readers a call to action, it's amazing how often people will do as they're told. I'll give you an example through something we did at Connex Network. We ran a series of 10 Internet marketing workshops for a large organization. Their staff and selected clients were invited to participate in any, some or all of the workshops. Their clients could include up to three employees. Since the workshops extended beyond the noon hour, lunch was provided.

Since Connex Network was responsible for organizing and managing the project, we needed to know the approximate number of people who would be attending each of the workshops to organize the luncheons. When we contacted each company's representatives by e-mail looking for participation RSVPs we conducted an experiment. We sent half the representatives one version of the message and a slightly different version of the message to the other half. The only difference between the two messages was that in one, we had a call to action: In one message we asked "RSVP before Wednesday at noon indicating if you will be attending as we must make arrangements for lunch," and in the other message, this same line read "Please let us know if you are planning to attend as we must make arrangements for lunch."

There was a 95% response rate from the group who received the first message. This is because we gave people a call to action and a deadline, and they felt obligated to respond more promptly. Meanwhile, less than 50% of the people in the second group responded to our message.

What does this tell us? To improve your response rate, give your readers a call to action when you send them e-mail. People will respond when told to do something, and they act with more urgency when there is a deadline.

Appropriate E-mail Reply Tips

Do not include the entire original message in your replies. This is unnecessary, aggravating to the original sender of the message, and often takes too long to **download**. However, you should use enough of the original message to refresh the recipient's memory.

Download Transmission of a file from one computer to another.

Remember to check the To and CC options before you reply. You would not want an entire mailing list to receive a response intended only for the sender. With most e-mail software, this will not be a problem. The same applies for selecting "Reply All" instead of "Reply." If you click on "Reply," only the From address will be included in the To field. If you select "Reply All," however, it is a good idea to double-check that only your intended recipients will receive your message.

Always Use Your Signature Files

As discussed previously, signature files are a great marketing tool. Always attach your signature file to your online communication. (See Chapter 6 on signature files.) Also, ensure that the signature files are appropriate for the intended audience.

Discerning Use of Attachments

If you are sending a fairly large volume of data, you may want to send it as a file attached to your e-mail message. However, only include an e-mail attachment if you have the recipient's permission to send it in an attached file. You would never consider going to someone's home, letting yourself in, finding your way into their living room and then leaving your brochure on the coffee table. However, people do the online equivalent of this when they send an unsolicited attachment. The attachment is sent across the Internet, to the recipient's computer and is downloaded and stored on the recipient's computer's hard drive. This is considered quite rude and, in most cases, unwanted.

Also, unless the recipient of your e-mail is aware of the file size and is expecting it, don't send an attachment that is larger than 50K. Although your Internet connection might be a cable modem or a T1 line and a 3 MB file is sent in seconds, the person who is receiving your message and attachment might be using a 14.4 Kbps modem and a slow machine. If you send a 3 MB file, it might take the person with the 14.4 Kbps modem over an hour to download the file. Needless to say, he or she won't be too pleased.

Another factor to consider when sending an unsolicited attachment is that the attachment you are sending may be incompatible with the operating system or the software the recipient has installed. Someone using a Macintosh with Corel WordPerfect installed will not be able to read a Microsoft Word 2000 document sent as an attachment. Thus, you will have wasted your time sending the file and the recipient's time downloading the file.

Finally, it is a well-known fact that e-mail attachments can act as carriers for computer **viruses.** You may unknowingly send someone an attachment with a virus, and even if the file you send is virus-free, you may still take the blame if recipients find a virus on their system, just because you sent them an attachment.

Basically, avoid sending e-mail attachments of any variety unless you have the recipient's permission. Be mindful of the size of the file you intend to send, its compatibility with other platforms, and computer viruses.

One alternative to sending a large attachment is to post the file on a web server, and in your e-mail message, direct users to a URL from which they can download the file.

Viruses
Programs that contaminate a user's hard drive, often with unwanted results.

Before You Click on "Send"

There are a number of things you should do before you send an important e-mail, especially if it is going to a number of people. Send a test message to yourself or a colleague so that you can check that the word wrap looks good and that the text is formatted properly and it displays as you want it to. Check that there are no typos, errors, or omissions.

Expressing Yourself with Emoticons and Shorthand

In verbal communication you provide details on your mood, meaning, and intention through voice inflections, tone, and volume. You also give clues about your meaning and intention through facial expression and body language. E-mail does not allow for the same expression of feeling. The closest thing we have to this online is the use of **emoticons.**

The word "emoticons" is an combination of "emotions" and "icons." Emoticons are combinations of keyboard characters that give the appearance of a stick figure's emotions.

Emoticons
Symbols made from punctuation marks and letters that look like facial expressions.

They have to be viewed sideways and are meant to be smiling, frowning, laughing, and so on. Emoticons let you communicate your meaning and intentions to your reader.

For example, if your boss gives you an assignment to be completed on the weekend via e-mail and your response is "Thanks a lot for unloading your dirty work on me," your boss may become upset at your obvious defiance. But if you replied with "Thanks a lot for unloading your dirty work on me :-)," your boss would understand that you were jokingly accepting the assignment.

Emoticons enable you to add a little personality and life to your text messages. However, their use is not universal and should generally not be used in business correspondence.

Some of the more commonly used emoticons include:

:-)	Smiling	:-0	Wow!
;-)	Wink	:-V	Shout
:-D	Laughing, big smile	:-@	Screaming
:-p	Tongue wagging	(-:	I'm left handed
:-o	Wow!	:-r	Tongue hanging out
:-#	My lips are sealed!	:-S	I'm totally confused
:-/	Skeptical	~~:-(	just got flamed!
:\\	Befuddled		

E-mail shorthand is used in newsgroups and other e-mail to represent commonly used phrases. Some common abbreviations are:

- BTW: By the way

- IMHO: In my humble opinion

- IMO: In my opinion

- IOW: In other words

- JFYI: Just for your information

- NBD: No big deal

- NOYB: None of your business

- TIA: Thanks in advance

- PMFJI: Pardon me for jumping in

- OIC: Oh, I see

- OTL: Out to lunch

- OTOH: On the other hand

- LOL: Laughing out loud

- LMHO: Laughing my head off

- ROFL: Rolling on the floor laughing

- BFN: Bye for now

- CYA: See ya!

- FWIW: For what it's worth

- IAE: In any event

- BBL: Be back later

- BRB: Be right back

- RS: Real soon

- TIC: Tongue in cheek

- TTFN: Ta-ta for now

- TTYL: Talk to you later

- TWF: That was fun

- YMBJ: You must be joking!

- WYSIWYG: What you see is what you get

- <g>: Adding a grin

Since e-mail shorthand is most commonly used in newsgroups and chat rooms, you will be most successful when using these acronyms with others who are familiar with them.

Using Automated Mail Responders— Mailbots and Infobots

Automated mail responders act like fax-back systems. They send requested information via e-mail automatically to the person that made the request. You can ask your Internet Service Provider (ISP) for details on autoresponder services they may offer. Alternatively, you can also do a search on "mailbots" or "autoresponders" to find any third-party companies that can provide you with these services.

You can make information on your operation, your area, your rates, and your marketing materials easily accessible 24 hours a day, 7 days a week, 365 days a year through mailbots. Examples of information that you can easily provide through this service are:

- Brochures

- Room rate schedules

- Scheduled activities

- Reviews and testimonials

- Press releases

- Newsletters

- Award announcements

These types of information could be placed on your web site. However, you may choose to promote them by way of an autoresponder so that you can obtain customer data prior to providing the customers with the information they are requesting from you. Ask them for their e-mail address, mailing address, and phone number so that you can follow up. You can also consider asking any marketing-related questions you may have. This type of data can be useful for targeting individuals in a future e-mail marketing campaign.

Autoresponders can also be used to personalize and build relationships and to provide outstanding customer service. For instance, even if you run a seasonal operation such as a ski resort, you may set an autoresponder during your off-season that might consist of something like the following:

Thanks for your e-mail. Sorry, we are closed for the season and not accessing our e-mail on a regular basis. We are scheduled to re-open on December 15th. If you would like to talk to us prior to then, please call Lynn at (902) 425-2578 and she will be happy to help you. Regards Susan

Obviously, it would be better to be able to respond immediately, but if you are indisposed, a "closed for the season" message such as the one just shown is an example of good customer service. You are letting your customers know that they are important to you even though you are unavailable.

Autoresponders also provide an excellent means of promoting your operation. Each time someone sends you a request for information, include a short marketing blurb in the autoresponder that includes the requested information. This marketing technique will not be viewed as unsolicited e-mail because the person asked for it. Change the autoresponder message until you find the one that generates the best response. Autoresponders are easy to set up and easy to change, so your marketing message can be modified in an instant. See the Internet Resources at the end of this chapter for more information.

people who have seen your e-mail address on letterhead, ads, business cards, and sig.files. Don't wait for the first inquiry before you begin to develop your operation's materials. Be prepared to respond by following these tips.

Brochure and Personal Note

Have an electronic brochure available that you can easily access and send via e-mail. Try to send a personal note in your e-mail along with any material requested.

Gather a Library of Responses

You will have different people asking a number of the same questions, and over time you will be able to develop a library of responses to these frequently asked questions. You can save a lot of time by copying and pasting the answers to frequently asked questions or FAQs into your e-mail responses. Again, always make sure to personalize your responses.

Have More Than One E-mail Box

By having a number of different e-mail accounts that you use for different marketing activities, you can develop databases of all the people who have sent you a message—sorted by their interests. (You will know their interests by which mailbox they choose to send an e-mail to.) For example, you may be able to tell that a person is interested in your golf weekend getaway promotion but not your catered business conference services, or interested in your whale watching tours but not in your mountain biking expeditions.

The tactic of using separate e-mail accounts and filtering them into different mailboxes can be used for many marketing purposes other than developing e-mail lists. An example would be to place the same advertisement in three different magazines. Associate a different e-mail address with each ad, and determine which ad generates the best response by reviewing the number of responses sent to the different e-mail addresses. You will then know in which magazine to advertise in the future for the best response.

Have More Than One E-mail Folder

You want to be able to target your customers based on their interests as much as possible. The more you can personalize you message to your target audience, the greater success you will achieve with your Internet marketing campaigns. Organizing your e-mail inbox into distinct folders will assist you with sorting your customers from your potential customers and further identifying these individuals by their interests.

For instance, if your travel agency markets travel packages to Hawaii, the Bahamas, and Europe, create a separate folder in your e-mail program to contain all of the e-mail inquiries you have received from people interested in going to Hawaii. Then, create folders for people who have written you about your Bahamas and European vacation packages, and so on. In the future, you will be able to market to these individuals directly based on their specific, expressed interest from the past.

Run An Opt-in E-mail Marketing Campaign

An opt-in e-mail marketing campaign is perhaps the best means to reach your target audience. "Opt-in" refers to the fact that people can willingly subscribe and unsubscribe from your e-mail list. This is important because if people do not want mail from you and you send them unsolicited e-mail, you could be accused of spamming. Spam is the scourge of the Internet and a pet peeve of many people. If it is reported to your ISP that you are sending unsolicited bulk e-mail, you could lose your Internet account.

Only send mail to people who have expressed prior interest in your business, and allow them to unsubscribe themselves from your mailing list if they choose. As mentioned earlier in this chapter, you can use the blind carbon copy method to conduct an e-mail marketing campaign, or you can use a specialized e-mail application. Most e-mail marketing software packages will permit you to easily add or subtract new subscribers from your mailing list. These applications also create more personalized messages than can be achieved using blind carbon copy.

Following Formalities with E-mail Netiquette

When writing e-mails remember the following:

- Be courteous—remember please and thank-you.

- Reply promptly—within 24 hours.

- Be brief.

- Use upper- and lowercase characters appropriately. Using all capitals indicates SHOUTING!

- Use emoticons where appropriate.

- Check your grammar and spelling.

- Use attachments sparingly.

- Do not send unsolicited bulk e-mail.

Reply Promptly

People expect an answer the same day or the next day at the latest. E-mail communication is like voice mail. If you do not respond within 24 hours, you send a very clear message to your visitors, potential visitors, and colleagues: "Your communication is not important to me."

Especially in the tourism industry, you want to get back to the people planning their vacations with all the answers to their questions as soon as you possibly can. You are in a very competitive environment. If your visitors find what they are looking for elsewhere on the Net before you have a chance to respond to their inquiry, you may be too late.

The Heart of Customer Service

Although most customer correspondence via e-mail is very pleasant and businesslike, you will occasionally encounter a person who is displeased with the service they have received from you. Very often, a series of courteous, prompt e-mail responses can turn a disgruntled customer into a customer for life. Taking a potentially disagreeable situation and reversing it to a positive one is the heart of customer service. Here is a real example of how a client turned such a situation around. This excerpt was provided to me by Donna Ross of the Shambhala Sun at a recent seminar and has been included with the permission of Donna and the Shambhala Sun magazine *(http:// www.shambhalasun.com)*. The name and address of the subscriber have been changed.

Customer 1st Message:

Dear Shambhala Sun Folk:
I sent in a change of address form back a few months ago, but I have not been receiving the latest issues of your magazine at my new address. The last one I received was the January 1999 issue at my old address. So let's try again:

Name: Joe Subscriber

Old Address:
100 Some Street
Anaheim, CA 92999

New Address:
49494 Another Street
San Jose, CA 92000

My home phone number is (999) 999-9999.

Thank you for your help and consideration on this matter.
Sincerely,
Joe Subscriber

Shambhala Sun Response:

Dear Joe:
We do have your new address in our system. Your May issue should be arriving there any minute now. I will send you the missed March issue in this evening's mail. I notice that we have the city for your new address listed as Laguna Hills. In your e-mail, you have it as San Jose. Please let me know which of the two is more accurate. Thanks.
Donna Ross
Shambhala Sun Subscriptions

Customer 2nd Message:
How did you know? The May issue arrived in my mailbox this very day! As I was just in a fairly bad auto accident and am laid up, it is most welcome. Thanks for your speedy reply.
Sincerely,
Joe Subscriber

Shambhala Sun Response:
Actually, it is my job to know. :-)
Sorry to hear you are hurt. Heal well.
Donna Ross
Shambhala Sun Subscriptions

Customer Final Message:
Thanks Donna for your concern. It's no surprise that Shambhala Sun has folks like you working there. Consider me a subscriber for life.
Sincerely,
Joe Subscriber
P.S.Although my car was totaled, I am doing fine and healing quickly.
End of Correspondence Thread

As has been clearly demonstrated by this example, the value of strong customer relations is immeasurable. If you take great care to respond quickly and courteously to your customers' e-mail messages (even when they're not happy), you can win them over for life. Nothing exceeds the value of a lifetime customer.

HTML or Text Messages?

E-mail messages are commonly sent and encoded as regular ASCII text. However, HTML mail is steadily making inroads into the e-mail world. See Figure 7.1 for an example. Many e-mail clients are capable of sending HTML-encoded messages, but should you use this format or just stick to text?

The benefit of sending an HTML-formatted message is that you can effectively send a message that acts and appears like a web page. It's like a colorful brochure and is much more attractive than a plain

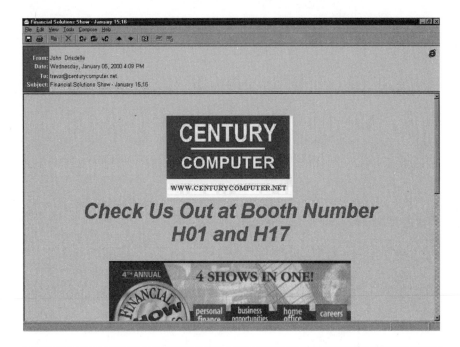

Figure 7.1. This image is an example of an HTML-formatted message. It includes a background image. Only current e-mail software can properly read HTML messages.

ASCII text message. The only drawback of HTML mail is that a lot of e-mail clients cannot properly decode the HTML. Thus, the message is converted to ASCII, loses its formatting, and looks unappealing. Your recipients will be inclined to delete such poorly formatted messages.

If you have ever received an e-mail message that contained a line of hyperlink text such as "Click here to visit our web site," this is one example of an HTML message. An e-mail client that can decode HTML will permit you to click on the highlighted text and access the web site. If your e-mail client only understands ASCII-formatted messages, the hyperlink might not work.

To ensure that URLs you insert in an e-mail message always display as hyperlink text, simply type the full URLs into your message. For instance, type Click on the link below to visit Connex Network: *http://www.connexnetwork.com*

Most e-mail clients will recognize the *http://* as the beginning of a hyperlink.

Regardless, if you want to try using HTML formatting in your e-mail correspondence, let your recipients decide which type of message they prefer. Send HTML-formatted messages only to the people who prefer it and ASCII messages to the rest of your recipients.

Some e-mail software packages can send both an HTML and an ASCII text version of an e-mail message at once. If your software has this capability, then you can send either type of message without any concern.

Internet Resources

E-mail Netiquette
http://ultra.santarosa.edu/net/email/netiquette.html
This document is from David Harris, author of Pegasus Mail, a popular PC and MAC e-mail package to help get the most from your e-mail.

Everything E-mail
http://everythingemail.net/
Information and links to make your e-mail account more productive and fun! Resources, guides, and a glossary to make things easier for

you to understand. Extensive web site dedicated exclusively to e-mail and e-mail services.

123 Promote
http://www.123promote.com/workbook/plan1.htm
E-mail guide to e-mail styles, mail-merging, autoresponders, autoreminders, Netiquette, headers, signature files, announcements, press releases, business administration, free designs, mailing list announcements, newsgroup announcements, office automation, mass e-mailing, publicity, form letters, form folders, e-mailed databases, programs, and software.

A Beginner's Guide to Effective E-mail
http://www.webfoot.com/advice/email.top.html
Help in writing the e-mail you need. Formats and why you need e-mail are all explained in detail.

Neophyte's Guide to Effective E-mail
http://www.webnovice.com/email.htm
This site goes through, step by step, the important issues you should keep in mind from start to send.

I Will Follow.com E-mail Tips
http://www.iwillfollow.com/email.htm
This site offers advice to beginners on all aspects of using e-mail.

Internet Marketing Newsletter
http://www.arrowweb.com/graphics/news/ap12.html
"The Secrets of E-mail Marketing Success," an article by Lesley Anne Lowe.

Windweaver
http://www.windweaver.com/emoticon.htm
Recommended emoticons for e-mail communication.

Dave Barry's Guide to Emoticons
http://www.randomhouse.com/features/davebarry/emoticon.html
Good resource for emoticons and shorthand. His site has an Emoticon Gallery with lots of examples (3069 at last count) and an area where you can make your own.

EmailAddresses.com
http://www.emailaddresses.com
A directory of numerous free e-mail services including POP accounts, e-mail forwarding, newsletters, and so on.

EEF's Extended Guide to the Internet
http://www.eff.org/papers/eegtti/eeg_286.html
This Unofficial Smiley Dictionary is only one of many different collections by various "editors" you'll come across at many places on the Net.

Aaron's Emoticons
http://www.teleport.com/~rhubarbs/faces.htm
Another extensive source of emoticons.

CyberAtlas
http://cyberatlas.internet.com
CyberAtlas is your guide to online facts. The site provides readers with valuable statistics and web marketing information, enabling them to understand their business environment and make more informed business decisions.

E-mail—The Mining Company
http://email.miningco.com/internet/email/
Updated weekly, this site consists of articles and links to e-mail resources on many topics: beginning e-mail, finding people, free e-mail, greeting cards, privacy, and much more.

8

Mailing Lists—Reach Out to Your Visitors

Internet mailing lists are quick and easy ways to distribute information to a large number of people. There are thousands of publicly available online lists, including hundreds of travel and tourism-related lists. You can also create your own Internet mailing lists to keep your clients and prospects informed of events, news, announcements, and press releases. If you operate an outdoor adventure business, perhaps you could use a mailing list to inform subscribers of upcoming events and scheduled activities. In this chapter we cover:

- How to identify appropriate publicly accessible mailing lists (discussion lists)

- Subscribing to the mailing list

- Writing messages that will be read

- Mailing list Netiquette

- Creating your own mailing list

Connecting with Your Target Audience

Discussion mailing lists are publicly available and focused on a particular subject matter. There are outdoor adventure mailing lists, bed and breakfast traveler mailing lists, seniors travel mailing lists, and all kinds of mailing lists for specific demographics related to travel and geographically related travel. Participating in a discussion list relevant to the travel and tourism industry and its target market can help you attract new customers. Discussion lists are organized hierarchically by subject matter in a way similar to Usenet newsgroups. Likewise, the membership rate of each discussion mailing list varies. People subscribe to particular lists to participate in that list and receive all of the postings that are sent to the group, generally because they have an interest in the topic. When you post a message to a mailing list, the message is sent out to everyone who has subscribed to the list by e-mail.

Discussion mailing lists are quick and easy ways to distribute information to a large number of people interested in a particular topic. The difference between discussion mailing lists and newsgroups is that anyone on the Internet can visit newsgroups at any time and read any articles of interest, whereas a discussion list delivers all messages posted directly to the subscribers' e-mail.

Note: Only discussion list subscribers can receive these messages. Newsgroups can be viewed by anyone with access to a newsserver. All they have to do is log onto the newsserver and enter the name of the newsgroup they wish to peruse, and they can view all postings made to that group. To subscribe to a discussion list, you have to send a subscription message to the list administrator and request permission to join the mailing list. Thus, newsgroup postings can be viewed anonymously, but permission is required to view postings to mailing lists.

Types of Mailing Lists

Publicly accessible mailing lists can be one of several types, each with varying degrees of control. Following is a discussion of the major types of lists.

Moderated Lists

This type of list is maintained by a "gatekeeper" who filters out unwanted or inappropriate messages. If you try to post an advertisement where they are not permitted, your message will never make it out to the list of subscribers. Similarly, flames (i.e.,publicly chastising another list member) are screened out. The gatekeeper will also keep the topic of discussion on track if a few members get off-topic.

Unmoderated Lists

An unmoderated list is operated without any centralized control or censorship. Most lists are of this type. All messages are automatically forwarded to subscribers. Unmoderated lists tend to have more blatant advertisements and flame wars because there is no gatekeeper to guide the discussion. It is then the responsibility of the list members to police their own actions. Otherwise, the list could end up being a landfill for spammers, or a lot of members will simply leave the list if a few individuals choose to ridicule them.

Targeting Appropriate Mailing Lists

There are thousands of publicly available lists online. There are a number of sites that provide lists of mailing lists. Three of the most popular and comprehensive are:

- The Liszt at *http://www.liszt.com* (see Figures 8.1 and 8.2)

- The List of Publicly Accessible Mailing Lists at *http://www.neosoft.com/internet/paml* (see Figures 8.3 and 8.4)

- TILE.NET at *http://tile.net/lists* (see Figures 8.5 and 8.6)

There are also companies online that specialize in providing targeted e-mail lists. One such company is Post Master Direct Response at *www.postmasterdirect.com*. This company rents e-mail lists of people who

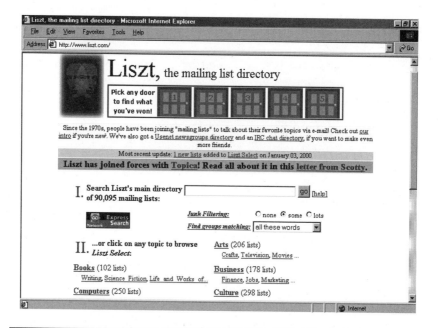

Figure 8.1. The Liszt has indexed over 90,000 publicly available mailing lists.

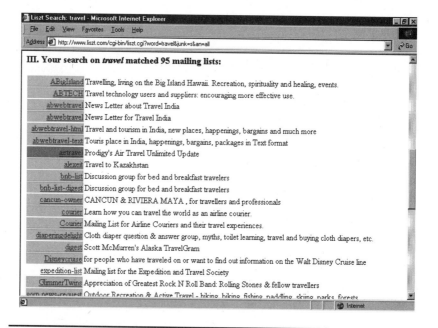

Figure 8.2. Search results for the word travel on The Liszt.

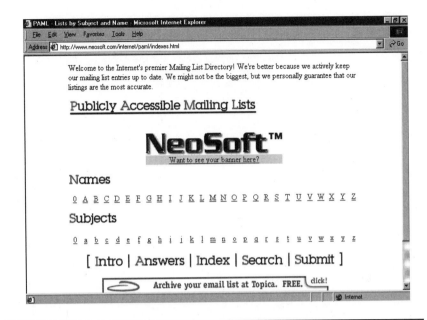

Figure 8.3. The List of Publicly Accessible Mailing Lists.

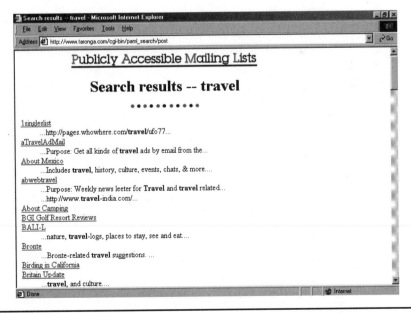

Figure 8.4. There's a good number of matches for the word travel on The List of Publicly Accessible Mailing Lists.

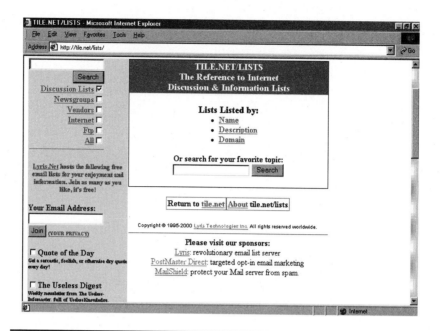

Figure 8.5. The TILE.NET offers more publicly accessible mailing lists.

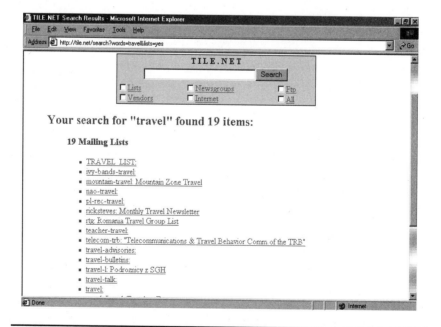

Figure 8.6. TILE.NET also returns a nice quantity of Travel mailing lists.

have requested information on a particular topic. However, these are different from the discussion mailing lists that we described earlier in this chapter. E-mail lists are simply that—lists of e-mail addresses. If you subscribe to one of these lists, you are not entering into a discussion, you are placing yourself on a mailing list that will receive e-mail postings. However, from a marketing perspective, e-mail lists can be useful tools if they are targeted.

Another option is to create your own publicly accessible mailing list. This is covered later in the chapter. Still another option is to purchase bulk e-mail lists. This is a questionable practice because it involves **spam**. Bulk e-mail lists are generally sold without the permission of the addressees, much like junk mailing lists. The recipients did not ask to be put on a mailing list. They are not aware of the fact that they are on a list and often do not appreciate being sent unsolicited e-mail. Another drawback is that usually these lists are not targeted. By using bulk e-mail lists you run the risk of not reaching any of your target market. You also risk annoying those addressees who under other circumstances may have been interested in what you were trying to promote.

Spam Inappropriate use of mailing lists as a broadcast medium by sending unsolicited messages to large numbers of people

The correct choice depends on the market you are targeting. Some people use the shotgun approach to reach as many people as possible. We've all received those e-mails—"reach 5 million with our mailing list available for $29.95." After all, one of the major benefits of the Internet is reaching large numbers of people quickly. There is no excuse for this kind of "marketing." Even if someone is marketing a product with broad-based appeal, that isn't a license to spam the world with their marketing message. If it isn't "opt-in," don't send it. Nobody is going to be too impressed by receiving spam. Either the message will be deleted without being read or some of the recipients of the spam could complain to the sender's ISP and have the sender's Internet access revoked.

However, the best approach is to choose a list whose subscribers fit your target market as closely as possible. For example, if you are offering advanced reservations for your campground, then you will want to consider a mailing list with a topic surrounding traveling, camping, or outdoor recreation. A shotgun approach is a waste of both your time and resources. By using bulk e-mail you raise the ire of thousands of recipients of your e-mail, destroy your image, and potentially damage your credibility. In this case, a much smaller targeted list, as noted earlier, should be used to get a much higher quality response rate. Less is better.

Finding the Right Mailing List

Whether you join a publicly accessible discussion mailing list or choose to purchase an opt-in e-mail list from one of the many online sources, you want to find a mailing list whose members are in your target market seeking a discussion on the types of tourism related products or services you are offering. You will have to do your homework here, because there are thousands of mailing lists to choose from.

There are various meta-indexes of publicly available mailing lists that you can search by title or by subject. Some of these sites provide detailed information on the mailing lists, such as their content and the commands used to subscribe. We have provided information on a number of these resources by category. There will be mailing lists that you might be interested in participating in that relate to your type of operation, your target demographic, your geographic location, and so on. Take a look at the following list of resources to find a list that is pertinent to your business. If none of the lists apply to your business, refer to Topica.com *(http://www.topica.com/)* or Liszt.com *(http://www.liszt.com)* for a more appropriate list.

Bed and Breakfasts

bbbb
Accommodation, bed and breakfast, cottages, chalets.
Subscription information: E-mail to *bbbb@xyz.net.*

bnb-list
Discussion group for bed and breakfast travelers.
Subscription information: You can mail a request for an "info" file to the server address, *majordomo@www.netconcepts.com.* Put this single line in the mail message: *info bnb-list.*

bnb-list-digest
Discussion group in digest format for bed and breakfast travelers.
Subscription information: You can mail a request for an "info" file to

the server address, *majordomo@www.netconcepts.com*. Put this single line in the mail message: *info bnb-list-digest*.

Country Inn

Getting-Inn
Getting-Inn is a moderated e-mail-based mailing list/discussion group exclusively for aspiring innkeepers. Its aim is to help facilitate communication and collaboration among participants and to provide a mechanism for them to pose questions, discuss issues and experiences, give advice and commentary, and just plain vent. Subscription information:Visit *http://www.paii.org/getting-inn/*

Outdoor Recreation and Camping

expedition-list
Mailing list for expedition and travel.
Subscription information: You can mail a request for an "info" file to the server address, *listserver@leicester.ac.uk*. Put this single line in the mail message: *info expedition-list*.

gilatrip
Gila wilderness camping trip discussion list.
Subscription information: You can mail a request for an "info" file to the server address, *listproc@lists.cc.utexas.edu*. Put this single line in the mail message: *info gilatrip*.

gorp.news-request
Outdoor recreation and active travel—hiking, biking, fishing, paddling, skiing, parks, forests, and so on.
Subscription information: Visit *http://www.gorp.com:81/guest/RemoteAvailableLists*.

green-travel
Moderated list about environmentally and culturally responsible tourism.

Subscription information: You can mail a request for an "info" file to the server address, *majordomo@igc.org*. Put this single line in the mail message: *review green-travel*.

Cruises

AllCruises
All you need to know about cruising.
Subscription information: Contact *going_cruising@hotmail.com*.

smartravel.com/cruises
Receive the best cruise ship berth liquidations available biweekly.
Subscription information: Contact *whodge@smartravel.com*.

Airline Travel

SKYONE-L
Discussion about airlines, aviation, airports, and travel.
Subscription information: Send your request to *ehuey@rush.edu*.

Travel Industry

Hospitality
Hotel, restaurant, and travel industry—sales, marketing and PR.
Subscription information: Contact *LTaverna@Hospitality-1st.com*.

travel_talk
Travel industry discussion.
Subscription information: You can mail a request for an "info" file to the server address, *listproc@lists.colorado.edu*. Put this single line in the mail message: *info travel_talk*.

Theme Parks

theme
Theme parks.

Subscription information: You can mail a request for an "info" file to the server address, *majordomo@listserv.prodigy.com.* Put this single line in the mail message: *info theme.*

theme-digest
Theme parks (digest format).
Subscription information: You can mail a request for an "info" file to the server address, *majordomo@listserv.prodigy.com.* Put this single line in the mail message: *info theme-digest.*

wdw
Discussion of the Walt Disney World theme parks, resorts, and so on. Subscription information: Visit *http://www.onelist.com/ subscribe.cgiwdw/*

Travel Deals

QTW
Travel specials, discounts, cruises, and lots more.
Subscription information:Contact *glagrow@quinwell.com.*

travplace
Weekly publication listing the hottest travel deals in the United States and the Caribbean.
Subscription information:Contact *travplace@aol.com.*

worldtravel
Great Deals, cruise steals, and fabulous vacations.
Subscription information: Contact *infoworldtravel@list1. channel1.com.*

General Travel

travel-ease
Discussion of leisure travel.
Subscription information: You can mail a request for an "info" file to the server address, *majordomo@kajor.com.* Put this single line in the mail message: *info travel-ease.*

traveller
The Traveller mailing list.
Subscription information: You can mail a request for an "info" file to the server address, *majordomo@lists.imagiconline.com*. Put this single line in the mail message: *info traveller.*

traveller-digest
The Traveller mailing list (digest version).
Subscription information: You can mail a request for an "info" file to the server address, *majordomo@lists.imagiconline.com*. Put this single line in the mail message: *info traveller-digest.*

TravelNotes
The TravelNotes discussion list is a Q&A for travelers connected to the web.
Subscription information: Contact *travelnotes@yahoo.com.*

ttbba-1
Travel and tourism.
Subscription information: You can mail a request for an "info" file to the server address, *listserv@unm.edu*. Put this single line in the mail message: *info ttbba.*

Geographic Specific Travel

abwebtravel
Newsletter about traveling in India.
Subscription information: Visit *http://www.travel-india.com/* for subscription information.

cancun-owner
Cancun and the Riviera Maya, for travelers and professionals.
Subscription information: Contact *cancun@iname.com.*

hondo1
Discussion of travel, retirement, vacation and investments in Honduras.
Subscription information: You can mail a request for an "info" file to the server address, *majordomo@maillist.peak.org*. Put this single line in the mail message: *info hondo1.*

jamaica
Jamaica Independent Travel discussion list.
Subscription information: You can mail a request for an "info" file to the server address, *majordomo@ezekiel.enteract.com*. Put this single line in the mail message: *info jamaica*.

London-Beyond
Group travel in London.
Subscription information: Contact *holiday@beechbrook.com*.

travel
Mailing list about international travel.
Subscription information: Mail the command *info travel* to *majordomo@cuy.net*.

Once you have identified mailing lists that have your target market as members, you will subscribe to those lists. To confirm that a list is appropriate for your marketing purposes, lurk awhile to monitor the discussion taking place. Once this has been confirmed, you can begin participating in the list by providing valuable content. If advertising is not allowed, abide by the rules. eGroups.com (see Figure 8.7) provides a description for each of the mail lists it hosts.

Subscribing to Your Target Mailing Lists

Liszt *(http://www.liszt.com)*, TILE.NET *(http://www.tile.net/lists)*, and the Internet Publicly Available Discussion Mailing Lists *(http://www.neosoft.com/internet/paml)* are great resources and will provide you with not only a huge list of accessible mailing lists but also specific instructions for joining the particular lists you are interested in. Most lists are subscribed to by sending an e-mail to the given address with *subscribe* in the subject or the body of the message. There are variations on this theme, so you must check the instructions for joining each specific mailing list. After you subscribe you generally will receive an e-mail response with the rules, FAQ files, and instructions on how to use the list.

For the most part, all of the rules for posting to newsgroups apply to mailing lists as well. Read the rules carefully and abide by

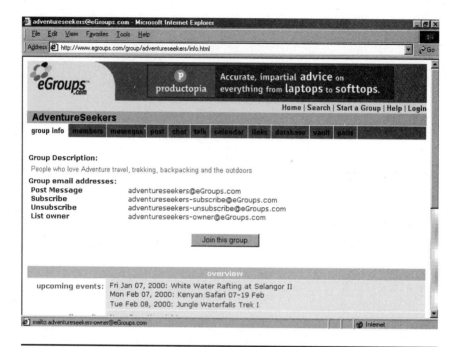

Figure 8.7. eGroups.com provides a description for each of the mail lists it hosts.

them. A lurking period should be considered before you post a message. This will help you observe what types of messages are posted and the commonly accepted practices for that particular group.

List Digests

Usually when you subscribe to a mailing list, you have the option to "subscribe digest." A digest is a compilation of many individual messages sent to each subscriber as one bulk message. Many digests contain a table of contents. The good thing about a digest is that you do not receive as many separate e-mails and your mailbox doesn't become clogged up. Also, the digest administrator chooses all or only the best postings to include in the list digest. Therefore, blatant advertisements, flames, and postings containing repetitive subject matter are filtered out. In an unmoderated list, you would receive every single message posted to the list. Most of these postings would not be of interest to you and would be deleted anyway. The digest format simplifies things so that you get the information you need without wasting a lot of time.

Composing Effective Messages

As discussed in the previous chapter, your e-mails must be carefully prepared before you post to a mailing list. Remember to make your subject line relevant, keep your messages short and to the point, and always include your sig.file. If you are unsure whether your posting is appropriate for the group, you can simply send a test message to the moderator asking for advice.

Unlike newsgroups, the members of mailing lists receive all the messages directly into their mailbox every day. Some people prefer to receive the postings in digest form, that is, as discussed earlier, all the messages for that day are compiled into one e-mail sent to the recipient at the end of the day. The digest provides, at the beginning of the e-mail, a listing of all the messages with the "From" and "Subject" identified, followed by the complete messages. Just as individuals who visit a newsgroup don't read all the messages, subscribers to publicly accessible discussion lists do not read every posting either. They decide which messages to review based on the subject line. Thus, the content of the "Subject" is extremely important.

You must never repeat the same or similar messages to a mailing list as you might do in a newsgroup. Once members of a mailing list have seen your posted message, they will not appreciate seeing it again, whereas a newsgroup has different readers all the time and similar postings are acceptable if they are timed appropriately.

The following tips on mailing list postings will assist you in becoming a respected member of their online community:

- Make sure that your messages are "on the subject." List subscribers don't want to read postings unrelated to their topic.

- You should be a regular contributor to your list before making anything resembling a commercial announcement. If your mailing list does not allow advertising (most do not), use your sig.file. Sig.files are generally accepted. Ensure that you make effective use of your tag line to get your mini-ad into discussion mailing lists where advertising is not permitted. (See Chapter 6 for advertising when advertising is not allowed.)

- Track and record your responses when you use a new mailing list. You should have a call to action in your posting, encouraging the readers to visit a specific page on your site or to send e-mail to an e-mail address designated solely for this purpose. Only by employing an appropriate mechanism to track responses will you know with any certainty which mailing lists are working for you and which are not. It's amazing how well calls to action work. For some reason, people tend to do what they're told.

- Set reasonable and achievable goals. As a benchmark, in most e-mail marketing campaigns a 1 to 3 percent response rate is considered a good response. However, if your mailing list is very targeted and you are offering something of interest or value to a particular group, your response rates should be significantly higher.

Building Your Own Private Mailing Lists

You may want to build your own mailing lists. Generating your own mailing lists is often beneficial because of the many marketing uses the lists have. They can be used to maintain an ongoing dialogue with existing customers regarding updates, news, specials, and so on. You can sign-up for 1 Stop-Travel's mail list (see Figure 8.8) to receive notice of specials and updated information. If you run a downhill ski operation, then you may want to have a mailing list to inform the users of the run conditions, advise them of how many runs are open, and so on. Mailing lists can also be used to communicate with current and prospective tourists through distribution of your operation's newsletters, rate schedule, accommodations, travel guides, improvements to your facility, new announcements, and upcoming events.

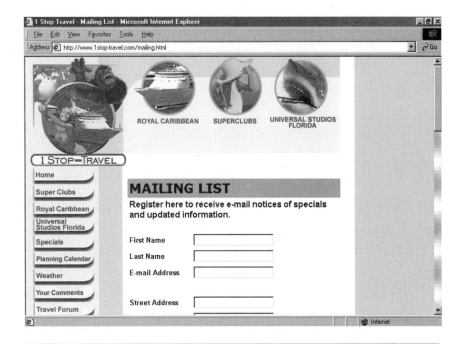

Figure 8.8. You can sign-up for 1 Stop-Travel's mail list to receive notice of specials and updated information.

You can use a number of methods for soliciting and collecting e-mail addresses, including an online guestbook or other type of registration form to be filled out on your web site. However, you must provide people with an incentive to leave their e-mail address with you. Anglers & Hunters Travel (see Figure 8.9) provides their subscribers with information on fishing and hunting opportunities.

Place a form with a "subscribe here" button on your site where visitors can sign up for the mailing list. Terminology such as "sign up now to receive our free newsletter" or " click here to receive our news every month" might be useful in convincing people to subscribe. Having people register for your mailing list by offering an informative newsletter is a great way to stay in touch with your target market. If you have valuable information that your customers and potential customers want, they will gladly give you their e-mail address to ob-

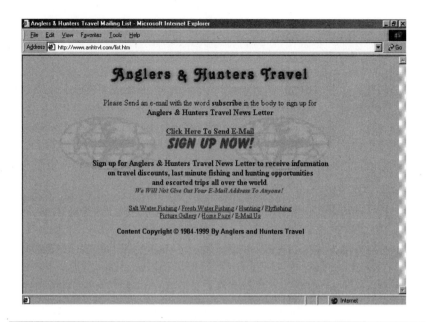

Figure 8.9. Anglers & Hunters Travel provides information on fishing and hunting opportunities.

tain your newsletter. Haynie Travel's mailing list (see Figure 8.10) offers travel information tailored to your interests.

A prime example would be @UK, the UK Travel and Tourist Guide's mailing list (see Figure 8.11), labeled ATUK-L. Their mailing list is intended for individuals involved in the UK's tourism industry and for those people interesting in a holiday or vacation in the UK. @UK also has another mail list named ATUK-COMPETITIONS (see Figure 8.12). All 600+ members gladly divulge their e-mail address to keep up to date on all @UK competitions. You can accomplish similar feats if you decide to administer your own newsletter.

Other newsletters provide freebie incentives such as T-shirts, software, or games. If you sign up for the newsletter at Lobster Direct *(www.lobsterdirect.com),* your name will be put in the monthly drawing for a lobster dinner for four, shipped live the next day via Fedex anywhere in North America.

Encourage customers and potential customers to subscribe to your electronic newsletter through traditional marketing techniques includ-

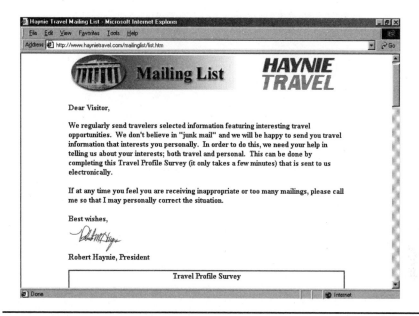

Figure 8.10. Haynie Travel's mailing list offers travel information tailored to your interests.

Figure 8.11. @UK's discussion list is a great resource for anyone planning a trip to the UK.

Figure 8.12. @UK's other mailing list keeps subscribers updated on competitions, prizes, and winners.

ing press releases, offline newsletters, advertising, letters, and so on. TheTravelzine.com (see Figure 8.13) has its own free travel discussion group that interested travelers can join.

If you use hardcopy direct mail, you can design a response system that requests the e-mail addresses through a fax-back, business reply card, or 1-800 number, or by asking respondents to go to your web site or e-mail you directly.

You can also ask people to sign up for your mailing list through newsgroup and mailing list postings, signature files, and other advertising. Just ensure that you make it easy for people to sign up for your mailing list. Have your mailing list signup form located in an easy-to-access place on your web site. (See Figure 8.14) A link should be provided from your home page to your newsletter signup form.

Furthermore, you can boost your response rate by guaranteeing that responders' e-mail addresses will be kept confidential and not sold to anyone else. People are concerned about the privacy of the

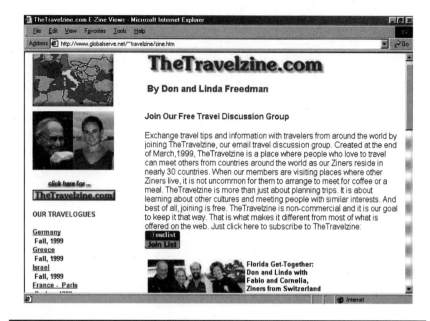

Figure 8.13. TheTravelzine.com has its own free travel discussion group.

information they provide you with. If you cannot assure them that your operation will use their e-mail address solely for your correspondence with them, they will not feel comfortable giving their e-mail address to you. Provide people with your private policy statement. Make them feel comfortable about divulging their e-mail address to your business.

Don't ever add someone's name to your mailing list without his or her permission. People really resent receiving unsolicited mail even if you give them the option to unsubscribe. However, one method of obtaining more e-mail addresses is to suggest to your subscribers that they recommend your mailing list to a friend (or a few friends). Let your subscribers spread the word about your mailing list. If your list provides useful information, your subscribers will recommend the list to their friends. Some of these people will then subscribe and tell their friends about your mailing list, and so forth. Word of mouth is a powerful force on the Internet.

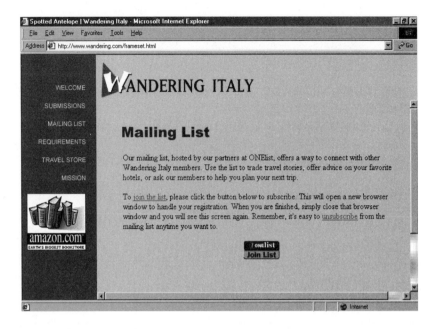

Figure 8.14. You can use Wandering Italy's mailing list to discuss planning your next trip.

Launching Your Own Publicly Available Mailing List

You can start your own publicly accessible mailing list. To create your Internet mailing list, you might want to do the following:

- First, give your list a name that reflects the discussion that will take place and is enticing for your target market.

- Draft a FAQ or charter containing information on what the list is all about.

- Develop guidelines for participation.

You will need to find a place to host your mail list. There are many ISPs that host mail lists or you can use one of the many online mailing list hosting services. (See Figure 8.15) For lists and links of

Figure 8.15.   Setting up your own mailing list on Topica is easy.

hosting service providers check out Vivian Neou's site at *http:// www.catalog.com/vivian/mailing-list-providers.html*

You should create a web page for your list to provide information about the list as well as its charter and guidelines. You should provide an opportunity to subscribe from the web site as well. This will add credibility to your mailing list. Once the list is up and running you will have to advertise it so that people will actually subscribe. You can promote your list by participating in newsgroups that relate to your mail list topic. Remember not to post blatant ads where advertising is not allowed. Contribute to the newsgroup with your postings and use a tag line in your signature file to promote your mail list. You can also trade e-mail sponsorships with other mailing lists for promotion purposes.

There are a number of places to appropriately announce your list. One recommendation is the Internet Scout's New List, which you can find at *http://scout.cs.wisc.edu/scout/new-list/index.html*

Net Happenings is another announcement resource for new Internet resources. Gleason Sackson, the moderator of this list, has a huge following. To subscribe to Net Happenings, send an e-mail to majordomo@is.internic.net with "subscribe net-happenings" in the message area.

Get your mail list linked from the many lists of lists on the Internet. We have provided some of these in the Internet Resources at the end of this chapter. And make your list worth reading by ensuring that you and others have valuable information on the topic to share.

Escape the Unsolicited Bulk E-mail Trend

Bulk e-mail is any message sent to a large number of e-mail addresses at one time. In some cases bulk e-mail lists have been developed from opt-in lists and the names are continually filtered through all of the universal remove lists. These lists are often categorized by subject and provide an acceptable marketing vehicle. If you are using opt-in e-mail lists and removing unsubscribe requests from your database, this is considered a legitimate e-mail marketing campaign.

However, there are many bulk e-mail lists that have been developed by unscrupulous means, and the people on the lists have no interest or desire to receive unsolicited e-mail. Unsolicited bulk e-mail is the single largest form of e-mail abuse we have seen to date.

Over the last couple of years, more and more businesses on the Internet focus on services and software products catering to the bulk e-mail market. Software products have been developed that collect e-mail addresses from Usenet newsgroups, online service members' directories and forums, bots that look for "mailto:" codes in HTML documents online, publicly available mailing list subscribers, or even your site's visitors. Service companies that collect e-mail addresses and perform bulk mailings abound today on the Internet. Be very careful when considering bulk e-mail for online marketing purposes.

Internet Resources for Chapter 8

Lists of Mail Lists

Search the List of Lists—Mailing Lists
http://www.catalog.com/vivian/interest-group-search.html

Search one of the largest directories of special interest group e-mail lists (also known as *listservs*) available on the Internet.

Liszt, the Mailing List Directory
http://www.liszt.com
A very big directory of mailing lists–over 90,000 to date. The Liszt has organized its lists into subject categories. The Liszt provides details on how to subscribe to each of the mail lists in its database and provides information on content as well.

List of Publicly Available Mailing Lists
http://www.neosoft.com/internet/paml
The List of Publicly Accessible Mailing Lists is posted on this site and once each month to the Usenet newsgroups news.lists.misc and news.answers. The Usenet version is the definitive copy—this web version is generated from the database and uploaded several days after the Usenet version is posted. They continually post to Usenet so that the PAML will be archived at rtfm.mit.edu.

Reference.com
http://www.reference.com/
Reference.com makes it easy to find, browse, search, and participate in more than 150,000 newsgroups, mailing lists, and web forums. Reference.com does not break their listings down by subject categories, but you can do a keyword search. Information is provided on content as well as on subscribe commands. Reference.com allows list owners to archive their content for free. A clipping service is also available from this site where you enter search criteria and Reference.com forwards incoming mailing list messages that match.

The List Exchange
http://www.listex.com/imark.html
The Internet's one-stop mailing list resource. It links to a number of list sites and sites with information on building your lists.

L-Soft's CataList
http://www.lsoft.com/lists/listref.html
CataList, the catalog of listserv lists! From this page, you can browse any of the 19,516 public listserv lists on the Internet, search for mailing lists of interest, and get information about listserv host sites. This

information is generated automatically from Listserv's Lists database and is always up to date.

The Internet Mailing List Network
http://www.listsnet.com/
ListsNet comprises a directory of publicly available mailing lists with browse and search capabilities. The mailing lists are categorized by subject and sub-topics.

Internet Marketing Mailing List
http://www.o-a.com
The Online Advertising Discussion List focuses on professional discussion of online advertising strategies, results, studies, tools, and media coverage. The list also welcomes discussion on the related topics of online promotion and public relations. The list encourages sharing of practical expertise and experiences between those who buy, sell, research, and develop tools for online advertising, as well as those providing online public relations and publicity services. The list also serves as a resource to members of the press who are writing about the subject of online advertising and promotion.

Usenet Newsgroup
news.lists
Gives you the list of new Usenet Newsgroups up and coming as well as the most popular ones.

AOL, Prodigy, and CompuServe
All have their own areas where you can search for mailing lists.

HTMARCOM
A mailing list that discusses high-tech marketing. To subscribe send the message "subscribe htmarcom your name" to the e-mail address *listserv@usa.net*.

I-Sales Digest
http://www.mmgco.com/isales
Formed in November, 1995, the goal of the Internet Sales Moderated Discussion List is to provide a forum for meaningful and helpful dis-

cussion of online sales issues by those engaged in the online sale of products and services. The list is moderated by John Audette, president of Multimedia Marketing Group, Inc.

E-mail List Builder Programs

The Direct E-mail List Source
http://www.copywriter.com/lists/index.htm
Thousands of e-mail lists where you can advertise without spamming.

Elmed Targeted Email Software
http://www.yug.com/tools/itools.htm
Information and links to e-mail marketing tools and software programs.

Campaign email marketing software
http://www.arialsoftware.com
This is e-mail marketing software used to conduct legitimate e-mail marketing campaigns. Campaign can import your contact database information and send personalized e-mail messages to all of your contacts.

MailKing
http://www.mailking.com
MailKing is similar to Campaign in that it can import your contact database information and send personalized e-mail messages to all of your contacts.

Web Crumbs
http://www.thinweb.com
Web Crumbs gathers the e-mail addresses of visitors to your web site. This intelligent program can also manipulate what the visitor sees based on rules. Downloadable demo available from this site.

LISTBOT
http://www.listbot.com/
ListBot makes starting your own free e-mail list quick and easy. Use a ListBot e-mail list to stay in touch with friends and family, notify customers of new products and specials, find out who is visiting your web site and send updates, let your clubs, teams, classes, etc., talk by

e-mail, create a forum for discussing favorite topic, publish an electronic newsletter, or connect any group of people by e-mail.

ONElist
http://www.onelist.com/
ONElist is a free email community service. The ONElist service empowers you to explore and create email communities where you can share views, ideas, and common interests with others. Create your own mail list today.

9

Grand Opening Tips for Your Web Site Virtual Launch

Just as you would have a grand opening for a new bed and breakfast establishment or a new golf course, you can have a web site launch. In preparation for the web site launch you must develop an appropriate launch strategy. In this chapter we cover:

- Development of your web site launch strategy

- Web site announcement mailing lists

- Direct e-mail postcards to your customers or prospective clients

Launching and Announcing Your Web Site

A new web site or your new location in **cyberspace** can be launched utilizing many of the same techniques you would use to promote a grand opening of your "real-world" tourism operation. This may involve both online and offline activities.

Cyber-space
A virtual location where web sites live.

Your Web Site Virtual Launch

Let's take a look at a traditional tourism operation grand opening. For the grand opening, which usually lasts for an evening or a day, there will be invitations to the media, press releases distributed, special invited guests, opening ceremonies, advertising, and possibly gift giveaways.

A web site virtual location launch occurs in cyberspace, and the "grand opening" can last for a day, a week, or a month. Many of the activities you include in your traditional grand opening can also be included in your Internet grand opening. The effectiveness of your launch can be increased with the following tips.

- Media attention can be generated through the distribution of press releases online and offline. (See Chapter 18 for press release distribution information.) Make your press releases interactive with hypertext links to your web site.

- Guests can be invited to your online opening through postings in newsgroups, newsletters, What's New sites, banner advertising, direct e-mail, and signature files, as well as offline direct mail and advertising.

- Opening ceremonies can be just as exciting online as offline. They can last for a month rather than a day. They must be designed to be of interest to the target market.

- You can feature special guests in chat areas for your grand opening or several special guests over the duration. Again, relate your guests and the topic to be discussed to the needs/wants of your target market. If you have a golf course, you could have the course designer, the golf pro, or a golf celebrity as your special guest.

- You can have contests or require visitors to visit various parts of your site to compete for prizes. Perhaps they have to complete a multiple-choice quiz the answers to which are found throughout your site. This way you encourage your guests to visit all those pages you want them to. Prizes could include a weekend stay at your inn or a set of golf clubs from your pro shop. You can also ask if they would like to be notified via e-mail of the winner. This gives you an opportunity to send them e-mail with their permission.

- Cross-promote your new web site with other partner web sites. Perhaps your partner or partners can contribute items to give away as prizes. Cross-promotion generates more exposure for your site because your partners will link to your site from theirs. Your online partners will benefit by receiving traffic from your site, so the benefits of cross-promotion are mutually shared. For example, if you operate a deep sea fishing charter, you could cross-promote it with tourism accommodation facilities in your area.

- You can have audio and video greetings from your site.

- There are many other innovative "grand opening" attention grabbers that can be brainstormed with appropriate marketing and public relations individuals.

- Special free gifts can be provided to the first 20 or 50 visitors to your site. You can also provide prizes to the first 100 to link to your site. Make the gifts and prizes things that will get them through your doors. Some good examples would be "two for the price of one" coupons for your restaurant, white water rafting trip, deep sea fishing expedition, ski lift tickets, and so forth, depending on your type of operation.

- Do some offline advertising for your new URL (see Chapter 21 for innovative offline opportunities) or take advantage of online advertising via Announcement Sites.

Whatever you decide to do, make it memorable, make it appropriate for your target market, and provide reasons for them to return.

Internet Resources

Netscape What's New

http:// netscape.com/home/whats-new.html
This site selectively publishes information on new sites. To warrant a mention your site must somehow be unique—perhaps using the latest Netscape technologies.

Best-Web-Sites Announcement List
You can join this mailing list by sending the message *sub BESTWEB your name* to *listserv@vm3090.ege.edu.tr.*

Site Launch
http://www.sitelaunch.net
Site Launch offers guides, tools, and information for webmasters. It takes you through everything you need to get more visitors.

Nerd World What's New
http://www.nerdworld.com/whatsnew.html
The newest links added to Nerd World and a place to show off your site. Not just for nerds.

LaunchBot
http://www.launchbot.com
A listing of what's new on the home page front. Instructions here on how to get your site listed with them.

10

Develop a Dynamite Links Strategy

The more appropriate links you have to your tourism Web site, the better! Expand your horizon by orchestrating links from different tourism-related Web pages to increase your traffic. In this chapter we cover:

- Developing a link strategy

- How to arrange links

- Getting noticed by providing an icon, tag line and hypertext for links to your site

- Link positioning

- Tools to check your competitors' links

- Using links to enhance your image

- Web rings and meta-indexes

- Getting links to your site

- Reciprocal link pages

- Associate programs

- How links can enhance your search engine placements

Links Have Staying Power

Developing your link strategy is one of the most crucial elements involved in Internet marketing. It is a very time-consuming task. However, it is time very well spent. Links are important for two reasons:

1. Appropriately placed, they can be a real traffic builder.

2. A number of the most frequently used search engines use link popularity as one of their ranking criteria. The more links to your site the more popular it is, so the number of links you have to your site can significantly impact your placement with the search engines.

Everything Links to You

When you post a message to a newsgroup where you promote your tourism web site through your brilliant contribution and your signature file, you will receive increased traffic while the message is current and being read by participants in the newsgroup. As time passes, your message appears further and further down the list until it disappears and then your traffic level returns to normal. This phenomenon also applies for a promotional effort in a mailing list. You can expect increased traffic for a short period of time after your mailing list posting, but as soon as everyone has read your posting and visited your site, traffic levels return to normal.

This is not the same for links. Traffic from links does not go away as easily as other forms of Internet marketing. Links generally stay active for a long period of time. When you have a link to your site placed on another web site, people will see it and will be enticed to click through to visit your site. As long as the site that hosts your link has new traffic, you will continue to receive traffic through it. The beauty of links is that in three months that link will still be there and people will still be clicking through.

Links are very important because if you have links placed appropriately on a high-traffic tourism-related web site, they can turn into traffic builders for your web site. They are also important because they can have a major impact on your search engine ranking in some of the major search engines, because some search engines use link popularity in their ranking criteria. These search engines include:

- AltaVista   *www.altavista.com*

- Excite   *www.excite.com*

- Google   *www.google.com*

- Go/Infoseek   *www.infoseek.com*

- Direct Hit   *www.directhit.com*

Once your link strategy is implemented and you begin to see an increase in the number of sites linking to your web site, you will see your ranking in the previous mentioned search engines improve. For more information on search engines and their ranking criteria see Chapter 4.

The more **links** you have to your site, the better chance you have that someone will be enticed to visit. However, a quid quo pro usually applies, and this means providing reciprocal links, giving people the opportunity to leave your site with the click of a button. To minimize this "flight effect," make sure you place outbound links two or three layers down in your site. Never place outbound links on your home page. You want your visitors to come into your site, see everything you want them to see, and do everything you want them to do before they have the opportunity to go elsewhere.

Regularly test all of the links from your site to ensure they are "live" and going to the appropriate locations. Dead links reflect poorly on your site and your tourism operation. There are tools avail-

Links
Selectable connections from one word, picture, or information object to another.

able online that can help you determine whether or not you have dead links. These tools, which include Net Mechanic *(www.netmechanic.com)* and SiteOwner.com *(www.siteowner.com)*, analyze your page, detecting any dead links that may be on your site. Each of these tools will be discussed in more depth in the Resources section at the end of this chapter.

Strategies for Finding Appropriate Link Sites

Ideally you should be linked from every high-traffic tourism-related site on the Internet because these sites would be of interest to your target market. However, you have to develop a strategy to find all of these sites and arrange links.

The first place to start is with the popular search engines. Most people use search engines and directories to find subjects of interest on the Internet. Most of the people searching never go beyond the first 20 to 30 results the search engine returns. Thus, these top 20 to 30 sites returned by the search engines must get a lot of traffic. Make sure you search relevant keywords in all the popular search engines and directories, and investigate these top sites for appropriate link sites. Some of these sites will be competitors and may not want to reciprocate links. The best opportunity for links is with noncompeting sites that have the same target market. I suggest you take your most important keywords, do a keyword search in the most popular 20 search engines and directories, and review the top 30 sites in each for potential link sites.

Another strategy to find appropriate link sites is to see from where the leaders in the tourism industry and your competitors are linked. I use the term "competitors" very loosely. Competitors include your direct competitors, your industry leaders, companies selling noncompeting products to your target market, companies selling similar types of products or services to your target market, and companies that compete with you for search engine ranking. See what your competition is doing. Determine where they are linked from, and decide whether these are sites that you should also be linked from. Learn what they are doing well, and also learn from their mistakes. You should be linked everywhere your competition is appropriately linked and then some.

Explore These URLs

There are many tools on the Internet to help you identify a web site's links. This is a great way to research where your site could be linked from but isn't—yet!

When determining which sites you should be linked from, you first have to develop a lengthy list of competitors. A competitor can be any business or site that offers the same products or services as you do, or anyone targeting the same demographic as you. Since the Internet creates a level playing field for all businesses, you are also competing against people in other countries. If people are using a search engine to find information on your tourism operation, they may see results from companies from all across the world in the top ten results.

Once you have developed your extensive list of competitors and have gathered their URLs, you must then find out what sites they are linked from. Tools have been developed to assist you in finding who is linking to your site. In most cases, you enter your URL and then these tools provide you with the list of sites linking to your URL. However, these tools can be used just as easily to determine which sites are linking to your competition and industry leaders by entering their URL instead of your own.

The more organized you are for this exercise the better. I suggest that you:

1. Gather an extensive list of competitors and their URLs.

2. Choose the tool or tools from the next section that you are going to use for this exercise.

3. Enter the first competitor URL to find the sites linking to it.

4. Copy and Paste the results into a Word, Notepad or other file that you can access later.

5. Enter the next competitor URL to find the sites linking to it.

6. Copy and Paste the results into the same Word, Notepad or other file adding to your list of potential link sites.

7. Repeat steps 5 and 6 until you have found all the sites linking to your competition. Now you have your potential link sites list.

8. Now develop a link request (see the next section for details) and keep it open on your desktop so that you can Copy and Paste it into an e-mail when you find a site you'd like to have a link from.

9. Next, visit each and every one of the potential link sites to determine whether the site is one that is appropriate for you to be linked from. If the site is appropriate, then send your link request. If the site is not appropriate for whatever reason, delete it from your list. This way when you get to the bottom of the list it now represents a list of the sites you have sent a link request to.

10. Follow through and follow up. Follow through and provide an appropriate link to those who have agreed to a reciprocal link. Follow up to make sure that they have provided the link as promised to your site, that the link works, and that it is pointing to the correct page on your site.

Tools To Identify Your Competitors' Links

The following tools can be used to obtain a list of locations on the Internet that are linked to your competitors' web sites:

SiteOwner
http://www.siteowner.com
SiteOwner.com (see Figure 10.1) will tell you who is linking to your site. It is a free service.

AltaVista
http://www.altavista.com
To find out where your competitors are linked using AltaVista, simply enter the competitor's URL in the search area like this:

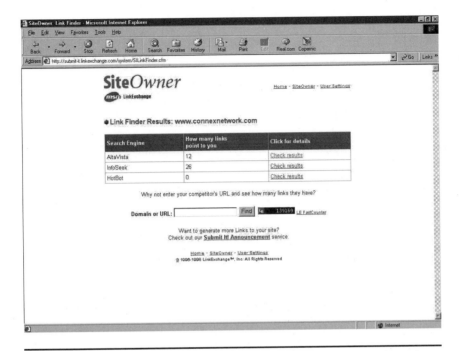

Figure 10.1. SiteOwner provides many valuable tools. Their Link Finder can be used to find who has linked to you from around the Internet. It can also provide valuable information on where your competitors are linked.

link:yourcompetitorsdomain.com. This will return all pages in AltaVista with a link to your competitor's web site.

HotBot
http://www.hotbot.com
Enter your competitor's URL in the search box and change the default from "all the words" to "links to this URL." When you type in the URL, remember to include *http://*. The results will contain all web sites linking to your competitor's web site.

WebCrawler
http://www.webcrawler.com/WebCrawler/Links.html
Enter your competitor's URL into the search query box to find out

how many links are provided to that page. WebCrawler provides the names of all the referring sites.

Infoseek
http://www.infoseek.com

Go to the Infoseek home page, and click on the Advanced Search link (see Figure 10.2). Select "WEB Advanced Search." Under "search the web for pages in which the:" choose "hyperlink" in the first drop-down menu. Select "must" in the second-drop down menu and "phrase" in the third drop-down menu. Then key in the URL you want to find in the space provided. Click on "Search," and the results will show listings, with descriptions, of the sites that provide a link to your selected URL.

Excite and other search engines: Just enter your competitors' URLs and see what comes up. Be sure to include the *http://*. If anything, the search query will include all web sites that are indexed that contain the URL searched.

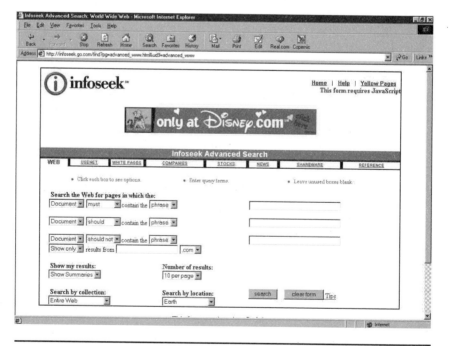

Figures 10.2. Infoseek and many other search engines offer advanced search capabilities to help you identify links to your site and links to your competitors' sites.

Other Potential Link Strategies

Another strategy for finding your competitors within the tourism industry is to visit the many different search engines and do a search on the keywords that you feel people would search on if they were looking for your site. For example, if you were a hotel operator, you might look up the keyword "hotel accommodations." The top results can also be considered your competition. You should add them to your list and repeat the procedures to find out where they are linked from and to see if they are appropriate links for your site.

Now you have a starting list of sites you want to link from. Your next activity is to request the link. Remember that although this is a time-consuming exercise, it is also an important activity. Developing a strong link strategy is critical if you want a large volume of traffic to your web site and if you want high placement in those search engines that give heavy weighting to link popularity.

Winning Approval for Potential Links

Now that you have a list of web sites sharing the same target audience that you would like to be linked from, the next step is to identify the appropriate company contact from whom to request the link. Usually this can be found on the site. Titles such as Webmaster@ or any variation on the theme are usually a pretty safe bet. If the site does not have an appropriate contact, then try feedback@. You can either send the request there or ask for the e-mail address of the appropriate person.

If you cannot find an e-mail address and you feel that you will benefit a great deal from being linked on their web site, you can visit Network Solutions *(www.networksolutions.com)* to find out contact information for that domain name. Click on the WHOIS Lookup link and submit the URL in the WHOIS Search field to do a search on the domain in question. The results will include the contacts, both technical and administrative, for that web site. The technical contact would most likely be the person you are looking for because that person is the one that most likely looks over the web site. The administrative contact is usually responsible for the renewal of the domain name, and the billing contact is usually the bill payer for the domain name.

Generally, a short note with the appropriate information in the subject line is most suitable. Your note should be courteous, briefly describe your site's content, and provide the rationale for why you think reciprocating links would result in a win-win situation. It doesn't hurt to compliment some aspect of the site that you think is particularly engaging.

It is a good idea to develop a generic "link request" letter that you can have on hand when you are surfing. You should always keep this letter open on your desktop when surfing the Internet so that you can quickly and easily Copy and Paste the letter into an e-mail. If you don't have a link request ready and you find a site that you are interested in requesting a link on, jot the site down as a reminder to return to request a link. However, if you have the request open on your desktop, when you find a site that is appealing from a linking perspective, you can simply Copy and Paste the link request into an e-mail, do a little editing or customizing, and hit the Send button. Here is an example of a link request e-mail:

Dear Web Site Owner,

I have just finished viewing your site and found it quite enjoyable. I found the content to be very valuable, particularly (customize here). My site visitors would appreciate your content as I think we appeal to the same demographic. My site, http://www.mysitename.com, focuses on (my site content) and would likely be of value to your visitors. If you have no objection, I would like to suggest we trade links.

Sincerely,

Andrew

HTML
Hypertext markup language; The coding language that tells a web browser how to display a web page's words and images.

When you get a response, it will usually say that they would appreciate a link to their site and will offer to provide a reciprocal link. To facilitate this, you should either have the **HTML** for the link ready to send, have it available on your site, or both.

Make sure to follow through and follow up. If you said you would provide a reciprocal link, follow through and do so within 24 hours. Follow up to make sure that your site has been linked from theirs.

Ensure that the link works properly and is linked to the appropriate page on your site.

Then remember to send a thank-you. Since they are doing you a favor by adding your site to their web page, you should strive to develop a good relationship with them. This way they may be more generous with the link that they give you. They may place it higher on the page, or even offer you the opportunity of having a small graphic link on their page, which would be dynamite for increasing traffic to your tourism operation's site. These graphic links will be explained in more detail later in the chapter.

Another way to get links is to ask for them on your site. In a prominent location on your site, place a link that says something like, "Would you like to provide a link to this site? Click here." Link this message to a separate page that holds several options for links. You can provide viewers with several different sizes of banner ads that they can place on their web site. You can also provide them with a thumbnail icon, the HTML, and your tag line, which they can simply Copy and Paste into the HTML code on their web site (see Figure 10.3). Quite often if you offer a viewer these opportunities for links, you will have a better chance of receiving these enhanced link features. If you make it easier for them to add the link, they will be more willing to provide the link, for they can do it at their convenience. By adding a small graphic to your link (see Figure 10.4), you can definitely make your link stand out from the others.

You might want to consider offering an incentive to people who will provide you with a link. It could be something that can be downloaded or a free sample of your product in exchange for a link. This also provides you with another opportunity to market your site, since you are giving something away for free. Thus you can be listed on the many Internet sites that identify sites with freebies. Another tactic that you can use is that if viewers provide a link to your site, they will be included in a draw for a prize. One prize could be related to your tourism operation—a weekend stay at your hotel, a round of golf, a whale watching expedition, ski lift tickets, and so on.

Meta-indexes and web rings are other sources for links. For a complete discussion of web rings and meta-indexes, see Chapters 12 and 20 respectively.

(a)

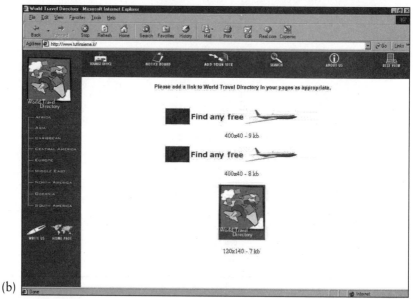

(b)

Figures 10.3. (a & b) By providing the HTML text and icons on your site, you can make it very easy for viewers to add your link to their site. It is best to supply them with the option of placing a text link, a small button, a large button, or a banner advertisement on their Web site.

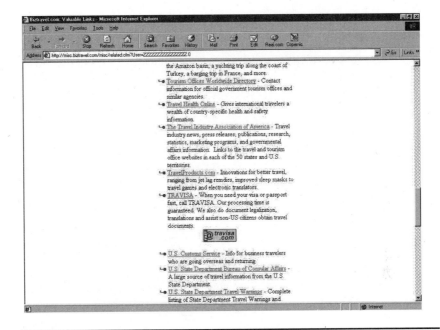

Figure 10.4. By adding a small graphic to your link, you can definitely make your link stand out from the others.

You may need to prompt sites to provide promised links. If you have made an arrangement for a link and, on following up, find that the link is not there, it is appropriate to send an e-mail reminder. When sending the follow-up e-mail, include your icon, HTML, URL, and any other information that may be helpful.

Making Your Link the Place to "Click"

You should take a proactive approach with linking arrangements. Explore every opportunity to have your link placed prominently and, if possible, to have it differentiated from the other links on the page for you want to differentiate yourself from your competition.

Icon
An image that represents an application, a capability, or some other concept.

Once you have an agreement with a site willing to provide a link, you should ask if you could send them an **icon** and the HTML for the link. The icon (GIF or JPG format) should be visually pleasing and representative of your company. Within the HTML, include a tag line that entices people to click on the link. With the icon or logo, the tag line, and your company's name, your link will stand out from the rest. Since another web site is going to be generous in providing a link to your site, your image should only be a thumbnail, because you don't want to take up too much space on their web site. This image could be your corporate logo or a graphic currently being use to promote for your tourism operation. By having this image and tag line strategically placed on a web site, the chances that a viewer will click through to visit your web site are dramatically increased.

This is an example of what it should look like:

<IMG SRC="your gif/tif/bmp name">
<A HREF="http://www.yourdomainname.com">Catchy tag line here</A>

To Add or Not To Add Your Site to Free For All Links

There are thousands of free for all links on the Net. Some of them are designed specifically for the tourism industry. These sites allow you to add your URL to a long list of links. These sites provide little in the way of traffic unless you can have your link stand out from the rest. One advantage you can get from being linked from these sites is in search engine ranking. As mentioned previously, some search engines use the number of links to your site in their ranking criterion.

Get Linked from Geographic Sites

People seeking information on places to stay and things to do within a particular city or region might visit the municipality's web site. You might be wise to try to obtain a link from any regional sites in your area that promote tourism to that region. Thus, by finding the Illinois Tourism site, a visitor might also find your Illinois bed and breakfast inn—if there is a link from the Illinois Tourism site to yours. By trading links with sites that are geographically affiliated with yours, you improve your chances of being discovered by prospective customers.

Add Value with Affiliate or Associate Programs

Another way of benefiting from links to your tourism operation's web site is by developing an associate program. Associate programs (also called reseller, partnership, or affiliate programs) are revenue sharing arrangements set up by companies selling products and services. When another site agrees to participate in your associate program, it is rewarded for sending customers to your tourism business. These customers are sent to your site through links on your associates' or affiliates' web site. By developing and offering this type of program, you generate increased revenue and increased links to your site. Associate programs will be explained in more depth during Chapter 14.

Maintaining a Marketing Log

Record all new links to your site in your Internet marketing log. It is important to maintain this log and review it on a regular basis. You must periodically check to make certain that links to your site are operational and going to the appropriate location. Along with the URL where your site is linked from, you should also keep track of all contact information you may have gathered when communicating with the webmaster.

A Word of Caution with Link Trading

You must be aware when trading links that all links are not created equal.

- If you provide a prominent link to another tourism-related site, make sure you receive a link of equal or greater prominence.

- Be aware: When trading your links with sites that receive substantially less traffic than you do, you will probably have more people "link out" than "link in" from this trade. Consider trading a banner ad and a link from their site for a link from your site, thus making it more of an equal trade. If their site has more traffic than yours, don't mention it unless they do.

- Don't ever put your outbound links directly on your home page. Have your outbound links located several levels down so that visitors to your site will likely have visited all the pages you want them to visit before they link out from your site.

- Sometimes when people update their site, they change the Internet address or delete a page altogether. If you have placed a link on your page to that page, and one of your viewers tries to link out to that page, and receives an HTTP 404 error, this reflects badly on your site. You should always check your Web site for dead links.

Internet Resources

Tourism Portals

Expedia.com
http://www.expedia.com/
This is Microsoft's foray into the world of travel. Book flights, reserve hotel rooms, and plan vacations.

Travelocity
http://www.travelocity.com/
Travelocity is one of the biggest players in the travel game, and one of the top e-commerce sites.

Trip.com
http://www.trip.com/

Once again, Trip.com is another huge travel portal site. You can book flights, reserve rooms, and plan vacations as you can with the other portal sites.

Yahoo! Travel
http://travel.yahoo.com/
This is Yahoo's travel portal site.

Vacation.com
http://www.vacation.com/
One of America's top vacation network sites.

Preview Travel
http://www.previewtravel.com/
Preview Travel is a provider of online travel services for leisure and small business travelers (book flights, vacations, etc.).

Hotel Online
http://www.hotel-online.com/
This is the hospitality industry's online meeting place, providing the latest and most relevant news, trends, discussion forums, employment opportunities, classified advertising, and product pricing available anywhere.

Places To Stay
http://www.placestostay.com/
Places To Stay works closely with over 10,000 bed and breakfasts, ski resorts, inns, and hotels worldwide.

Cruise.com
http://www.cruise.com/
Planning a cruise? Come here first.

Tools That Check For Dead Links

Web Site Garage
http://www.websitegarage.com.
This site has a dead link check in its Web site diagnosis. It has a link

popularity tool as well, which tells you how many links a particular site has pointing to it and also from where a URL is linked.

Net Mechanic
http://www.netmechanic.com
To find out if you have any dead links with Net Mechanic simply enter your URL into the query box and view the results. The site will generate a detailed report that will outline whether or not you have any dead links, and if so where.

SiteOwner
http://www.siteowner.com
When using SiteOwner, you can check your site for various web site criteria. To check for dead links, you must enter your URL into the query box, then select "Dead Link." The results will outline any dead links that are on your site.

Reciprocal Link Information

Virtual Promote
http://www.virtualpromote.com/guest6.html
This tutorial covers how to promote traffic to your web site with reciprocal links. This is a free service for all web site developers who want to learn more about announcing their web site and promoting more traffic to the Internet.

Free For All Link Sites

Mega Linkage List
http://www.netmegs.com/linkage/
An exhaustive listing of over 1500 directories, classified ad sites, little-known search engines, FFA pages, and more - all compiled for you alphabetically. Although there are some dead/broken links here, a large majority are active, and you will be hard-pressed to visit each one.

Entrepreneurial Trend
http://www.angelfire.com/ct/suremoney/page2.html

Links to hundreds of places to list your site! Free for all link pages and search engines. Free classifieds and message boards. Free newsletters and reciprocal links.

Auto Link/Master Link

http://www.career-pro.com/autolink/index.cgi?autolink

AutoLink allows you to type in your site's URL and with one click automatically list it on over 350 FFA pages, directories, and search engines. MasterLink is a brand new tool, and you must see it to truly appreciate this new concept in web site promotion. Highly recommended.

Link-O-Matic

http://www.linkomatic.com/index.cgi?10000

This site allows you to submit your URL to 450+ quality promotional sites with one click, driving traffic to your web site and saving you loads of time.

FFA Net

http://www.ffanet.com/links/list.pl

This page has a detailed listing of thousands of free for all link pages. It also offers you the opportunity to set up your own free for all link pages on the FFA network.

11

Winning Awards/
Cool Sites and More

There are literally hundreds of Cool Sites, Sites of the Day, Hot Sites, and Pick of the Week Sites. Some of these sites require you to submit; others are selected based on such things as:

- Awesome graphics

- Dynamite content that is useful and interesting

- Uniqueness

- Fun features

If you are selected for one of these sites, it can mean a huge increase in the number of hits to your tourism site. You must be prepared for the increased traffic flow as well as the increased demand for online offerings. In this chapter we cover:

- Where to submit your tourism site for award consideration

- How to win Site of the Day—tips, tools, and techniques

- Getting listed in What's New

- Posting your awards on your site

- Hosting your own Site of the Day

It's an Honor Just To Be Nominated

There are sites that find and evaluate other sites on the Internet and recognize those that are outstanding by giving them an award. The award sites are generally very discriminating in terms of which sites are selected to be the recipients of their award. They have established criteria defining what is considered "hot" or "cool" and base their award selection on those criteria. There are all kinds of popular award sites on the Web (see Figure 11.1).

What's New web sites are designed to inform Internet users of new sites and updates to existing sites, and are often selective about

Figure 11.1.   Here is a collage of several of the more popular award sites.

which new sites they will promote. The owner of each site also selectively chooses awards for Site of the Day, Week, Month, and Year.

As discussed earlier, some of these sites require you to submit an announcement or site description, and the awards are granted based on criteria such as graphics, dynamic content, uniqueness, and the "fun" quality of your site. Other sites grant their awards based solely on the personal likes and dislikes of the owner of the site and do not adhere to any criteria at all.

Some awards are taken just as seriously as the Academy Awards. The Webby Awards have a very comprehensive nomination procedure. The following information regarding their process is available on their web site:

How to Win a Webby—Web Site Nomination Procedure

The International Academy of Digital Arts and Sciences (IADAS) is responsible for nominating and awarding each year's Webby Award and People's Voice Award winners. The 1999 awards were given out in 24 different content categories, including Arts, Commerce, Community, Education, Fashion, Film, Finance, Games, Health, Humor, Living, Music, News, Politics, Print and Zines, Radio, Science, Sports, Tech Achievement, Travel, TV, and Weird. The site plans to expand the number of categories for The 2000 Webby Awards; possible new categories include Kids, Services, and Webcast. Nominees are selected by the International Academy of Digital Arts and Sciences' nominating committee for each category. Composed of 240 journalists, experts, critics, scholars, or new-media professionals, the committee for each category collaborates to select five Webby Award nominees. The Academy now accepts web site nominations in exchange for a $50 fee. Figure 11.2 shows the 1999 award winner for Travel Sites.

When you win an award, you post the award on your site for all to see. The award icon is usually a link back to the site that bestowed the honor on you.

Figure 11.2. Biztravel.com (*http://www.biztravel.com*), winner of the 1999 Webby award for travel sites.

Choosing Your Awards and Submitting to Win

Some awards are easier to receive than others, such as those from commercial sites that give out awards in an attempt to increase the traffic to their own site. Traffic increases because the award is a graphic link displayed on the winner's site that visitors can follow back to the award giver's site. Other webmasters give out awards to anybody and everybody who makes a submission. The award is granted with the sole purpose of building traffic.

There are a large number of award sites available; however, many will direct fairly generic traffic unless you select topic specific awards and award sites. As a tourism operator you should look for respectable award sites that pertain specifically to the tourism industry or that offer awards based on categories, including tourism—this will return the most accurate and targeted results. Some options available to you are listed below. For further details, please refer to the resource section at the end of this chapter.

- Webby Awards

- Epicurus Awards

- Golden Eagle Awards

- Travelseeker Web Awards

- Mountain Valley Properties' "Solid Site" Awards

Mountain Valley Properties *(http://mountainvalley.com/)* offers the Solid Site award (see Figure 11.3). To submit your site to the Solid Site award, your site must be travel related, offer either excep-

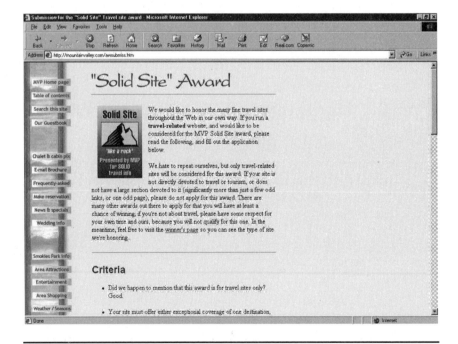

Figure 11.3. Qualifying travel sites are eligible for the Mountain Valley Properties' Solid Site award (*http://mountainvalley.com/awsubmiss.htm*).

tional coverage of one destination or a wide range of coverage of several destinations, and be creative, well organized, well written, and well maintained. Most awards for travel sites are based on similar criteria.

The bottom line is that awards such as the Solid Site award are valuable assets for tourism sites. The average web user cannot tell which awards are the prestigious ones and which are given to anyone that submits. So, submit for any awards that you choose to, as long as your site is ready. A sample award submission form is shown in Figure 11.4.

Where you place these awards is important. If you win a lot of awards, you will be expected to place a promotional graphic and a link on your home page for each award you win. Your home page can become quite cluttered and load more slowly as a result. If you have been fortunate enough to be in this situation, consider develop-

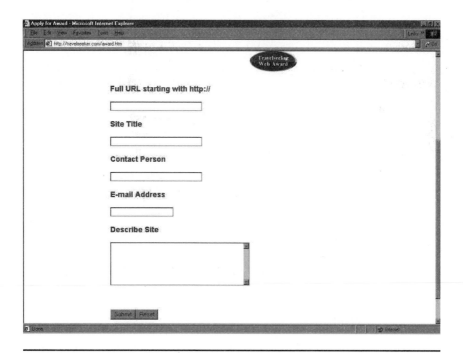

Figure 11.4. As with most travel site awards, you only need to submit some basic information about yourself and your site to become eligible for the award.

ing an awards page, with a link from your navigation bar, to house them.

Another item to determine before you submit for an award is whether the huge amount of new traffic will benefit your site. If you have a travel agency, then any traffic is good traffic, and awards will benefit your site. On the other hand, if you are a marine biologist specializing in red tides in the Arctic, then the traffic that Site of the Day would bring may be more of a hindrance than a help in marketing your services. Always determine if the marketing tools and techniques will increase hits from your target market before deciding whether to include them in your online marketing strategy.

Getting mentioned on one of the Cool Sites lists is one of the single biggest ways to draw traffic to your site. Cool Sites does not just list anybody, and the traffic they send to your site is like a flash flood—fast and furious. Be careful what you wish for—you might just get it!

The traffic will be swift and plentiful after you win one of these awards. Be prepared! Have a plan that you can implement on a moment's notice. If you offer something free from your site, ensure you can access a huge volume of whatever it is and ensure you have a plan to distribute quickly. If you offer a free download from your site, plan to have a number of alternate **FTP** sites available to your visitors. If you have a "call in" offer, ensure you have a telephone response system in place and staff to handle the huge volume of calls you may get. You will need a plan to handle the huge volume of e-mails you will get as well.

FTP
File
Transfer
Protocol.

What's New sites accept submissions for sites that they review. The best of the best are then placed prominently on their home page for all to see. It is considered to be quite an honor to develop or own a site that has been selected by some of the more discriminating What's New sites.

Once you have decided that the type of traffic that comes along with winning the award fits with your marketing strategy, you should make sure your site has the makings of a winner and then submit to as many award sites as you can.

- First, make a list of the URLs of these award sites.

- Understand the submission form and guidelines. Review a number of forms to determine the common information requested.

- Develop a document with the answers to the various questions from which you can Copy and Paste into the different submission forms (this will save you time).

- Submission forms will capture the following types of information:

  - URL

  - Title of your site

  - Contact person (name, e-mail, phone, address)

  - Owner of the site

- Submission guidelines will tell you what type of sites can be submitted (i.e., some awards do not accept personal pages; others do not include commercial sites). The submission guidelines will also tell you what meets their definition of "Cool" or "New" and what doesn't.

- Some award sites require that you display their award icon on your site. Posting an award on your site can provide a number of positive results—including enhanced credibility.

There are different levels of prestige associated with each of the different award sites. Some are an honor to receive, such as a Starting Point Hot Site *(http://www.stpt.com)* award. These awards are highly competitive because of the number of submissions they receive.

What's Hot and What's Not in the Name of Cool

Most of the award sites will provide you with their selection criteria. Some award sites look for and base their selection on valuable content; other award sites look for innovative and unique capabilities. Although sites differ on what they consider "Hot" or "Cool," they are fairly consistent on what doesn't make the grade, as summarized next.

What's Hot	What's Not
Awesome graphics	Single-page sites
Great, original content	Single-product promotion
Broad appeal	Offensive language or graphics
Fun feature	Lengthy download time

Displaying Awards on Your Site

If you have managed to collect a few awards for your web site, you will want to display them somehow. After all, any award is a good award, and the award site that granted you a particular award will expect you to display it in return for the recognition.

Posting the awards on your home page might not be the best idea, though. For one, the additional graphics that will have to be downloaded will slow the load time for your home page. Second, by posting the awards on your home page, you are placing links leading out of your site on the first page. Thus, you are giving people the opportunity to leave your site before they have even had a chance to explore it.

Where should you post your well deserved awards then? Simply create an Awards section on your web site. Here, you can list all of your awards without adversely affecting the load time of your home page or losing traffic.

Starting Your Own Award Program

You can also create your own award program in order to draw traffic to your site; however, this requires a huge amount of work to maintain. You will need to work at it on a daily or weekly basis, so you must be committed to it. Be sure there is a benefit from a marketing perspective before you design and develop your own award program. You must also be prepared to conduct your own searches at the outset to find sites to promote if the quality of sites being submitted to you is poor.

- You will first have to develop the criteria you will use in your site selection.

- You will have to develop several web pages related to the award (information on selection criteria, submission forms, today's or this week's award winner, past award recipients page, etc.) in order to promote the award. (Ensure that you stipulate that you are looking for submissions from commercial sites or personal pages and what criteria will be used in judging the submissions.)

- You will have to have your award icon developed. Have this icon link back to your site. The award distinguishes the winner, so the link will probably be displayed prominently on the their site. This is a great traffic builder.

- Finally, you have to announce the award and market, market, market.

Internet Resources

Awards

Webby Awards
http://www.webbyawards.com
The Webby Awards have been embraced by the online community as the leading creative honors for digital media. The awards recognize the most creative and innovative web sites of the year and the talented editorial, technical, and design teams behind them. The travel site award winner can be found at *http://www.webbyawards.com/nominees/winners/travel_w.html*.

The Epicurus Awards
http://www.epicurus.com/500best.htm
Grants awards for the best hospitality/tourism web sites in 14 different categories.

Golden Eagle Awards
http://www.photojournal.com/american/notesoftheday/blueaward.html
The best travel and home web sites are honored by the American Photojournal.

Mountain Valley Properties' Solid Site Award
http://mountainvalley.com/awsubmiss.htm
If you have a travel-related web site that offers either exceptional coverage of one destination or a wide range of coverage of several destinations, and is creative, well organized, well written, and well maintained, you are eligible for this award.

TravelPage.com
http://www.travelpage.com/
Suggest your tourism site to TravelPage.com, and you will be listed in their searchable directory and become eligible for their Select Site award.

Travelseeker Award
http://travelseeker.com/award.htm
This award is open to any travel-oriented web site.

Best of the Planet Awards
http://www.2ask.com
Called the people's choice award, where you can decide who's best.

Best of the Web Awards
http://botw.org/
This award aims to highlight those places that best show the quality, versatility, and power of the World Wide Web.

PC Magazine's Top 100 Web Sites
http://www.zdnet.com/pcmag/special/web100/index.html
A list of top sites listed in five categories, everything from amazing online stores to essential computing resources, with a couple of stops along the way for fun and entertainment.

High Five Award
http://www.highfive.com
Each week they review well-designed web sites and discuss how to make your site become a killer.

People Chase
http://www.rainfrog.com/pc/

Award-winning sites become part of the People Chase web ring. Web site design and content are judged to determine the winner.

Jayde.com
http://www.jayde.com/goldlnks.html
Awards the Gold Diamond Award to sites with great style, design and content. Jayde.com also has an award for commercial sites.

What's New

Yahoo!
http://www.yahoo.com/new
Yahoo's What's New on the web.

Netscape What's New
http://www.netscape.com/netcenter/new.html
Netscape features a few new web sites every day and gives them ratings. You can submit your site to Netscape for review.

What's New Too
http://newtoo.manifest.com
New announcements are posted to this site within 36 hours of submission, and the list, which is lengthy, is updated daily.

Whatsnew.com
http:www.whatsnew.com
This is a seven-days-a-week, continuously updated, fully searchable directory of new Internet web sites.

Hot Sites/Cool Sites

USA Today Hot Sites
http://www.usatoday.com/life/cyber/ch.htm
USA Today scours the web for sites that are hot, new, and notable. Visit their daily list to find some of the best sites the web has to offer. They look for sites that may stretch the design envelope and show

where the web is headed—sites that offer something unusual or unexpected, or something just plain useful.

Starting Point Hot Site
http://www.starting-point.com
Votes are taken from their What's New section for sites worthy of a Hot Site Award.

Lycos Top 5%
http://www.lycos.com/help/top5-help.html
Lycos Top 5% is the oldest and most prestigious web site directory. Each site in the Top 5% directory includes a detailed review describing its editorial and visual merits.

100 Hot Web sites
http://www.100hot.com/
Directory of web sites based on web traffic and organized by category.

The All Original Web Site Awards
http://www.oliveplace.com/originalwebs.html
Awards for Web sites that are completely original in their design, graphics and content. No clip art allowed!!!

A Comprehensive Guide to Receiving Web Site Awards for Free
http://www.fonesave.com/websave/freeawards.htm
Includes links to submission pages for award sites plus links to other free web resources

Cool Site of the Day
http://www.coolsiteoftheday.com
Cool Site of the Day is a wildly popular Internet award site that features interesting, provocative, and irreverent web sites from around the world.

Cool Central Site of the Hour
http://www.coolcentral.com
Delivers the best new web sites the moment they are discovered. Featuring Cool Central Site of the Moment or Hour, and Nick Click, Private Eye.

CoolStop
http://www.coolstop.com/
The Best of the Cool Award consistently recognizes truly outstanding sites in terms of design, originality, and content.

Netscape What's Cool
http://home.netscape.com/netcenter/cool.html
Netscape's picks of the coolest web sites.

Virtual Reference Meta-Index of Award Sites
http://www.refdesk.com//textcool.html
A listing of different sites that host site of the day, hot sites, and so on.

The Bottom 95%
http://www.dartmouth.edu/~jaundice/bottom95/
If your web site has never received a top 5% award, the bottom 95% could be for you.

Web Pages That Suck
http://www.webpagesthatsuck.com
Keep your site from being nominated to Web Pages That Suck, and you are probably doing well. However, you can learn a lot from Web Pages That Suck about how to properly design your site from a marketing perspective.

Tools

Free Links Award Sites
http://www.freelinks.com/awards.html
This is a free service to aid and simplify your web site promotion efforts. You can also find information on databases, search engines, and link pages where you can list your site for free.

Links2Go: Site Awards
http://www.links2go.com/topic/Awards
Find links to dozens of award sites.

12

Maximizing Promotion with Meta-Indexes

Meta-indexes are intended to be useful resources for people who have a specific interest in a particular topic. Meta-indexes are a large and valuable resource to reaching your target audience and should be utilized to their full potential. In this chapter we cover:

- What meta-indexes are

- Why meta-indexes are useful to the tourism industry

- How to make the link to your site stand out

- How to create your own travel or tourism meta-index

What Are Meta-Indexes?

Meta-indexes are lists of Internet resources pertaining to a specific subject category and are intended as a resource for people who have a specific interest in that topic. These lists, like the one for Lodging in

Dominica shown in Figure 12.1, consist of a collection of URLs of related Internet resources and are arranged on a web page by their titles. The owners or creators of meta-indexes put a lot of effort into compiling these lists and are eager to find new sites to add to them. They will often list your site for free because they desire to have the most meta of the meta-indexes—they strive to have the largest of the large indexes and more sites means a larger index. So if you come across a meta-index that is associated with your type of operation or offering, feel free to ask for a link.

Some of these meta-indexes have a "Submit to add your site" area; for others you have to develop an inclusion request e-mail and send it to the owner of the site. In your inclusion request e-mail, you would let the owner know that you had visited the site and feel that your site would be appropriate to be included. Give the reasons you think your site appropriate and request the link. You should provide the HTML for the link as well. Review the techniques discussed in Chapter 10 to have your link stand out with a graphical icon, hypertext link, and tag line.

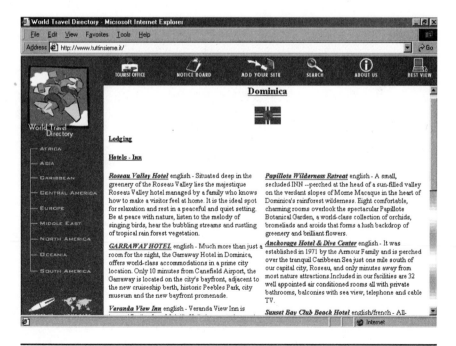

Figure 12.1. World Travel Directory's lodging index for Dominica.

Meta-indexes are directed at a specific topic, such as New England Country Inn, Kid-Friendly Travel Destinations, or Outdoor Adventure Sites. Meta-indexes provide easy access to a number of sites on a specific topic, and they are a great way to draw targeted, interested people to your web site. In addition, some users may rely on meta-indexes as their only search effort. They may not use a search engine to perform a query on Mexican resorts, for example, if they know a certain meta-index contains 200 sites on Mexican resorts. Meta-indexes can increase your chances of being found by people who are interested in what you have to offer.

You may want to consider placing a banner ad on one or some of the meta-indexes you find given that the target audience you want to reach will be the people using these indexes. Choose carefully, though, you don't want to buy a banner ad on a meta-index that is not up to par and doesn't provide you with the traffic you want to acquire. Take your time and investigate the meta-index before advertising on it. Does it appeal to the eye? Is it of good quality? Are there a lot of dead links? Is it updated frequently? Does it have sufficient traffic?

How To Find Appropriate Meta-Indexes

Now that you know what a meta-index is, how do you find them? You might find them when you're browsing on the web and happen to come across one. If you do, bookmark it for future use. A better way to find meta-indexes is through the search engines and directories on the web.

When you're searching the search engines for meta-indexes, we recommend you perform a focused search by looking for the word "directory" or "meta-index" plus the most appropriate keyword or phrase related to your tourism operation. By doing so, you will increase your chances of finding appropriate meta-indexes. Search for "golf resorts" and "meta-index" or "outdoor adventure" and "directory." You should refine your searches to achieve more accurate results. Some general techniques using the words "golf" and "directory" as examples you can apply in your search for meta-indexes are:

- *golf directory* generally means look for all sites containing the word "golf" or "directory," but try to gather those sites with "golf" and "directory" together

- *"golf directory"* often means look for all sites containing the words "golf" and "directory" next to each other

- *+golf directory* means find all sites with the word "golf" and preferably the word "directory" as well

- *+golf +directory* means find all sites with both words

Search engines look for information in different ways and allow different techniques to be applied in order to narrow or broaden the search criteria. This information can be obtained by looking at the respective search engine's help page. See Figure 12.2 for Alta Vista's help page.

Figure 12.2. AltaVista's help page and quick search guide.

Many search engines and directories have or give you the option to use an "advanced" search or search "options" page that present you with the ability to perform more detailed searches without using the parameters outlined above. Yahoo (see Figure 12.3) and Infoseek (see Figure 12.4) are two such sites.

We have done a little research and provide you with some tourism related meta-indexes below that may be useful.

Hotels/Motels/Accommodations Meta-Indexes

HotelsTravel.com
http://www.hotelstravel.com/
Claims to be the most complete, comprehensive, and up-to-date lodging directory on the web

Inntopia.com
http://www.inntopia.com/

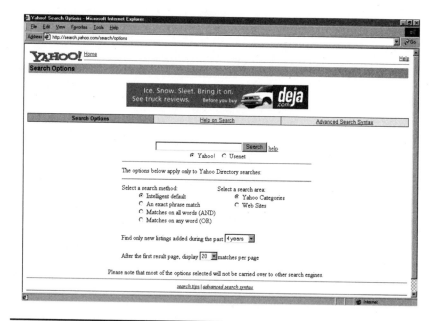

Figure 12.3. Yahoo's advanced search.

Figure 12.4. Infoseek's search options.

A search engine for fine inns, lodges, hotels, and resorts worldwide, with real-time booking and confirming reservations for your next leisure travel vacation.

International Lodging Directory
http://www.usa-lodging.com/
A searchable database of over 60,000 U.S. hotels and motels.

The National Lodging Directory
http://www.guests.com/toc.htm
An online directory of hotels, motels, bed and breakfasts, inns, and vacation rentals.

The Register
http://www.travelassist.com/reg/reg_home.html
Lists over 850 bed and breakfasts, inns, and small hotels in the United States.

World Travel Directory
http://www.tuttinsieme.it/
Find and book accommodations anywhere in the world.

Bed and Breakfasts and Country Inns Meta-Indexes

Bed & Breakfast Inns of North America
http://cimarron.net/index.html
Find a bed and breakfast inn anywhere in the United States, Canada, Mexico, or the Caribbean.

Bed & Breakfast Inns Online
http://www.bbonline.com/
A searchable meta-index of 2400 bed and breakfasts and country inns.

BedandBreakfast.com
http://www.bedandbreakfast.com/
The name says it all.

Elizabeth Arneson's list of Canadian Bed and Breakfasts
http://bandb.miningco.com/travel/bandb/msubmenu3.htm
Lists Canadian bed and breakfast operations by province.

Elizabeth Arneson's List of Caribbean Bed and Breakfasts
http://bandb.miningco.com/travel/bandb/msub1f.htm
Lists Caribbean bed and breakfast businesses.

Elizabeth Arneson's list of European Bed and Breakfasts
http://bandb.miningco.com/travel/bandb/msubmenu2.htm
Lists bed and breakfast operations by country.

Elizabeth Arneson's list of U.S. Bed and Breakfasts
http://bandb.miningco.com/travel/bandb/msubmenu.htm
Lists bed and breakfast organizations by state.

Elizabeth Arneson's Miscellaneous List of Bed and Breakfasts
http://bandb.miningco.com/travel/bandb/msub1a.htm
Find links to more bed and breakfast resources

Outdoor Recreation and Camping Meta-Indexes

Adventure Tour Links
http://carver.pinc.com/home/adventure/tours.html
Discover links to outdoor adventure tours including sailing, canoe-ing, hiking, biking, and riding, plus links to spas and relaxation resorts.

GORP's Links to U.S. National Parks
http://www.gorp.com/gorp/resource/US_National_Park/main.htm
Links to U.S. national parks organized by state.

International Holiday Guide - Find a Campground
http://www.holidayguide.com/camp.html
Links to campgrounds, RV parks, charters, and marinas.

Links to World National Parks
http://www.edgamesandart.com/parkslinks.html
Find a national park anywhere in the world.

OnSafari.com
http://www.onsafari.com/
Find a safari tour operator anywhere in the world.

Cruise Meta-Indexes

About.com - Linda Coffman - Cruises
http://cruises.tqn.com/travel/cruises/
There is no shortage of information on cruises and cruise lines here.

Cruising.org
http://www.cruising.org/links.htm
Cruise line links.

Dan Youra's Ferry Travel Guide
http://www.youra.com/ferry/cruises.html
Cruises and cruise lines on the WWW.

Seamax
http://www.seamax.com/acompletecruise.htm
Includes links to numerous cruise lines.

Shopspy
http://www.shopspy.com/cruise/title-cruises.html
A searchable index of available cruise lines from around the world.

TravelUSA Links to Cruiselines
http://www.travusa.com/cruiselinks.html
Cruiselines have never been easier to find.

Airline Travel Meta-Indexes

Airline Directory
http://www.airlines.com/directory.cfm
A complete directory of U.S. and world airline operators.

Airline Homepages, Etc.
http://www-nrg.ee.lbl.gov/kfall/air.html
Airline home pages, schedules, fare searches, and general information.

Airline Toll-Free Numbers and Web Sites
http://www.princeton.edu/Main/air800.html
Princeton's meta-index of world airlines' numbers and URLs

International Lodging Directory's Airfare Specials
http://www.usa-lodging.com/motel/airlines.htm
Includes links to major North American airlines and their current specials.

Travel Industry Meta-Indexes

ASTAnet Links
http://www.astanet.com/www/asta/pub/link/links.htmlx
Links to important travel industry resources.

The List of Travel URLs
http://soshome.com/URLs.htm
Your guide to travel information on the Net.

Travel Industry Association of America
http://www.tia.org/links.asp
Travelers within the United States will want to take note of this important resource.

Travigator
http://www.travigator.com/
The travel industry's search engine directory.

United States Tour Operators Association
http://www.ustoa.com/
Find links to member tour operator sites.

Theme Park Meta-Indexes

About.com - Theme Parks
http://themeparks.tqn.com/travel/themeparks/
A meta-index with links to theme parks worldwide.

Amusement Parks and Rollercoaster Links
http://users.sgi.net/~rollocst/amuse.html
The web's first directory of amusement park related links.

Californian Theme Parks
http://www.caohwy.com/t/themepar.htm
Find a theme park in California.

CATA Holiday Adventures
http://www.chycor.co.uk/tourism/cata/
Cornwall (UK) Association of Tourist Attractions.

Disney Theme Parks
http://asp.disney.go.com/disneyworld/db/seetheworld/themeparks/index.asp
Find a Disney theme park near you.

General Theme Parks
http://www.geocities.com/TheTropics/Paradise/5599/other.html
Links to a few choice U.S. theme parks.

Golden Coast Attractions
http://www.reflections.com.au/GoldCoast/ThemeParks
AndAttractions/index.html
Links to Australian theme parks.

New Hampshire Theme Parks
http://www.greatnorthwoods.org/thingstodo/theme.htm
Theme parks along the southern edge of the Great North Woods in
New Hampshire.

The Ultimate Rollercoaster
http://www.ultimaterollercoaster.com/
A great resource to find rollercoaster theme parks.

Theme Parks
http://pages.prodigy.com/joshman/theme.htm
Links mostly to Disney theme parks and rollercoasters.

Travel Deals Meta-Indexes

Airfare Specials
http://www.airlines.com/airfares.html
Find airfare specials as they are announced.

Webflyer
http://www.webflyer.com/
A great source for great airfare deals.

General Travel Meta-Indexes

ASE.net
http://www.ase.net/
A search engine for business and leisure travelers seeking to find the

right hotel, motel, hostel, self-catering flat, bed and breakfast, and so on.

Everything's Travel
http://members.aol.com/~trvlevery/
A travel directory of accommodations, destinations, lodgings, and transportation.

Festivals.com
http://www.festivals.com/
A searchable meta-index of festivals and attractions around the world.

Galaxy Travel
http://galaxy.einet.net/galaxy/Leisure-and-Recreation/Travel.html
Another searchable travel directory.

MapQuest
http://www.mapquest.com/
Find a map of your vacation destination.

NetGuide: Travel Guide
http://www.netguide.com/Travel
A general directory of destinations, travel resources, and vacation planning tools.

Travel Reports and Links
http://tourism-industry.net/
Obtain the latest travel reports on almost any region or recreational activity.

Yahoo! Travel
http://travel.yahoo.com/
Find all you need here to plan your next vacation.

Geographic Specific Meta-Indexes

African Travel Industry
http://www.mbendi.co.za/indy/trvl/trvlaf.htm

Provides an overview of the African travel and accommodation industry.

Australia Travel
http://www.anzac.com/aust/aust.htm
In-depth, state-by-state information on Australia.

Bahamas Travel Directory
http://www.caribbeansupersite.com/bahamas/links.htm
Your guide to the Bahamas.

CIA - World Factbook
http://www.odci.gov/cia/publications/factbook/country.html
A meta-index of every country in the world.

Hugh's Asia Travel Guide
http://www.mcs.net/~hwebb/travel.html
A guide to travel sources and country information for Southeast and East Asia.

Information USA
http://www.information-usa.com/
Complete listings of anyone and anything important to travel and tourism in the United States.

Infotec-Travel
http://www.infotec-travel.com/
A tourism meta-index with too much information. If you are looking for tourism-related topics, software, web rings, and so forth, go here.

Personnel Guide to Canada's Travel Industry
http://pguide.baxter.net/
Find Canadian travel agencies, tour operators, hotel owners, and so on.

Specialty Travel
http://specialtytravel.com/
Find almost anything travel related in any country.

Timeshare Meta-Indexes

Fern Modena's Timeshare and Travel Page
http://www.geocities.com/RodeoDrive/1060/mag.html
A tremendous resource with links to other travel meta-indexes.

JourneyQuest
http://www.journeyquest.com/apartments.html
Apartments for rent.

Specialty Travel Timeshares
http://specialtytravel.com/
Go to the Interest/Activity directory and then click on "Timesharing" or "Apartment/Condo Rental."

Enlisting Meta-Indexes for Optimal Exposure

To ensure that you are taking full advantage of meta-indexes, do the following:

- Source the meta-indexes related to your travel-related offering

- Request a link

- Provide the details necessary

- Look at sponsorship or banner advertising opportunities

Meta-indexes can be arranged by subject (sites that provide information on theme park destinations), by geography (tourist sites in Alaska), or by demographic (senior travel destinations). As mentioned before, the major search engines are a good place to start. For example, to find tourist sites in Alaska, conduct a search on "+Alaska+tourist+directory" or "Alaska+tourist+metaindex." Once you find a good list and start to check the links, you will likely find other lists through the first list. Bookmark or keep a record of the meta-indexes you like for future reference.

If you are not sure if your site will be accepted by a certain meta-index, send a request anyway. Meta-lists draw more traffic when they provide more resources to their readers, so list owners may be fairly lenient on what's acceptable.

When you are requesting a link to your site, send an e-mail with *site addition request* in the subject area of your message. Include the following in the body of the message:

- Your URL

- A description of your site

- Why you feel your site is appropriate for the list

- Your contact information in your signature file (see Chapter 6)

Once you have identified the appropriate indexes that appeal to your target market, determine whether additional opportunities might exist for sponsorship or purchasing banner advertising on the site. Meta-indexes that relate to your market are a great place to advertise because they are accessed by your target customer.

Keep in mind that the compilers of meta-indexes are motivated by noncommercial reasons and are under no obligation to add your site to their list or process your request quickly. However, because of the banner advertising revenue potential, more and more meta-index sites have a commercial focus.

To make your link stand out among the many others listed, inquire about adding a prominent link or icon to the meta-index page along with a short tag line, in addition to your company name. If you provide the GIF and the HTML coding, the meta-index owner may be happy to include it.

Review the Work of Some Meta-Index Giants

The National Lodging Directory (see Figure 12.5)
http://www.guests.com/toc.htm

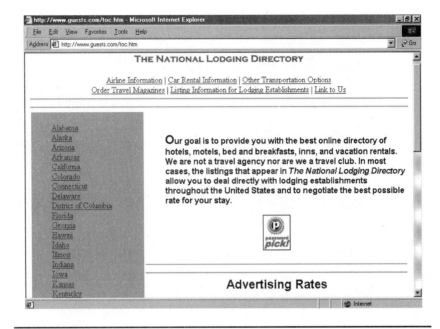

Figure 12.5.   A meta-index of lodging locations across the United States.

Hugh's Asia Travel Guide (see Figure 12.6)
http://www.mcs.net/~hwebb/travel.html

Travel Reports and Links (see Figure 12.7)
http://tourism-industry.net/

Australia Travel (see Figure 12.8)
http://www.anzac.com/aust/aust.htm

World Travel Directory (see Figure 12.9)
http://www.tuttinsieme.it/

Internet Resources

WWW Meta-Indexes and Search Tools
http://www.fys.ruu.nl/~kruis/h3.html
A Library of Congress Internet resource page.

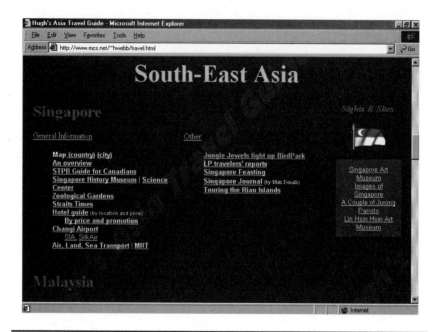

Figure 12.6. A travel meta-index for Asia.

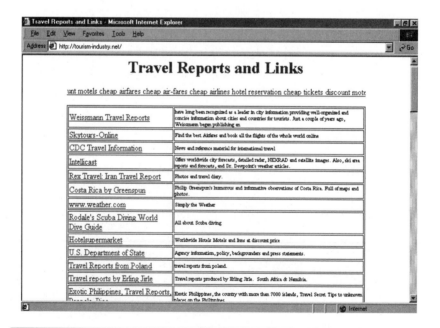

Figure 12.7. A meta-index of sites related to travel information.

Figure 12.8. Meta-index of Australian travel related sites.

Figure 12.9. A meta-index covering travel information around the world.

Argus Clearinghouse
http://www.clearinghouse.net
The premier Internet research library (or meta-index) to locate everything you need to find on the web.

The Ultimate Directory - InfoSpace
http://www.infospace.com
InfoSpace calls itself the ultimate directory. You'll find yellow pages, white pages, classifieds, shopping sites, investing information, government listings, chat rooms, and much more.

Virtual Library
http://vlib.org/Overview.html
The Virtual Library is the oldest catalog of the web, started by Tim Berners-Lee, the creator of the web itself. Unlike commercial catalogs, it is run by a loose confederation of volunteers, who compile pages of key links for particular areas in which they are expert. Even though it isn't the biggest index of the web, the VL pages are widely recognized as being among the highest-quality guides to particular sections of the web.

W.E.D. The World E-mail Directory
http://www.worldemail.com/
The World E-mail Directory has estimated access to more than 18,000,000 e-mail addresses and more than 140,000,000 business and phone addresses worldwide. One of the fastest growing engines for people, businesses, and organizations.

Essential Links: Portal to the Internet
http://www.el.com/
Essential Links to the Internet and the World Wide Web. Essential Links is a portal to the Internet portal sites, news headlines, search engines, web directories, references, and utilities.

@LinkPad
http://www.referthem.com/pad/links.htm
A meta-index of meta-indexes. This site has indexes ranging from advertising, e-zines, and e-mail to web graphics and real estate.

13

Online Advertising

There have been numerous studies on banner advertising over the last couple of years. Some say banner advertising works; others are not so positive. I find it very interesting that such a blanket statement can be made. It really depends on what your objectives are, what type of ad you develop, and your ad placement strategy. Advertising online provides visibility for your tourism operation—just as offline advertising does. You must develop a banner advertising strategy that works with your organization, your marketing objectives, and your budget. In this chapter we cover:

- Your tourism operation's online advertising strategy

- Advertising opportunities on the web

- Banner ad design and impact on click-throughs

- Banner ad sizes and locations

- Placing classifieds

- Tips to creating dynamite banner ads that work

- The cost of advertising online

- Measuring ad effectiveness

- Banner ad exchange networks

- Using an online advertising agency

- Sources of net advertising information

Expanding Your Exposure Through Internet Advertising

Today, Internet advertising is being recognized in the advertising budgets of tourism operations around the globe. Banner ads represent one way to create awareness of your web site and increase the traffic to it. Your web site is your online presence. When your banner ads are placed on tourism-related web sites, people interested in what you're offering are encouraged to click through and visit your site.

The Internet offers many different advertising spaces. Banner ads can be placed on search engines, content sites, advertising sites, and online magazines. Where you decide to place your ad will depend on the objectives you wish to achieve with your online advertising strategy. There are a number of advantages to online advertising:

- The response from these ads can be easily measured within one day.

- The amount of information that can be delivered, if your web site is visited, far surpasses that of a traditional advertising campaign.

- The cost of developing and running an online advertising campaign is much less than using traditional media.

Traditionally, advertising used to be handled by a PR/advertising company, who would come up with your advertising concept. Tourism operators, as clients, would review and approve (usually after several attempts) the concepts before they were ever released to the public eye. The PR/advertising firms would be responsible for developing TV, radio, and printed ads for their clients around this concept. They would come up with the media buy strategy after reviewing appropriate publications, editorial calendars, pricing, and the discounts that they would receive for multiple placements. The ads would then be gradually released over the period of the campaign and finally viewed by the public. At the end of the campaign, the PR/advertising company would evaluate the success of the marketing campaign. Success would be very easy to evaluate if the objective of the campaign was to achieve a given number of reservations, but such an evaluation would be much more difficult if the goal of your campaign was to generate brand awareness.

Today, online banner ads are developed in much less time and can be placed on web sites quickly. Web traffic analysis software can tell you the next day whether or not the banner ad is effective by tracking the number of visitors who clicked through and visited your site. If a banner ad is proving to be ineffective, you can move it to another site or change the banner ad you are using to see if you can attract a greater audience.

Maximize Advertising with Your Objectives in Mind

When you are developing an advertising strategy for your tourism operation, you will need to determine the objectives of your advertising campaign. When tourism operators are developing an online advertising campaign, their most common objectives:

- Building awareness

- Increasing web site traffic

- Generating leads, reservations, and sales

You have a number of choices to make. What type of advertising should you use? What sites would be the most effective to advertise my tourism operation? These choices should be made based on your objectives. If one of your objectives was to increase the overall recognition of your tourism operation, then a nicely designed banner ad on one of the high-traffic search engines would be effective. If you would like to develop and increase your reservations, then a more targeted approach should be taken. For instance, you might wish to try placing a banner ad on a high-traffic tourism-related web site.

When you are deciding how to proceed with your advertising strategy, consider how many people you want to reach. Do you want a high-quality response from a small number of very targeted people, or do you want to reach a mass-market audience?

Think about the people you are targeting. If you have a golf resort, you want to target people who are interested in playing golf. It would not make much sense to put an ad on AltaVista when you could advertise on a site targeted to the golf enthusiast.

Always keep your budget in mind when you are developing your online advertising strategy. There are many ways to stretch your advertising dollar. If you have the time, you can find appropriate sites to trade banners. Participating in banner exchange programs is another option.

Online Advertising Terminology

Banner Ads

Banner ads are small advertisements that are placed on a web site. Companies usually develop their banner ads, find appropriate sites for placement, and then either purchase or trade banner space.

Click-Throughs

When viewers click on a banner ad with their mouse and go to the site advertised, it is called a "click-through." The number of click-throughs often determines the banner advertising rates.

Hits

Hits to a site are the number of times that another computer has requested a site (or a particular file on a site). This does not mean that if your site has 1000 hits, 1000 people have visited your site. If your home page has a number of graphic files on it, this number could be very misleading. A hit is counted when the home page main file is accessed, but a hit is also counted for every graphic file that loads along with the home page. So, if a person visits 6 pages on a site and each page has 4 graphics, there would be a minimum of 30 hits generated. Quite often the number would be much higher, because the pages usually include files for navigation bars, banner ads, and so forth.

Impression

When someone views a banner ad, it is called an impression. Banner advertising prices are often calculated by impressions. If a person visits a page six times, this will generate six impressions.

CPM

Cost per thousand impressions, or CPM, is a standard advertising term. CPM is often used to calculate the cost of banner advertising. If the price of banner advertising on a site was $40 CPM, and the number of impressions the ad had was 2000, then the advertiser would have to pay $80 for displaying the ad.

Keywords

You can purchase keywords on search engines. This allows your banner ad to appear when someone does a search on the keyword that you purchase. This is very good for zooming in on your target market. For example, if you operate a white water rafting company, you can purchase the keywords "white water rafting." Your banner ad will be displayed when and only when a person searches for the keyword phrase "white water rafting." When your banner ad does appear, there is a good chance you will receive a click-through from it, because the person who searched for "white water rafting" is obviously interested in services similar to those your operation is offering. Therefore, purchasing keywords and linking your banner advertising to these keywords can help attract your target market to your site.

IP Addresses (Geo Targeting)

Purchasing IP numbers is one of the latest trends in Internet marketing. Every device that connects to the Internet has its own, unique IP address. These are assigned centrally by a designated authority for each country. We are now seeing search engines sell banner advertising by IP addresses to help businesses pinpoint their target demographic. For example, John Doe is from Boston and is going on vacation in Kentucky. He is searching for bed and breakfast accommodations. Dooley's Bed and Breakfast in Kentucky happens to be marketing over the Internet, and as part of their banner advertising campaign, they have purchased banner ads by keyword and by IP address. Simply stated, they have said they only want their banner ad to appear when the keyword "bed and breakfast" is searched on by individuals whose IP address is within a certain range (the range being those existing in Boston). When John Doe does his search on the keyword "bed and breakfast," the Dooley Bed and Breakfast banner ad is displayed at the top of the page holding the search results. Someone in Michigan searching for the keyword "bed and breakfast" will see a different banner ad.

Jump on the Banner Wagon

Banner advertising is the most common and most recognized form of online advertising. Banner ads are available in various sizes, but the most common banners are displayed at roughly 468 × 60 pixels. Banners usually have an enticing message or call to action that coaxes the viewer to click on it. "What is on the other side?" you ask. The advertiser's web site, of course. A banner ad can also be static, just displaying the advertiser's logo and slogan, or it can be animated.

If you use an advertising or PR company to develop the offline advertisements for your tourism operation, quite often they will provide you with a library of different banner ads that you can use for your online advertising campaign. If you choose not to use an advertising or PR company, you can outsource the banner ad creation activity to another company or you can create your own.

The banner ad is designed to have a direct impact on the number of click-throughs it will achieve. There are a number of resources online to assist you in developing dynamic banner ads. The Banner Generator at *http://www.coder.com/creations/banner* allows you to create banners online at no charge. The Media Builder at *http://www.mediabuilder.com/abm.html* provides you the opportunity to develop animated banner ads directly from their site. Other resources to assist you in designing and building banner ads are identified in the Internet Resources section at the end of this chapter.

A wide variety of banner sizes are available (see Figure 13.1). You should consult with the owners of the web sites on which you want to advertise before creating your banner ad or having one created professionally for you to make sure your banner ads will fit.

The objective of your banner ad is to have someone click on it. Do not try to include all of your information in your ad. A banner that is too small and cluttered is difficult to read and is not visually appealing. Many banners simply include a logo and a tag line entic-

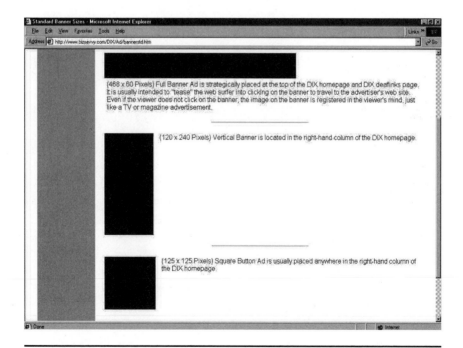

Figure 13.1. There are many different marketing resource Web sites available online that can provide you with the different size possibilities for your banner ads.

ing the user to click on it. Free offers or contest giveaways are also quite effective for click-throughs, since they tend to appeal to the user's curiosity. A common example used by tourism operations is to promote a contest giving away a free night's accommodation at their lodging. This is great, because these banners entice the viewers to click through to the tourism operator's web site, where they get to learn more about the resort.

Exploring Your Banner Ad Options

Static banners are what the name suggests. They remain static on the same web page until they are removed. Your banner ad will be visible on that particular page until your reader moves to another page.

Animated banners use a series of slides to create the illusion of motion (much like the old flip-through comics). Animated banners are usually in GIF89a (GIF stands for graphics interchange format) and contain a group of images in one file that are presented in a specific order. When using animated banner ads (see Figures 13.2 a, b and c) you can choose to loop the file so that the banner will continue to move between the images in the files, or you have the option to make it stop after a complete cycle.

Rotating banners are banner ads that rotate among different web pages on the same site. Other rotating banner ads rotate every time there is a new visitor to the page. Rotating banners are commonly used in high-traffic web sites.

Scrolling banners are similar to modern billboards. Here the visitor will see a number of billboard ads scrolling to show a different advertisement every 10 to 30 seconds.

Tips for Designing Your Banner Ads

Follow these tips to ensure that your banner ad will achieve your marketing objectives:

- Make sure your banner ad is quick to load. If the web page loads in its entirety before the banner, then the viewer may

Figure 13.2.(a)   This is the first stage in this animated banner ad. It catches the visitors attention, and makes them think that the banner is doing a search on popular keywords related to skiing.

Figure 13.2.(b)   This is the second stage in this animated banner ad. It acts as though the banner is doing a search on the keywords inputted into the query box.

Figure 13.2.(c)   This is the final stage in this animated banner ad. It appears as though the search is complete, and now promotes *Ski Canada* magazine. This is great because by the time they are ready to promote the *Ski Canada* magazine they have the viewer's full attention.

click away before ever seeing it. Ideally you should have a fast-loading banner ad on a relatively slow loading site. This way visitors have nothing to do but read your banner ad while they are waiting for the site to load. You should always try to keep your banner ad size under 10K.

- To see how large banner ad files are when using any version of Internet Explorer, you must follow these steps:

1. Right mouse click on the banner ad.

2. Select "Properties."

3. In the Properties window you will see a Size line, which will tell you the banner size.

- To see how large banner ad files are when using any version of Netscape Navigator, you must follow these steps:

  1. Right mouse click on the banner ad.

  2. Select "View Image" and the banner ad will appear on a page of its own.

  3. Right click on the banner and select "View Info". Another page will pop up and give you the information on the banner ad size.

- Keep it simple! If your banner contains too much text, (as seen in Figure 13.2) animation, or too many colors and fonts, viewers will experience information overload. Viewers will not be encouraged to read or click on your banner.

- Make sure your banner ad is legible. Many banners on the Internet are nicely designed, but are difficult to read. Use an easy-to-read font with the appropriate size. Be careful in your choice of color.

- You should always use Alt tags for those visitors who surf the Internet with their graphics turned off or cannot see your banner ad for whatever reason.

- Make sure your banner ad links to the appropriate page in your site. It is not uncommon to click on an interesting banner only to find an error message waiting for you. This is very annoying to Internet users and counterproductive to your marketing effort.

- Check your banner ads on a regular basis to verify that the link remains active and is pointing to the appropriate page on your web site.

- If you are using animated banner ads, you should limit your ads to two to four frames.

- You should always include a call to action like "Click here." It is amazing how many people will do what they are told. You still have to make your ad interesting and attention-grabbing. Don't simply say "Click here," give your audience a compelling reason to do so.

- Test your banner ads with the different browsers, the different versions of these browsers, and at different screen resolutions to make sure that they look the way you want them to.

- If you are not well versed in the fields of advertising and graphic design, do not try to create a banner on your own. Go to a professional. If you do design your own banner, get a second opinion and maybe a third.

Advanced Banner Ad Options

The following are more technologically advanced forms of banner advertising. They are interesting to the viewer because they have attributes that are unique or different in some way. These attributes may be more apt to grab viewers' attention and entice them to click on the banner ad.

Expanding Banner Ads
An expanding banner ad (see Figure 13.3 a, b and c) is one that looks like a normal banner ad, but expands when you click on it, keeping you on the same site rather than transporting you to another site on the Internet. Usually they say "Click to expand," and the viewer then can learn more about what it is that the banner is promoting. Some of the more advanced expanding banner ads have e-commerce capabilities, which allow you to actually order products from the banner without actually ever going to the web site.

Animated Banner Ads
Animated banner ads contain a group of images in one file that rotate in a specific order. These banner ads are more likely to receive a

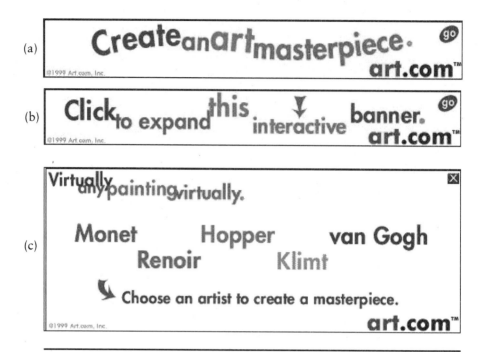

Figure 13.3. In this example, the user can click on "go" (a & b) to expand the banner ad (c).

click-through than a normal banner ad, because with moving images on the web site your chances of the viewer reading the banner are increased. These banners also offer you the chance to deliver more information to the viewer than a normal banner ad, for you can show different files, which contain different data. You should limit your banner ads to two to four frames to keep your loading time fast and to make sure your viewer reads your information before continuing to surf the Internet.

Banners Containing Embedded HTML
Lately we have been seeing an increase in banner ads containing embedded HTML. This allows viewers to choose commands from a drop-down menu (see Figure 13.4 a and b) that relate to the web site the banner ad is promoting. These banners are great because instead of making viewers click through and navigate through your site as with a conventional banner, HTML banners can direct your viewers to the specific page of interest on your site.

Figure 13.4. In this banner ad (a), the user can select a travel destination from the drop-down menu to find an air fare (b). This is an example of having HTML code embedded in a banner ad.

Interstitial ads are advertisements that appear in a separate browser window while you wait for a web page to load. (See Figure 13.5) Interstitial ads are likely to contain large graphics, streaming presentations, and more applets than a conventional banner ad. Studies have found that more users click on interstitial ads than on banner ads. Some users, however, have complained that interstitial ads slow access to destination pages.

Java and Flash banner ads allow you to use rich media in your advertisements. By using Java and Flash technology, you can incorporate animation and sound into your banner advertisement (see Figure 13.6 a to d). Although Java banners are more technologically advanced and offer more features, they also take much longer to download and risk not being viewed. Flash was designed to generate faster-loading web sites, online animation, and advertising. If you want to incorporate rich media into your banners, you may want to try Flash, because you want your visitors to see your banner ads as quickly as possible.

Figure 13.5. Here is an example of a pop-up banner ad or interstitial ad. Although pop-up ads annoy a lot of users, this form of advertising can be quite effective if targeted properly.

Location, Location, Location

As with all types of advertising, the location of the ad is extremely important. There are any number of targeted tourism related web sites on which you can place your banner ads. Always ensure that your banner advertising location is consistent with your objectives.

Search Engines

If your goal is to reach as many different people as possible to create awareness about your tourism operation, high-traffic search engines are where you should be. Cost per thousand (CPM) impressions is usually $20 to $50. If your target market is more selective, then a more targeted buy within the search engine is appropriate. Targeted buys

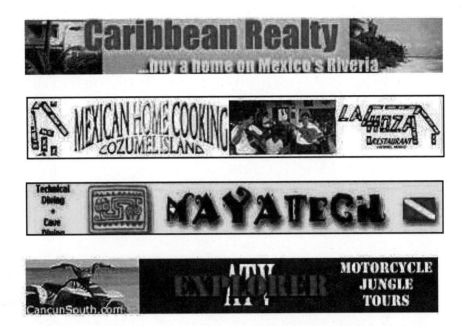

Figure 13.6. Although it is difficult to depict on paper, these slides are all taken from the same rotating banner ad. A JavaScript function rotates the image shown on the banner and loads the corresponding URL.

can include tying your banner ad to specific keywords (i.e., every time the keyword is used in a search your banner ad would appear) or specific IP addresses so that your ad would be seen only by those in a specific geographic area. Targeted ads generally range in price from $40 to $90 CPM but are quite often worth the extra price because of the correlation to the targeted buyer. If you owned a bed and breakfast and purchased "bed and breakfast" as a keyword, whenever someone searched for "bed and breakfast" your banner would appear.

Content Sites

If your objectives include attracting more prospective tourists to your site, then advertising on appropriate content sites would be extremely effective. These are sites that concentrate on a specific topic. For example, if you have a bed and breakfast or country inn in the New

England area, you should consider placing your banner ads on sites whose content deals with New England country inns. Much like buying keywords from a search engine, when you advertise on sites containing content that is relevant to your tourism operation, you are advertising directly to your target market. Travelers who are looking for a country inn in New England will naturally be drawn to the host's web site because of its content. When they visit the New England Country Inns site, they will see your banner ad. Chances are, you will receive click-throughs from these visitors and some sales will result. The cost of advertising on content sites ranges from $25 to $50 CPM, depending on the traffic volume.

Banner Ad Price Factors

The price of banner ad space varies from site to site. Banner ads are often sold based on the number of impressions or number of click-throughs. As stated earlier, an impression is an ad view and click-throughs represent actual clicks on the banner. The price per impression should be less than the price per click-through. Banner ad pricing CPM (cost per 1000 impressions) is between $10 and $90 depending on the site where you are advertising—how targeted the audience is, and how much traffic it receives. Search-engine banner ads range between $20 and $50 CPM. Keyword advertising ranges between $40 and $70 CPM. The cost to run a Geo Tracking campaign can be very costly. For example, Excite *(http://www.excite.com)* charges approximately $10,000 for the purchase of an IP address. The click-through pricing is somewhere between $0.20 and $1.20 per click-through, again depending on the site and the traffic. Before you sign anything, make sure that you understand what you are paying for. Based on industry standards, Ad Resource *(http://www.adresource.com)* has average CPM advertising rates, which are updated quite frequently.

When site owners charge per impression, there is usually a guarantee that your ad will be seen by a certain number of people. The burden is on the sellers to generate traffic to their site. When the charges are on a per-click-through basis, the responsibility is on you, the advertiser, to design an ad that will encourage visitors to click on it. Sites that charge per impression are more common than those that charge per click-through. There are obvious advantages to advertisers when paying per click-through. They don't have to pay a cent for the 10,000 people who saw their banner but did not pursue the link. Sites that do not have a large volume of traffic often charge a flat rate for a specified period of time.

Make Sure Your Banner Ad Is Seen

One major factor that is often overlooked is that some people surf the Internet with their graphics turned off. Not a big deal, right? What if you purchased a banner ad? They are not going to see it, so the chances that they will click through to your site via the banner ad are not great. An easy way to make sure that the viewer still knows that your banner is there is to include the Alt attribute in the IMG (or "image") tag for your banner. The Alt attribute provides descriptive text for the browser to display if the graphic cannot be viewed. Here you should develop a clever tag line that will still entice the viewer to click through to your web site. Remember that it is important to include Alt attributes for all of the graphics on your web site.

Banner Ad Placement—Where Should You Place Your Ad?

As for an advertisement in a newspaper or in a magazine, the location of your banner ad on a web site is very important. A past study by graduate students at the University of Michigan showed that by placing a banner ad on the lower right-hand corner, next to the scroll bar, you receive a higher click-through rate. This is because when people scroll down the page, their eyes are in the bottom corner, so they see your ad. The study also showed us that placing a banner ad one third of the way down the page received a 77% higher click-through rate compared to those placed at the top. It is very common for the search engines to place their banners one third of the way down the page for prime advertising exposure.

When placing a banner ad, you must always go back to your objective, which is to increase the traffic to your site. Always conduct research on a web site before you place an ad on it. You want to discern whether or not it receives high traffic. There is no point in paying for an ad that will not be seen by anyone. You should try to place an ad on a site that is aimed to your target audience. Ensure that your banner is eye pleasing and includes a call to action that will entice the visitor to click through.

Making It Easy with Online Advertising Agencies

If your objective is to reach a large number of users through a wide variety of sites, Internet ad networks may be appropriate. Ad networks work with a wide range of different web sites viewed by thousands of people everyday. You have to supply your banners to the ad network and determine how you want them to promote you. B2B Works (*http://www.b2bworks.com*) is an example of a very popular ad network. B2B Works (see Figure 13.7) has well over 70 different industries in their network and are emerging as an ad network leader. They can specifically target sites related to the tourism industry or advertise your banner to a mass audience. For a more targeted audience, you will have to pay a higher CPM. Although you have to pay a little more initially, you will save money in the long run. If you are targeting tourism-related web sites, you are placing your banner advertisement in front of the eyes of your target audience, because they will be visiting these sites.

The benefit of joining an ad network is that not only can they target your audience, they also provide you with real-time reports that indicate the success of your banner ads. This allows you to evaluate the success of your current banner ad campaign and offers you the chance to change your marketing strategy if you are not happy with your results. Maybe you want to take a different approach, or maybe a different banner design might work better for you. Whatever it may be, the data that the ad network can provide you with is very beneficial to determining the strength of your banner ad campaign.

You can also join an ad network as a publisher. Publishers are the web sites that banners are placed on. If you have a web site and would like to make some additional online revenue from your site, you can join an ad network, and they will place banner ads on your site and

Figure 13.7. B2B Works (*http://www.b2bworks.com*) is an example of a popular online ad network.

pay you for the use of this space. Very similar to an affiliate program or banner exchange, by joining an ad network, you can dramatically increase your online revenue. A detailed list of banner ad networks will be listed in the resource section at the end of this chapter.

Saving Money with Banner Exchange Programs

Banner exchanges work much as you would expect. Your ad is placed on other sites in exchange for someone else's banner ad being placed on your web site.

To register with a banner exchange you often have to go through a qualifying process. What this means is that your site has to meet certain minimum standards. Once you have passed the test, the banner exchange will provide you with HTML code to insert into pages of your site where the banner ads will appear. Every time this HTML is accessed, a random banner ad appears for the viewer to see.

This process is monitored and tracked. Each banner that is accessed from the exchange and displayed to a visitor earns you some sort of credit or token. These credits or tokens are used within the banner exchange like a bartering system. The credits you earn are exchanged for having your banner displayed on another site.

Sometimes some of the credits you earn go to the banner exchange itself as a fee for managing the process. The banner exchange will sell the credits to paying advertisers or use them to promote the exchange. Some banner exchanges, like the ad networks, will allow you to focus your exposure on your target market by only advertising your banner on tourism-related web sites.

When determining which banner exchanges to belong to, look for restrictions. When banner exchanges have no restrictions, you never know what could be loading to your pages. Don't join banner exchanges without size specifications for the banners. Your site could be displaying huge 150 × 600-pixel banners that make your visitors wait while they load. Ensure that the loading time of every banner displayed on your site will be reasonable.

Applying to join a banner exchange is very easy. For an example we will use LinkExchange *(http://www.linkexchange.com)* (see Figures 13.8, 13.9, 13.10). To apply to join MSN's LinkExchange program, you have to follow a few short steps. First, you have to agree to their terms and agreements. Next, you must fill out a few forms containing your personal and web site information. Then simply submit this information to LinkExchange for review. If you are accepted, they will contact you and give you the appropriate HTML code to place on your site to enable you to start the program.

LinkExchange offers you the chance to promote your banner ad on over 450,000 different web sites across the world. In exchange, you must agree to display the LinkExchange HTML on your site. This HTML will enable LinkExchange to display different banner advertisements for LinkExchange sponsors and LinkExchange members on your site in return for their free service. You will have your banner ad displayed once for every two banners you display on your web site. This can generate a lot of exposure for your site.

Here are some of the other popular online banner exchange programs. A more complete listing is available in the Internet Resources section of this chapter.

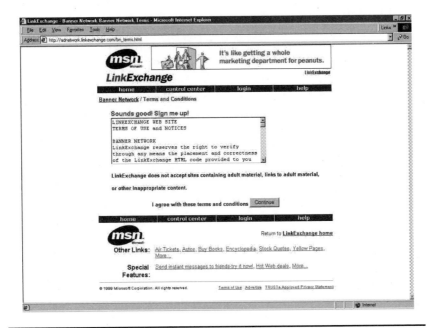

Figure 13.8. The first step to signing up for the LinkExchange program is accepting the terms and conditions of the program. By doing so you certify that you fully understand not only what is involved in the program, but also what you cannot do.

- Net-On: *http://www.net-on.se:81/banner/index.html*

- SmartClicks: *http://www.SmartClicks.com*

- BannerSwap: *http://www.bannerswap.com/*

- Banner-X-change.net: *http://banner-x-change.net/*

Bartering for Mutual Benefits with Banner Trading

Using this technique requires you to barter with other web sites to trade banners with their sites. If you are browsing the Internet and find a site that may appeal to your target market, then ask for a

Figure 13.9. The second step in the LinkExchange program is very easy. You simply fill out some personal information about yourself and your Web site.

trade. Send the webmaster an e-mail outlining your proposition. Include the reasons why you think it would be mutually beneficial, a description of your site, where you would place their banner on your site, and where you think your banner should go on their site.

When you make arrangements like this, be sure to monitor the results. If the other site has low traffic, then more visitors may be leaving your site through their banner than are being attracted to yours. Also, check the other site regularly to make sure that they are still displaying your banners for the duration agreed to.

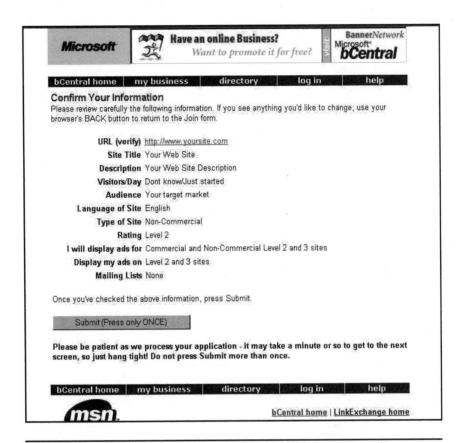

Figure 13.10. The third step is simply to review your information to make sure it is correct. Then submit the information for review. If you get accepted to the program, you will be contacted by MSN and they will provide you with the information that you will need to immediately setup your exchange program.

Tips for Succeeding with Classified Ads

Classified ads are also displayed on the Internet on various web sites. Some sites offer to display classified ads for free; others will charge a small fee.

Here are some great tips for creating effective classified ads:

- **Headlines.** The headline of your ad is very important. The subject line determines how many people will read the rest of your ad. Look at the subject lines of other ads and see what attracts your eye.

- **Entice.** Use your classified ad to get people to request more information. You can then send them a personalized letter outlining all of the information and making a great pitch to attract their reservation or purchase.

- **Be friendly.** Your classified shouldn't be formal and business like. Make your ad light and friendly.

- **Call to action.** Do not only offer information about what you are selling. Call the reader to action; for instance, to make a reservation now!

- **Do some tests.** Run a number of different ads and use a different e-mail address for each one. This way you can determine which ad receives the most responses. You can then run the best ad in a number of different places to find out which place gets the biggest response.

- **Keep a record.** Keep records of your responses so that you will know which ads were the most successful.

Form Lasting Advertising with Sponsorships

Sponsorships are another form of advertising, one that usually involves strong, long-lasting relationships between the sponsors and the site owners. Sponsors may donate money, web development, web hosting, web site maintenance, or other products and services to web site owners in this mutually beneficial relationship. By sponsoring tourism-related web sites on the Internet, you can achieve great exposure for your tourism operation. People appreciate sponsorships and will look at banner ads that are from a sponsor. The benefits of sponsorships on the Internet is that you can target a specific audience, you usually get first call on banner ad placement, and you show your target market that you care about their interest. Overall, by sponsoring sites on the Internet, you have the opportunity to get directly in the face of your target market.

There are a number of different ways that you can advertise online through sponsorships. The following is a list of the more common forms of online sponsorship:

- E-zines and Newsletters—an example of this would be Taylor Made sponsoring a Golf Resort Digest e-zine.

- Content Sites—an example of this would be United Airlines sponsoring an Airline Travel web site.

- Online Chat Sessions—an example of this would be Trip.com sponsoring a Chat on the Scotland Online *(http://www.discussion.scotland.net/)*.

- Events—an example of this would be a travel site such as Trip.com (partial sponsor) sponsoring the Customer Relationship Management for the Travel Industry conference *(http://www.firstconf.com/travel/crm/)*.

Commercial Links

Another form of online advertising is commercial links. Numerous web sites provide a lengthy list of URLs related to the tourism industry. These sites will often provide your listing for free but charge a fee to have a hypertext link activated from their site to yours. There are also web sites where you can be listed if you don't have a web site and would prefer to only have your business name and phone number or e-mail address listed. These are great sites, especially since they are targeted toward your demographic. An example of this would be Roomz.com *(http://www.roomz.com)* (see Figure 13.11). This site has a database of travel accommodations targeted toward people who are planning a vacation. If you have a tourism operation that provides accommodations to travelers, you may want to have a link on this web site because your target market will visit a web site like this. Roomz.com allows tourism operators to post links on its site for free, but also gives them the opportunity to enhance their listings by providing more detailed information about their operation.

Figure 13.11. Roomz.com is one of the largest lodging directories on the Internet.

Sponsoring a Mailing List

Another online advertising opportunity is presented by mailing lists. Tourism-related mailing lists provide a very targeted advertising vehicle. Mailing list subscribers are all interested in the list topic. If they are subscribing to a tourism-related mailing list, they are your potential clients. Best of all, the rates for sponsoring lists are quite low. The cost is determined on a price-per-reader basis and is usually between 1 and 10 cents per reader. Subscribe to the lists that have appeal to your target market and read the FAQs to determine whether advertising or sponsorship opportunities exist for each mailing list. If the mailing list allows sponsorship, contact the mailing list administrator to inquire the cost of sponsoring, and if it is reasonable, negotiate your sponsorship. All of the members of the mailing list have subscribed and want to be on the list; therefore, it is likely that they will read this e-mail. This is an excellent opportunity for you to expose your tourism operation to these potential clients. A good example of this would be Trip.com sponsoring a mailing list about different vacation destinations around the world. Since the readers are interested in the topic, they may be encouraged to click through and book a trip to the destination of their choice. For more information on mailing lists, refer to Chapter 8.

Cross-Promoting Your Tourism Web Site

A great way to promote your tourism operation is to jointly promote it with a noncompeting tourism-related business targeting the same demographic. For example, you might own a hotel near a ski hill. If this is the case, you want to inquire with the ski hill to see whether or not you could exchange banner ads or links, or offer a special online cross-promotional deal to their customers. For instance, the ski hill could offer a 10% room discount to their customers and you could offer $5 off the price of ski lift tickets to your guests. These offers can be promoted through banner ads on each site. Cross-promotion can be mutually beneficial to both tourism operations.

Online and Offline Promotion

Your advertising strategy shouldn't be limited to online activities. It is important to integrate your offline advertising strategy to include promotion of your tourism web site. For more information on offline promotion see Chapter 21.

Internet Resources

Banner Ad Tools

The Banner Generator
http://www.coder.com/creations/banner

The Banner Generator is a free service to let you create graphical banners for your web pages.

The Media Builder
http://www.mediabuilder.com/abm.html
Create your own custom animated banners right here. No fancy plug-ins or hard thinking required.

Animation Online
www.animationonline.com
Create your own animated banner in minutes for free from this site.

Animated Communications
http://www.animation.com
Another online resource to build your own animated banners in minutes.

Creative Connectivity
http://www.crecon.com
Home of the Instant Online Banner Creator.

Online Advertising Agencies

MMG, The Online Agency
http://www.mmgco.com/index.html
MMG specializes exclusively in online media planning, buying, tracking, and reporting. They combine state-of-the-art technology with expert knowledge to place advertising for clients in the right place, before the right audience, at the right time, and for the right price. For companies with quarterly online advertising budgets of $100,000 or more.

Thielen Online
http://www.thielenonline.com/index.htm
A full-service advertising agency, located in Fresno and Sacramento, California, with strategic online marketing and complete web site development capabilities.

Lunar Group Interactive
http://www.lunargrp.com/
Lunar Group Interactive is a full-service advertising agency with expertise in traditional mediums, as well as one that embraces the future of marketing. Clients include Casio and Imtech.

Ad Networks

24/7 Media
http://www.247media.com
24/7 Media is a top-reach network of branded sites in a vast variety of categories. This allows their advertisers to zone in on their target market and get the results they want from their online marketing efforts.

AdForce
http://www.adforce.com
AdForce offers a powerful central server-based system that provides an end-to-end online ad management service for both web publishers (the sellers of advertising space) and advertisers and their agencies (the buyers).

Adsmart Network
http://www.adsmart.net
Adsmart, a majority-owned operating company of CMGI, Inc., is an online advertising network composed of more than 375 web sites totaling 2 billion monthly impressions.

Ad-Up Advertiser Services
http://www.ad-up.com
With a targeted ad buy, Ad-Up guarantees you'll get at least a 3% click-through rate (the industry average is close to 0.5%) That's a 600% improvement in response over the industry average.

B2B Works
http://www.b2bworks.com

B2B Works has well over 70 different industries in their network and are emerging as an ad network leader. They can target a specific industry of your choice, or advertise your banner to a mass audience.

BURST! Media
http://www.burstmedia.com
BURST! helps manage more than 13 million advertising impressions per day in more than 400 purchase categories for its more than 2800 publisher members.

Click-Through Services
http://www.clickthrough.com
Click-Through's combined network of online newspapers and other media sites delivers 50 million page views per month.

DoubleClick
http://www.doubleclick.com
The DoubleClick ad network goal is to provide solutions to make advertising work for companies on the Internet. They offer five different types of services to help advertisers prosper on the Internet. They will enable you to market globally and locally. They can help you to build brand awareness or to close the loop on your target market. DoubleClick also offers its clients the opportunity to participate in the e-commerce world by offering online sales technology to their advertisers who would like to sell products online.

Flycast Communications
http://www.flycast.com
Flycast Communications is the leading provider of Internet direct-response advertising solutions. They strive to help companies get the best return on investment for their marketing dollar.

ValueClick
http://www.valueclick.com
ValueClick is the Internet's largest results-based advertising network. They use a cost-per-click model, which enables participants to pay only for the viewers that click through to their web site.

Banner Exchanges

The Banner Exchange
http://www.bannerexchange.com
When you register, you agree to show banners on your site. Each time a banner is displayed on your site you receive half a credit. For every full credit you accumulate, your banner will be shown on the Banner Exchange network of web pages.

Link Exchange
http://www.linkexchange.com
Free banner advertising on over 450,000 web sites. Support for over 3000 geographic regions and subject categories and over 30 languages. They also provide reports and statistics about the people who visit your site.

Smart Clicks
http://www.smartclicks.com
Free banner exchange with automatic or manual targeting, animation allowed, real-time reporting, and much more!

BannerExchange.com
http://www.bannerexchange.com
The BannerExchange.com offers you the opportunity to advertise on their growing network of web sites. They will display your banner on a 2:1 display ratio.

GSAnet
http://bs.gsanet.com
GSAnet Banner Swap is unique in that it offers up to a 1:1 display ratio to members depending on where you locate the banner on your web page(s). In addition, small sites (sites with few visitors) see an even greater ratio due to what are called "charity banners."

Link Media
http://www.linkmedia.com/network
LinkMedia Free Exchange is a free service for the Internet community. As a member, you will receive free banner advertising on other member sites. In return, you will display banner ads on your site.

Banner Advertising Price Information

Ad Resource
http://www.adresource.com
Web advertising, marketing resources, and secrets. Ad Resource offers an extensive price guide about Internet advertising, including what the top 100 sites are charging. This site also has a large number of web advertising related links.

Online Advertising Education

Nielsens Net Ratings
http://www.netratings.com
Nielsens Net Ratings provides you with continuously updated statistics on the top advertisers on the Internet, and which banner advertisements are the most commonly viewed on the Internet. They also offer a wide range of other Internet-related statistics that may prove important to your marketing needs.

Web Site Promoters Resource Center
http://www.wprc.com
The focus of the Web Site Promoters Resource Center is to stay on the cutting edge of the developing web site promotion industry. If you are looking for resources to help conduct your own promotional campaign or seek to hire a professional staff to conduct it for you, this is a good place to start.

Four Corners Effective Banners
http://www.bannertips.com/
This site is dedicated to the study of all things banner-like, including banners, click-through ratios, banner advertising, banner link exchanging, and so on. You'll learn how to improve your banners and increase your site traffic. The best part is that this entire site is free!

Mark Welch's Web Site Banner Advertising Site
http://www.markwelch.com/bannerad
A great site about ad networks, brokers, exchanges, pay-per-click and pay-per-sale (commission) ads, counters, trackers, software, and much more.

Advertising Age Magazine
http://adage.com/news_and_features/deadline
This advertising industry publication always has interesting articles on advertising online.

Internet Advertising Bureau Online Advertising Effectiveness Study
http://www.mbinteractive.com/site/iab/study.html
The IAB Online Advertising Effectiveness Study is the most comprehensive and projectable test of online advertising effectiveness to date. With 12 major web sites and over 16,000 individual users taking part in the test, the study ranks as the largest, most rigorous test of advertising effectiveness conducted to date in any medium.

14

Associate and Affiliate Programs

Associate and affiliate programs began in 1996 when Amazon.com *(www.amazon.com)* began to pay Web sites for referring customers to their site. If you joined Amazon's affiliate program and properly coded a link on your web site that directed a visitor to the Amazon.com web site, and the visitor then decided to purchase an item, you received a percentage of that sale. Today we see many sites following in the footsteps of Amazon.com. These affiliate programs, also known as associate programs and referral programs, are now very common in the Internet marketplace.

Many different affiliate programs are available on the Internet. These programs all vary in terms of reliability, quality, and the amount of commissions offered. E-tailers have these programs to develop repeat business and increase sales. A side benefit to having an affiliate program is that every affiliate provides a link to your site, which in turn improves link popularity, which in turn improves search engine ranking in a number of the popular search engines. On the downside, developing and implementing the affiliate program takes time and effort, and you have to be competitive with other affiliate programs to encourage participation. In this chapter you will learn:

- How to distinguish between the different types of affiliate programs

- How to pick the appropriate affiliate program for your tourism operation

- Tips to succeed with affiliate programs

- The benefits of affiliate programs

- How to start your own tourism affiliate programs

- Important features for affiliate tracking software

- Affiliate program resources

Affiliate Programs—Increase Traffic to Your Tourism Site

To understand the opportunities available with affiliate programs, you must first understand the different types of affiliate programs. All pay for referral business, but in different ways. Before you decide to participate in an affiliate program, you must first look at your objectives, your products and services, your target market, and, more important whether you take reservations or sell products or services directly from your site. Then decide whether an affiliate program is appropriate for your tourism operation. Most of these programs are designed to electronically track your visitors from the referring site to the final purchase and electronically calculate the commission due to the referring site. If your tourism operation does not do electronic reservations or sell products via e-commerce on your site, you will have to assess how an affiliate program would work for you and how you would monitor and track the results. Once you have affirmed that an affiliate program is appropriate for your operation, you then choose the type of program that works for you.

Commission-Based Affiliate Programs

The most common type of affiliate program is the commission-based program. The commission-based program offers Web sites a chance to make a percentage of sales resulting from their referrals. Commissions typically range from 1% to 15%. Some programs offer a two-tier commission structure, and some offer an increased amount of commission for those who have higher traffic sites. 1TravelNow.com is a great example of a more popular tourism-related affiliate program (see Figure 14.1). They offer affiliates the opportunity to earn up to 50% of commissions made on sales through referrals from their web sites. Other examples of tourism-related commission based affiliate programs include:

- TravelNow.com   *www.travelnow.com*

- Inntopia.com   *www.inntopia.com*

- 1travel.com   *www.onetravel.com*

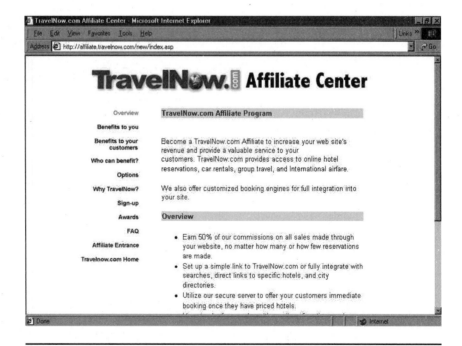

Figure 14.1.   TravelNow.com's affiliate program is a geat example of a commission-based program.

Flat-Fee Referral Programs

The flat-fee referral programs will pay a web site a fixed amount for every new visitor who links from the referring site to the host site and takes certain predefined actions. The required action is quite often making a purchase on the host site. Other flat-fee programs do not require the purchase of an item. The predetermined actions might be making a reservation, ordering a brochure, requesting further information, or another action desired by the host site. A good example of this is HotelGuide.com (see Figure 14.2) where you can make hotel reservations online. If you join the HotelGuide.com affiliate program and place a link on your site that encourages a viewer to make a reservation using the HotelGuide.com web site, you will receive a flat-fee commission. Here are the links to HotelGuide.com and two other tourism related web sites that offer flat-fee affiliate programs from their web site.

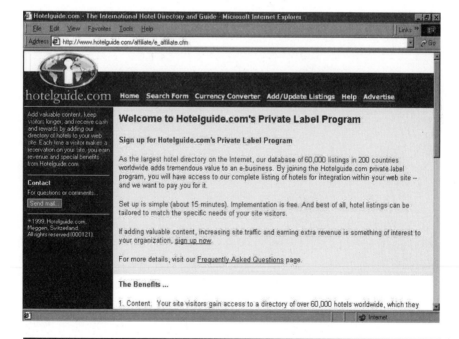

Figure 14.2. HotelGuide.com has a unique program offering its affiliates money for every person that makes a hotel reservation from the HotelGuide.com Web site. This is an example of a flat rate referral program.

- HotelGuide.com *http://www.hotelguide.com/*

- Travelocity.com *http://www.travelocity.com/*

- Online Reservationz *http://www.onlinerez.com/*

Click-Through Programs

A click-through program is one in which affiliates receive a fee for every unique visitor that clicks through from the affiliate's site. The click-through will come from a referring link or banner ad that has been placed on their web site. The typical click-through fee would be between 1 and 10 cents. There are many click-through programs available on the Internet. A good example would be CruiseDirectOnline.com (see Figure 14.3). If you join the CruiseDirectOnline.com affiliate program, you will receive a click-through fee when you send a unique visitor to the CruiseDirectOnline.com web site. Some popular tourism-related click-through programs are:

- CruiseDirectOnline.com *http:www.cruisedirecton line.com/*

- Discover Afrika *http://www.discover-afrika.com/*

- Priceline.com *http://www.priceline.com/*

Selecting an Affiliate Program That Is Right for You

The first thing that you should do when deciding whether to start an affiliate program is to ask yourself if this fits in with your tourism operation's web site objectives and if the program is something that would be of interest to your target audience. Click-through programs that work with banner ads can serve to increase traffic to your web site as long as your banner ad is designed with your target market in mind and the banner ad is placed on tourism-related sites that are of interest

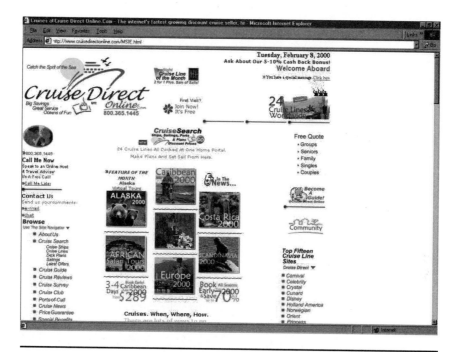

Figure 14.3. The CruiseDirectOnline.com affiliate program is an excellent example of a click-through program.

to your target market. Commission-based and flat-fee affiliate programs can go further in having the referred visitors do what you want them to do when they get to your site. The referring site knows that they only receive their commission when a certain action has been taken by the visitor, whether that action be an online reservation, a quote request, or something else. The referring site has a vested interest in having the referred visitor take that action, and they are in a position to suggest or recommend that the visitor take that action.

How To Succeed With Your Affiliate Site

You may have an affiliate program, but are you really doing all that you can to exploit it? There are several things that you can do to be successful with an affiliate program. You should go out of your way to help make the links stand out on your affiliates' sites. Provide different-sized icons that grab visitors' attention and are designed with the target market in mind. Also, prepare the proper HTML coding and a tag line linking to your web site, and you will help your affiliates get the attention of their visitors. You can also inspect your affiliates' web sites regularly to determine whether or not you can do anything to help them add value to the links on their pages. You could offer them advice about where they should locate their links if they have them in an obscure place on their web site. Remember that you don't run their web sites, so make it clear that you are simply offering advice and not trying to run their site.

You should also make sure that you, the affiliate program administrator, do your best to be prompt with reporting and referral payments. People will not want to participate in your program if you are late with payments or don't provide them with detailed reports of their referrals from the last reporting period. By sticking to the program schedule and doing the best you can for your affiliates, you will not only keep your affiliates happy, you will also advance the interest of your tourism operation's affiliate program.

How Affiliate Programs Can Benefit Your Tourism Operation

There are many benefits to having an affiliate program for your tourism operation's Web site. There are also some not-so-obvious advantages. By creating your own affiliate program you may generate a significant increase in traffic to your tourism-oriented web site. When your affiliates place links on their web sites linking to your site, you will increase your link popularity. This generates a significant amount of traffic to your site and also helps to increase your search engine rankings. Some of the major search engines use link popularity in their search engine ranking criteria. Once you have successfully launched your affiliate program and have developed a wide sales force on the Internet, you may be surprised with the amount of new traffic you have to your tourism operation's web site.

Your greatest advantage is the opportunity to expand your sales force to thousands of people. If you run a good affiliate program, your sales force could consist of people all over the world, thus expanding your target market into different cultures your personal sales force might have otherwise not been able to penetrate.

Starting Your Own Affiliate Program

If you have a tourism-related product or service that you are trying to sell online, you should consider starting your own affiliate program. It is an easy way to generate a wide sales force for your products or services while continuing to retain most of the profits, but what is involved in starting your own affiliate program?

First you must decide which type of program you want to offer to your affiliates—click-through, flat rate, or commission based.

The second, more important step in setting up your tourism operation's affiliate program is deciding which type of tracking software you are going to use to monitor your affiliate program. This is important, because like any other part of your web site, you want it to be as user friendly as possible. You should make it easy for your affiliates to verify how well they are doing with your program. There are several options for tracking your affiliates' success: developing mirror sites for each of your affiliates, using an affiliate program service, and purchasing affiliate tracking software.

Develop Mirror Sites for Each of Your Affiliates

This is one of the original ways of tracking affiliates. What you actually have to do is set up a mirror site for each of your affiliates. This is a separate page for each of your affiliates to use when directing consumers to your tourism site.

For example, let's say that you are developing your mirror page for your first affiliate. Your site is *http://www.yourdomain.com,* but you can assign your first affiliate the URL of *http://www.yourdomain.com/index1.html.* Your first affiliate would be indexed as affiliate number one, and all sales that came from this mirror page would be traced to her. You would repeat this process for the next affiliate, and so on.

The problems that occur when using mirror sites to track your affiliates is that they are aimed more specifically at people who have only one product to sell. If you had more than one product, you would have to design multiple mirror pages for each of your affiliates, and this would be very time-consuming. With more pages for each of your affiliates, tracking sales may become confusing due to sheer volume. When changes are made to any of the pages—for example, a graphic is updated—you would have to modify the graphic on each of your affiliates' mirror pages. This is very time-consuming. If you didn't host your site on your own server, you would also have to be concerned with the cost for hosting. With more pages on your ISP's server, you would have to pay more, and if each of these pages was receiving high amounts of traffic (as you hope) you would have to pay for more bandwidth.

Pay an Affiliate Program Service To Track Your Affiliates' Success

Another avenue you can explore when starting your own affiliate program is to pay an affiliate program service to track your affiliates' traffic and their activities (see Figure 14.4). The affiliate program service can provide everything you need to have a good affiliate program. Full tracking services provide real-time statistics for your affiliates so that they know how they are doing with sales, and the tracking service takes care of the accounting side as well. They calculate the amount due to your affiliates at the end of every reporting period. The affiliate program service providers charge a fee for their services. Some of the more popular affiliate program services are:

- Affiliate Shop   *http://www.affiliateshop.com*

- ClickTrade   *http://www.clicktrade.com*

These services take care of everything for you from developing and implementing the program to providing you with activity reports. However, if your objective for starting your tourism operation's affiliate program is to make more money, you might want to do a few calculations to determine the cost. With the affiliate program service, you not only have to pay your affiliates, you also have to pay for the tracking service, which in turn cuts into your profits.

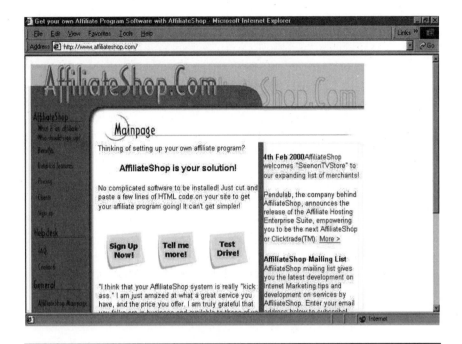

Figure 14.4. AffiliateShop.Com is just one of many affiliate service providers available if you want to start your own affiliate program. They will manage your program and make tracking your affiliate sales easy, which can save you a lot of time.

Purchasing Affiliate Tracking Software

If you want to bring the tracking of your affiliates in-house, your best bet is to purchase affiliate tracking software. Companies have developed comprehensive tracking software that allow you to provide maximum service to your affiliates. Depending on what features you would like to provide to your affiliates, the cost of tracking software ranges anywhere from $300 to $15,000.

There are many varieties of affiliate tracking software. Some software programs are quite unsophisticated and offer very few features, and others offer them all. There are some features that you should watch for when purchasing your software. They can help you to run a very smooth affiliate program and can save you a lot of time. Outlined here are some of the more important features available.

Automated Signup

You should always look for this feature because you want to make it as easy as possible for your affiliates to sign up for your program. It should not take them days to officially sign up for your program. They should be able to do so automatically. You want them to get started as quickly as possible, so as soon as they sign up they should automatically be sent all information that you feel necessary for them to quickly incorporate your program on their web site.

Automated Tracking Systems

This is one of the most important features that you must look for. You want to make sure that your software is capable of tracking all sales made so that you can reward your affiliates with the appropriate commission. You don't want to have to calculate which web sites the sales came from at the end of the month. You want to be able to let the software do all of the tracking for you and at the end of the reporting period provide you with a report outlining payment due to your affiliates.

Automatic Contact Systems

You should be able to contact all of your affiliates whenever you find it necessary. Some software allows you to send messages to all of your affiliates at the click of a button. It compiles their e-mail addresses in a database.

Real-Time Statistics

Real-time statistics allow your affiliates to view their current sales statistics. This will let them know how many people clicked through from their site and how many of those people actually purchased something. This is a very good feature because it is important to keep your affiliates informed about their current sales status in your program.

Variable-Payment Option

Another important feature that you should look for is the variable-payment option. Some forms of affiliate software will only let you work with so many variables, meaning the fixed fee, percentage, or flat rate per click-through that you multiply by the referral from your affiliates' sites. Some software is only designed for certain types of programs. You might purchase software designed to calculate payments for a click-through program. If you wanted to have a commission-based program that pays a percentage of sales resulting from each click-through, this software would not be good for you. It would not be able to comprehend and manipulate data to calculate the payments, because it is incapable of using the percentage of sales variable. You should remember to check this out before you purchase any software.

Automatic Check Payment

As soon as your tourism operation's affiliate program is up and running and you have developed an extensive list of affiliates, it can become a hassle to write checks at the end of each payment period. Some software comes equipped with an automatic check payment option that allows your computer to print off the checks payable at the end of the payment periods. This can make your tourism operation's affiliate program run very smoothly and can also save you lots of time.

Automatic Reporting Period Statistic Distribution

Some of the more advanced affiliate tracking software will automatically e-mail each of your affiliates at the end of the reporting period, which is usually one week. This keeps your affiliates informed as to how much success they are having with your program, and allows them to adjust their marketing strategy to help them to succeed with your program.

Here are some of the more popular affiliate tracking software programs that are available to people wanting to start their own affiliate program:

Affiliate Link
http://www.affiliatezone.com
Affiliate Link enables you to do everything from signing up affiliates to checking on both administrative and individual affiliate statistics.

Affiliate Program
http://www.theaffiliateprogram.com/entry.htm
This affiliate tracking software allows you to manage all of your affiliate members and track impressions, click-throughs, and online sales.

The Travelocity.com Example

Travelocity.com has a well-organized affiliate program for its travel site. For this reason, we will now walk through how they have set up their affiliate program. The Travelocity.com affiliate program model is a good one for you to follow if you intend to establish an affiliate program of your own.

Travelocity.com describes their affiliate program as follows:

The Travelocity.com on-line affiliate program not only gives you the links that connect your users to the leading travel site on the Internet, but also pays you when your site visitors book and purchase. You choose the kind of links, the number of links, and their placement on your site. Each time your site visitors click-through to Travelocity.com and book and purchase an airline ticket or VIA Rail Canada ticket, you earn a commission!

As Travelocity.com describes it, the affiliate program sounds easy for both the affiliate and Travelocity.com. Upon further inspection, we can see that this is the case. Prospective affiliate members can link through to the Travelocity.com affiliate program information page directly from Travelocity.com's home page (see Figure 14.5). You should also make your affiliate program this easy to find on your site.

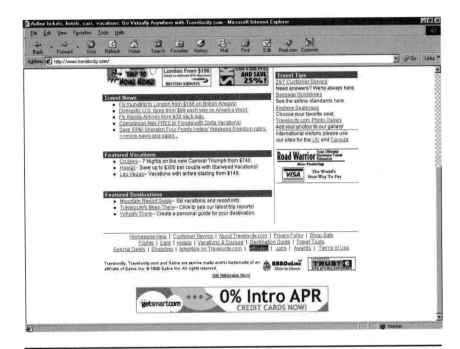

Figure 14.5. Visitors can access the Travelocity.com afflilate program page directly from the Travelocity.com homepage.

Like Travelocity.com, you will need an information page or section of pages explaining the details of your affiliate program to visitors. Figure 14.6 shows you the Travelocity.com information page. It is well written and walks potential affiliate members through a series of steps that describe the details of the program (what the affiliate program is, the commission rate, how commissions are paid, and so on). Current affiliate program members can also log in to their account from this page and inspect their sales statistics. Ensure that you provide a place on your site for affiliate members to log in and provide adequate information about your affiliate program so that potential affiliates understand its potential.

Next you will require a sign-up form for your affiliate program. Figure 14.7 displays a portion of Travelocity.com's associate program application form. Only ask applicants for necessary information. This will keep the length of your signup form brief and encourage more new members to join.

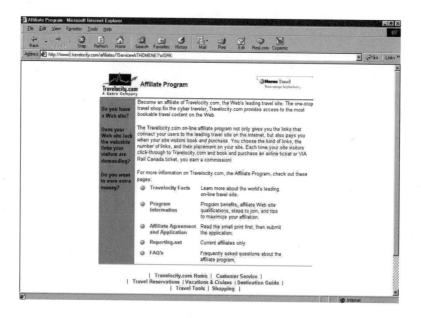

Figure 14.6. The affiliate program information page on Travelocity.com.

Figure 14.7. Like Travelocity.com, make it easy for new members to join your affiliate program by providing a concise application form on your site.

Once people complete and submits the affiliate program application form, Travelocity.com immediately sends the linking code to the new members to include on their sites. The following code is an example of what you might receive from Travelocity.com:

<A HREF="http://service.bfast.com/bfast/click/travelocity?sourceid=814396&categoryid=homepage">img SRC="http://www2.travelocity.com/affiliates/bttns4affils/header_1.gif" BORDER="0" WIDTH="460" HEIGHT="82" ALT="Travelocity"></a>

As you can see, the URL to the affiliate's page is quite lengthy. However, there is no need to memorize it. Affiliate members simply have to Copy and Paste this linking text into the HTML code of the pages of their site. As described earlier, provide affiliate members with tips on where to include and how to present the affiliate link on their site. On the site shown in Figure 14.8, the affiliate simply links to the Travelocity.com affiliate page by inserting the linking text

Figure 14.8. Persuade your affiliate members to make the link to your site prominent as The Internationalist (*http://www.internationalist.com/*) has done with their Travelocity.com affiliate program link.

around the Travelocity.com banner ad. The affiliate link is prominently displayed on the affiliate's site, so if visitors are interested in Travelocity.com's services, they click on the banner ad and are linked through to Travelocity.com, where they can proceed with the transaction (see Figure 14.9).

Thus, Travelocity.com receives the sale request, processes the order, and books the accommodations and travel arrangements, and the affiliate member receives a 15% commission from the order. Travelocity.com sends the affiliate a weekly sales report and a check for the commissions earned after affiliate sales reach a certain level.

Once again, the point of presenting this example of how the Travelocity.com affiliate program operates is to give you some ideas about what you should include in your affiliate program and how

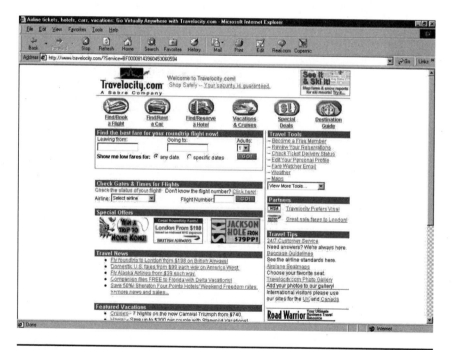

Figure 14.9.   Visitors to your affiliate members' sites can link through to your site. The affiliate members receive a commission for each sale they generate. In this image, a visitor has clicked through from The Internationalist site to the Travelocity.com site. The Internationalist will receive a commission if a sale is made.

you should present the information. With this example and the other details provided in this chapter in mind, you should now be sufficiently informed to initiate an affiliate program of your own.

Internet Resources

AssociatePrograms.com
http://www.associateprograms.com/
The AssociatePrograms.com directory helps you find the best associate programs—also known as referral, partner, revenue sharing, or affiliate programs—to earn money from your Web site.

Refer-it.com
http://www.refer-it.com
Refer-it.com is the authoritative guide to Internet affiliate programs, associate programs, and referral programs. Refer-it is a great resource for merchants with affiliate programs and webmasters with affiliate web sites.

AssociatePrograms.co.uk
http://www.associateprograms.co.uk/
A UK guide to affiliate marketing and associate programs. Listings and ratings of many programs by category. Includes headlines, tips, advice, and free weekly news updates.

Associate-It
http://www.associate-it.com/
Claims to be the Web's biggest directory of associate programs.

I-Revenue.net
http://www.I-Revenue.net
Claims to be one of the largest affiliate program directories on the Internet.

ClickQuick: Affiliate and Pay-per-Click Program Reviews
http://www.clickquick.com/
In-depth reviews of webmaster affiliate, associate, and pay-per-click programs that offer opportunities to make money on the Internet.

Also reviews of banner ad networks and helpful articles on improving affiliate program performance.

CashPile.com
http://www.cashpile.com/
Comprehensive directory/search engine for revenue sharing (affiliate, associate, referral, and bounty) programs.

AssociateCash.com
http://www.associatecash.com/
AssociateCash.com reviews different associate and affiliate programs and rates them. Learn which affiliate programs earn webmasters money.

Popular Tourism Sites With Affiliate Programs

Travelocity.com
www.travelocity.com
Travelocity.com has one of the number one rated tourism related affiliate programs online. At Travelocity.com you can find low air fares on the Internet with the best fare finder, make hotel and car reservations, and research vacation destinations online.

Inntopia.com
www.inntopia.com
Inntopia.com is your real-time online leisure travel reservation network.

Priceline.com
www.priceline.com
Priceline Travel is the only way consumers can name their own price for airline tickets, hotel rooms, groceries, new cars, home finance, and more.

TravelNow
www.travelnow.com
TravelNow.com provides access to online hotel reservations, car rentals, group travel, and International airfare

FareAgent.com
www.fareagent.com
Your personal travel service, where you name the price and schedule
and they continue to look while you sleep.

More Popular Affiliate Programs

Amazon.com
www.amazon.com
A pioneer in the affiliate program industry, Amazon.com boasts earth's
biggest selection of products, including free electronic greeting cards,
online auctions, and millions of books, CDs, videos, DVDs, toys and
games, and electronics.

CDNow
www.cdnow.com
CDNOW is the world's leading online music store.

Reel.com
www.reel.com
Reel.com is one of the biggest places online to buy movies.

Barnes and Noble
www.barnesandnoble.com
BarnesandNoble.com offers a wide selection of books, and has over
120,000 Web sites participating in their affiliate program.

Tunes.com
www.tunes.com
Steal Our Sites is Tunes.com's affiliate program. Tunes.com is the
Internet's definitive music hub, combining the Web's largest collec-
tion of music content with programming and content from
RollingStone.com, TheSource.com, and DownBeatJazz.com.

15

The Cybermall Advantage

Cybermalls are Internet shopping centers that contain "stores" related to a specific theme. Some of the more successful malls concentrate on a specific type of product or service category. These cybermalls bring in targeted, interested people, looking for a specific type of product or service—including tourism destinations. In this chapter we cover:

- Can your site benefit from being linked in cybermalls?

- Cybermall features

- Types of cybermalls—which is best suited to your business?

- Where to look for cybermalls

- Discounts and coupons to lure customers

- Selecting the appropriate cybermall

- What will it cost?

- Checking visitor statistics

The Advantages of Internet Shopping Centers

Cybermalls are collections of commercial web sites on the Internet. There are literally thousands of cybermalls, and they are increasingly growing in popularity. Cybermalls provide an arena where people can shop online via the Internet. As in traditional malls, cybermall merchants benefit by receiving more traffic due to the promotional power of, and services offered by, the mall owner and the other participants. These malls are accessed by the consumer through a common Internet address.

Some cybermalls will design, build, and host your web site, and offer ongoing maintenance of your site for a fee that is comparable to other web developers and service providers. Other malls simply provide a link to your site on another server. If you already have a web site and choose this option, the charges are generally a lot less.

Cyber-malls
Internet shopping centers.

When Are Cybermalls Appropriate?

There are many different reasons that tourism operations choose the cybermall route. Some companies choose to participate in a cybermall and also offer their accommodations, products, or services from their own site. Some companies choose to participate in a number of different cybermalls. Any one of the following may provide sound reasoning for their business decision.

- *You don't know how or don't have the time to work on building traffic to your site.* In a cybermall the onus is on the mall to perform online and offline marketing activities to increase the traffic to their site. Your site will benefit from the general traffic that comes through the mall doors as long as your product is of interest to the incoming mall visitors.

- *You don't have a secure server.* The fact that a cybermall has a secure server may be reason enough to locate your online business there. If you are going to be selling online you need a **secure server**, and the volume of business you are going to do may not warrant

Secure server
A server allowing secure credit card transactions.

the purchase price and expertise required to set up your own secure server.

- *You can locate your online storefront in a niche mall that caters to your segment of the travel or tourism industry.*

- *You don't have a credit card merchant account.* Some financial institutions charge a premium for small business merchant accounts when the business is going to be selling online or may even refuse to provide a merchant account for online vendors. The cybermall may provide merchant accounts or merchant account services to its tenants.

E-com- merce The buying and selling of goods and ser- vices on the Internet.

- *You don't have credit card validation.* Many malls provide electronic commerce or **e-commerce** solutions for their tenants. Credit card validation online means that once the purchasers provide their credit card number as payment, the transaction is then authorized and approved by their financial institution. The transaction amount is automatically deposited into the bank account of the vendor, minus, of course, the credit card commission and usually the credit card validation charge.

- *You don't have shopping cart capability.* Shopping carts online allow mall visitors to drop items into their shopping cart as they travel through an online store or cybermall with a click of their mouse. When they have finished their shopping they can review and edit their invoice online. They may decide they wanted to purchase two luggage sets rather than one, and can make the change with one keystroke. Similarly, a golf pro shop may establish an e-commerce system to allow customers to pick and choose items for purchase. Customers may delete a few items when they see that the total of the invoice is more than they were planning to spend. When the online invoice reflects exactly what they want, they complete the transaction by providing their credit card for payment. Where a tourism operator does not have the technical or financial resources to put shopping carts on its site, a cybermall might provide this valuable service.

Cybermall Categories

Cybermalls can be organized in a number of ways. These are described next.

Geographic Region

All of the tenants are located in the same geographic region. Many of these cybermalls are provided by an ISP for its clients. In many cases participation in these types of malls is done to provide easy access through a variety of means for the customer, to build name recognition with the local customer base, and as a means of advertising and cross-promotion. You may wish to consider joining a cybermall that is associated with your geographic region if your target market is more likely to look for information about your specific region before they would look for your tourism operation. Figure 15.1 offers an example of a regional tourism cybermall.

Figure 15.1. Victoria British Columbia Tourism Mall (*http://
tourismmall.victoria.bc.ca*).

Products and/or Services

All of the tenants provide similar types of products. These types of cybermalls are of interest to the same target market. A tourism or travel cybermall would consist of a number of merchants all providing products or services related to traveling and vacationing. Figures 15.2 and 15.3 illustrate a couple of the cybermalls available.

Industry

All of the tenants would be in the same industry. A financial services industry cybermall would provide a wide range of different products and services in insurance, banking, investment, and accounting. Likewise there are tourism/travel/vacation cybermalls that focus on companies that provide products and services related to the industry.

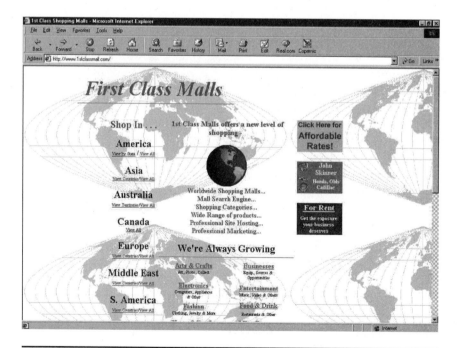

Figure 15.2. First Class Shopping Malls (*http://www.1stclassmall.com/*) hosts regional malls from all over the world and also provides listings by type of product or service.

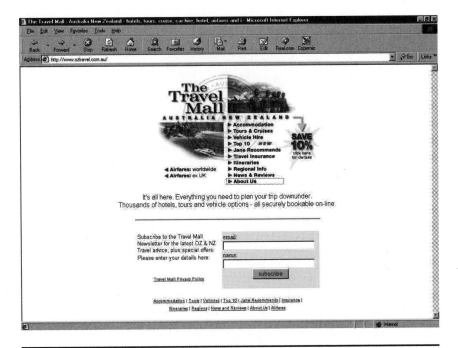

Figure 15.3.   The Travel Mall, Australia and New Zealand (*http://www. oztravel.com.au*) provides travel-related products and services in Australia and New Zealand.

Unrelated Products and Services Catering to One Demographic

Some cybermalls have tenants that provide a variety of unrelated products and services to the same demographic. There should always be some common theme that ties the visitors together for target marketing purposes. A seniors' cybermall that has vendors providing everything from travel to insurance to financial services to medical aids would be a good example of this type of cybermall.

Typical Cybermall Products and Services

Most of the items you would find in your local shopping malls are appropriate for a cybermall. Some items that are not typically found in retail shopping centers because of the space requirements, such as car dealerships, are also appropriate for cybermalls. Products and services that are popular in cybermalls today include:

- Travel

- Software

- Books

- Computers

- Electronics

- Gifts

- Games

- Clothing

- Arts and collectibles

- Automotive

- Food

- Health and fitness

- Housewares

- Financial products and services

- Professional services

- Sports and recreation

- Specialty shops

Some malls choose to concentrate on a specific niche, such as the one shown in Figure 15.4. The niche can be a type of product or service category. These malls bring in very targeted, interested people looking

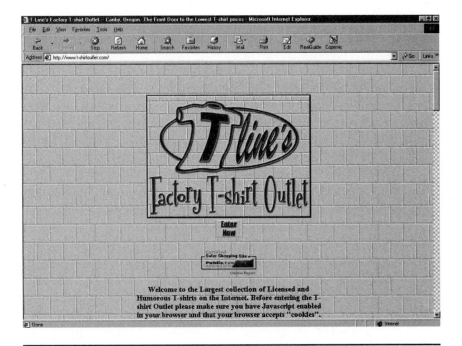

Figure 15.4. The Factory T-shirt Outlet is a storefront that focuses on one product but provides a range of services such as gift-wrapping, delivery, and a "dressing room."

for a specific type of product or service. There are a number of cybermalls focusing on niche categories in the travel and tourism industry.

Selecting the Right Cybermall

Before you commit to a cybermall that is going to host your tourism operation's web site, you should check a number of things in your evaluation process. Choosing a successful mall is tricky, but if you use the following guidelines you will be better equipped to make the right decision.

High-Speed Access

The cybermall merchant should have a high-speed connection (T1, ISDN, ADSL, or cable). If access is slow, the visitors will not wait.

This is very similar to traditional retail outlets. If the line at the cash register is too long, customers will not wait and will shop elsewhere.

Home Page and Interface

A good cybermall should have a good-quality, attractive home page with consistent navigation throughout the site. It is great if there is space for specials, coupons or other advertising that you might choose to participate in.

Domain Name

The mall you choose should have a logical and easy-to-remember domain name.

Hardware

The cybermall's server should be reliable, state-of-the-art, fast, and have lots of capacity to handle the anticipated volume. There should be technicians available to provide technical support and quickly resolve any problems that occur.

Categories

Before choosing a mall, make sure that your operation fits within one of the categories in the mall. Don't join a mall that is targeting a different demographic than yours.

Online and Offline Promotion

Make sure that the mall you choose is promoted both online and offline. Many of the malls only promote online. The cybermall owner should be able to provide you with details of its Internet marketing strategy to increase the traffic of its targeted market to their site.

Site Maintenance Activities

Successful web sites must be updated on a continual basis. Ensure that the mall provides software tools to make it easy for you to maintain your own site or, if the mall provides the updates, that their fees regarding changes are not too expensive.

Traffic

Obtain details on mall traffic and the number of unique visitors to the home page of the mall, if possible. Any other count of hits may include hits to the pages of merchants in the mall, which would be misleading. Talk with other merchants residing in the mall about their traffic, as well as their experience with the mall itself (fee increases, hidden costs, server downtime, etc.). Many progressive malls now provide their tenants with access to their web traffic analysis reports.

Secure Server

Ensure that the mall has a secure server, allowing you to offer secure credit card sales transactions. Most consumers will not purchase on-line without it.

Credit Card Merchant Account

Merchant accounts for the popular credit cards are usually difficult to obtain for businesses with only a virtual presence. If you don't have a merchant account, you will want to choose a mall that offers this service.

Promotions

Find out what promotional efforts the mall is involved in. Many malls indicate that they promote extensively but ensure they are actually targeting shoppers not merchants.

Commission Fees

Some malls charge a commission on every sale. Check the details on all commissions, transaction fees, and other charges. If the mall is responsible for all the traffic to your site, they should be compensated for this activity through your monthly rental charge or a commission on sales. If you are making an effort to promote your tourism operation's site yourself and the traffic to your site is a result of your marketing efforts, it is unreasonable for the mall to expect to be compensated for each and every transaction on your site.

Cybermall History and Reputation

Find out how long the mall has been in existence. Talk to existing tenants and past tenants about their experience.

Other Features and Services Provided by the Cybermall

Cybermalls may include a variety of other products and services to their tenants, as shown in Figure 15.5. When comparing cybermalls, make sure you are comparing apples with apples. Some additional features and services provided by cybermalls might include the supply of mailing lists or autoresponders, or the provision of chat rooms and bulletin boards.

Cybermall Features

Cybermalls may provide a number of features to their tenants as well as to the tenant's customers.

Electronic Shopping Carts

Shopping carts, like the one shown in Figure 15.6, are a necessity if you offer a variety of products from your site. They enable users to click on items they would like to purchase from mall vendors and

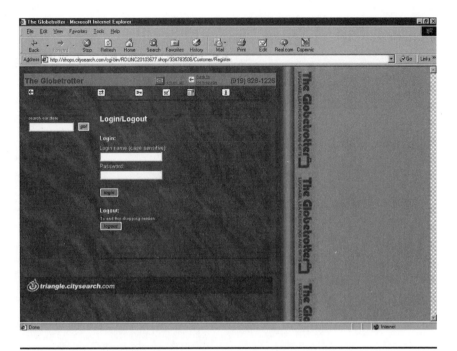

Figure 15.5.   TheGlobetrotter.com (*http://www.theglobetrotter.com*) allows you to register your billing information and ship to addresses to expedite your checkout process.

put them in their shopping cart. At the end of their online shopping trip, the users have an opportunity to review the contents of their cart as well as the invoice. Purchases can be edited before an order is placed.

Secure Ordering

Most cybermalls offer a secure server and encrypted transactions for their tenants' online transactions. Technology is advancing rapidly in the area of e-commerce, and the cybermalls are among the first web sites on the Internet to make use of the latest capabilities. Some malls now offer online charge card authorization and automatic deposit for their tenants as well as storing client billing, credit card, and shipping information for return visits to the cybermall.

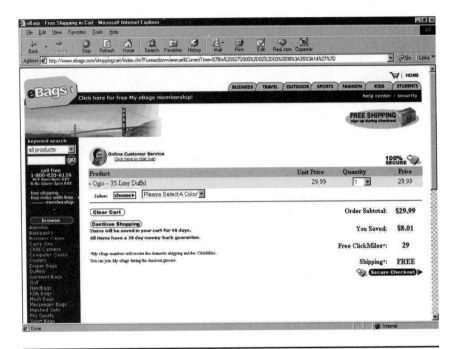

Figure 15.6. eBags (*http://www.ebags.com*) has an online shopping cart system to facilitate your online purchases.

Search Capabilities

Many cybermalls will provide a site search capability to assist shoppers with finding the items they are looking for.

More Than One Cybermall?

It may be appropriate to join more than one cybermall, especially if you have your own site and are just paying a monthly fee for the link from your storefront in the mall to your site. If you decide that this is appropriate for your business, you should have some mechanism in place to track the traffic to your site to determine which malls are effective. This can be accomplished quite easily these days with all the web traffic analysis tools that are available. See Chapter 23 for a full discussion of web traffic analysis.

Cybermall Pricing

Malls charge their tenants in a variety of ways. If you choose a mall that hosts one page as a storefront and a link from that storefront to your site on a different server than the cybermall, the charge is generally a flat fee per month. If your web site is hosted by the cybermall, you may be charged on a flat-fee basis, a basic fee with add-ons, or a commission-on-sales basis. The variable charges are generally on either a commission or set-fee-per-transaction basis.

Cybermall charges to be linked to their storefront can be anywhere from $25 a month to over $1000 a month, depending on the services and number of features provided by the host.

Where to Look for Cybermalls

A number of meta-indexes of cybermalls can be found online. There are cybermall web rings that can be researched and also cybermalls of cybermalls. There are all kinds of locations and sites listed in the Internet Resources at the end of this chapter to assist you in finding the appropriate cybermall for your tourism operation. Listed next are a number of travel- and tourism-related cybermalls that you may wish to investigate.

Travel Malls

1st Class Shopping Malls
http://www.1stclassmall.com/
This cybermall hosts regional malls from all over the world. This could also be a good resource if you are looking for a particular geographically located cybermall.

CyQuest Malls—Adventure Vacations
http://www.cyquest.com/advent.html
Includes resort vacation opportunities from around the globe. CyQuest also has listings for golf and ski products and vacations.

MallPark
http://www2.mallpark.com
Thousands of online merchants by shopping category! Instant searching. Secure order forms, shopping carts, merchant accounts to accept credit cards, and merchants can link for free.

Mallpark's Travel Mall
http://www.mallpark.com/travel/destin.htm
Destinations Mallpark takes the chaos out of shopping on the Internet. Fast, easy, and productive one-stop shoppers' paradise for your every need. Their 54 cybermalls are made up of 1250 shopping centers by shopping category.

Virtual Cities Electronic Mall
http://www.virtualcities.com
Featuring 1st Traveler's Choice bed and breakfasts, country inns and small hotels; vacation rentals and nonhosted lodging, Internet real estate classifieds with a specialty of inns for sale.

Geographic Travel Cybermalls

New England Cybermall Travel & Tourism
http://www.necybermall.com/travel.htm
The travel and tourism pavilion at the New England Cybermall. A virtual guide to New England lighthouses.

Northwest Cybermall
http://www.nwcybermall.com/depts/shopping/travel.html
Shop for and buy travel and leisure opportunities from the Northwest Shop, and buy travel and leisure opportunities from Northwest merchants at the premier online shopping mall.

South Dakota Online
http://www.sdonline.com/
Shop from the directory of South Dakota vendors.

The Mall of America
http://www.mallofamerica.com/
An American tourism cybermall.

The Travel Mall - Australia New Zealand
http://www.oztravel.com.au
Everything you need to plan your trip down under, including thousands of hotels, tours, and vehicle options—all securely bookable online.

Tourism Calgary
http://www.visitor.calgary.ab.ca/travel/shopping.html
A directory of shopping resources in Calgary, Alberta (Canada).

UNLV
http://www.unlv.edu/Tourism/retail.html
The University of Nevada at Las Vegas has established a cybermall for their region.

Victoria British Columbia Tourism Mall
http://tourismmall.victoria.bc.ca
A tourism mall dedicated to the Victoria, BC (Canada) region.

VR Metro Malls
http://www.vrmetro.com/
VR Metro Malls of metropolitan Detroit, serving the southeast Michigan area.

Enticing Customers with Coupons and Discounts

To increase the traffic to your cybermall site, you can post coupons either as banner ads or links from other sites. The sites you choose to host these banner ads or links should be those that appeal to your target market, or you might consider purchasing a keyword from a search engine. See Chapter 13 for advice on appropriate banner advertising.

You can also use online coupons, which can be printed from your site, to increase the traffic to your offline locations. If your customers know they can check your weekly coupons or sales, it will encourage repeat visits.

You might also consider trading coupons with other online vendors who offer products or tourism services complementary to what you do.

Internet Resources

2000 Cybermall Avenue
http://www.cybermallavenue.com
The place to buy anything online. 2000 Cybermall Avenue is an Internet mall where you can purchase almost anything you want online.

The Most Frequently Shopped Malls on the Internet
http://ourworld.compuserve.com/homepages/asappub/CYBER.HTM
Listing the more commonly visited cybermalls on the Internet.

The Hall of Malls
http://nsns.com/MouseTracks/HallofMalls.html
The most comprehensive listing of all known online malls located on the Net.

National Travel & Tourism Mall
http://www.buyersusa.com/malls/malls/travel.cfm
This is a U.S.-based cybermall that is just in its early beginnings. There is a lot of space for rent.

The Cybermall.com Directory
http://www.cybermall.com
Evaluations of hundreds of online malls and a selection of only what they determine are the very best. Malls cannot purchase a listing on this site (unlike other directories) and are selected exclusively because they provide you with a positive home shopping experience. You get

access to the better shopping malls. Their categorical listings include brief site reviews to help you find the quality shopping sites you want without all the work.

Malls.com
http://malls.com
Besides providing a range of products and services from their mall, Malls.com provides a huge meta-index of all the malls on the Net at *http://malls.com/metalist.html*. This list is a great starting point when doing your cybermall research.

ShopNow Market
http://www.internet-mall.com
ShopNow Market's merchandising program gives you two key components to successful online marketing: strategic positioning and targeted, focused traffic generation programs. You'll benefit from their partnerships with high-traffic sites such as Yahoo and PC World as well as from an aggressive advertising and marketing campaign designed to drive hordes of shoppers to this portal—and to your business. They provide merchant listings with options ranging anywhere from an entry tenant position with a listing on the department level for just $25 a year—to virtually owning the category with top-level placement and other "spotlight" positioning as a $995 per month anchor tenant. They provide à la carte programs for banner, sponsorship, and e-mail advertising. They also offer sponsorship and promotional packages.

Internet Plaza
http://internet-plaza.net
This site is actually a "cybertown," with addresses for each category of product/service they provide. They have Travel Avenue, Card and Gift Drive, Fashion Blvd., Finance Street, Home and Garden Row, Career Way, Sport and Recreation Street, BookEnd, Gourmet Lane, Health Care Place, Impression Avenue, Industry Parkway, and Kids Alley. Neat site!

Access Market Square
http://www.icw.com/mall.html
Access Market Square has an occasion (birthday, anniversary, etc.) reminder service that also provides personalized gift ideas. They also

have a great search engine that allows you to enter names of items, brand names, product types, or store names. They provide a wide variety of products by category including art, audio-video, automotive, books, clothes, computers, electronics, flowers, food, health, jewelry, music, sports, travel, and others. Access Market Square uses VeriSign for secure ordering capabilities.

American Shopping Mall
http://www.greenearth.com
The American Shopping Mall has been rated among the top most visited sites on the Internet by *PC Magazine.* They profess to be one of the busiest virtual shopping malls on the World Wide Web, with over 32 million visitors last year and over 50 million visitors since their opening in 1995.

iMall
http://www.imall.com
This is an electronic commerce enabler of small and medium-sized businesses allowing them to cost-effectively engage in electronic commerce through the use of iMall's proprietary e-commerce tools and services. iMall offers its electronic commerce services directly to merchants, as well as through partnerships with leading ISPs, web hosting firms, and financial service companies with an Internet focus. The company professes to operate the largest shopping mall on the Internet, with more than 1600 hosted storefronts and millions of visitors monthly.

16

E-commerce—Accept
Online Reservations

You have established your tourism web site and have been busily promoting it with your target market in mind. Now, you want to make it easy for people in your target market to become your customers. They should be able to make a reservation online or purchase your product or service without a lot of effort. How will these transactions be handled? In this chapter, we discuss:

- The E-commerce concept

- E-commerce on the rise

- Features of e-commerce web sites

- Web trust—the challenge of e-commerce

Online Travel and E-commerce—We've Just Begun

E-commerce is a rapidly growing sector in the world's economy, and the travel and tourism industry is riding the wave. EStats *(http://*

www.estats.com) announced the GartnerGroup's finding, which revealed that travel has moved ahead of computers as the top consumer e-commerce category. In 1999, travel-oriented e-commerce transactions reached $5 billion. Consumer spending on the online travel industry is expected to climb to $30 billion by 2001 (see Figure 16.1).

The GartnerGroup also noted the following demographics:

- In 1999, 75% of people with Internet access researched travel schedules, vacation packages, flights, and travel discounts online (four times more than in 1998).

- Sixteen percent of Internet users booked flights or purchased airline tickets online (eight times more than in 1998).

- Seventy percent of online users said they would make all of their personal travel arrangements online if more choices were available.

- Thirty percent of individuals with Internet access claimed that purchasing tickets online is still too complicated and too risky.

From these figures, a lot of people are using the Internet to plan their vacations and business trips. However, there is still a great deal of concern over the safety of booking reservations online. Although three-quarters of Internet users research travel schedules online, only a slight percentage of them actually book flights and purchase tickets

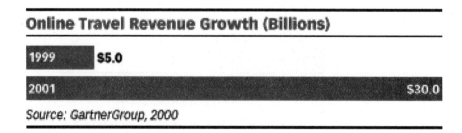

Online Travel Revenue Growth (Billions)

| 1999 | $5.0 |
| 2001 | $30.0 |

Source: GartnerGroup, 2000

Figure 16.1. eStats (*http://www.estats.com*) reports a GartnerGroup study that indicates the online travel industry is on the rise.

online. E-commerce is a new medium for conducting financial transactions, and the hesitation on the part of consumers to make online reservations en masse is understandable. Online travel and tourism operations will have to earn the trust of consumers. Web trust is discussed in detail later in this chapter.

As for the makeup of the online travel industry, more than half of the market share belongs to travel agencies (according to PhoCusWright in their 1998 study). Figure 16.2 notes the three other major sectors of the online tourism industry as being airlines, hotels, and car rental companies. Travel agencies, airlines, hotels, and car rental companies were most likely to have been the major players in the travel industry last year and will continue to be in the future.

Further Evidence of E-commerce on the Rise

In general, e-commerce beyond its application in the travel industry is on the rise. The top e-commerce retailer, Amazon.com, has managed to see a 50% increase in the number of buyers from its site.

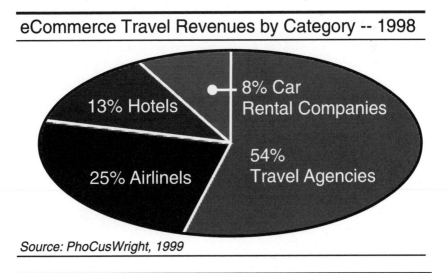

eCommerce Travel Revenues by Category -- 1998

13% Hotels

8% Car Rental Companies

25% Airlinels

54% Travel Agencies

Source: PhoCusWright, 1999

Figure 16.2. Travel agencies represent the largest portion of the online travel sector.

Amazon.com processed orders from approximately 1.8 million home-based buyers in November 1999. Buy.com and eToys.com both saw significant sales gains as well, but not to the level of success that Amazon.com experienced. Winning the home-based market is the key to success for these businesses focused on e-commerce. Following are PC Data Online's list of the Top 20 Web Retailers Among US Home Users for the month of November 1999 (total home users in brackets):

1. Amazon.com (1,805,000)

2. buy.com (876,000)

3. eToys.com (403,000)

4. barnesandnoble.com (362,000)

5. iprint.com (331,000)

6. drugstore.com (316,000)

7. planetrx.com (286,000)

8. landsend.com (283,000)

9. ticketmaster.com (261,000)

10. mothernature.com (239,000)

11. gap.com (228,000)

12. gateway.com (160,000)

13. SmarterKids.com (152,000)

14. cdnow.com (139,000)

15. enews.com (109,000)

16. officemax.com (101,000)

17. 1800flowers.com (97,000)

18. petopia.com (86,000)

19. chipshot.com (85,000)

20. kbkids.com (84,000)

Although no travel sites cracked the top 20 e-commerce sites, the travel industry itself is still a significant part of the e-commerce world. The GartnerGroup's prediction of a $30 billion travel industry by 2001 (noted earlier) suggests that the industry is one to be reckoned with.

What Is E-commerce?

The term "e-commerce" is commonly used, but e-commerce represents different things to different people. To some people, e-commerce is simply having a web site with a toll-free number customers can call to place an order. Other people think e-commerce is having a web site that enables customers to submit their credit card information online, even though their orders may then be processed manually, just like a fax or telephone order.

Others still believe that e-commerce means being able to place a secure online order, having immediate credit card verification and having a fully integrated back end database that dynamically updates and informs the customer of the latest prices and whether or not an item is in stock. The point is this: How you define e-commerce and how you implement e-commerce on your site will depend upon your tourism operation and the type of products or services you currently (or intend to) market on the web.

For instance, a ski hill has no inventory per se. They can basically sell as many lift tickets as people are willing to buy. Therefore, they would not necessarily require a back end inventory database to be integrated with their e-commerce system. All they might need is an e-commerce system that accepts payment online and provides the customer with proof of purchase to be traded for the lift ticket at the hill. On the other hand, if you manage a pro shop at a golf and country club, you might require a full-blown, full-featured e-commerce system to compete with other online golf supply retailers. Otherwise, potential customers will shop at another golf supplier whose e-commerce system is more convenient and easy to use. We discuss the features of an e-commerce site in the next section.

Features of E-commerce Sites

The consumer is king. This statement is especially true in the e-commerce realm. For instance, let's assume you are doing some holiday shopping and you have a number of golfers on your list. If you were to visit an offline golf supplies retail store, you might browse through the aisles for a few hours, pick out some new irons, a few sleeves of golf balls, and a new golf umbrella, and take them to the cashier to pay for them. If you asked the cashier whether the golf retailer offered gift-wrapping or shipping services, the response from the vendor would probably be "no, we don't provide those services." You would be satisfied with this and make the purchase anyway. You would then take the gifts home, wrap them, and ship them out to several different destinations.

Online it's a whole different world. You have higher expectations. Often you are shopping online for the convenience, and you expect the online merchant to meet your needs. You expect the online merchant to deliver what you want, when you want, and how you want. If you are making the same gift purchases at an online golf supplies retailer, you expect to be able to have them gift-wrapped and delivered to any address you desire. It defeats the purpose somewhat to have the clubs, balls, and umbrella delivered to your address only to turn around and ship them someplace else. If you are purchasing these items as gifts, you want to have them gift-wrapped. Again, it defeats the purpose to have the clubs, balls, and umbrella sent to your address so that you can gift-wrap them and then re-ship.

Shopping online is all about the consumers, their convenience, their shopping experience, and their expectations. If you don't provide what they want the way they want it, another vendor is just a click away.

Not all possible features of an e-commerce site are applicable to every tourism operation, but if you intend to be competitive online, you must give your consumers what they are looking for. You might have something they want, but if they cannot conduct transactions easily on your site and if your competitors offer more point-of-sale service, people will leave your site and shop at another site that is easier to buy from. This section focuses on some possible e-commerce features that you might want to include on your site. Decide which features are most applicable to your business, and implement them into your e-commerce system.

Shopping Carts

An e-commerce shopping cart is an excellent feature for sites selling multiple products or services. The online shopping cart system operates much like an actual shopping cart. You can add items to your cart as you please, and you can remove items just as easily. As the customers add and subtract items from their shopping cart, a running total of their purchase choices is dynamically updated.

Figure 16.3 demonstrates how an online luggage vendor's shopping cart system operates. Notice the customer has the power to add and subtract items from the cart. Customers can also modify the quantities of the items they wish to purchase, continue shopping, or proceed to the "checkout counter" at any time. In all ways, the customers have the same options with the online shopping cart as they do with a cart in an actual storefront. The customer is in control.

Database Integration

To create a one-to-one, personal relationship with each of your customers, you will require specific information about them. Generally speaking, a database is the best place to store customer data. This facilitates easy referencing of information for a particular customer on demand.

Wouldn't it be great if you could tie your customer database into your web site? This is exactly what major travel e-commerce operations are doing today. For instance, Travelocity.com *(http://www.travelocity.com)* will save each customer's profile. This makes it more efficient for customers to order from Travelocity.com in the future because they do not have to reenter their personal information

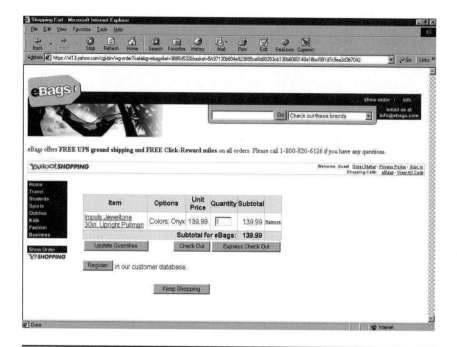

Figure 16.3. eBags.com (*http://www.ebags.com*) demonstrates how a shopping cart system works.

for each order. As seen in Figure 16.4, once your customer profile is in the Travelocity.com database, you can book flights and make reservations. You enter your information the first time, and that's it. Each customer is issued a username and password that permits access to the customer's account at any time. This database integration enables the vendor to implement loyalty programs, volume discounts, and other features affected by a consumer's history.

Aside from linking your customer database to your web site, it is possible to link into your inventory database as well. Doing so can instantly inform customers if the items they want to purchase are in stock or if they have to be backordered.

Gift-Wrapping

A well run e-commerce site should allow its customers to have each item they purchase gift-wrapped. Many online vendors such as

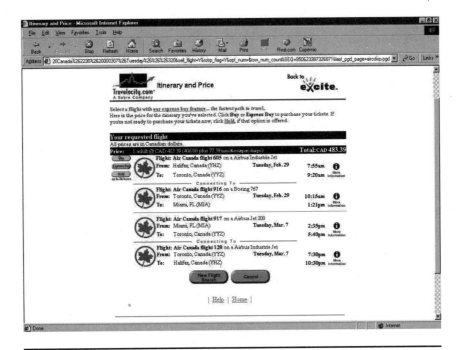

Figure 16.4. Travelocity (*http://www.travelocity.com/*) lists available flights and allows you to book a flight online.

Amazon.com (not a tourism operation, but they present the best example) offer gift-wrapping services. If you wish, you can purchase a Christmas present or birthday gift, and Amazon.com will gift-wrap it for a nominal fee. This convenience can be a great time-saver for your customers and an additional source of revenue for your business.

Amazon.com has two tiers of gift-wrapping service. Basic gift-wrapping costs $1.95 per parcel. This includes a choice of gift-wrap and the option to attach a personalized message to the gift. However, for $4.95, Amazon.com gives their customers fancier gift-wrapping options. Thus, Amazon.com upsells its gift-wrapping service for increased revenue.

Remember, the consumer is king. For some people, gift-wrapping services are a requirement of an e-commerce site. If your site does not have this service, your customers can leave your site at the click of their mouse and order from another site that offers gift-wrapping.

Shipping Options

Having a variety of shipping options is a popular e-commerce feature. For example, people might be on your site doing all their holiday shopping. They want to be able to identify different "ship to" addresses for different items in their basket (see Figure 16.5). A tourism operation with a well-run e-commerce site should allow the customer to have each purchase gift-wrapped and shipped directly to the address of their choice. It is more convenient for the customer to specify a different shipping address and have your company mail the gifts to the intended recipients than for the customer to have to transport or re-send the gifts themselves.

Aside from allowing for unique shipping addresses for each parcel, good e-commerce sites offer a number of different delivery options as seen in Figure 16.6. Permit your customers to choose the

Figure 16.5. Ideally, an e-commerce site will allow you to specify separate shipping addresses for each parcel. Also, you can track promotions by accepting promotional codes from customers.

Figure 16.6. Offer different levels of shipping service with each order.

level of service they desire. Give them the option of next-day delivery, airmail, or surface mail. If they want their parcels delivered quickly, they will gladly pay for it. E-commerce sites are great if you're one of those last-minute shoppers—you can do your shopping in minutes, make your purchase, have them gift-wrapped, personalize your card, and have your gifts delivered the next day.

Tracking Promotions

Tracking your promotional efforts is easy with e-commerce. You can include a special, unique promotion code with each advertising campaign you run. Then, set up your order form to accept promotion codes from your customers. Figure 16.5 shows us an example of this. This will allow you to track which ads are more successful. To convince people to enter the promotion codes, offer them an incentive such as free shipping, or 10% off. The feedback you receive from your advertising campaigns is valuable, and promotion codes are a great way to gain it.

Reminder Services

Another useful technique employed by e-commerce sites is a reminder service. I find the reminder service to be an especially great feature. Travelocity.com has a "fare watcher" e-mail service that updates you on the lowest airfares to your favorite destinations. You receive the e-mail as the fares become available. In this way, you are reminded of travel plans you have been putting on hold, and you are encouraged to visit Travelocity.com to purchase your airline tickets in order to take advantage of the low fare. However, you could take the reminder service idea even further. Your tourism operation could send a reminder notice confirming customers' reservations for the following week. In the e-mail message, you could upsell to them by asking the customers if they would like to make dinner reservations at your hotel's restaurant, invite them to visit your fitness center's top-notch facilities, or ask them if they would like to have a bottle of champagne delivered to their room. Reminder services keep your business name, products, and services in the minds of your customers. Since the messages are personalized, people will be encouraged to act on their reminder notice, visit your site, or make a reservation depending on the content of the reminder notice.

Taking Reservations Online with E-commerce

Microsoft's Expedia.com illustrates how your hotel or bed and breakfast can accept reservations online. Actually, the process is quite simple for the visitor. As shown in Figure 16.7, the customer is interested in visiting New Orleans, Louisiana for four nights and needs a room for two people. When this information is submitted to Expedia.com's searchable hotel database, the results are returned immediately (Figure 16.8). From these results, the customer can choose a hotel to book a reservation or find out more about a particular hotel. Once the decision has been made, the customer hits "Book Now" and is taken to an online form stored on a secure e-commerce server (see Figure 16.9). The form then accepts the customer's personal and credit

Figure 16.7. Expedia.com (*http://www.expedia.com/*) allows customers to find a hotel room in any city thanks to Expedia's online searchable database.

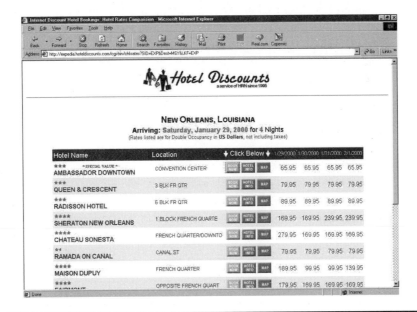

Figure 16.8. A list of hotels with rooms available in a particular city for a specified period of time is generated.

Figure 16.9. The customers enter their personal and credit card information into the form, submit the information using the secure e-commerce Web server, and makes the reservation.

card information, which is submitted to the hotel's reservation list. The customer's credit card is charged for the reservation and the hotel in New Orleans reserves a room for two people for four nights beginning January 29, 2000.

If your hotel, bed and breakfast, or travel agency has the resources, you might want to consider an e-commerce reservation system similar to the one used by Expedia.com. It will make it easy for your customers to book vacations and rooms online in a secure environment.

Putting It All Together

As can clearly be seen, there are a lot of steps to the e-commerce process. There are many decisions to be made. The services you offer offline may be quite different from the services you offer online. While it may be quite acceptable not to provide gift wrapping in your offline golf retail store, it may be a necessity online.

Unless you are a coding genius yourself, you will likely require e-commerce software, a web development firm, or your ISP to customize an e-commerce system that works for your business. The methods used to reach an effective e-commerce solution will vary depending on your business, your products and/or services, and the expertise of the particular contractor you are working with.

Please keep in mind that customized e-commerce solutions can be rather expensive to have designed and maintained. If your tourism business is a small startup operation, if you develop and manage your own web site, or if you have a limited budget for this project, you may want to start small and add e-commerce components, as your business or your budget grows. Companies such as Amazon.com and CDNow *(http://www.cdnow.com)* have had years to design and refine their e-commerce presence. These enterprises are also well capitalized and can afford their own in-house e-commerce team. However, if you have a tourism product or service that a lot of people want, the e-commerce system can pay for itself.

E-commerce is the buzzword in today's business world. Despite all the excitement surrounding e-commerce, Internet transactions represent only a small fraction of retail sales. However, online revenue is expected to increase rapidly, and you are well advised to do everything you can to reap some of the benefits from e-commerce. If you make it easy for your customers to buy your products and travel services and encourage repeat business, your online tourism company will succeed. Remember, word of mouth remains a powerful marketing vehicle in the e-commerce environment, and the customer rules.

Web Trust

Online privacy has been a major issue with e-commerce ever since the day e-commerce began to propagate across the Internet. Thanks to recent innovative technologies, consumers are feeling better about the security measures many e-commerce sites now employ. Although consumer fear of conducting online transactions has dissipated to some extent, there are still a lot of folks who need convincing. This section addresses the issues surrounding consumer confidence and e-commerce security.

THE CHALLENGE OF E-COMMERCE

This section was written and provided compliments of Stefan Gashus, CA. Stefan owns and operates a professional services firm that specializes in e-commerce consultation, information technology and, assurance services. He represents CA4IT *(http://www.ca4it.com),* which specializes in the needs of the IT contractor. You can visit Stefan's informative web site at *http://www.gashus.com* for more information on security issues related to e-commerce on your site.

Technology alone will not drive e-commerce; trust among the parties involved is also necessary. Even the most sophisticated website will not inspire consumers to buy if consumers do not feel they can trust the merchant company behind the web site. Consumers must trust the vendor, or in the very least, believe they have some recourse against the vendor if their order is not fulfilled correctly. A vendor needs to project integrity and credibility to win the sale. This has always been the case in business, and the challenge of e-commerce is to gain the trust of people you have never met and possibly never will.

Common sense tells us not to trust people or companies we don't know, so how will companies assure potential customers to engage in e-commerce? Gaining credibility from brand recognition the company may currently hold will certainly help, however how long will the company's brand be perceived as "the best"? The new economy of e-commerce has dramatically altered the costs of doing business, squeezed margins and has reduced many of the barriers of entry for new competition. As e-commerce continues to shift the balance of power towards the consumer, brand management will become even more synonymous with quality control and sound business practices. The new economy has begun to level the playing field among competitors, making consumers more in control of what and how they buy, while providing them with a range of selection never before enjoyed.

For less established brands, a means to create trust with online customers is essential. In order to compete and maintain customer loyalty and trust, all brands need to clearly define their business practices and outline their commitment to offer quality, price and superior customer service. Building trust is a function of integrity and competence, and above all, is an exercise of judgment. Of course, building trust with consumers or business partners is a complex matter, both on organizational and social levels. A successful e-commerce business will implement strategic initiatives to achieve and monitor customer trust, satisfaction and loyalty. In other words a useful e-commerce plan will strive to place the company ahead of its competitors by utilizing the Internet to improve customer service and quality.

Web Seals of Assurance

Web seals certifying that a particular web site practices "good" e-commerce have become more common in recent years. The Cheskin Research Group produced a study in January 1999 that established that placing a seal of assurance on a merchant's web site can be effective in increasing consumer confidence in the merchant, its technology, and the network behind it.

The value of a web seal is derived from any increase in online sales that can be attributed to consumers being more comfortable in dealing with the merchant who displays the seal. In other words, consumers may come to trust the merchant because the consumers already trust the organization behind the seal. This concept has been referred to as third-party trust. However, it is unlikely consumers will be heavily influenced by a mere rubber stamp that a merchant has paid to have placed on its web site.

In many respects, the web seals being used on the Internet today are extensions of traditional assurance services provided by not-for-profit organizations and the public accounting and auditing professions. The more common web seals are Trust-e, BBB online, VeriSign, and WebTrust. A good example of all four seals can be found at *http:/ /www.altusmortgage.com/safety.htm.*

BBB online
http://www.bbbonline.org
The Better Business Bureau, a not-for-profit organization sponsored in part by Dun & Bradstreet, instigated its seal program in 1997. The BBB web seal can also be obtained online, with a registration fee of $75 and annual registration of approximately $150 for a business with revenues under $1,000,000. Records are maintained for any customer complaints, and members must remain in good standing to continue displaying the seal. BBB also provides a seal for web sites targeted at children aged under 13.

Truste
http://www.truste.org
Truste is a not-for-profit organization established in 1997 and is based in Silicon Valley. The Truste seal demonstrates a web site has disclosed its business policy with respect to privacy and that management has agreed to a process of arbitration, in case of any consumer complaints or disputes. The web seal can be obtained by registering online and paying an annual fee of approximately $300 for a business with annual revenues under $1,000,000.

VeriSign
http://www.verisign.com
VeriSign is the leading certificate authority, providing online businesses with the infrastructure necessary to encrypt Internet transmissions. VeriSign, Inc., (NASDAQ: VRSN), is a darling stock, which after a 2 for 1 stock split, has moved from $11 to $143 in 1999. VeriSign creates public and private keys or digital certificates that work in conjunction with Microsoft and Netscape browsers. The digital certificates enable SSL (secure socket layer), a connection on the Internet between a server and a browser that is protected by encryption.

When a server is registered with VeriSign and has been issued a digital certificate, which resides on the particular server, a web site located on the server may display the VeriSign Secure Server Seal. The VeriSign Web Seal (see Figure 16.10) signifies that a digital certificate has been issued and that the web site is capable of sending

Figure 16.10. Verisign (*http://www.verisign.com*) enables businesses to implement encrypted Web site security to allow for secure credit card transactions.

and receiving encrypted information. The annual cost of the Secure Server Seal starts at approximately $1300 and includes Lloyd's of London insurance, which protects VeriSign Server certificate customers against economic loss resulting from the theft, corruption, impersonation, or loss of use of a certificate, or damages due to the digital certificates not working correctly. The following certificate authorities also provide digital certificates: Entrust, Thawte, GlobalSign, and the government of Canada (Internal).

WebTrust
http://www.cica.ca/cica/cicawebsite.nsf/Public/SPASWebTrust
WebTrust is the highest level of assurance that can be obtained from a web seal. The American Institute of Certified Public Accountants (AICPA) and the Canadian Institute of Chartered Accountants (CICA) initially developed the WebTrust standard in 1997. These organiza-

tions represent the public accounting and auditing professions and are renowned for setting standards that help regulate financial reporting for the stock markets and government. Standard setting for the Internet is of course no less important, and the standards and criteria for WebTrust provide for an in-depth investigation of a business's web site and business practices.

A WebTrust seal includes a VeriSign secure server digital certificate and costs $2000 per year. In addition, an independent Certified Public Accountant (CPA) or Chartered Accountant (CA) must be involved in the process of acquiring the WebTrust seal, and these professionals will also charge for their time. The time spent by a CA and CPA should be valued because they can also impart valuable professional advice with respect to business practices and business strategy.

The CA or CPA broadly examines the e-commerce entity no less than every three months. The WebTrust audit covers the three major areas of e-commerce: (1) transaction security, (2) protection and use of confidential information, and (3) disclosure of business practices. The disclosure of business practices includes disclosure of how customer disputes will be resolved, and The National Arbitration Forum *(http://www.arb-forum.com)* has assisted in the design of a program for e-commerce and specifically WebTrust.

The decision to invite a CPA or CA to review a business's web site clearly demonstrates the business's commitment to consumer's concerns. Only CPAs and CAs are personally accountable and liable for the assurance they provide.

Security Matters

There is no doubt that SSL technology protects Internet transmissions by encryption. The real question is what happens to the information once it is decrypted and residing on someone's private network somewhere. There is a risk that highly skilled network hackers or novices will attack. Experts agree that the only truly impenetrable networks are those with the connection to the Internet turned off! A business's internal controls always have inherent limitations because they are always subject to human error, fraud, or being overridden by management. Therefore judgment must be exercised in implementing controls for protecting a network from unauthorized use. Every network security program needs to weigh the costs of protection and performance against the benefits of further security.

Between the Internet and a private network resides a firewall or proxy. The firewall can be thought of as a gap between two networks, filled with something that lets only a few selected forms of traffic through. There is a growing number of types and configurations of firewalls, but each can be easily reconfigured or bypassed. This places significant responsibility on network administrators and management to ensure that the company's control procedures are in fact effective. Testing firewalls can be expensive and can only be performed at a particular moment in time. It is always possible that a firewall will be improperly reconfigured after the test. Rather than trust the firewall itself, it is much more practical for consumers to place their trust in someone who is accountable for security practices. This is why business practice disclosure is vital to successful e-commerce, because it sets up boundaries and accountability in return for trust.

Who Will Consumers Trust?

Considering the proliferation of franchised businesses in recent years, consumers clearly look for familiarity and consistency in many of their buying decisions. Trusted Internet search engines or Internet infomediaries, who provide consumers with a service of finding particular merchants online, can provide an element of trust and assurance for dealing with the merchant if they themselves are trusted. Internet service providers that host merchant sites may also be able to provide additional assurance for consumers. Brands will continue to play an important role of signifying quality and assurance to consumers, because of their known business practices.

For all the players in e-commerce, it is advisable to take the concept of third-party trust very seriously. The organizations that can win the trust of consumers, and keep it, should be very successful.

Forrester Research, in the table below, estimated the total amount of dollars lost to fraud with Internet transactions versus other types of transactions. Internet transactions had far fewer instances of fraud.

DOLLARS LOST TO FRAUD PER $1000 IN REVENUE TRANSACTIONS

Types of Fraud	Dollars per $1000 Lost
Cellular phones	$19.83
Toll calls	$16.00
MasterCard	$1.41
Expected Internet fraud	$1.00

Consumers want transactions to occur instantly on the Web. This helps to reduce anxiety and gives them more confidence about conducting business on your site. In the end, efficiency and security represent good customer service. The better your customers are serviced, the more likely the possibility of having repeat business from your clients.

After all, the consumer is truly in control in the Internet world. Not only is it nice to have a strong e-commerce system these days, it's imperative. Consumers have many more choices in an online shopping environment than they do in a shopping mall in the physical world. Therefore, your tourism operation's e-commerce system had better be up to the standards of your customers, or they will take their business elsewhere.

Internet Resources

Related Links

Internet.com's Electronic Commerce Guide
http://ecommerce.internet.com
Includes links and information for companies seeking an e-commerce environment.

ECNow
http://www.ecnow.com/Internet_Marketing.htm
Thirty Internet marketing techniques to implement for your business.

Electronic Commerce Modeling Language
http://www.ecml.org
A collaborative effort by several large players in the e-commerce

industry to develop a universal format for wallets and merchant web sites.

Electronic Commerce Resource Center
http://www.ecrc.ctc.com
ECRC serves as a catalyst for a vast network of small and medium-sized enterprises to adopt electronic commerce.

Resources

Mercury Web Technologies
http://www.mercurywebtech.com
Features a variety of resources and information to help you launch your business on the web.

Forrester Research
http://www.forrester.com
Provides statistical analysis of technology change and its impact on business, consumers, and society.

eMarketer
http://www.estats.com
Aggregates, filters, organizes, and analyzes the statistics, news, and information that businesses need to succeed on the Web.

Successful E-commerce Sites

Amazon.com
http://www.amazon.com
Books, music, toys, electronics, e-cards, auctions, and so on.

Barnesandnoble.com
http://www.barnesandnoble.com
Books, music, software, and magazines.

Ebay
http://www.ebay.com
The best-known and largest auction site on the web.

eBags.com
http://www.ebags.com
Lots and lots of luggage.

Expedia.com
http://www.expedia.com
Make reservations, book a vacation.

CDNow.com
http://www.cdnow.com
One of the original music and video vendors on the web.

MotherNature.com
http://www.mothernature.com
Vendor of all natural products, supplements, shampoos, luggage,
mattresses, and so on.

Travelocity
http://www.travelocity.com
Book vacations, business trips, flights, rent cars, and so on.

The Gap
http://www.gap.com
Designer clothing at your fingertips.

L.L.Bean
http://www.llbean.com
More clothing and specialty items.

Dell.com
http://www.dell.com
Customizable computer solutions.

Gateway
http://www.gateway.com
Customizable computer solutions.

Egghead.com
http://www.egghead.com
One of the largest software vendors on the web.

E-Trade
http://www.etrade.com
Online brokerage that services merchant accounts.

VeriSign
http://www.verisign.com

Carefree Community Solutions
http://www.carefreesolutions.com

RealTime Commerce Solutions
http://www.realtimecommerce.com

Business Solutions Merchant Account Services
http://ourshops.com/paycard

17

Keep 'Em Coming Back

There are many little things that will spice up your Tourism web site to "keep 'em coming back." Learn the tips, tools, and techniques to create "stickiness" for your site and get visitors to return to your site again and again. In this chapter we cover:

- Attractive web site content

- Having your own What's New page

- Ensuring you are bookmarked

- Cartoons, contests, jokes, and trivia

- Calendar of events and reminder services

- Interesting bulletin boards

- Having your own newsletter

- Special guests or celebrity appearances

- Giveaways and awards

- Offline tactics for promotion

Encourage Repeat Visits

Just as you would want clients to visit your tourism operation frequently, so too in cyberspace you want clients and potential clients to visit often. The more often people visit your site, the more likely they are to make a booking and visit your tourism operation. You want to ensure that the techniques you use to get repeat traffic are appropriate for your target market. For example, if you were having a contest on your site targeted toward children you would not want to give away a bread maker as the prize. That would be okay if your target market was families or homemakers. You would want to offer something of interest to the market you are targeting. For tourism operators, something like a free night's accommodation at your tourism operation would be appropriate. If your target market was skiers, then a weekend in Vail might be appropriate. You should always remember your objectives when doing any form of online marketing because you don't want to do something inappropriate that might drive your target audience away from your site.

Use a What's New Page for Repeat Hits

A What's New page can mean different things to different sites. For some, this page updates the users with the summaries of the most recent features and additions to a particular site, as in Figure 17.1. You should have your What's New page accessible from your home page so that when people visit your site they will not have to search through your entire site to find out what is new. If visitors repeatedly find interesting additions in the What's New section, in whatever context you use it, they will come back to your site on a regular basis to check out what's new. Without this they may visit and search through

Figure 17.1. The Park Hotel Web site has a great example of a What's New page.

your site and find that nothing was new and they just wasted 20 minutes looking for anything new.

Here, too, you can ask if visitors would like to be notified via e-mail when you've added something to the What's New section. It's all about getting their permission to send them e-mail and therefore include them in your community.

There are many other appropriate What's New sections for your Web site that can encourage repeat traffic. What's new with your tourism operation, what's new in your geographic area that may be of interest to tourists, or what's new in the tourism industry. Whatever it is, you should always make sure that it is of interest to your target market. You can also ask your visitors if they would like to be notified when there are updates to these sections. This once again gives you permission to e-mail them and present them with new information that will make them want to come back to your site again.

Everyone Loves Free Stuff

Giving items away for free is a great way to increase traffic—everybody likes a freebie. If you give something away each week, you are sure to have a steady stream of repeat traffic. When you have freebies or giveaways on your site, your pages can also be listed and linked from the many sites on the Internet that list places people can receive free stuff. To find these listings of free stuff, simply go to a search engine and do a search on "free index," or "free stuff links." You will be overwhelmed by how many people are giving things away online.

You don't have to give something away to everyone. You could simply have a drawing every week. You could then ask them if they would like you to notify them of the winner, which again gives you permission to e-mail them. An example of a site that has a monthly draw would be RaceRock.com at *http://www.racerock.com*. Race Rock is a popular theme restaurant with locations in Orlando, Florida, and Las Vegas, Nevada. Their restaurants target racing enthusiasts, providing the ultimate atmosphere for race fans. RaceRock.com provides monthly giveaways of RaceRock.com merchandise such as sweatshirts, caps, and so on, so every month many people enter their draw for their chance to win one of these prizes. When the draw is done, Race Rock e-mails all the entrants to inform them of the winner and takes the opportunity to remind them of the monthly specials, and upcoming giveaways that their restaurant will have. This certainly can't hurt sales.

You want to target tourists to your site, so you would be less inclined to give away mainstream things like screen savers (unless it was a graphic of your tourism operation), shareware games, utilities, and so on. Try to give away something that only people interested in your tourism operation would want, like a free romantic weekend for two, or a free round of golf, or a free ski lesson, depending on what you offer.

If you don't care what traffic comes your way, and any traffic is good traffic, then give away useful things that everybody needs. Try to have your logo and URL displayed on the item. For example, a neat screen saver can be made that displays your logo and URL. When this is made available as a download, there are no handling or shipping charges associated with it. If your freebie is something that has your URL on it (see Figure 17.2) and is something that is generally kept around a computer it reminds and encourages people to visit your site. A mousepad with your URL would be a good example.

Figure 17.2. The Race Rock theme restaurant regularly gives away Race Rock apparel to lucky visitors.

Resisting a Deal Is Hard with Coupons and Discounts

Offer coupons and discount vouchers that can be printed from your site. You can change the coupon daily or weekly to encourage repeat visits. People will come back to your site again and again if they know they will find good deals there. You can also ask people if they would like to be notified by e-mail when you update the coupons on your Web site. This, once again, gives you the opportunity to present them with new information about your tourism operation.

Offering coupons is a great way to encourage people to visit your tourism operation. These can be your loss leader to encourage tourists to come in to your tourism operation. An example of a tourism-related coupon site (Figure 17.3) is the Las Vegas Fun Book. Here you can go online and find various coupons for different attractions in Las Vegas. When you find a coupon that you are interested in you can print it and use it at the physical location when you visit. Provid-

Figure 17.3. The Las Vegas Fun Book enables visitors to print coupons from their Web site.

ing the coupons online makes it very easy for tourists to receive them and will encourage them to visit your location.

You can develop a coupon banner ad for you tourism operation that links to your site, where the coupon can be printed. The banner ads should be placed on high-traffic sites frequented by your target market.

You can trade coupons with other tourism-related sites that target the same market that you do, but offer noncompeting products or services. For example, you can trade your country inn banner ad with a theme park in your geographic location. Your coupon on their site links to your site, and their coupon on your site links to their site.

By offering coupons from your tourism Web site you also cut down your overhead cost because people are printing the coupons on their own printers. Remember that you should have terms and conditions on the coupons that are available for printing. For example, you should have an expiration date. Someone could print a coupon, then visit your tourism operation in three years time and try to use it.

You should try to have the expiration date close to the release of the coupon. This will entice the visitor to use the coupon quicker and then come back for more coupons.

Today we are seeing an increase in the number of coupon-related sites that are appearing on the Internet. CoolSavings.com *(http:// www.coolsavings.com)* is an online coupon network where businesses of all kinds can advertise and place coupons for their products and services. They even have a section of their site dedicated to travel coupons, as seen in Figure 17.4. They provide their services to businesses in the United States only, and have been doing so since 1997. Sites like this are a good way to promote your tourism operation, for they receive a high amount of traffic. CoolSavings.com has been a household name since they launched their national advertising campaign during 1999. If you offer coupons from your site, it would benefit you to be listed on these sites. If you are not aiming for a national appeal, you should search to find out if there are coupon

Figure 17.4. CoolSavings.com offers tourism operators the opportunity to advertise their coupons on their Web site.

networks in the geographic location that you are targeting. Other coupon sites are listed in the resource section at the end of this chapter. There are meta-indexes of sites with coupons or discounts from which you can be linked for greater exposure.

Offer a Virtual Tour of Your Tourism Operation

A great way to encourage traffic to your tourism web site is by offering your visitors a virtual tour of your tourism operation. A virtual tour could be as simple as a picture tour through the different rooms of your country inn or as complex as a complete streaming video tour of your tourism operation. Virtual tours are a great way to encourage people to visit your site, because they will actually be able to see what your tourism operation has to offer. The Batcheller Mansion Inn Bed and Breakfast (see Figure 17.5) offers a virtual tour that takes their visitors through every room of their bed and breakfast so that they will know what to expect if they decide to make a reservation. This is a great way to provide your target visitors with a comfort level and everything they need to make a reservation at your tourism operation. For more information on virtual tours see Chapter 23.

After your visitors take the virtual tour of your tourism operation, you should give them the opportunity to notify a friend via e-mail about your site. This e-mail will be sent directly from your Web site and will inform the receivers that a friend thought that they would be interested in the site. They will then be prompted to follow a hypertext link that will direct them toward your virtual tour. This is a great way to generate traffic to your Web site.

A Calendar of Events Keeps Visitors Informed

A comprehensive, current calendar of events related to your tourism operation or your community will help you to encourage repeat visits. A sample calendar is shown in Figure 17.6. Your calendar should always be kept up to date and be of value to your visitors. A calendar of events for a hotel might show upcoming events that will take place there such as conferences and conventions. A calendar of events of

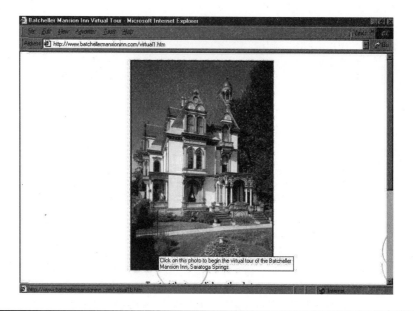

Figure 17.5. The Batcheller Mansion Inn takes their visitors on a virtual tour of their tourism operation.

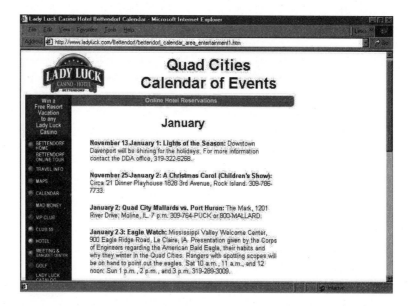

Figure 17.6. The Lady Luck Hotel's calendar of events keeps visitors informed about upcoming events in the quad city area.

what is going on in the community is also appropriate for tourism operations, because these events will inform your visitors of what they can do in your area when they visit. By providing a calendar of events you will encourage a lot of repeat traffic as long as it is current and complete. Calendars of events are also appropriate on tourist bureaus and community sites because these are accessed often by the community and they can stay posted on what is going on.

Lure Customers with Contests and Competitions

Contests and competitions are great traffic builders. Some tourism sites hold regular contests on a weekly or monthly basis to generate repeat visitors. Holding contests is also a great way to find out about your target market by requesting information on the entry form.

What type of contest you hold depends upon your Internet marketing objectives. You want to attract potential customers from your target market, so you give away something that relates to your tourism operation. A common example used is a free night's accommodation at your tourism operation. As seen in Figure 17.7, Bed and Breakfast Inns Online *(http://www.bbonline.com)* offers a monthly contest for two free nights lodging at various bed and breakfast locations across North America. By changing the location for the draw each month, Bed and Breakfast Inns Online generates a lot of repeat traffic.

If you develop your own contest, you could simply request that people fill out an electronic ballot including their name, address, phone number, and e-mail address if they wish to enter. If you want to find out something about the people entering or want to do some market research, ask them a question or two. You can also take this further. If the prize is a free weekend for two at your tourism operation, consider asking entrants to write a short essay outlining why they would like to receive this prize you are giving away. You can award the winner or winners with the prize and follow up with the other entrants via e-mail and encourage them to enter the contest again. This encourages a lot of repeat traffic.

If your products or services are appropriate for a prize that would be of interest to many different types of people, you might consider finding tourism-related contest sites that might like to offer your products or services as a prize on their site. A good example of this would

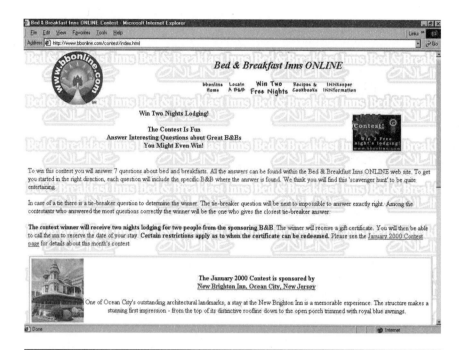

Figure 17.7.   Bed & Breakfast Inns Online holds monthly contests for a free night's lodging at various bed and breakfast operations.

be if you were interested in offering a free night's accommodation at your tourism operation as a prize for their contest. You could ask other tourism-related sites in your area if they would like to offer this prize for the contest on their web site. You could have it set up on their site so that it shows a picture of your tourism operation with a link to your site. The contest site should be more than happy to do this, because you are offering to give away something that adds value to their site. This will generate brand awareness for your tourism operation and will encourage people to visit your site.

Other competitions may include such things as best short story about past visits to your tourism operation. This creates an opportunity for your past visitors to promote your operation. When potential visitors read about past visitors' experiences, they may be encouraged to make the reservation. The closer the contest relates to your tourism operation, the better. Instead of offering just one prize, offer a number of smaller prizes as well. This makes the odds look better, and people feel they have a better chance of winning.

Before you go ahead with holding any kind of contest, check out all of the legal issues. There may be restrictions that you don't know about (e.g., you may be required to purchase a legal permit to hold lotteries or there may be an age restriction). You should also remember to ask the entrants the e-mail address at which they would like to be notified of the winner. This, again, grants you permission to e-mail them to tell them who the winner was, and also to inform them of the specials that you may have at your site that month.

Create Useful Links from Your Site

Provide visitors with links to other tourism sites in your area or a meta-index of links to other sites that would be of interest to your target market. When people plan their vacation, they are always interested in knowing what else there is to do in the area. Do not put outbound links on your home page. Place them down a level or two after the visitors have seen all the information you want them to see before you provide the links away from your site.

Try exchanging links with others so that you receive a link from their site to your site. As long as the links are of value to your visitors, people will come back to see if you have found any new and interesting sites for them to visit.

You might consider asking if your visitors would be interested in being notified when you update your list of links, or just updates to your site in general. If they accept your offer, you have the opportunity to send them an e-mail message and remind them about your operation while presenting them with new information about what might be going on with your site. Remember to use your signature file containing your URL. This way the viewer can link through to your Web site directly from the e-mail.

Tips Can Encourage Repeat Visits

Have a section that offers cool tips that relate to your tourism operation, your products or services, or your target market, as in Figure 17.8. If you have a golf resort or a ski hill, golf tips or ski tips respec-

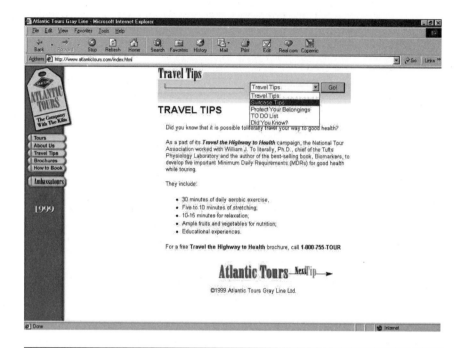

Figure 17.8. The Intrepid Traveler provides their visitors with a new travel tip every day.

tively would be appropriate. These tips can be one sentence to one paragraph long. If visitors find your advice helpful, they will return repeatedly to see what interesting piece of information you have displayed that day. Ask your visitors if they would be interested in receiving the tip via e-mail or notification when the tip has been updated so they could then visit your Web site.

Ensuring Your Site Gets Bookmarked

Encourage visitors to add you to their bookmark list. Somewhere on your site display the call to action "Bookmark me now!" (see Figure 17.9). A call to action is often effective. Make sure the title of the page that has the "Bookmark me now!" clearly identifies your site and its contents in an enticing way because the title is what will ap-

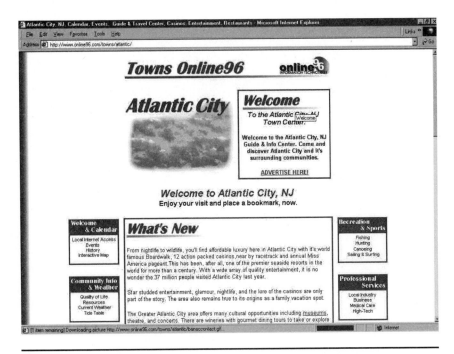

Figure 17.9. Towns Online reminds you to bookmark their site right away.

pear in the bookmark file as a description. Whenever I see "Bookmark this site now!" I always consider it. Sometimes I do, sometimes I don't, but I always consider it. Often, when the call to action is not presented, I don't think about it, and don't bookmark it. Then days later when I want to go back there and wish I had remembered to bookmark.

World Interaction with Bulletin Boards

It can be very satisfying to see people join in from all over the world just to interact with each other about a topic that relates to your tourism web site, as shown in Figure 17.10. Beware, you will have to keep an eye on the messages and may even have to play referee occasionally. This is usually appropriate for larger operations that may have multiple locations. A bulletin board where people could discuss

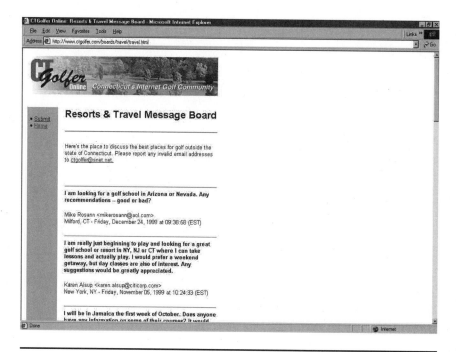

Figure 17.10. The CT Golfer Web site has a resort and travel message board.

their experiences with various locations with others would be appropriate for the Club Med site.

Encourage Repeat Visits with Your Site of the Day

Having your own Site of the Day or Site of the Week listing will mean a lot of work searching the Internet for a cool site to add or looking through all the submissions. However, if your picks are interesting to your audience, you may find that avid Internet users come back every day to see what great new site is listed. Again, larger operations might profile one of their locations every week. Club Med could have a Profiled Village of the Week, or Carnival could have a Profiled Cruise of the Week. Remember that if you have a Site of the Week, it must be updated on schedule; displaying a week-old Tourism Site of the Day will reflect poorly on your site and your company. You should also ask if your visitors would like to be notified via e-mail when you update your profiled site of the week. This gives you the opportunity to remind your visitors about your site and will encourage them to return. For more information about hosting your own award site see Chapter 11.

Keep Them Happy with Cartoons

Displaying relevant cartoons keeps your site dynamic and fun. You do not necessarily have to create all of the content and features yourself. If you update this weekly, ask visitors if they'd like to be notified via e-mail when you update your Cartoon of the Week. A good example of a Web site that uses cartoons is Cartoons Online *(http://www.mervm.com/trav.htm)*, which continuously provides humor to its viewers (see Figure 17.11).

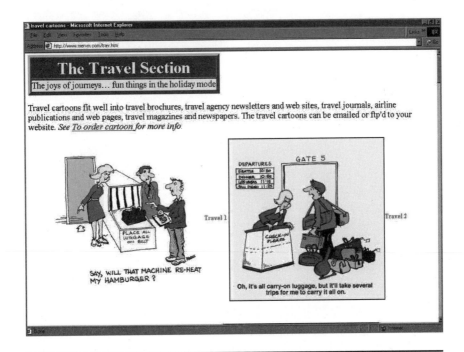

Figure 17.11. Travel cartoons are great for adding humor to your Web site.

Sending Postcards Around the Internet

Visitors can create original postcards (see Figure 17.12) that can be e-mailed to their family and friends. The postcards should be able to be identified as coming from your site—have your logo and URL displayed somewhere on them. An example of this would be Carlson Wagonlit Travel at *http://www.carlsontravel.com,* a site that gives their visitors the opportunity to send their friends colorful postcards via e-mail from different locations around the world. When you send a postcard to your friends, they receive an e-mail, which contains a link to the page where they can view their postcard. When you click through to view the postcard there is also a Carlson Wagonlit Travel logo and links to other sections of their Web site. Offering electronic postcards is a great way to generate repeat visitors to your site and to encourage new visitors to visit your tourism operation.

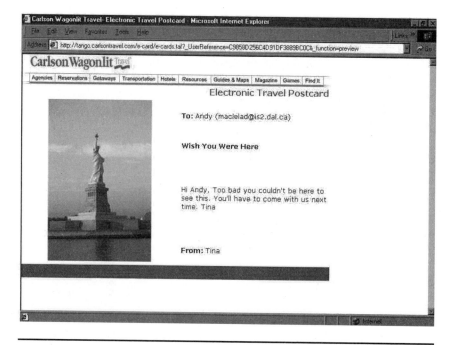

Figure 17.12. Carlson Wagonlit Travel offers personalized electronic postcards to their visitors.

Similar to offering postcards from your tourism web site, you can also offer your visitors the opportunity to send their friends pictures of your tourism operation. You can display a variety of pictures of your tourism operation on your web site that visitors can choose from to send to their friends. This is very convenient for people who are planning vacations. If they visit your web site and like what they see, they can simply select pictures from your photo gallery and send a message regarding them to their friends via e-mail. The e-mail will inform the viewers that their friend thought that they would be interested in this tourism operation and will prompt the viewers to follow a hypertext link to the site where they can view the photographs. When the viewers click through to look at the photographs, they are then able to travel through the rest of your web site to find out more about your tourism operation. Never send the pictures as an attachment—remember we covered all the reasons why in the e-mail chapter!

Benefiting from Humor with Jokes and Trivia

"Laughter is the best medicine" and could prove to be a popular feature of your web page, as in Figure 17.13. People enjoy trivia, or a "thought of the day," and there are many sources for you to draw from. Perhaps providing trivia related to your geographic area may peak their interest in making that visit. Be sure to update regularly. Again, this gives you the opportunity to ask if your visitors would like to be notified when you update this section of your web site.

Everybody Loves Games

More and more, tourism sites are featuring fun activities and games on their sites. (A sample game site is shown in Figure 17.14.) Just about anything goes here. You can host anything from a tourism trivia contest to having guests play an interactive game with other visitors. Relate the game to your target market. If your operation caters to family vacations, kids games may be appropriate—quite often kids influence where the family goes for vacation. If you have a golf re-

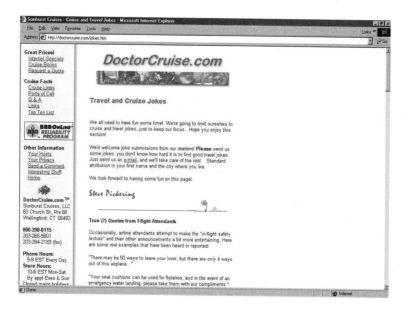

Figure 17.13. DoctorCruise.com has a variety of travel and cruise jokes on their Web site.

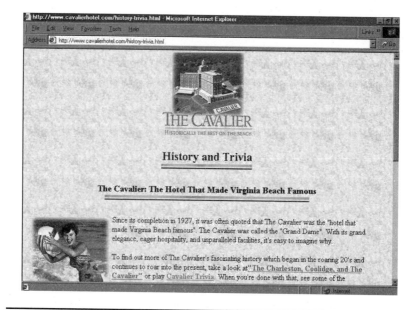

Figure 17.14. The Cavalier Hotel has a hotel trivia section that sees a lot of repeat traffic.

sort, there are lots of golf-related games or simulators that can be included on your site.

Keep Customers in Touch with Update Reminders

Ask visitors to your site if they'd like to be notified when there are updates or content changes to your pages. This is similar to a mailing list except you only write to the "list" when changes have been made. This is effective when you have a newsletter or a frequently visited calendar of events on your site.

If you take reservations at your tourism operation, you can offer your visitors the opportunity to be notified via e-mail one or two weeks before they are scheduled to visit your tourism operation. This will not only remind your visitors of their reservation at your tourism operation, it will show them that their business is important to you.

Special Events Reminder Services

People can sign up to be reminded of something via e-mail on a specified date. This feature was originally thought of by a florist to remind people about important dates like birthdays and anniversaries (where flowers might be an appropriate gift). You can remind people about any number of things relating to your tourism operation. If you have a golf course, you could get people to sign up to be reminded when certain tournaments are being held at your location. In your reminder you can also include information regarding different items that may be on special at your pro shop.

Adding Image with Advice Columns

Some tourism web sites are incorporating travel advice columns, as in Figure 17.15, or ski advice columns, or fly fishing advice columns, or golf advice columns, or cruise advice columns, and so on. People will return again and again to read the e-mails asking for advice and

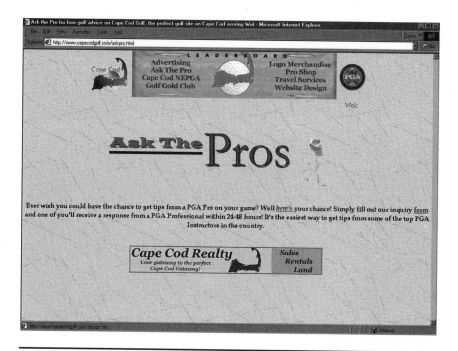

Figure 17.15. Cape Cod Golf has an Ask The Pros advice section on their Web site.

reviewing the responses that are given. This also helps perpetuate an image of expertise in your given field. You might want to offer advice on things that tourist could do while visiting your area.

Using Reward Programs to Your Advantage

There are many programs available for tourism operators that enable them to reward customers for their business. Most common are airline travel bonus programs like Delta Airlines' SkyMiles program and Air Canada's Aeroplan program (see Figure 17.16). These programs reward customers with mileage that they can use to receive free flights with the airlines. Tourism operators partner with these airlines to offer tourists the opportunity to receive mileage points that they can use toward their next flight with the airline.

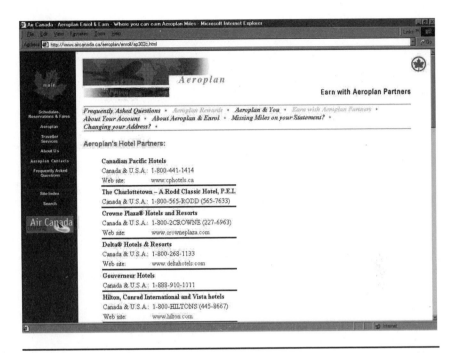

Figure 17.16. The Aeroplan program has many tourism operators as their strategic partners.

If you participate in such programs, you should advertise this on your Web site. Visitors may be doing research on where they would like to stay while on their vacations and will be more willing to stay at your location if they know that they can receive points with their preferred airline for staying at your tourism operation. You should also promote the current promotions on your site. For example, if a visitor receives bonus points for staying at your location during a particular time period, you should advertise this on your tourism Web site. This will generate repeat traffic from people who travel frequently because they will return to your site to see what the latest rewards are for visiting your operation. You should also offer your visitors the opportunity to be notified via e-mail of the latest reward program promotions. This gives you the opportunity to remind visitors about your tourism operation and will encourage them to return to your web site.

Internet Resources

More Hits for Your WWW Site
http://www.adze.com/zine/morehits.html
Teachings on how to get people to keep coming back to your site.

Web Developers Virtual Library
http://www.stars.com\ul
A comprehensive illustrated encyclopedia of web technology, the WDVL is for webmasters and Internet developers. It's a well-organized gold mine of tutorials, demos, and links to great resources.

10 Secrets of the Web Masters
http://www.i-strategies.com/10secret.html
A guide to web design and strategy to get visitors and make them return.

Guide to Web Style
http://www.sun.com/styleguide
Sun Microsystem's cookbook for better web site design to encourage repeat visitors.

Design Tips

Five Most Serious Web Design Errors
http://www.hp.com/Ebusiness/webdesign.html
Web designer tips to avoid fatal flaws that could cause your site to fail.

Yale Style Manual—Table of Contents
http://info.med.yale.edu/caim/manual/contents.html
A good example of a detailed web design manual to keep visitors coming back.

Web Architect
http://argus-inc.com/design/webarch.html
Archive of Web Review site design features to help you get the perfect layout.

Web Page Design—Introduction
http://www.wpdfd.com
Web design from the perspective of typography and graphics to keep visitors happy; no HTML.

Pulling the Plug-Ins
http://www.cio.com/archive/webbusiness/060198_main_content.html
Web plug-ins are finally on the outs with web designers. So how should you cram all that interactivity in your web pages without alienating your visitors? Go here and find out.

Conservatism of Web Users
http://www.useit.com/alertbox/980322.html
Statistics show that web users are adopting new web technologies at slower rates, affecting how you should design your site.

Features—how to—elements of web design
http://www.builder.com/Graphics/Design
CNET's elements of good web design to help in your web page design.

18

Maximizing Media Relations

Your online media strategy can be extremely effective in building traffic to your site. Press release distribution can be done easily. Build the right list of e-mail addresses or make use of one of the online press distribution services. Most reporters and writers have e-mail addresses. Some do not like to receive e-mail press releases; others prefer e-mail versions. When you send your press releases via e-mail, expect that reporters may reply by e-mail and will expect your response within 24 hours. Develop a media kit that you can e-mail out to editors. In this chapter we cover:

- Developing an online media strategy for your tourism operation

- Public relations vs. advertising

- Online public relations vs. traditional public relations

- Effective press releases

- Press release distribution services online

- How to distribute interactive press releases online

- Providing an area for media on your site

- How to find reporters online

- How reporters want to receive your information

- Encouraging re-publication of your article with a direct link to your site or article

- Providing press kits online

- Electronic newsletters

- Resources

Managing Effective Public Relations

Press release distribution can be accomplished easily if you have an established list of reporters and editors, or if you make use of a press distribution service. There are many publications, both online and offline, devoted to the travel industry that may be interested in your story.

Media relations are very important to your marketing efforts. The best results are achieved when you integrate both online and offline publicity campaigns. Maintaining effective public relations will deliver a number of benefits to your tourism operation. Your operation can be given exposure through press releases, and a positive image of your operation will be portrayed. Your relationship with current clients will be reinforced and new relationships will be formed.

Benefits of Publicity vs. Advertising

Media coverage, or publicity, has a major advantage over paid advertisements. Articles written by a reporter carry more weight and are given more credibility with the public than are ads, because the media and reporters are seen as unbiased third parties. Articles printed in media publications are given more credibility by the public than paid advertisements.

Another advantage of distributing press releases is that it is more cost effective than advertising. You have to pay for advertising space on a web site or time on the radio, but the costs of writing and distributing press releases are minimal.

One of the disadvantages of press releases vs. advertising is that you don't have control over what is published. If the editor decides to cast your operation in a negative light, then there is nothing you can do to stop him or her. If the writer of the piece does not like your operation, for whatever reason, this may come across in the article. Basically, after your press release is distributed, you have no control over what will be written about your operation.

It is important to note that when generating publicity, you may lose control over the timing of your release as well. For example, you may want an article released the day before you open your doors for this year's tourist season or the week before your big fishing contest so that you will see more traffic, but the editor relegates it to a date the following week. There is nothing you can do about this. It is not a good idea to rely exclusively on publicity for important or newsworthy events because if the release is not reviewed and considered newsworthy, you may be stuck with no promotion at all.

What Is a Press Release?

Before you begin your media campaign you should know what press releases are and how to write them. Press releases are designed to inform reporters of events concerning your operation that the public may consider newsworthy. Press releases can get your operation free public attention. A press release is a standard form of communication with the media. Press releases must contain newsworthy information. A tourism operation that continually sends worthless information in a blatant attempt to get their name in the press will not establish a good relationship with the media.

Writing a Press Release

Your press release should follow a standard format, which is described in the following paragraphs.

Notice of Release

The first thing the reader sees should be

FOR IMMEDIATE RELEASE

unless you have sent the information in advance of the time you would like it published. In that case state it as follows:

FOR RELEASE: Wednesday, December 14, 2000 (using the date you want it released.)

Remember that no matter what date you put here, the publication can release the information before or after the specified date. If the news is really big, it is not likely that the publication will hold it until the date you have specified.

Header

The header should be in the upper-left corner. It should contain all of the contact information for one or two key media contacts. These contacts should be able to answer any questions regarding the press release. If reporters cannot get in touch with someone to answer their questions, then they may print incorrect information or even drop the article all together. Here is a sample header:

Connex Network Incorporated
Suite 301
800 Windmill Road
Dartmouth, Nova Scotia
Canada B3B 1L1

Tel 902-468-2578 Fax 902-468-2233

Contact: Susan Sweeney

Headline

Your headline should summarize your message and make the reader want to continue reading.

City and Date

Name the city you are reporting from and the date you wrote the press release.

The Body

Your first sentence within the body of the press release should sum up your headline and immediately tell the reader why this is newsworthy. With the number of press releases reporters receive, if you don't grab their attention immediately they won't read your release. Begin by listing all of the most relevant information first, leaving the supporting information last.

Ask yourself the five Ws (who, what, where, when, and why) and answer them up front. Write the press release just as if you were writing a newspaper article for publication. Include some quotes from key individuals in your operation and any other relevant outside sources that are credible. If there are any statistics that support your main message, include them as well. Your last paragraph should be a short description of your operation.

The Close

If your release is two pages long, center the word "-more-" at the bottom of the first page. To end your release, there are three ways of standard notation to do this: center the symbol "#," the word "end," or the number "-30-" at the end of your message.

Advantages of Interactive Press Releases

Online press releases take the same standard format as offline press releases, but the online press release can be interactive, with links to a variety of interesting information that supports your message. Reporters can easily find out other facts by following your hypertext links. Additional items included in your interactive press releases are:

- A hypertext link to the e-mail address of the media contact person in your operation.

- Hypertext links to your web site.

- Hypertext links to articles and related issues both on your web site and on other sites.

- Hypertext links to graphics and pictures for illustration. If your story relates to your country inn, have a link to a gallery of pictures of your country inn (interior, exterior, the grounds, the rooms, etc.). Reporters can simply right mouse click, "Save picture as," and incorporate the images into their story.

- Hypertext links to key individuals, their biographies, their photos, and possibly some quotes. Journalists usually include quotes in their stories.

- Hypertext link to a FAQ section where you can have frequently asked questions and perhaps a few that you wish were frequently asked.

Figures 18.1 through 18.5 are examples of some online tourism-related press releases.

Sending Press Releases on Your Own vs. Using a Distribution Service

When distributing press releases on your own, you save the money it would cost to have a service do it. You can also be more targeted in your efforts than a service might. Some services' lists may be outdated or incomplete. Their lists of reporters and editors may not be comprehensive and may not have been updated recently.

On the other hand, some services may get your press release taken more seriously. If reporters recognize the name of the service, they may be more receptive than if the release came from an unknown company. Using a service is bound to save you a lot of time.

If you decide to send your press releases on your own, you will have to build a list of journalists. When reading tourism publications that are read by your target market, look for the names of reporters and find out their contact information. If you don't know who to

Figure 18.1. A press release on Hotel Online referring to Extended Stay America.

Figure 18.2. This press release has sufficient contact information included at the bottom of the press release's content.

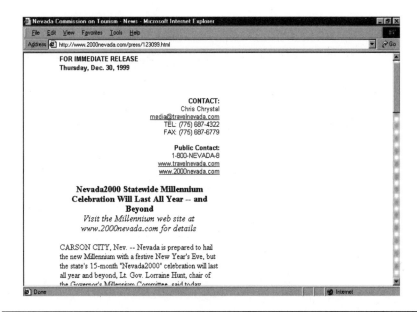

Figure 18.3. 2000Nevada.com has a press section on their site. Notice they include their URL, e-mail address and full contact information in the press release.

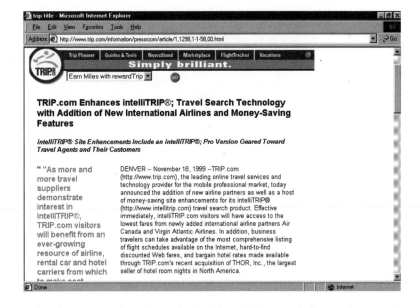

Figure 18.4. Trip.com uses an attractive layout for their press releases.

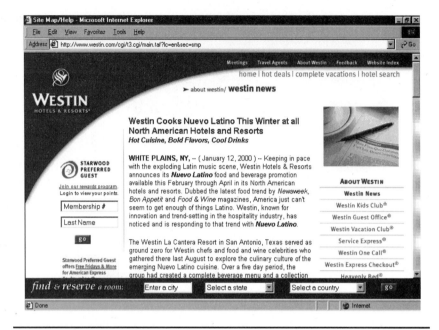

Figure 18.5. Westin Hotels & Resorts bolds specific keywords to make them stand out to readers of their press releases.

send a press release to at any publication, you can always call and ask for the name of the appropriate editor.

Subscribe to a personalized news service to receive articles about the tourism industry. This is a great way to find the names of journalists who might be interested in what you have to say.

There are a number of online resources to assist you in building your press distribution list, such as the one shown in Figure 18.6. MediaFinder *(http://www.mediafinder.com)* is a web site that may be useful. It provides access to a database of thousands of media outlets including magazines, journals, newspapers, newsletters, and catalogs. Press Access *(http://www.pressaccess.com),* as shown in Figure 18.7, has a large database of journalists and industry analysts. Their press access editorial database is available online, 24 hours a day, and contains in-depth information on journalists, publications, calendars, and so on.

MediaMap *(http://www.mediamap.com)* (see Figure 18.8) is an excellent public relations resource that has in-depth profiles on

Figure 18.6.   You can use MediaFinder to locate relevant media.

Figure 18.7.   Press Access is a great source for finding editors and publications.

Figure 18.8. MediaMap provides in-depth information on thousands of media contacts.

20,000+ of the top media contacts, their publications, and respective profiles that include their phone number, fax number, e-mail address, work preferences, and likes and dislikes pertaining to public relations professionals. Editorial calendars are included that inform the user who is writing what when. Through MediaMap you can gain access to Bacon's information on more than 200,000 media contacts (e.g., 1500 U.S. and Canadian daily papers, all U.S. weekly papers, 11,000+ business, trade, and consumer magazines, etc.). The inclusion of Bacon's information also enables you to access 24,000+ radio, TV, and cable contacts. MediaMap continually updates their media and calendar database to ensure 100% accuracy.

There are numerous press release distribution services online. You will find a number of them in the Internet Resources at the end of this chapter.

Where To Submit Your Tourism-Related Press Release

You should submit your press releases to all appropriate sites of interest to your target audience. Many sites post "news" or have monthly newsletters that may be appropriate recipients of your press release. Consider submitting to tourism accommodation sites and general tourism sites, and targeting your press releases by geographic area. Following are a few examples that may be of interest.

Hotel Online
http://www.hotel-online.com/
Submit your press release to Hotel Online (see Figure 18.9); the hospitality industry's online meeting place, providing the latest and most relevant news, trends, discussion forums, employment opportunities, classified advertising, and product pricing available anywhere.

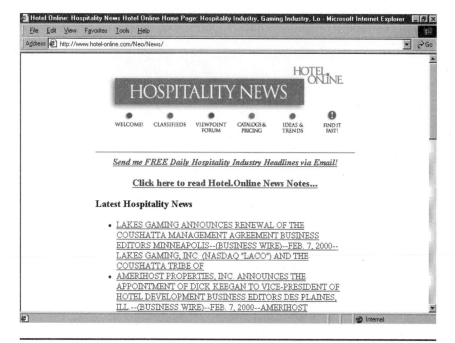

Figure 18.9. You can submit news pertaining to the hospitality industry, free, on Hotel Online.

Accommodation Search Engine
http://www.ase.net/
This accommodation-oriented search engine (see Figure 18.10) allows you to list your site and promote your press release or current news through their monthly newsletter.

Attracthits.com
http://www.attracthits.com/press.htm
Submit your press release to a pool of approximately 200 travel-oriented journalists (see Figure 18.11).

Golden Tips for Press Release Distribution

When distributing your press releases, don't send them to the news desk unaddressed. Know which editor handles the tourism and travel

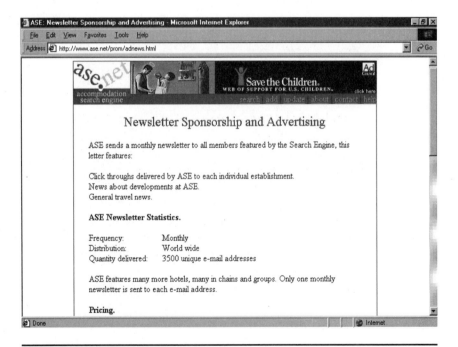

Figure 18.10. You might consider submitting your press release to the Accommodation Search Engine; they may include it in their newsletter.

Figure 18.11. For a fee, Attracthits.com allows you to submit your press release to a pool of approximately 200 travel-oriented journalists.

beat, and address the press release to that person. Don't send the press release to more than one editor in any organization unless there is more than one angle to the information in the press release.

Call ahead, if possible, to discuss and solicit the editor's interest in your press release before sending it. Also, follow up with a phone call a few days later to be sure the release was received and to answer any questions.

Be sure to review editorial calendars of publications in the tourism industry to see if there are upcoming articles where your story may make a contribution.

Timing and Deadlines

One of the most important things to remember when sending a press release or advisory is the deadline. Know how far in advance you should send your information for each of the different media. Here are some time guidelines for your press release distribution.

Monthly Magazines

For monthly magazines you should submit your press releases at least two to three months before the issue you want it to appear in. Magazines are planned far in advance because it often takes a number of weeks to have the magazine printed and in subscribers' mailboxes.

Daily Newspapers

It is a good idea to have your press release arrive on the editor's desk at least several weeks in advance. If it concerns a special holiday, you should send it even earlier.

TV and Radio

When submitting press releases to TV and radio, remember that you may be asked to appear on a show as a guest. Be prepared for this before you submit the release. TV and radio move very quickly; a story that has been given to the news director in the morning may appear on that evening's news.

Formatting Your E-mail Press Release

Your press releases can be e-mailed. Some reporters prefer e-mailed releases; others say they prefer mailed or faxed releases. Check the reporter's preference before you send your press release. If you send e-mailed press releases, make sure that your e-mails are formatted properly and that your press release is included in the body of the e-mail rather than as an attachment. Refer to Chapter 7 for guidelines on how to create effective e-mail messages.

Keep your e-mailed press releases to one or two pages with short paragraphs. It is best to include the press release in the body of the e-mail. Do not send your press release as an attachment. You don't know which platform or word processing program the reporter is using. You might be using Microsoft Word 2000, but the reporter could be using WordPerfect 3.0 and may not be able to open the file. There may also be problems downloading, which may prevent your release from being read. The person on the receiving end of your e-mail may be using an old computer with a slow dialup connection, meaning that what may take you 2 minutes to transfer might take them 20 minutes to download. In addition, you may be using a PC platform but the recipient may be using a Mac. Someone who spends 20 minutes downloading your e-mail only to find out it's useless won't be impressed—great start to getting the journalist to do a positive story on you!

Make sure the subject line of your e-mail is compelling. E-mailed releases can be easily deleted, unopened, by the journalist, and quite often they are, because journalists receive large volumes of these daily. Make sure your e-mail is clear and concise. Get to the point with the first sentence. If you don't grab the reader's attention at the beginning of the release, the recipient may not keep reading to find out what your news is.

It's very important to be able to send press release information in digital format. The journalist, with a quick Copy and Paste, will then have the "first draft" of the story. You have made it very easy for the journalist, who can then edit the draft and have a story very quickly. Everybody loves to save time, and a lot of these journalists are under tight deadlines.

What Is Considered Newsworthy?

Your press release has to contain newsworthy information for it to be published. One of the main concerns for public relations representatives is figuring out what is considered newsworthy and what isn't. You have to have a catch, and, if possible, it should appeal to some sort of emotion. Following is a list of newsworthy items:

- An exciting event taking place at your operation

- A free service or resource offered by your operation to the general public

- The appearance of a celebrity at your operation, an event, or an upcoming online promotion

- A contribution to charity

- A milestone anniversary that your operation is celebrating

- An award presented by or to your operation

What Isn't Considered Newsworthy?

Some things that aren't news to the general public may be news to targeted trade magazines and journals. Use your own judgment when trying to determine if your press release is news or just an excuse to get your operation's name in the press.

The launch of a new web site has not been news for a number of years now. Unless the site serves the public interest in an innovative way, you won't get a mention in the news. Nor is a new feature or change to your web site newsworthy information. Even if your site has undergone a major overhaul, this is not news to the general public.

Preparing Your Press Kits/Media Kits

Your press kit is an essential item at press conferences and interviews. This kit can also be sent to reporters when they request more information about a press release you have sent to them.

Your press kit should start with a folder displaying your tourism operation's logo and basic contact information. The folder should have pockets inside so that different sheets of information can be inserted. The following items should be included in your press kit:

- A press release outlining the newsworthy event

- A history of your operation

- Brochures

- Other articles written about your operation

- Pictures

- Background information on key players

- FAQ files and answers to anticipated questions

- Quotes from key individuals

- Contact information

- Your business card

Develop an Online Media Center for Public Relations

If publicity is a significant part of your public relations strategy, you should consider developing an online media center as part of your site (see Figure 18.12). The media center should be easily accessible from your navigation bar. It would include all the components needed by a journalist when doing a story on your tourism operation. The journalist should be able to find pictures to include in the story and all the information necessary to do their due diligence. The journalist should be able to send a question to the appropriate media contact within the organization with one click.

The media center should include:

- A chronology of press releases distributed by the company

- Your operation's history and background information

- An electronic brochure

- A link to other articles written about your operation

- A link to pictures of your operation or related products or services. Perhaps have a gallery where journalists can choose the pictures they want to include in their story with a right mouse click and "Save image as"

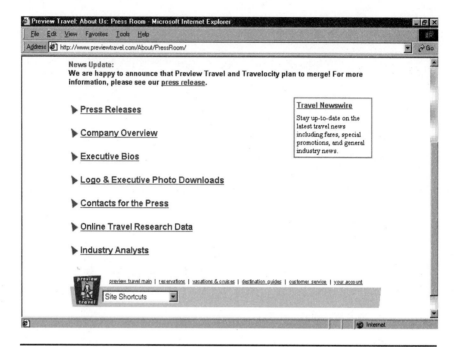

Figure 18.12. Preview Travel's Press Room has a number of important options available that would be of interest to the media.

- Background information on key personnel, along with their pics, bios, and quotes

- An e-mail link to your tourism operation's media and all contact information

- FAQ files and answers to anticipated questions

By having a media center on your site you are sending a clear message to the journalist. You are saying, "You're very important to me! I want to provide you with everything you need to quickly and easily complete your story on our operation." With the media center you are providing all the information, in a format journalists can use, to enable them to do the story no matter when they choose to do it.

Internet Resources

Press Releases

Press Release Tips for PR People
http://marketing.tenagra.com/releases.html
Talks about what one expects to receive and how you should write releases.

Executive Summary: Understanding News
http://www.x-summary.com/tips/980526.phtml
Improve the reception of your press releases by knowing what is news and what isn't.

PR Tips
http://www.profilepr.co.uk/prforum/PRTIPS/PRTIPS6.HTM
A British agency reviews the pros and cons of e-mail press releases.

Care & Feeding of the Press
http://www.netpress.org/careandfeeding.html
Journalist's manifesto for how PR people should work with the media.

Don't Drop the PR Ball
http://www.searchz.com/wmo/dontdroppr.shtml
A brief example of how a PR pro blew it with a reporter.

Xpress Press—Email Press Release Information
http://www.xpresspress.com/PRnotes.html
Information on how to write and format a press release to be distributed by e-mail.

A Template for a Killer Press Release
http://www.netrageousresults.com/pr/prtemplate.html
Example format for a successful press release to get yours noticed.

Where to Submit Your Press Releases

E-Releases
http://www.ereleases.com/

Submit your press release to a list of more than 10,000 opt-in journalists.

eworldwire
http://www.eworldwire.com/
eworldwire targets the larger publications and smaller regional, well-read, and respected publications such as those of private organizations and chambers of commerce, the freelance writers that write for these publications, and thousands of Internet-only publications otherwise known as e-zines (including travel zines).

Internet Wire Travel News
http://www.internetwire.com/travel/
This company is a premier Internet-based press release distribution service. Internet Wire also creates tailored information delivery services for public relations agencies and in-house PR departments.

E-mail Press Release Service Comparison
http://www.urlwire.com/email-releases.html
A decent comparison between different e-mail press release services.

Partyline
http://www.partylinepublishing.com
The standard media placement newsletter for the public relations trade.

PR Newswire Home Page
http://www.prnewswire.com
A leading source for worldwide corporate media, business, the financial community, and the individual investor.

Internet News Bureau Press Release Service
http://www.newsbureau.com
For a fee you can distribute your press release to thousands of online media outlets here. Also links to a number of good PR resources.

WebWire
http://www.webwire.com/
An Internet press release resource.

Promote Mailing Lists and Newsletters

Tell Liszt about Lists
http://www.liszt.com/submit.html
Register your mailing list with a major online database to get yourself noticed.

NewJour Welcome Page
http://gort.ucsd.edu/newjour/NewJourWel.html
Home for many Internet newsletters.

The List Exchange
http://www.listex.com
Directory of mailing lists and resources for those who run them.

Paid Help

Internet Media Fax
http://www.imediafax.com
Custom online news distribution service that creates targeted media lists "on the fly."

Internet Wire
http://www.internetwire.com
The Internet Wire offers online press release distribution via e-mail.

Xpress Press News Release Distribution Service
http://www.xpresspress.com
Press releases delivered electronically by e-mail to 4000 journalists and media members in the United States and internationally.

Tips for Printed Press Releases

13 Tips for Sending Effective Press Releases
http://www.poewar.com/articles/releases.htm
Tips to get the best results with press releases.

19

Online Publications

More than 60 percent of Internet users frequently read online publications, many of which relate to travel and the tourism industry. Identify appropriate marketing opportunities by searching for and reading e-zines that are relevant to the tourism industry. In this chapter, we will cover:

- What electronic magazines are

- Finding online sites to advertise or arrange links

- How to find appropriate travel-related e-zines for marketing purposes

- Submitting articles to appropriate e-zines

- Advertising in appropriate e-zines

- E-zine resources online

Appealing to Magazine Subscribers on the Net

A recent NPD Online Research survey shows that six out of ten web users frequently read online publications or e-zines. This is one of the reasons they are among the most popular marketing tools on the Internet. Five years ago there were a few hundred e-zines in publication. Now there are thousands of e-zines dedicated to a wide variety of general topics such as travel, business opportunities, food, child care—you name it. There are also many magazines that are more specific in content such as travel in Vermont, tourism in Southern New Mexico (see Figure 19.1), or adventure travel (see Figure 19.2). For any topic you are interested in, there are quite likely several e-zines dedicated to it.

E-zines, Ezines
Electronic magazines.

What Exactly Are E-zines?

E-zines, or electronic magazines, are the online version of magazines. They contain information regarding a certain topic in the form of magazine articles and features. Some e-zines are web site based and others are e-mail based.

Many offline magazines provide a version online as well. *Backpacker* (see Figure 19.3), *Outside Online* (see Figure 19.4), and *101 Things to Do in Hawaii* (see Figure 19.5) are all accessible via the Internet. Some offline magazines provide the full version of their traditional magazine. Others are selective about the articles they provide, and still others provide last month's edition.

Web-Based E-zines

There are web-based e-zines that have only an online presence (Figure 19.6). These e-zines are accessed through their web sites by browsing from page to page. They have the look and feel of a traditional magazine. They include lots of glossy pictures and advertisements similar to traditional magazines. Usually there is no charge to view the web-based e-zines, but some do charge a subscription fee.

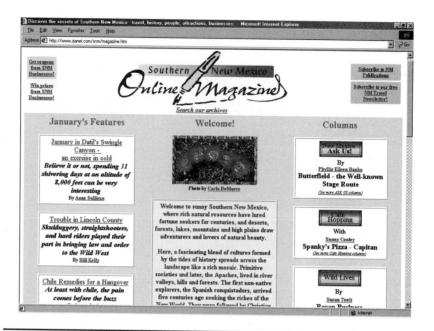

Figure 19.1. An online magazine for tourism in southern New Mexico.

Figure 19.2. An example of an adventure travel Ezine.

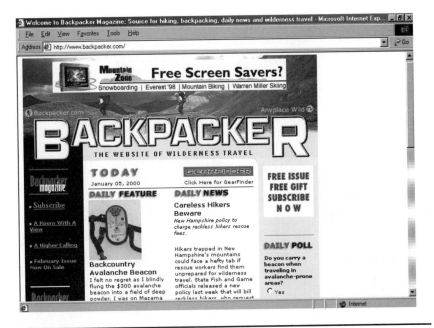

Figure 19.3. *Backpacker Magazine* has an online presence as well.

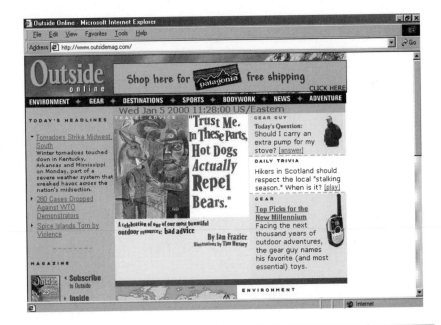

Figure 19.4. *Outside Magazine* also has an online presence.

Figure 19.5. 101 Things to Do in Hawaii has a Web site.

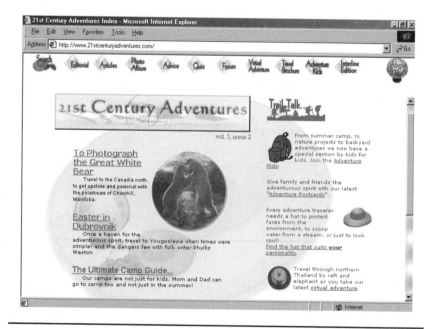

Figure 19.6. 21st Century Adventures is a Web-only Ezine.

These web-based e-zines tend to be as graphically pleasing as offline magazines. Many web-based e-zines relate to the tourism industry specifically; others are more general but certainly appropriate for travel stories and information.

E-mail E-zines

E-mail based e-zines are not nearly as pretty as the web-based e-zines. They tend to be more content oriented and, as such, tend to be more of a target marketing mechanism. E-mail e-zines tend to be several pages in length with several articles and often have some sort of advertising. Circulation of these e-zines is often in the thousands. Most of these e-zines run weekly or biweekly editions. Here too there are many that relate to the travel and tourism market.

Individuals interested in receiving these e-zines subscribe, and the e-zine is delivered straight into their e-mail boxes. Those individuals who are interested in the subject have taken the time to subscribe and ask to receive the information directly in their e-mail box. Once you have found an e-zine that caters to your target market, it may be a very valuable marketing vehicle.

Subscribers to an e-mail-based e-zine have access to the Internet. They regularly receive and send e-mail, and quite likely surf the Net. If you advertise in this type of medium and place your Internet address in the ad, your prospective customer is not more than a couple of clicks away from your site.

People subscribe because they are interested. Even if they don't read it immediately when it is received, they usually read the e-zine eventually. Otherwise, they would not have subscribed. Therefore, subscribers will see your URL and product advertisements. For this reason, e-mail e-zines are a great marketing tool for all tourism operators.

Using E-zines as Marketing Tools

Online publications are superior marketing tools for a number of reasons. They can be used in a number of different ways to increase the traffic to your web site. You can:

- Advertise directly

- Be a sponsor

- Submit articles

- Send press releases

- Start your own

Finding Appropriate E-zines for Your Marketing Effort

There are many locations online to find lists and links to both web-based and e-mail based e-zines. The most important element in choosing an e-zine is to choose one that reaches your target market. The reason e-zine ads are effective is that there is a high correlation between the target audience and the magazine's subscribers. If you advertise in an e-zine simply because it has the largest subscriber base, you will probably be disappointed unless your products or services have mass market appeal.

You should review a number of the e-zine-listing sites. Some of these sites have search capabilities on appropriate keywords. Others have their e-zines listed by category. Figure 19.7 is an example of a site that allows you to search for e-zines by keyword or by category. Once you have a list of e-zines you feel fit well with your marketing objectives, you should subscribe and begin receiving and reviewing these e-zines.

We have done a little research and have provided you with a number of tourism-related e-zines that may be appropriate for your marketing efforts.

Tourism Accommodation E-zines/Newsletters

Innfo—Bed and Breakfast Updates
Bed and breakfast information update from Sage Blossom Consulting, the B&B education and realty specialists. Monthly updates to

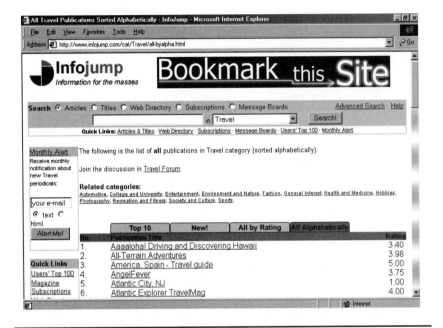

Figure 19.7. Infojump can be used to find a variety of travel Ezines and articles.

share the latest in our seminar schedule, conference news, B&Bs for sale, and industry related topics and issues.
Subscription information: Send an e-mail to *innfosubscribe @topica.com*.

Marketing Opps
Timely information for innkeepers comes directly to you so you can respond right away instead of waiting for the newsletter to arrive.
Subscription information: Send an e-mail to *info@paii.org* and mention the name of the list.

Weekly Quickie
A weekly update on what's news in innkeeping, and what's coming up from PAII.
Subscription information: Send an e-mail to *info@paii.org* and mention the name of the list.

Outdoor Recreation and Camping E-zines/Newsletters

AdventurousTraveler.com
http://www.adventuroustraveler.com
AdventurousTraveler.com is the destination to find the most current outdoor travel guidebooks, maps, CD-ROMs, videos, language courses, and more. Sign up for the AdventurousTraveler.com Trail Blazer titles and weekly newsletter.
Subscription information: Send an e-mail to *adventuroustraveler-subscribe@topica.com*.

Cyberwest Magazine
http://www.cyberwest.com/
A webzine affiliated with GORP, The Great Outdoor Recreation Pages. Read it online.

National Park Explorer
For discussion of America's National Parks, including history, science, recreation, and social issues.
Subscription information:Send an e-mail to *National_Parks-subscribe@topica.com*.

Where in the World
http://www.whereintheworld.co.uk
Online newsletter for adventurers, travelers, and explorers. Adventures and events you never knew existed. Fly a jetfighter at 70,000 feet or dive to the *Titanic*. Ride Route 66 on a Harley or walk the South Pole. Their aim is to inspire travelers to try something different.
Subscription information: Send an e-mail to *whereintheworld-subscribe@topica.com*.

Cruise E-zines/Newsletters

Cruise News
http://www.cruise-news.com/
The latest information on cruises and cruise operators.

HOTCruiseBargains
This list is for people looking for group rate cruise prices without

having to join or form a group. New subscribers require the list owner's approval to join.

Subscription information: Send an e-mail to *HOTCruiseBargains-subscribe@topica.com.*

Just Cruises
http://www.justcruises.com/
Just Cruises' E-News, distributed twice monthly, provides current information about cruising as well as special cruise offers direct from the cruise lines.

Subscription information: Send an e-mail to *justcruises-subscribe@topica.com.*

Sealetter Cruise Magazine
http://www.sealetter.com/current/
Cruise reviews and information.

The CruiseLetter by Doctor Cruise
http://DrCruise.com/
The CruiseLetter by Doctor Cruise is a weekly newsletter specializing in leisure cruises.

Subscription information: Send an e-mail to *cruise-subscribe@topica.com.*

Airline Travel E-zines/Newsletters

The FrequentFlier Crier
http://frequentflier.com/
The Internet's premier e-mail newsletter for frequent travelers. Frequent flyer program promotions, special fares, industry news and trends.

Subscription information: Send an e-mail to *frequentflier-subscribe@topica.com.*

Travel Industry E-zines/Newsletters

Tourism Promote Newsletter
http://www.marl.com/lds/
Provides tips to help you build a successful online tourist business.

Travel Deals E-zines/Newsletters

All-Out's Hot Spots
Plan your next vacation. Find great wholesale discounted rates on vacation packages.
http://www.alloutmktg.com/hstravel.html.
Subscription information: Send an e-mail to *allouthotspots-subscribe@topica.com.*

bizTRAVELER@Biztravel.com
http://www.biztravel.com/biztraveler
Geared toward frequent business travelers who want to make their time on the road or in the air more productive and fulfilling.

Condo Hot List
http://www.condohotlist.com/
Cheapest condos around. Rent them for as little as $250.00 a week. They are unused time share rooms.
Subscription information: Send an e-mail to *condos-subscribe@topica.com.*

Discount Travel
Lists discount travel programs and free travel promotions. Huge discounts on airfare, cruises, vacation condos, hotels, dining, golf, car rentals, and so on.
Subscription information: Send an e-mail to *travelfair-subscribe@topica.com.*

Have Fun Will Travel
http://travel-right.com/
Special travel deals from airlines, tour operators, cruiselines, resorts, and so on.
Subscription information: Send an e-mail to *travel_deals-subscribe@topica.com.*

T-Saaver Alert
http://www.travelsites.com/
A weekly e-mail that sends you all the best travel deals and information.
Subscription information: Send an e-mail to *webmaster@ travelsites.com.*

General Travel E-zines/Newsletters

Andy Graham's Tips for Long-Term Travelers & Travelogue
http://www.hoteltrade.com/
Travel tips for travelers (e.g., theft, what to pack, e-mail access) plus links of stories, pictures.
Subscription information: Send an e-mail to *andy_graham-subscribe@topica.com.*

BizTraveler
http://magazine.biztravel.com/biztraveler/
A weekly travelzine for the business scene.

Globe Hopping
http://GraceWeb.org/
Check out travel destinations, tips, and resources—almost 1000 subscribers.
Subscription information: Send an e-mail to *GlobeHopping-subscribe@topica.com.*

Online Rez News
http://www.onlinerez.com/
Periodical mailing of travel specials and what's new at ONLINE REZervationz.
Subscription information: Send an e-mail to *onlinerez-subscribe@topica.com.*

TravelASSIST Magazine
http://travelassist.com/mag/mag_home.html
It's a webzine all about travel. Visit the URL and read it for yourself.

Travel and Leisure
http://www.pathfinder.com/travel/
A real print magazine that also has an online version.

Geographic Specific E-zines/Newsletters

Atlantic Explorer TravelMag
http://atlanticonline.ns.ca/travmag/

Contains the most comprehensive information and list of links to travel, accommodations, and recreation in Canada's Eastern Provinces of Nova Scotia, New Brunswick, Prince Edward Island, and Newfoundland/Labrador.
Subscription information: Send an e-mail to *tonyt@explore.ca*

Intrepid Traveler
http://itfs99.virtualave.net/welcome.shtml
News and updates concerning the Intrepid Traveler as he works in and explores Yellowstone National Park.
Subscription information: Send an e-mail to *IT99-subscribe@topica.com.*

Topica Mig2
Tourist news.
Subscription information: Send an e-mail to *tourists-subscribe@topica.com.*

Tropi-Ties
http://tt.kia.net/ezine/
An e-zine for people who dream about a tropical paradise.

Visit USA
http://www.usabound.com/
Information on leisure and corporate travel to the United States and Canada, for overseas professional travel planners.
Subscription information: Send an e-mail to *america@topica.com.*

Totally Costa Rica Newsletter
http://www.ipee.com/newsletter.html
Dedicated to providing links, essays, and content about education, travel, recreation, discount air fares, relocation to Costa Rica, law and politics, agriculture, and culture in Costa Rica.

Yellowstone Net Newspaper
http://www.yellowstone.net/newspaper/
Provides a variety of current information and news about the Yellowstone National Park region.

The Multiple Advantages of E-zine Advertising

One of the major advantages of e-zine advertising is the life span of your ads. E-zines that are delivered to e-mail addresses will be read by the recipient and sometimes saved for future reference. Many e-zines archive their issues with the ads intact. Advertisers have received responses to ads that are several months old! Keep in mind, the immediate results of this advertising method will not be as impressive as a banner ad displayed for a limited time.

Another advantage of e-zine advertising is that e-zines are often shared with friends and associates. Your ad may be passed around a number of times after it first entered the mailbox of the subscriber. You are being charged for the ad based on the number of e-mail subscribers. Therefore, the extra viewers of your ad will be at no cost to you.

One of the most tangible advantages of e-zine advertising is the relatively low cost. E-zines need to fill all of their available space. If an e-zine advertising section has empty spaces, they are often willing to negotiate. Some will even barter with you, advertising space at a discounted price in exchange for their e-zine promotion on your web site.

E-zines provide a very targeted advertising medium. People subscribe to various e-zines because they have a genuine interest in the topics covered. This provides a major advantage over other advertising media. E-zine ads have been shown to have very high response rates due to their targeted nature. If someone subscribes to an e-zine on Caribbean cruises, you know they are interested in Caribbean cruises and therefore are a prime target for a cruise line to advertise to.

Guidelines for Your Advertising

Once you have found e-zines that are applicable to your niche in the tourism industry, you should consider a number of other factors before you make your final decision on placing your ad.

- Check the ads displayed in the e-zine for repetition. If advertisers have not advertised more than once, then they probably did not see very positive results.

- Respond to some of the ads and ask the advertisers what their experiences were with advertising in that particular e-zine. Be sure to tell them who you are and why you are contacting them. If you are up front, they will probably be receptive to your inquiry.

- Talk to the e-zine publisher and ask questions—for instance, how many subscribers there are. Ask what other advertisers have had to say about their results. Find out what types of ads they accept and if there are any restrictions. Maybe the e-zine has a set of advertising policies that you can receive via e-mail.

- Find out if your ad can have a hypertext link to your web site. If the e-zine allows hypertext links, make sure you link to an appropriate page, one that is a continuation of the advertisement or a page that provides details on the item you were advertising. Provide a link to the order form from this page to assist the transaction.

- In some cases the e-zine will have an editorial calendar available to assist you with the timing of your ad. The editorial calendar will tell you what articles will be included in upcoming issues. If an upcoming issue will have an article relating to your type of tourism operation, your products, or your services, you may choose to advertise in that issue. You might contact the editor regarding a product review or submit an article relevant to the issue topics.

- Make sure that the advertising rates are reasonable based on the number of subscribers, and ask yourself if you can afford it. If you are not in a position to pay for the advertising now, ask if there are any other arrangements that could be made. For example, the publisher may accept a link on your web site in exchange for the ad.

- You should develop your ads with your target audience in mind. They should attract your best prospects. Wherever possible you should link to your site or provide an e-mail link to the appropriate individual within your organization.

- You should develop a mechanism to track advertising responses. You could use different e-mail accounts for different ads to determine which ads are bringing you the responses. You can also use different URLs to point the viewer to different pages within your site. If you have a good traffic analysis package, you will be able to track the increase in visitors as a result of your ad.

- Make sure you are versed in the publication's advertising deadlines and ad format preferences.

Other Marketing Opportunities with E-zines

Besides advertising, a number of other marketing opportunities can be explored with e-zines.

Once you have found the e-zines that cater to your target market, these e-zines may be appropriate recipients for your press releases. Refer to Chapter 18 for recommendations on press release development and distribution.

The editors may also accept articles of interest to their readership. You might be able to incorporate information on your products and services in an interesting article that would fit the editor's guidelines.

Starting Your Own E-zine

You can start your own e-zine. Don't make this decision without lots of thought. There are lots of resources online regarding e-zine development and administration. If you do start your own e-zine, you should do the following:

- *Promote it to your target market through newsgroups, mailing lists, your web site, and your e-mail signature file.* If you do promote your e-zine in newsgroups and mailing lists, be sure it is appropriate to advertise your e-zine in a given newsgroup or mail list before you post. You do not want to be accused of spamming. However, promote your e-zine shamelessly on your site (let people subscribe to the e-zine on your site) and in your signature file.

- *Provide an opportunity for subscribers to let others know.* In your online e-zine, have a form that allows subscribers to e-mail a copy of the e-zine to their friends and colleagues. Use a call to action statement like "Send a friend of copy of this e-zine. Click here." This is a great way to pick up additional subscribers because some of the nonsubscribers who read your e-zine might then become subscribers if your content is interesting to them.

- *Make it easy for people to subscribe to your e-zine.* Provide clear subscription instructions in each e-mail version of your e-zine and on the online version of your e-zine. Have a form handy on your site to collect e-mail addresses from people who wish to subscribe.

- *Don't provide your list of subscribers to anyone.* This will protect your subscribers' privacy and keep your list spam-free. Thus, when you mail your e-zine, use the BCC feature or use a specialized e-mail program that hides all the recipients' addresses so the entire list is not compromised. People will not be happy if they start receiving spam as the result of your e-zine.

- *Provide great content.* This goes without saying. If you have content that people want to read, they will remain subscribers. As the word about your e-zine spreads, you will have a large community of people who fit your target market reading it.

Internet Resources

The Magazine Rack
http://magazine-rack.com

Provides a searchable directory of online magazines, newspapers, journals, and e-zines.

Factsheet Five
http://www.factsheet5.com
A site dedicated to e-zines. How to's, reviews, FAQ files, and a list of e-zines on the Internet. This is a selection of favorite web sites.

The Etext Archives
http://www.etext.org/Zines
Complete with a search engine, this site offers places to find all of your online publication resources.

Electronic Newsstand
http://www.enews.com
Founded in 1993, this was one of the first content-based sites on the Internet. Since then, the site has grown to become the largest and most diverse magazine-related resource anywhere on the web.

MediaFinder
http://www.mediafinder.com/magazines/mag0020.cfm
A national directory of magazines with details on target audience, publisher, contact, telephone numbers, web addresses, e-mail addresses, editorial descriptions, issue frequency, and subscription price. In a lot of cases an Information Request form is attached should you want further details. Great resource!

WebPlaces
http://www.webplaces.com/e-zines.htm
A meta-index of e-zines sorted by category.

Ecola Newsstand
http://www.ecola.com
Ecola's Newsstand has over 6800 magazines, newspapers, and publications. There are over 100 categories of magazines to choose from.

Ezine Search
http://www.homeincome.com/search-it/ezine

Billed as the world's ultimate e-magazine database. Searchable by category.

InfoJump
http://www.infojump.com
Browse a huge directory of e-zines by category.

LinkPad—Electronic Magazines
http://www.referthem.com/pad/ezines.htm
A list of electronic magazines and directories.

20

Web Rings as a Promotion Tool

Web rings provide a different way to organize sites. They are a free service offered to the Internet community. Web rings arrange sites with similar content by linking them together in a circle, or a ring. Each link in the ring is directed to a CGI script on the web ring's server that sends the viewer on to the next site in the ring. There are literally thousands of rings with such subjects as travel and tourism, communications, games, art, real estate, and so on. If there isn't a ring suitable for your site, you can create your own. The types of visitors you will receive from participating in the web ring will be potential customers who are responsive to the content of your site and curious about your services. In this chapter, we cover:

- What web rings are and how they work

- Promotion possibilities with web rings

- How to participate and what it will cost

- Where to find web rings that work for your tourism operation

- Web ring resources on the Net

An Effective Alternative to Search Engines and Directories

Web rings are a fast-growing medium providing one of the easiest ways for visitors to navigate the Internet. In each of its tens of thousands of topic-specific rings, member web sites have linked their sites together, thus permitting more targeted visitors to reach the joined sites quickly and easily.

People have been becoming increasingly dissatisfied with search engines and directories as tools to identify specific topic-related sites. Searches on a specific keyword have yielded results that often include totally unrelated sites. For instance, if you were planning a vacation to Mexico and you wanted to search for resorts in Mexico, the search engine results would likely include sites somewhat related but not exactly what you were looking for. The results would include book titles at Amazon related to Mexico travel, personal pages with other people's experiences traveling in Mexico (complete with pictures from their family vacation), travel agencies, and tour company sites. The web ring provides an alternative to these tools.

Site owners typically trade links with other web sites to help advertise each other's sites. The web ring was initially developed to enlarge the scope of link trading. A web ring joins together many sites with a common topic. Two of the major web ring sites are:

- WebRing at *http://www.webring.org/*

- LoopLink at *http://www.looplink.com/*

What Are Web Rings?

A web ring is made up of a number of topic-specific sites that are grouped together, as shown in Figure 20.1. There are *Titanic* web rings, Beanie Baby web rings, prenatal care web rings, outdoor adventure web rings, and remote sensing web rings as well as bed and breakfast web rings in the list of over 80,000 web rings that exist today. At webring.org, web rings fit into several major categories:

Figure 20.1. The Travel Industry Network Web ring displays the common Web ring graphic at the bottom of the page. The navigation tool allows you to travel easily throughout the ring.

- Arts and Humanities

- Computers

- Business and Economy

- Internet

- Health

- Recreation and Sports

- Entertainment

- Society and Culture

- Miscellaneous

At looplink.com, they too have many categories:

- Arts and Entertainment

- Business

- Computers

- Health

- Home and Leisure

- Information Sources

- Internet

- Online Shopping

- Science and Technology

- Society and Culture

- Sports

- Travel

- Multimedia

Each of these major categories has a number of subcategories, and each of the subcategories has a number of individual rings.

Rings can contain any number of sites. There must be at least five before the ring will be listed in the directories. Generally, the rings will contain somewhere between 20 and 200 sites. Some rings are smaller and some rings are substantially larger, with close to a thousand sites included.

Each ring was started and is maintained by an individual web site owner. Through navigation links, found most often at the bottom of member pages, visitors can travel to all or any of the sites in a ring. They can move through a ring in either direction, going to the next or previous site, or listing the next five sites in the ring. Visitors can also jump to a random site in the ring or survey all the sites that make up the ring.

An extraordinary system, web rings are entirely open and free of charge to both visitors and members. As more and more people discover web rings, we will see phenomenal growth in this as a preferred method to surf the Net. Today web rings are experiencing growth rates in excess of 10% monthly. Member sites total over 1,300,000 and web rings total over 80,000.

How Do Web Rings Work?

To surf a ring, all you have to do is use the links at the bottom of the page in the "web ring block." At the bottom of web ring participant's pages, you will find the web ring navigation aid. A common web ring graphic will include links to the Next site in the ring, the Previous site in the ring, or a Random site in the ring. You also have the option, in many cases, to see a list of the Next 5 sites in the ring or to view the entire Index of the ring's sites. Once you begin surfing a ring, there is no clear beginning or ending, just a circle of related sites. The web ring program compensates for sites that are unreachable because they no longer exist or have server problems. You will always be able to navigate the loop.

When using a search engine, you are provided with a list of resulting sites, only some of which are appropriate. You visit the sites listed and then, depending on which browser you are using, you may use your Back button to return to the results page to make another selection. With a web ring this backing out is unnecessary. Once you're finished reviewing a site in the ring, you proceed to the next site that is of interest or simply surf through the connected sites one by one.

How to Participate in Web Rings

The first thing to do is find web rings that are appropriate for your operation, your product, or your service, those that cater to your target market. You can review the directories at the WebRing site *(http://www.webring.org)* and also at the LoopLink site *(http://www.looplink.com)*.

We have done some research and provide you with a number of travel and tourism web rings that may be appropriate for your tourism web site.

Hotels/Motels/Accommodations

All Small Hotels Around the World
224 sites
http://www.hotellinks.com/smallhotels/welcome.cfm

Hotels with under 100 rooms, most of which are family owned and operated.

Vacation Villas Worldwide Web Ring
Membership size not listed
http://www.villanet.com/villaring/index.html
Selected web sites featuring private homes and villas in all parts of the world that you can rent for your vacation.

Bed and Breakfasts and Country Inns

Bed and Breakfast Web Ring
98 sites
http://bandb.miningco.com/travel/bandb/blring.htm
Bed and breakfast sites around the Internet.

Outdoor Recreation and Camping

Adventure Travel Web Ring
12 sites
http://www.adventurering.com/
A wide variety of reputable, top-notch specialized tour operators.

Campgrounds (RVPark) International Web Ring
103 sites
http://homepages.go.com/~rvpark/rvpark.html
Campgrounds and RV parks directory worldwide. One-stop resource for information about private campgrounds and private RV parks. A web ring designed to make searching for campgrounds and RV parks user friendlier, if you like. Added to fifty search machines. Banners allowed with descriptions. Resources now allowed to display their banner for more exposure to users.

RV TRAVELIN' Web Ring
39 sites
http://www.webring.org/cgi-bin/webring?ring=falcor;index
This site is for anyone or anything RV, whether you live in your RV

full time, or just travel a few months of the year. They want clubs, campgrounds, RV personal pages, seasonal employers, anything RV. If you think your site will benefit the RVing community—come on in and join the campfire!

Ecotourism Web Ring
47 sites
http://www.ecotourism.cc/
Features sites offering outdoor adventure tours.

Carnivals, Fairs, Festivals, and Outdoor Amusement Events Webring
50 sites
http://nav.webring.org/cgi-bin/navcgi?ring=carnivals;list
Carnivals, fairs, festivals, and outdoor amusement events are the mainstay of entertainment through out the world. This web ring links together all members of the OAB industry and those sites that showcase the fun that is had all over the world every Saturday night as families head out for their local events. Of special interest are web sites featuring information on carnival ride companies, theme parks, thrill rides, industry providers, and home pages that are just plain *fun!*

Camping in the United Kingdom
9 sites
http://www.crosswinds.net/maidstone/~campinguk/index.htm
This web ring brings together people who enjoy camping in the UK. It covers all forms of camping, from backpacking to RVs. So if you enjoy the joys of camping join them and spread the word.

Backpackers Traveling
26 sites
http://travelers.israel.net/backpack/
For budget travelers who use their backpack to travel.

Cruises

Seacruise Web Ring
19 sites
http://www.permafrost.com/cmgarven/seacruise.htm

Sites related in some way to the world of cruise travel; personal, commercial, and informational sites welcome.

Travel Industry

The Travel Industry Network
48 sites
http://www.gulfcoast.net/tin/
The Travel Industry Network promotes any form of travel industry on the Internet. They offer links to travel agents and agencies, cruise companies, tour companies, resorts, and much more. If you are going to travel, you must visit these sites!

Travelring
1063 sites
http://www.actionsites.com/travelring/index1.htm
Listing lots of travel organization web sites.

Travel the World
26 sites
http://www.geocities.com/starscroll.geo/webring.htm
Features sites with travel information and vacation photos from around the globe.

Travel Report Ring
152 sites
http://www.bielefeld.netsurf.de:8080/~u_mueller/ring.html
Connects pages with travel reports from all over the world.

Tourism Research Web Ring
27 sites
http://www.waksberg.com/webring/
Links together tourism research web sites.

The Top 100 Recreation and Travel Web Rings
http://stats.webring.org/cgi-*bin/wrstats?group=rec%2*
Etravel&toprings
A list of the top 100 travel and recreation web rings that includes the number of hits obtained by each ring and the number of sites in each.

Theme Parks

Theme Parks, Coasters, and Thrill Rides
199 sites
http://nav.webring.org/cgi-bin/navcgi?ring=tpcoaster;list
The Theme Parks and Coasters ring is for quality sites that feature theme and amusement parks, roller coasters, rides, and the like.

Geographic Specific

Canada Travel Ring
57 sites
http://www.fortunecity.com/oasis/niagara/26/ring.html
For Canadian travel-oriented sites.

Atlantic Canada Tourism Partnership
http://actp.net/
The Atlantic Canada Tourism web ring is designed to bring more tourism operators online into the exciting world of the World Wide Web (WWW) and connected throughout Atlantic Canada, including Nova Scotia, New Brunswick, Prince Edward Island, Newfoundland, and Labrador.

Caribbean Travel Web Ring
62 sites
http://www.grenadaexplorer.com/Caribbeantravel.htm
Making it easier for visitor to plan a vacation or visit the Caribbean.

Las Vegas Web Ring
82 sites
http://www.lvol.com/webring.html
Featuring sites containing Las Vegas content.

ScenarioUSA Online Sponsors
166 sites
http://scenariousa.dstylus.com/faqs.html
Links U.S. sites geared toward travel and tourism.

0-Delay Bed and Breakfast Inns of Florida
21 sites

http://innformation.com/fl/ring/
Bed and breakfast inns located in Florida.

Discover Washington State
11 sites
http://www.westernwashington.com/direc.shtml
Discover Washington state. Useful web sites to aid the viewer in a search for information about Washington state. These sites will contain more information than just local business pages. All sites will contain some if not all of the following, information about recreation, tourism, businesses, accommodations, parks, maps, dining, weather, news, sports, employment, travel, and whatever you may be looking for in the way of Washington state information.

State of Michigan Web Ring
143 sites
http://www.fascinatingferrets.com/mich.htm
Linking Michigan-related web pages, whether personal or business. You must live in Michigan to join.

The Australian Travel Web Sites Ring
34 sites
http://www.overland.com.au/webring/travel.htm
The objective of this ring is to promote web sites that deal primarily with travel within Australia.

The Blue Paradise Web Ring
Membership size not listed
http://www.geocities.com/TheTropics/Shores/8770/Blue.html
Promotes and connects web sites with travel-related content.

Zimbabwe Travel Ring
11 sites
http://www.lind.org.zw/zimtravelring.htm
Travel in and around Zimbabwe including hotels, tour and safaris companies, travel agents, airlines, car hire and tourism-related services and information.

Arizona Tourism Web Ring
26 sites

http://www.pageviews.com/aztourism/
Sites that provide Arizona-specific content or services such as lodging, tours, maps, ghost towns, golf courses, and vacation destinations.

Alaska Travel Web Ring
58 sites
http://www.ktn.net/webring/
Dedicated to Alaska tourism, vacations, lodging, sportfishing charters, outdoors, city information, and more.

European Bed and Breakfast Ring
4 sites
http://users.skynet.be/brugge/bbeuro/
European bed and breakfast sites.

0-Delay Colorado Bed and Breakfast Webring
8 sites
http://innformation.com/co/ring/
A list of great bed and breakfast inns in Colorado.

Timeshares

Timeshare Web Ring
64 sites
http://goldenstrand.com/Webring/
Dedicated to web sites about timeshare vacations, timeshare resorts, timeshare information, timeshare brokers, and much more.

Once you have found an appropriate web ring, you contact the owner to ask permission to join. See Figure 20.2 for an example of this. The owner will review your site to determine your "fit" with the theme. Once you are accepted, the owner will provide you with the required code and accompanying graphics, which you will insert on your page. The ring owner provides all the required material, you slip it into your HTML file, and that's that.

Once the code is on your site, webring.org or looplink.com monitors the traffic and collects the statistics for your site as they do for all web ring sites. This is very beneficial to you because you can see how much traffic you are getting through the web ring.

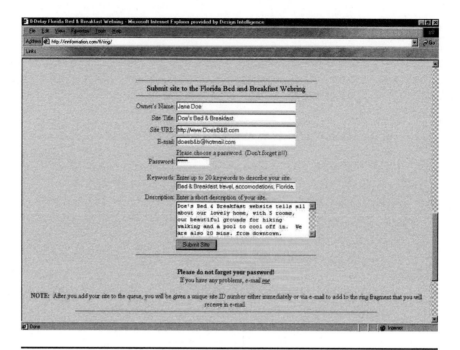

Figure 20.2. Joining a Web ring is as simple as filling out an online application and submitting it for approval.

Any web site owner can apply to create a new ring. If the application is approved, webring.org or looplink.com will provide all the necessary code and instructions. New web rings are listed in the directory once they contain at least five sites.

Web Ring Participation Costs

The cost to participate in these web rings is absolutely nil. There is no application fee, no charge for the approval, no charge for the code to be inserted on your pages, and no charge for the increased traffic a web ring brings.

The Benefits of Web Rings

There are many benefits to both the users of web rings and the participating web sites. Benefits to the user include the following:

- Web rings provide a great navigation tool for people looking for more information on a specific topic.

- Web rings are easy to use. They provide one of the most efficient ways to find specific content on the Internet.

- Web rings avoid the duplication found in search engines, where a site may appear several times in one search. Each site is linked only once in each web ring.

- Web rings speed up search time.

- Web rings eliminate sifting through mounds of search engine results for appropriate sites.

Benefits to participating web sites include these:

- Web ring participation increases the number of targeted visitors to your web site.

- The organizers of the web rings make it easy to monitor how successful your ring is. Traffic reports and "top" rings statistics are made available to participants.

- Web rings drive traffic to your site.

Business Reluctance to Participate in Web Rings

One of the biggest hurdles web rings face to being adopted by the tourism sector is that when you join a ring, you are linking to the competition, as shown in Figure 20.3 and Figure 20.4.

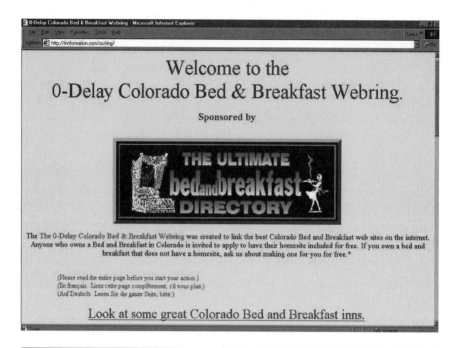

Figure 20.3. Although Web rings can contain links to your competition they can still generate large amounts of targeted traffic to your Web site.

It is likely that this mentality explains why web rings have been so popular for personal sites and special interest groups, but have failed to catch on in today's business. But, again, tourism-related web sites have not shied away from web rings. Lately we have seen a growth in commercial application of web rings. There are a few reasons for this:

- A number of articles have appeared in Internet marketing magazines related to the high volume of traffic through these web rings. Businesses have sometimes found that the bulk of the traffic to their site is coming through the web ring.

- Other articles talked about the benefits of being conveniently located near your competition bringing more traffic for everyone. Several likened it to what happens in the real world in the fast food industry. When a McDonald's opens, you

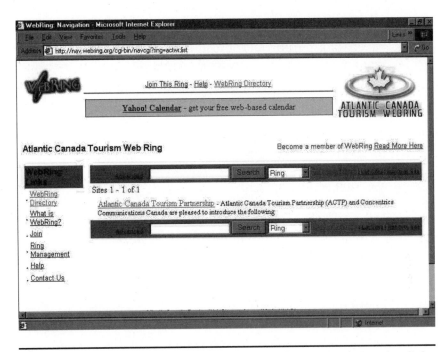

Figure 20.4. The Atlantic Canada Tourism Web ring was designed to link Atlantic Canadian tourism operators' Web sites.

quickly see a Burger King, Wendy's, Pizza Hut, KFC, and Taco Bell all open up close by. This means more business for everyone.

Other Marketing Opportunities Provided by Web Rings

When you have found a tourism-related web ring that attracts your target market, you can participate and enjoy the increase in visitors to your site. Web rings provide an array of other opportunities as well.

You can search through the list of participants in a web ring to arrange reciprocal links. You can also search a web ring for banner advertising purposes. You can either exchange banners or purchase advertising on these sites.

You can find travel sites that may be appropriate for cooperative advertising purposes. You can exchange coupons with another site you are linked to, which works especially well when you sell non-competing services to the same target market.

Internet Resources

Webring—The Shape of Things to Come
http://www.webring.org
One of the fastest and most exciting ways to navigate the World Wide Web. In each of its tens of thousands of rings, member web sites have banded together to form their sites into linked circles. Their purpose is to allow more visitors to reach them quickly and easily.

LoopLink—The Traffic Building Site
http://www.looplink.com
Sites of a particular subject together in a loop. A visitor to any loop site can easily move forward or backward through the loop and visit other loop sites within that subject area. This drives targeted quali-fied traffic to all the loop sites. Surfers don't want to deal with mounds of irrelevant search engine results. They want to visit sites on topics they love. It's so simple, and everybody's a winner.

RingSurf
http://www.ringsurf.com
RingSurf is a completely free service that lets users quickly, easily, and reliably navigate thousands of related web sites organized by areas of interest. Joining a Net ring is great way to increase traffic to your site.

21

Effective Offline Promotion

The benefits of using traditional media and print materials to cross-promote your web site are numerous. Your web site can provide prospective tourists and members of the press with the latest information and quickly answer a lot of their questions. The web also facilitates an easier way to present more information than you can print in a magazine or newspaper ad (due to cost and space restraints). People can then request additional information or order online. In this chapter, we cover:

- Tips for offline promotion of your tourism-related web site

- Offline promotion opportunities

Offline Promotion Objectives

Since visitors can be directed from offline promotion to request additional information or order online, you should promote your URL on every piece of promotional material you produce. The more exposure your URL receives, the more likely it is that people will remember it when they go online.

Be creative with your offline promotional campaign. Brainstorm with your marketing team to generate a number of lucrative channels through which to promote your URL; for example, try displaying your URL in TV and radio commercials, magazine and newspaper ads, and billboards. The more places your URL appears, the more it will get noticed. Some businesses even incorporate their URL into their building and vehicle signage. Answer your telephone "YourTourismOperation.com, good morning." This is quite effective in letting people know that you want them to visit your web site and providing them with your URL at the same time. Next time they have a question or want to place an order or make a reservation, they may go directly to the web site.

By displaying your URL in traditional media, you encourage people to visit your site for more information about your tourism operation. Another benefit is that people can usually order or make a reservation from your web site. Naturally, your site should be up-to-date with all of the latest rates and sales promotions. If a six-month old advertisement is seen in a magazine, as long as the URL is displayed in the ad, readers can go to your site and get current information. Your web site is your most effective means of advertising, but people have to know about it before they can view it.

Exposing Your URL Using Corporate Literature and Material

It is important that your corporate image be consistent in your online and offline promotional campaigns. You should use the same colors, style, fonts, logo, and tag lines on all of your marketing materials. As a rule of thumb, try to place your URL on everything you put your logo on—which means just about every piece of corporate literature. Make sure to include your URL on the following:

- Letterhead

- Business cards

- Brochures

- Envelopes

- Checks

- Fax coversheets

- Flyers

- Advertisements

- Direct mail pieces

- Newsletters

- Press releases

- Media kits

URL Exposure Through Promotional Items

If your tourism operation uses promotional items as giveaways at trade shows and events, it is a good idea to promote your web site with these items. Figures 21.1 and 21.2 are some examples of the different promotional products that you can order on the Internet for your tourism business. Promotional items that are used in and around computer workstations are ideal because your URL is visible when people are in a position to actually visit your site. Some examples are:

- Mousepads

- Diskette holders

- Screen cleaning kits

- Software

- Screen savers

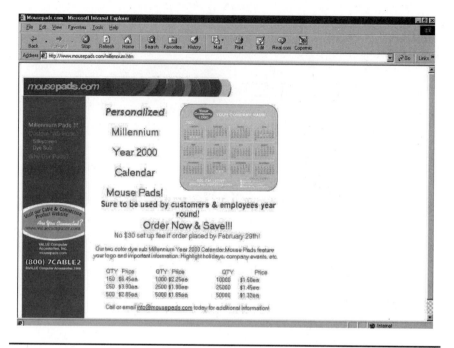

Figure 21.1. Mousepads.com (*http://www.mousepads.com/*) allows you to place your tourism operation's information on customized mousepads.

- Pens and pencils

- Scratch pads

- Coffee mugs

- Coasters

- Letter openers

- Stress balls

- Calendars

- Sticky notes

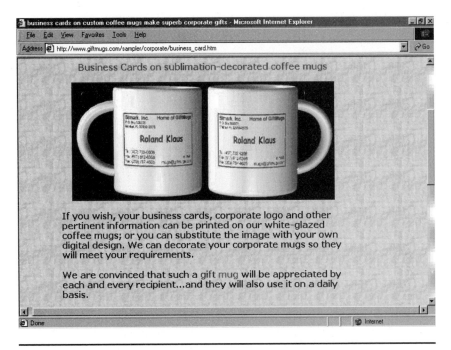

Figure 21.2. Put your tourism operation's company information on mugs courtesy of Giftmugs.com (*http://www.giftmugs.com/*).

Promoting Your URL on Clothing

Articles of clothing are another great promotional item. When people wear an article of clothing with your URL on it, they become a walking billboard for your site. Most golf and country clubs and a high percentage of tourism operations have their own line of clothing. Tourists often purchase articles of clothing as mementos of their trip, so clothing with your URL and logo on it is a great promotional vehicle. If you have a corporate uniform, your URL should be displayed. Figure 21.3 demonstrates just a few of the items that you can put your URL on. Put your URL and a catchy phrase or tag line on such items as:

- Golf shirts

- T-shirts

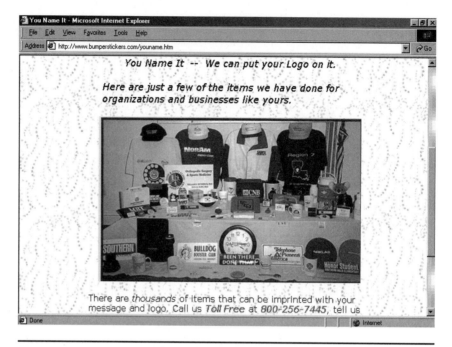

Figure 21.3. Bumperstickers (*http://www.bumperstickers.com/*) can embroider your company's logo onto t-shirts, hats, pens, stickers and so forth.

- Sweatshirts

- Hats

- Aprons

- Jackets

Promoting Your URL on Novelty Items

Novelty items can be an effective place to print your URL. Figure 21.4 illustrates quite a unique method of displaying a URL. If your target market is a younger audience, then put your URL on items that will appeal to them, such as:

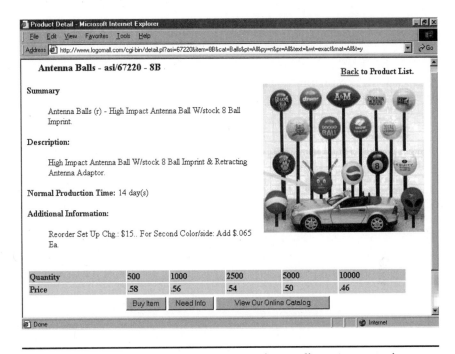

Figure 21.4. At logmall.com *(http://www.logomall.com/)* you can have antenna balls customized with your tourism organization's logo.

- Frisbees

- Balls

- Beach towels

- Sunglasses

- Key chains

- Magnets

- Chocolate bars

- Bumper stickers

Promotion with a Touch of Creativity

Be creative and come up with catchy slogans that have a connection with the promotional item. For example,

- Clocks: "Take some time to visit our web site at"

- Rulers: "For a measurable difference visit us at"

- Coffee mugs: "Take a break and visit our web site at"

- Tape measures: "Visit our web site at *http:// www.YourURL.com* and see how our site measures up."

- Magnifying glasses: "You don't need one of these to see that our site is the best. Come visit us online at"

- Watches: "Isn't it about time you visited us at"

- Bookmarks: "Take a break from reading and visit our web site at"

Internet Resources

Promotional Webstickers
http://www.websticker.com/products.htm
Simple ideas to effectively promote your web site offline.

Bizine
http://www.bizine.com/profit.htm
Increase your profits by coordinating online and traditional offline marketing. An article by Bob LeDuc.

Free Pint
http://www.freepint.co.uk/issues/040399.htm
12 Offline Ways of Promoting Your URL, by Nikki Pilkington.

HCS
http://www.hcsweb.net/OfflinePromotion.htm
This includes a checklist of possible places where you can include your web site address.

Digital-Women.com
http://www.digital-women.com/unique.htm
This includes unique ideas for online and offline promotion.

WebCMO
http://www.webcmo.com/report/opss1/offline.htm
A survey report on offline promoting.

PC Mojo
http://pcmojo.com/pcmojo/offline.htm
Information on why you need to promote your site off the Internet.

Advertising Concepts
http://www.bumperstickers.com/ad.htm
Why use promotional products? This site gives you good promotional ideas and shows what these promotional products will do for you.

Mohawk Advertising
http://www.logomall.com
Mohawk advertising sells hundreds of promotional items online for your business.

22

Where Are Your Visitors Coming From? Web Traffic Analysis

Online advertisers are constantly seeking ways to better target the people who visit their web site. Fortunately, the technology exists to assist them with this task. Many tourism web sites are now using web traffic analysis software to gain valuable marketing information on their visitors and their visitors' experiences traveling through their site. This software enables them to analyze not only what page of the web site their visitors came to first, but also where they came from, and how long they spent on your site. In this chapter you will learn:

- What your web server's log files can tell you about your site's visitors (what browser your visitors is using, what version of the browser they are using, their country of origin, etc.)

- How analyzing log files with web traffic analysis software can benefit your tourism web site

- How to develop a profile of your visitors

- How to optimize your web site to accommodate your visitors

- Getting the most for your marketing dollar

- Generating leads for your tourism operation

- How analysis software can help you to manage your online advertising

- How you can get web traffic analysis software for your web site

- Popular brands of web traffic analysis software

Do You Know Who Your Visitors Are?

Retailers have always spent endless hours trying to analyze the shoppers who visit their stores. They are constantly trying to collect data about their markets so that they can decide what the best form of advertising is for their target market, what services are important to that market, and what features that market is looking for. The same thing is happening today on the Internet for all types of businesses— tourism operators included. Tourism operators are constantly collecting data on their target market—their needs, wants, preferences, and desires. Most people are unaware that they are even doing this.

Web traffic analysis software is helping tourism operations focus on their target market like never before. It is helping them to understand the traffic on their web site, and is enabling them to make the necessary changes that are critical to increasing web site traffic. But how do they do it, you ask?

Using Log Files to Your Advantage

All web servers log a list of all the requests for individual files that people have requested from a web site. These log files will include the HTML files and their embedded images, and any other associated files that have been transmitted through the server. These files can be analyzed by web traffic analysis tools to generate important data, such as:

- The number of visitors to your home page

- Where the visitors came from in terms of their IP address

- Where your visitors were on the Internet immediately before your site

- Where they entered your site

- Which pages they visited

- How long they stayed on your site

- What page they left your site from

- Where they went immediately after they left your site

- How many times each page on your web site was requested

- What time, day of the week, and season people accessed your site

- Which browser and version of that browser your visitors are using

- Which keywords or phrases your visitors are using to find your site using a search engine

- Which advertisements are viewed the most on your web site

- Detailed information on visitors and demographics

This is phenomenal information from a marketing perspective! There are some amazing things you can do with this data. Like any good experiment, you must collect the data first, review or analyze the data, and then make the recommendations.

Analyzing Log Files with Web Traffic Analysis Software

By analyzing the data from your log files, you can generate results that could significantly increase the popularity and success of your tourism operation's web site. By tracking the visitors on your web site in terms of where they spend their time, how they came to your site, and if they do what you want them to do, you can fine-tune your web site to fit your objectives as well as the specific needs of your target market.

Developing a Profile of Your Web Site Visitors

By analyzing the log files, you can find out a lot about your audience. You can see how the majority of your audience came to your site, and what they like to do while they are there. Did they request information? Did they join your mailing list? Were they interested in the free giveaways? You can use this information to find out if your site needs to be changed to accommodate the needs of your visitors. For example, if you find that many of your visitors are spending a lot of time on your What's New page, maybe it would be in your best interest to start a monthly mailing list to inform your audience of the happenings of your web site.

The log files can tell you when your audience is entering your site. For example, if the log files indicate that your traffic is mostly at night, you could predict that most people visit your site from home. Since most homes do not have high-speed access, you may want to check your graphic sizes to make sure that it is not taking too long for your site to load. If your analysis tells you that not many people visit your site on Saturday, you may want to select this day as your maintenance day. You don't want to make changes to your site on days when you receive high traffic because it is very displeasing if your visitors receive HTTP 404 errors because your site is temporarily down.

You can also see your visitors' IP addresses, which the software will translate into the geographical location of your visitors (see Figures 22.1 and 22.2). Some software is even capable of narrowing the data down to the city from which each visitor accessed your site. From a marketing perspective, this can benefit you in planning your

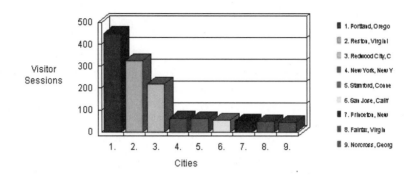

Figure 22.1. WebTrends can tell you what cities are bringing you the most online traffic.

Most Active Cities		?
	City, State	Visitor Sessions
1	Portland, Oregon, United States	449
2	Reston, Virginia, United States	325
3	Redwood City, California, United States	218
4	New York, New York, United States	62
5	Stamford, Connecticut, United States	60
6	San Jose, California, United States	55
7	Princeton, New Jersey, United States	49
8	Fairfax, Virginia, United States	48
9	Norcross, Georgia, United States	44
10	Washington, D.C., United States	39
11	New Berlin, Wisconsin, United States	33
12	Mountain View, California, United States	32
13	Houston, Texas, United States	31
14	Cambridge, Massachusetts, United States	30
15	San Diego, California, United States	30
16	Chicago, Illinois, United States	29
17	San Francisco, California, United States	28
18	Dallas, Texas, United States	26
19	Palo Alto, California, United States	24
20	Santa Clara, California, United States	23
Total For the Cities Above		**1,635**

Figure 22.2. The data of Figure 22.1 presented in a table.

marketing efforts in other media. If you notice that a large portion of your traffic is coming from a certain city, you may want to plan a television or newspaper campaign in this area. This would enable you to have these potential clients view your tourism operation online as well as offline.

It is very common for web traffic analysis software to indicate which browser your visitors are using when visiting your web site (see Figure 22.3). Although you want to have a web site designed to be compatible with older and newer browsers, this data can be used to your advantage. Older browsers that cannot read Java scripting properly and that do not have the proper plug-ins for a Macromedia Flash introduction may still be in use by your viewers. However, if most of your visitors are using the latest browsers, you could incorporate more current day technologies into your site. Remember that you should always offer a "skip Flash" option on your site and the latest Java plug-ins for people using older browsers.

Which Pages Are Popular, and Which Pages Are Not

When you look at the log files and see where your audience is spending most of their time on your tourism site, you can also tell where

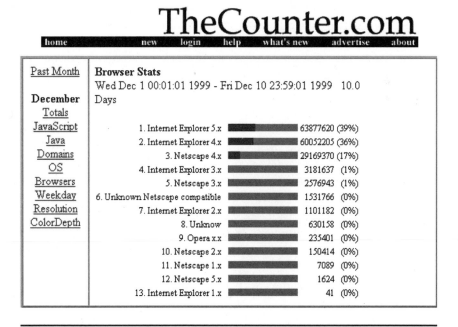

Figure 22.3. TheCounter.com offers a free service that can analyze many aspects of Web traffic, including what browsers people used to view your site.

they are not. You can then take this information to determine what the popular pages on your site incorporate that the less popular ones do not. Perhaps the popular pages are similar to the less popular, but are visited by a specific source (e.g., search engines, newsgroups). Maybe there is a content problem on the less popular pages, or maybe they take longer to load than the other pages and visitors do not want to wait for them to load. Whatever the case may be, you can take this information and attempt to fix those problems that would keep visitors from spending time on all the pages of your tourism site.

Find Out How Each Visitor Found Your Site

By finding out how each visitor came to your site, sometimes you can boost your traffic tremendously. You can use this information to help you with the allocation of your online advertising budget. For example, if most of your traffic is derived from a link that you have developed on a high-traffic tourism web site or a specific search engine (see Figure 22.4), you could consider purchasing a banner advertisement on that page. The same theory goes if your traffic is coming from a tourism-related newsgroup, meta-index, and so on.

If you have a number of doorway pages (for more info on doorway pages, see Chapter 4), it would be good to know which ones are drawing the most attention. If the statistics reveal that 4 out of 10 of your doorway pages are sending traffic to your site, you should analyze the other 6 doorways to see if you can make them more effective. Maybe the keyword prominence is too low, and they are not as effective as you thought when you designed them. If so you should tweak these pages, then resubmit them to their corresponding search engines.

You can also find out where your visitors go when they leave your web site. You want your viewers to stay at your site as long as possible. If you notice that the majority of your viewers are not traveling through your entire site and are not viewing important information that you want them to see, you may want to manipulate the layout of your web site. If you notice that your top exit page is your home page, you may want to try a whole new approach.

Single access pages are pages on your web site that are accessed through a link, or search engine, and then are immediately exited. If a high percentage of your web site traffic is a result of these pages, it

Figure 22.4. HitBox Enterprise allows you to view what search engines people are using to find your site.

is very important that you convey a strong message while you have the visitors' attention. If you have pages like this, you should reevaluate what is on those pages and try to come up with content that will entice your visitors to search through the rest of your site.

Some of the more advanced web traffic analysis software can indicate which keywords and phrases your visitors used to find your site using a search engine. This is extremely valuable information because you can use these keywords to increase your popularity in the search engines. By knowing the most popular keywords your visitors are using to locate your site, you can make sure you use them in your meta-tags, Alt attributes, page titles, and page text for higher placement in the search engines. Also, after seeing which search engines are being used by the majority of your visitors, you may choose to purchase a banner ad or keywords for that engine to achieve maximum visibility.

Another benefit of observing who is visiting your site is that you can see when spiders and crawlers from search engines have crawled to your page. This means that you will most likely have your site indexed on their corresponding search engine. This is good to know, because it not only reassures you that you are going to be indexed, but also because by knowing this you do not resubmit your site to the search engine and risk spamming. As was explained in Chapter 4, if you are caught spamming the search engines, you could be banned from their indexes.

Identifying Your Target Market

After you have collected data from your log files and used the web traffic analysis software to determine which demographics are actually visiting your site, you then must determine whether this is the demographic that you want to target. If it is not, you must then determine how you are going to reach your target market. For example, maybe you will find that you should change your online advertising campaign. Or perhaps you should reevaluate your Internet marketing strategy, taking into consideration the new data that you have collected.

Finding Out What Forms of Online Promotion Work

When you first launch your web site, you are going to aggressively implement your Internet marketing strategy by experimenting with all of the different forms of online marketing. However, when you analyze who is actually visiting your site and find out where the majority of your traffic is coming from, you can then determine where to focus the majority of your marketing effort. You may find that a link on a high-traffic tourism web site is resulting in a high amount of traffic to your site; therefore, you may want to consider purchasing a banner advertisement on that site. The same goes for all of the other forms of Internet marketing. If, after a short period of time, your analysis software tells you that you are receiving low traffic (if any) from a banner ad that you had purchased, you may want to pull it from that site and designate your investment to another tourism-related site on the Internet. This is a good way to make sure you get the most for your investments in online marketing.

Managing Your Online Tourism Operation

If you are involved in selling online advertising on your site, web traffic analysis software can save you a lot of work. When you place your client's banner advertisement on your site, the analysis software can track not only how many people have viewed that specific banner, but also how many people have clicked through. This makes billing your clients very easy, for all you have to do is read the reports generated by your software. If your clients pay per click-through, you simply look up the figure and charge them the appropriate fee. The same goes for paying based on impressions or unique visitors.

How To Get Web Traffic Analysis Software

If you would like to purchase web traffic analysis software, you can do so, but it will have to be installed on the server where you host your web site. If you host your own web site, you will definitely have to purchase your own software; however, if you are paying an ISP to host your web site, they should already be able to provide some sort of analysis software. Most people don't take advantage of the tremendous marketing opportunities available by analyzing their traffic, and they do not ask their ISP about the software. It should be available to you, for you are paying for their services. If it is not, simply ask them to purchase the web traffic analysis software of your choice. They will likely purchase the software in order to remain competitive with other ISPs. In some cases they may charge you an additional fee for this service.

Popular Web Traffic Analysis Software

If you do decide to purchase your own web traffic analysis software, there are many different brands with a variety of features. The following is a list of the more popular brands of web traffic analysis software:

Web Crumbs
http://www.thinweb.com/products/webcrumbs/

WebCrumbs (see Figure 22.5), brought to us by ThinWeb.com, is a web site analysis tool that provides real-time performance analysis reports by using Dynamic Navigation Technology (DNT). You will be able to monitor usage patterns, judge your web site's overall effectiveness, and customize your web page to best fit your target audience. WebCrumbs allows you to analyze your visitors' patterns, where they came from and what they do while visiting your web site. You can track banner ads that are pointed toward your web site to calculate the best investment for your online marketing budget. WebCrumbs easily plugs into web servers, which cuts down on the large cost of purchasing additional technical products to run the software. The easy to use graphical administrator allows you to simply point and click.

WebTrends Enterprise Suite
http://www.webtrends.com/
The WebTrends Enterprise Suite is one of the most comprehensive web site analysis software packages available. It provides reports on

Figure 22.5.   WebCrumbs from ThinWeb is an excellent Web site traffic analyzing tool.

everything from the number of views your banner ads receive on another web page to which keyword was used when a visitor found your site using a search engine. You can easily target specific hits and user sessions that include file types and names, entry pages, time and day, user addresses, or any other medium that may have pointed a visitor to your page. WebTrends develops detailed advertising reports, which tell you how often banners on your web site are viewed and how often people click through. This assists you in selling and billing space to your clients. This is an all in one piece of web traffic analysis software that does more than answers the question of who is actually visiting your site.

ARIA Enterprise
http://www.andromedia.com
One of the higher-end web traffic analysis tools, ARIA can help you to develop comprehensive Internet marketing reports, including daily, weekly, and monthly traffic trend reports, demographic and geographic reports, and top visitor domain reports. With the capability of handling sites with larger amounts of traffic, ARIA has the power to report visitors' behavior in real-time on multi-server sites that receive tens of millions of page views per day. ARIA Enterprise is a piece of e-intelligence that can help you optimize your marketing strategy. Know your customers' needs, and keep them coming back for more.

net.Analysis by net.Genesis
http://netgen.com
net.Genesis offers one of the best log analyzing systems. It is one of the first and one of the best web traffic analysis tools for medium to large sites. It's great for Intranet access and for analysis by non-tech-savvy users. net.Analysis also has solid integration with IBM Net.Commerce.

Net Tracker eBusiness edition
www.sane.com/products/NetTracker/ebiz.html
Net Tracker uses an Oracle database engine. It is perfect for most companies because they don't need a database administrator to use it. The Business Edition can handle really large log files with the speed and agility of an Oracle8 database. This Business Edition also lets you access your data for additional analysisusing standard reporting tools such as Crystal Reports and products from Cognos, Informa-

tion Builders, and more. This product contains 79 standardized summaries plus you can create and save your own. Finally, Net Tracker eBusiness edition also generates usage reports for multiple web sites, proxy servers, firewalls, and FTP sites.

Internet Resources

Free Web Traffic Analysis Services

TheCounter.com
http://www.thecounter.com
The counter provides free tracking services to its members. By placing a small image on your web site, they will tell you information such as when your visitors came, where they came from and what browser they used. If you are just experimenting with Web traffic analysis, you can't go wrong with The Counter.com.

The Hitometer
http://www.hitometer.com
The free Hitometer service offers an extensive choice of counters and reporting of URL statistics, such as how many visitors visit your site per day, month, and year. You can receive your reports online or have them sent to your e-mail.

eXTReMe Tracker
http://www.extreme-dm.com/tracking/
The eXTReMe Tracker is a free service that offers comprehensive real-time reporting with no limit on the amount of traffic that you receive on your Web site. It is capable of tracking your visitors' geographic location, their domain, their e-mail address, the browser that they are using, and much more. The eXTReMe Tracker is a very comprehensive service that is completely free.

HitBox
http://www.get.hitbox.com
HitBox is designed for ad-supported, personal, or e-commerce sites. It is capable of developing user profiles and tracking which sites refer your visitors to your site and how much traffic you receive on a daily,

monthly, and annual basis. HitBox can also track how your visitors navigate around your Web site, which can help you in customizing your Web site to your viewers' needs.

SuperStats.com
http://www.superstats.com
SuperStats.com is a free service that allows you to retrieve real-time statistics for your web site 24 hours a day, 7 days a week. Find out who's visiting your site, how they found it, and when they were there.

Pagecount
http://www.pagecount.com
They provide you with a free graphical page counter that shows how many times your page has been viewed. Their statistics show how many people viewed your page, a breakdown of page views by date, day, and time, and a list of where the requests for your page originated. This sounds fantastic, and the only catch is that you must display one of their banner ads on every page of your site that contains the counter.

AccessWatch
http://www.accesswatch.com
AccessWatch is open source shareware that generates browser statistics, referrers, page views, and other web site traffic statistics.

Web Traffic Analysis Education

Demystify Your Log Files
http://www.builder.com/Servers/LogFile/index.html
This article written by Olufemi Anthony explains in detail how your log files produce traffic analysis data. Although this article was written in 1998, it goes over different terminology and gives descriptive examples that can help you to understand what exactly goes on in your web server's log files.

There's Gold in Them There Log Files
http://www.wdvl.com/Internet/Management/index.html
This article written by Charlie Morris touches on the different things that you can interpret from log files when analyzed by web traffic

analysis software. It touches on different features that are available with different software.

Web Traffic Analysis Software Comparison
http://www.iw.com/extra/logchart.html
This is a chart that breaks down the different features that are available with the different types of software. It compares the different features from low- to high-end software and also gives the cost of purchasing the software to assist you in your decision making when preparing to purchase your own software.

23

Give Them a Virtual Tour with Webcasting

Webcasting is defined by Netlingo *(http://www.netlingo.com)* as "using the Internet, and the World Wide Web in particular, to broadcast information. Unlike typical surfing, which relies on a pull method of transferring Web pages, Webcasting uses push technologies."

According to a study conducted by Arbitron New Media and Northstar Interactive, 70 percent of the webcast audience clicks for content information, and while listening/viewing streaming media, nearly 60 percent click through for advertising information. Their study also states that approximately half of the webcast audience buy online advertised products and 44 percent click on online ads. The majority of webcast users tune in from home (63%), followed by users at work (47%). In this chapter, the topics covered include:

- Streaming versus non-streaming media (also known as rich media)

- Advertising with rich media (a few ways your tourism operation can use rich media to reach your target market)

- Barriers to acceptance of webcasting

- Uses of webcasting

- Prominent webcasters

Streaming Versus Nonstreaming Media

Before we explain the marketing implications of webcasting or rich media, it is important to explain some of the terms and what is required by the end user to view them. Webcasting consists primarily of video and audio. Whatis.com defines rich media as follows:

> *Rich media is an Internet advertising term for a Web page ad that uses advanced technology such as streaming video, downloaded applets (programs) that interact instantly with the user, and ads that change when the user's mouse passes over it. For example:*

- *A streaming video tour for a tourism destination*

- *A mouse cursor that is changed to an image on a particular web site if the user requests it*

- *A standard size banner ad that includes an inquiry form about booking a flight, capturing the personal information filled in by the user, and telling the users they will be contacted by a company representative—all simply by interacting with an ad on an online publisher's web page.*

We will talk about streaming and nonstreaming content, with most emphasis placed on streaming because it has the highest promotional potential. What is the difference between streaming and non-streaming? To put it simply, streaming is presented as it arrives. RealAudio files are an example of streaming media. Meanwhile, non-streaming requires you to download the entire clip/file before you can listen/view it. AVI, MP3, and MOV are non-streaming file formats.

- **Video.** This category would include both streaming (Real Audio, G2, and Windows Media Player) and non-streaming video formats (such as AVI and MOV files). Streaming video is often sent from pre-prepared files but is usually distributed as a live broadcast feed. Examples of this include tourism accommodations, video clips of a white water rafting expedition, or a video tour of a theme park.

- **Audio.** Audio includes streaming and non-streaming formats. RealNetworks is by far the current king with their RealAudio. Another major leading provider of streaming audio is Macromedia with their Shockwave.

Obviously, streaming video file formats contain an audio element to them as well. After all, a video clip is much more interesting when there is sound associated with it.

Other popular webcasting or push technologies formats include:

- **ASF** (Advanced Streaming Format). Designed to store synchronized multimedia data and deliver the data over a large variety of networks and protocols.

- **CDF** (Channel Definition Format). Permits web developers to push information to users through the use of channels.

Push technologies involve sending information to your target market across the Internet. Internet users install software on their system that receives content from the webcaster. For example, they might receive the latest airfare rates, the current weather conditions in vacation resorts around the world, or special offers from a specialty cruiseline operator. The information is "pushed" to the client's system. This differs from "pull" marketing, in which clients specifically request content from a web site by loading it into their browser.

Technically speaking, e-mail is one of the earliest forms of push technology. Internet marketers send e-mail messages to individuals in their target market without permission to do so from each of the recipients. However, we all know that this is spam. Savvy Internet marketers can still use e-mail to push their message to potential clients, but they must have a potential client's permission beforehand.

Webcasters can utilize push technologies much as Internet marketers do with e-mail marketing campaigns. Real Networks *(http://www.real.com)* has been involved in the webcasting field for several years. Their RealPlayer software is a prime example of how to utilize push technology. The basic version of the player can be downloaded for free from the Real Networks web site. Observing Figure 23.1, you can see how active channels have been incorporated into the RealPlayer application. Clicking on one of the active channels in the Channels menu automatically connects the user to a streaming audio/video presentation from the site of one of Real Network's partners. In this way, Real Networks helps its partners (ESPN, Fox, ZDNet, etc.) brand them-

Figure 23.1. RealPlayer receives Internet channels. You can subscribe to new channels or view the channel information of Real Network's partners.

selves through the RealPlayer webcasting software, and Real Networks likely receives a healthy sum of money in exchange for this advertising.

The RealPlayer software permits you to subscribe to other channels as well. Thus, Real Networks gives users a free application, but the company profits from RealPlayer by selling advertising space. Real Networks is the perfect example of how webcasting can be used to quickly achieve brand recognition and earn additional revenue.

Aside from Real Networks, these other companies also provide software to allow for the distribution of channels:

- Microsoft Active Channels software *(http://www. microsoft.com)*

- Netscape Communicator's Netcaster *(http://www. netscape.com)*

- PointCast EntryPoint software *(http://www.entrypoint.com)*

Advertising Your Tourism Operation with Rich Media

Rich media can be used by tourism operators by purchasing a "commercial" that precedes an online presentation or audio event, or they can be developed and used by tourism operators on their own web sites to provide a greater sense of interactivity, which will result in more repeat traffic. For an example of this, go to Broadcast.com *(http://www.broadcast.com)*. Broadcast.com provides current streaming audio and video footage of almost any event you could imagine. For instance, you can listen to the commentary of an entire NHL hockey game. However, just before the game gets underway, you will be greeted by a 25-second audio advertisement. You can also download full-featured promotional videos for tourism destinations and resorts (see *http://www.broadcast.com/travel/*) (see Figure 23.2). Why is this good advertising?

- Rich media averages higher recall.

- Rich media advertising leaves a deeper impression on customers than a static banner ad.

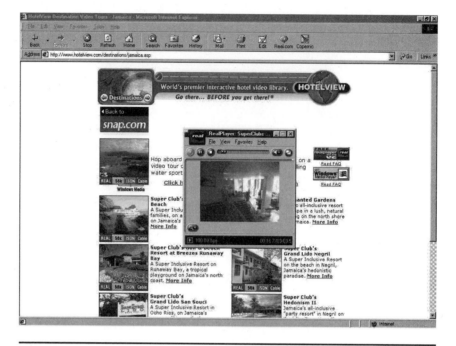

Figure 23.2. Broadcast.com (*http://www.broadcast.com*) links to HotelView (http://www.hotelview.com) where interested tourists look inside popular resort hotels using streaming rich media presentations.

- Higher customer recall of rich media makes it easier to brand a company name or product.

- Rich media has higher click-through rates.

- Rich media is more "likeable."

Higher Recall

@Home *(http://www.home.com)* and Intel *(http://www.intel.com)* recently conducted a rich-media study consisting of 30,000 survey responses. In their study, rich-media (broadband) advertising averaged 34% higher recall than standard narrowband advertising. This means people are more likely to remember your company's streaming media presentation than a static banner ad. Therefore, you can attract more tourists by advertising with rich media because people will remember your ads.

Better Branding

It goes without saying that better customer recall leads to better branding and more tourists. Creating brand awareness with banner ads is difficult because banner ads are not very interactive. The combination of sight and sound possible with rich media advertising makes it much more effective than a static image or looping animated GIF.

More Click-Throughs

A banner ad incorporating Java or Flash Media will have more than twice as many click-throughs as a static banner ad. Static banner ads generally average less than one click-through per hundred impressions. If you have a banner ad that actively engages the customer, you can achieve higher click-through rates and generate more sales leads.

More Likeable

@Home and Intel concluded that a nonstreaming interactive banner ad offers a 20% potential increase in likeability. People will be more likely to interact with a banner ad that has a game of some sort built into it as opposed to a static image. Therefore, an interactive banner ad has the potential to attract a lot of people who are not usually inclined to click on banner ads. Likewise, a 30-second spot in a streaming multimedia presentation (e.g., watching the Superbowl online) is going to be more acceptable to a user than a pop-up banner ad. The bottom line is that if people like you, they will probably patronize your tourism operation. Both streaming and non-streaming broadband media advertising increase your chances of making a positive impression on the customer.

You can create a streaming, interactive tour of your bed and breakfast operation, your resort, your golf course, your fishing expedition and so forth. Then, visitors to your site can take the tour and make a more informed decision about where they would like to spend their travel dollars. Chances are, if you can show the people what they are looking for, they will become your customers.

More Reasons To Use Rich Media Advertising

Given the high recall rates, the cost per branding impression (i.e., the number of times customers must view the ad before they become familiar with your brand) decreases. This increases your ROI (return on investment) because you do not have to invest as much in rich-media advertising to get your message across as you would with traditional advertising. For instance, to brand your tourism operation's name, products, or services using television advertising would require a substantial financial investment. People change the channel during commercial breaks, so it is harder to reach television viewers.

However, when people intentionally subscribe to an Internet channel, they are viewing and listening to information they are interested in. Plus, it is more of an effort to switch channels on the Net than it is to do so watching television. Therefore, the user's tendency to remain tuned-in is higher. Thus, you could create your own Internet channel that focuses on information relevant to your potential tourists. They could then subscribe to your channel, and you could send them the timely information on your tourism operation straight to their desktop.

Also, the Internet is a worldwide network. Television, magazines, and other traditional marketing vehicles are more regionalized. Therefore, a rich-media advertisement streaming across the Internet has the potential to reach a much larger audience of potential tourists.

The Barriers to Webcasting (Rich-Media) Acceptance

With every new medium, there are bound to be barriers to its public acceptance. Webcasting, both streaming and non-streaming, is no different. There are six primary obstacles that webcasting must overcome before it becomes a widely acceptable advertising medium.

Cost

The possibilities are there, but so are the costs, and you must be aware of this. Developing streaming media and non-streaming media can be quite expensive. Moreover, if you're looking to advertise on a site that applies video and audio content, then you must be made aware that most of the sites that apply this technology are high-budget, high-volume, and high-bandwidth sites, and will likely ask for quite a fee to advertise.

You must also consider the potential return on investment. We described earlier how rich-media advertising has a higher recall rate than standard web advertising. Also, rich media is more cost effective and efficient for branding purposes. Therefore, the initial expense of producing a rich-media advertisement may be quickly recovered by the interest and sales the ad will generate.

Rich-Media Advertising Is Not Accepted by All Sites

Although many tourism operation sites do not have the resources to offer webcast advertising opportunities, many major sites do. Content sites such as Launch.com and RollingStone.com place ads in front of some of the videos you can view on their site. These streaming media sites offer tremendous exposure opportunities for companies that advertise with them.

There are also sites such as MP3.com *(http://www.mp3.com)* that offer free webcast advertising. On MP3.com (see Figure 23.3), unsigned music artists can post MP3 versions of their songs for the world to hear. MP3.com is a high-traffic site as a result of the community of artists they have created, and the artists themselves benefit from the increased exposure. Given the number of webcast companies and major companies getting involved with webcasting, companies that do not utilize it may be left behind.

Bandwidth Constraints

Both streaming and non-streaming media require that users have high connection speeds to experience a webcast as it is intended.

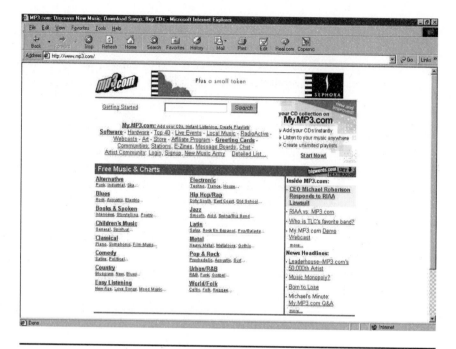

Figure 23.3. MP3.com (*http://www.mp3.com*) permits independent artists to stream their music across the Internet.

To view streaming content you will need a plug-in or player of some sort. Popular applications used to view/hear streaming content are:

- Windows Media Player

- Quicktime

- RealPlayer

- Macromedia Shockwave Player

It is important to note that the higher the connection speed the more convenient the use of streaming content will be. If your target market, the family making their vacation decision, is still using a 14.4 modem, they're simply not going to get the performance needed to make it worthwhile. This presents an obstacle to people with slower Internet connection rates. Also, some people simply do not wish to download and install the plug-ins necessary to play rich-media files. You will not be able to target your webcasting advertising campaign toward these users.

Irritates User

Does webcasting annoy users? Sure it does, but this will only be the case for people with low bandwidth or less robust machines. Also, some people despise advertising in any form, so you probably won't win over any of these individuals either. You will have to hope you can reach such potential tourists using offline media and more traditional forms of advertising.

However, @Home and Intel discovered from their rich-media study that 75% of their users either "enjoyed" or "did not mind" rich-media advertising on the @Home site. Could @Home boast the same level of advertising acceptance for a television ad? It's very unlikely they could.

Too Complicated

The software to create rich-media content exists and, with a little initiative, can be learned by anyone. You first have to determine if your target market is likely to be a user of rich media. Here are some software applications you should inspect if you have an interest in creating rich-media/webcasting files for your tourism operation:

Streaming Media Creation/Encoding Software

- RealSlideshow Plus *(http://www.real.com)*. This product allows you to create your own streaming media slideshow.

- Emblaze *(http://www.emblaze.com)*. Designed to enable delivery of rich media over any IP network, over any platform, and under any bandwidth.

- Liquid Audio *(http://www.liquidaudio.com)*. Offers solutions for encoding your music and serving it in a streaming media format.

- Stream Anywhere *(http://www.sonicfoundry.com)*. The all-in-one solution for preparing audio and video multimedia for distribution over the web

- Quick Time 4 *(http://www.apple.com/quicktime)*. Create/edit streaming and nonstreaming video and audio files.

Nonstreaming Media Creation/Encoding Software

- Macromedia Director 7 Shockwave Internet Studio and Flash *(http://www.macromedia.com)*. Generate powerful presentations and content for your web site.

- AudioCatalyst 2.1 and Xing MPEG software *(http://www.xingtech.com)*. Create MP3 and MPEG files from source files.

- Real JukeBox *(http://www.real.com)*. Create MP3 files from CDs.

It is obvious that the software to create rich media exists, and most of it is not too difficult to learn. It just requires a little bit of initiative and patience.

The Technology Changes Too Often

Webcasting is a relatively new medium. Of course, new standards are being introduced every few months. The key here is to watch the technologies the major Internet sites are using. If you see some of the major tourism sites starting to use a particular webcasting technology, you should investigate it. Generally, the learning curve for new technologies is not very steep because they are based on previous technologies.

Uses of Webcasting

Despite the existence of a few barriers to using webcasting as a promotional vehicle, you should investigate it if you think your potential visitors may include early adapters to technology. Some important uses of providing rich-media content to the general public include:

- Online tours of vacation resorts

- Coverage of sporting events (both streaming and nonstreaming footage) such as golf tournaments and ski races

- Live continuous broadcasts of radio stations and networks

- Broadcasts of cable networks and television stations

- Live music including concerts and club performances (both streaming and non-streaming footage)

- On-demand shows, corporate events, CDs, audiobooks, video titles, and so on.

As bandwidth increases and more people have access to higher-end technology, webcasting will become a regular part of our lives and be more accepted as an advertising medium. The transition to webcasting has already begun, as is evidenced by the large number of prominent players already entrenched in the field.

Prominent Webcasters

Yack.com *(http://www.yack.com)* (see Figure 23.4) is an excellent resource to locate sites with streaming audio and video content. It divides the information into easy to follow categories such as sports, music, and news. It also provides the time and location of the respective events.

Because the public enjoys using streaming media for a variety of purposes, a tourism operator can benefit from enhanced branding campaigns and increased recognition, ultimately leading to higher reservations and sales.

Recently, Broadcast.com *(http://www.broadcast.com)* and Yahoo *(http://www.yahoo.com)* merged. Yahoo's Broadcast (see Figure 23.5) has webcast over 36,000 live events including the last Super Bowl,

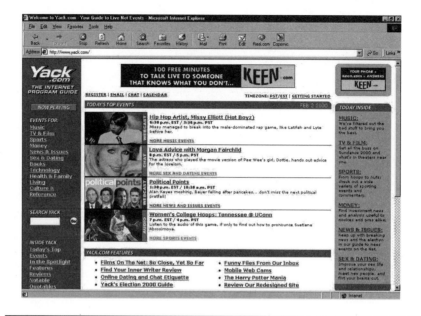

Figure 23.4. Yack.com offers streaming audio and video content.

Figure 23.5. Recently acquired by Yahoo!, Broadcast.com is perhaps the largest and best-known provider of streaming media events.

the NHL regular season and Stanley Cup Playoffs, and even the on-line premiere of *Casablanca*. Visit *http://advertising.broadcast.com/ ad_demos/index.html* to learn more about their advertising opportunities for your tourism operation. They offer gateway ads, channel and event sponsorships, multimedia ads, and traditional banner ads. More appropriate to this chapter is the ability to purchase slots and insert Internet-only commercials within Yahoo's programming.

Figure 23.6 was taken from a streaming video demonstration on *http://www.broadcast.com*. You can think of it in terms of watching a commercial on TV in some respects. When the user clicks on "Webcast of Court TV," Real Player loads as well as a pop-up window for Volvo. Before the show begins, Real Player presents a commercial, much like one you would watch on your television.

As one can imagine, you're going to pay a premium to have an ad of this caliber placed on a site similar to this one, and it may not be within the budget of a small tourism operation; however, we do not want to leave any options uncovered.

Figure 23.6. Volvo's streaming media advertisement on Broadcast.com.

Similarly, EntertainmentBlvd.com's *(http://www.entertainment blvd.com)* Vidnet plays video commercials before allowing you to view a video. They also have a section of their site strictly for "Netfomercials." Your tourism operation could create a streaming video to include in EntertainmentBlvd.com's Netfomercial section, as did the company that markets The Pocket Fisherman (see Figure 23.7). Although there is currently no Travel section on EntertainmentBlvd.com, they would certainly create one if you wanted to display your commercial on their site.

Staying within the EntertainmentBlvd.com network, you can go to another section of their site called NetFomercial.com (see Figure 23.8). The purpose of this site is to sell products using streaming video infomercials, much like the ones you watch on TV.

DiscJockey.com (see Figure 23.9) is another popular site that offers a host of interactive advertising opportunities for multiple demographic segments. Of importance to this chapter is the ability to

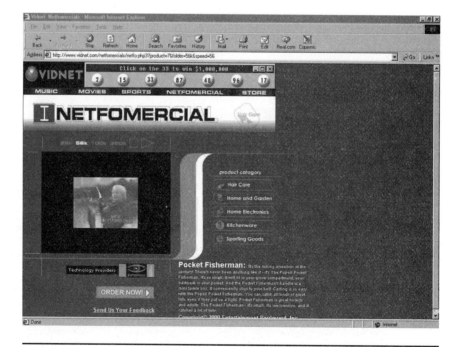

Figure 23.7.   EntertainmentBlvd.com's Netfomercial section allows advertisers to include a streaming commercial video on their site.

Figure 23.8. If you are interested in streaming media advertising, NewFomercial.com is the place to visit.

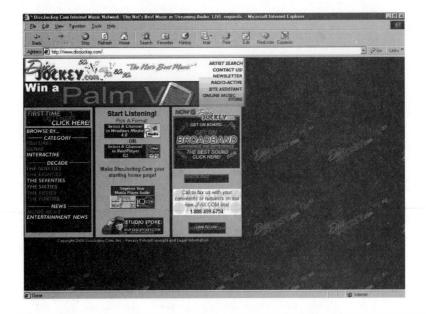

Figure 23.9. Advertise on Web radio stations courtesy of DiscJockey.com.

purchase audio advertisements. Before you hear your selected station, an audio advertisement is played. You can contact DiscJockey.com through their web site *(http://www.discjockey.com)* for more information.

A major use of streaming audio comes in the form of Internet-only radio stations and traditional radio stations that broadcast their signal online. For the radio stations it's an ideal opportunity to increase market share and increase the number of loyal listeners. Web-Radio.com *(http://www.web-radio.com)* (see Figure 23.10) has a large directory of over 2700 radio stations broadcasting over the Internet. InternetNews.com *(http://www.internetnews.com)* reported in September 1999 that one of every four radio stations with a web site is webcasting. At that time, they projected that over 3000 radio stations would be webcasting by the beginning of year 2000.

Figure 23.10. Almost 3000 radio stations now stream their programming across the Internet. The existence of Web-Radio.com is evidence of the growth in this field.

The benefits here are twofold. A radio station will benefit from the broader exposure (worldwide as opposed to regional); however, these online radio stations provide an excellent opportunity for others to advertise online. Since online radio listeners broaden the potential audience for a radio station, the station could charge advertisers higher rates. This source of revenue is unquestionably attractive, which is why radio stations are scrambling to establish themselves in the webcasting world.

HotelView's web site *(http://www.hotelview.com)* (see Figure 23.11) is an interactive video library of hotels. Perhaps you own a bed and breakfast near a waterfront location. You can use a streaming or non-streaming video clip to display the scenery, much like a travel agency can provide a videotape demonstrating the beauty of a potential vacation destination.

Figure 23.11. HotelView.com helps hotels and bed and breakfast businesses promote themselves online with streaming media.

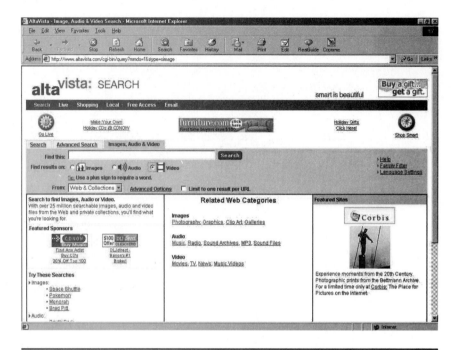

Figure 23.12. You can search for streaming audio and video on Altavista.com.

AltaVista *(http://www.altavista.com)* has recently redesigned their site to claim title as the number one search engine on the web and has applied much more emphasis on webcasts (see Figure 23.12). Why did they do this? The popularity of audio and video on the web is exploding, so they needed to include this information. As well, their competitors are doing it.

Webcasting is a technological phenomenon that offers tourism operators a new way to reach potential customers. Whether you create a streaming video tour or place streaming audio advertisements on web radio stations during other online events, webcasting offers an excellent advertising opportunity for the tourism industry. Many Internet giants have already seized the webcasting reins and now deliver rich-media content and advertising to the world. Perhaps you would be wise to investigate webcasting for your tourism operation and do the same.

Internet Resources

HotelView
http://www.hotelview.com/
HotelView provides a fully narrated video "walking" tour through select hotels worldwide. Take an inside look at the accommodations, amenities, recreation, and entertainment before you leave home.

OII—Webcasting Standards
http://www2.echo.lu/oii/en/webcast.html#RDF
Explanation of webcasting standards.

Broadcast.com
http://www.broadcast.com
Broadcasting over 36,000 live events, this streaming media industry giant was recently purchased by Yahoo.

Castanet
http://www.marimba.com/doc/general/current/introducing/introducing.html
Marimba's Castanet is a system for distributing, installing, and updating software and content over intranets and the Internet.

ChannelSEEK
http://channelseek.com
ChannelSEEK is a comprehensive webcast and streaming media guide for the web. Even streaming MP3 audio from multiple sites. Watch hundreds of movies and listen to music with your computer.

ChannelSeven.com
http://www.channelseven.com
A large resource for Internet development, marketing, and advertising executives. This site contains information on rich-media advertising.

Dick Becker's LIVE Radio Stations
http://www.geocities.com/ResearchTriangle/1803/
Radio and TV stations broadcasting live on the Net via RealAudio, RealVideo, NetShow, Windows Media Player, Streamworks, and AudioActive.

Digital Librarian: Audio, Video, Rich Media
http://www.servtech.com/~mvail/audio.html
A librarian's choice of the best audio and sound resources on the internet. Updated weekly. Meta-index.

International Webcasting Association
http://www.webcasters.org
The IWA serves as the meeting place for companies active or interested in the delivery of multimedia (audio and video) services to consumers or business customers via the Net and other networks.

OnTheAir.com
http://www.ontheair.com
A reference site listing the best sites who provide links to live radio and television from across the United States and around the world. Over 1000 stations available live on your computer.

Real Networks
http://www.real.com
Innovators in the field of streaming media, Real Networks has several popular webcasting software applications including RealPlayer, RealJukebox, and RealSlideshow.

Scour
http://www.scour.net
Find audio, video, images, and animation at this guide to online multimedia. Search the index for multimedia files or navigate through their category directory.

Streaming Media World
http://www.streamingmediaworld.com
Streaming Media World offers media player reviews, news, tools, tutorials, discussion forums, and cool links devoted to streaming video, audio, MP3, multimedia, and GIF animation.

The Media CHANNEL
http://www.mediachannel.com
A guide to video on the Internet.

Web-Radio
http://www.web-radio.com
A comprehensive directory of radio stations (broadcasting) on the
Web.

Webreference.com
http://www.webreference.com/multimedia/video.html
A directory of multimedia tools including Windows Media Player,
Real, Emblaze, and Macromedia.

VideoDome.Com Networks Inc.
http://www.videodome.com
Offers a variety of Internet OnDemand video solutions to meet your
online video needs.

VideoSeeker
http://www.videoseeker.com
The leading Internet video service offers a wealth of streaming video
clips and a complete online video guide. Check out exclusive must-
see video from NBC, including comedy from *SNL, The Tonight Show,*
and *Late Night with Conan O'Brien,* as well as the latest music videos, celebrity interviews, movie trailers, MSNBC news, live webcasts,
and more.

VirtualTuner.com
http://www.virtualtuner.com
Directory of live and on-demand radio links for the Internet.

Yack!
http://www.yack.com
A guide to online events with co-branding and personalized event
services, Yack is the main portal for searching and finding all Internet
events. Yack.com has a list of Webcasts.

About the Author

Susan Sweeney, C.A.

Renowned industry expert and consultant, Susan Sweeney C.A., tailors lively keynote speeches, full and half day seminars and workshops for companies, industries, and associations interested in improving their Internet presence and increasing their Web site traffic and sales. Susan is the founder and President of **Connex Network Inc.** an international Internet marketing and consulting firm. Susan holds both her Chartered Accountant and Certified General Accountant designations. She is an experienced Internet Marketing professional with a background in computers, marketing, and the Internet. Susan is the author of several books on Internet Marketing as well as numerous articles concerning Marketing on the Internet, Export Marketing, and The Internet and Business. She is a member of the Canadian Association of Professional Speakers, the National Speakers Association, and the International Federation for Professional Speakers. Susan is also the Treasurer and an executive on the Board of Directors of the Information Technology Industry Association of Nova Scotia, as well as a member of the Board of Directors for the Canadian Association of Professional Speakers.

Connex Network is a marketing firm, providing Internet and international marketing consulting and training services to industry and government. Their clients range in size from single person start-up operations to multi-million dollar international firms. Their primary services include Internet Marketing Workshops, Internet Marketing Strategies, Web Site Report Cards, Internet Marketing Consulting, Market Research and Competitive Analysis. During their workshops and training sessions they ensure their clients have a complete understanding of the principles involved with developing a strong online presence. The team of Internet marketing analysts at Connex is highly trained in the area of Internet marketing and all stay up to date with the latest technological advancements and industry trends in the on-line marketing world. Every person on the team has extensive practical hands-on experience and the necessary skills to use proven tips, tools, and techniques to generate high volumes of traffic to your site.

As a result of technological change and global competitiveness the need for a strong Internet presence is essential. Susan instructs individuals with her enthusiastic personality combined with her vast hands-on international marketing experience, which keeps her listeners informed, and captivated. Let Susan help you increase your traffic and make your business prosper!

Susan Sweeney, C.A.
Connex Network Inc.
Suite 300, 800 Windmill Road
Dartmouth, Nova Scotia, Canada B3B 1L1
Phone: 902-468-2578 Fax: 902-468-2233
www.connexnetwork.com
susan@connexnetwork.com

Appendix A

Terminology

404–File Not Found This message is returned from a web server when a requested document cannot be found.

Animated GIF Special image-editing applications can meld several GIF images into a single image, much like slides in a slide show. Each of the images is displayed briefly in turn to create the illusion of motion (similar to cartoon flipbooks).

ASCII Text File (American Standard Code for Information Interchange) The worldwide standard format for text files in computers and on the Internet. The code represents all the uppercase and lowercase letters, numbers, punctuation, etc. There are 128 standard ASCII codes in which a 7-digit binary number, 0000000 through 1111111, represents each character.

Autoresponder A program that automatically responds to incoming e-mail. It is like an electronic fax-back system for e-mail.

Backbone Large transmission lines that carry data being transferred from smaller lines. These lines or paths connect local or regional networks together for long-distance communication. The connection points are known as network nodes or telecommunication data switching exchanges (DSEs).

Banner Ad A graphical advertisement on a web site that links to a particular promotion when the user clicks on it. Banner ads are used to increase product awareness and company and brand identity, and can be a source of revenue (advertising revenue) to the site that hosts the banner ad.

BBS—Bulletin Board System A computer that can be reached by computer modem dialing (or by Telnet) for the purpose of sharing or exchanging messages or other files. Some BBSs are devoted to specific interests; others offer a more general service. The definitive BBS List says that there are over 40,000 BBSs worldwide.

BCC (Blind Carbon Copy) Including e-mail addresses in the BCC field of an e-mail message will hide all the addresses aside from each recipient's address.

Benchmark A point of reference by which something can be measured or compared. In surveying, a "bench mark" (two words) is a post or other permanent mark used as the basis for measuring the elevation of other topographical points.

Branding Creating public awareness of a company, product, or service so that the company, product, or service is quickly and immediately identified and associated.

Browser The software used to view the various kinds of Internet resources, or sites.

Bulk e-mail A group of identical messages e-mailed to a large number of addresses at once. This is a technique commonly employed by spammers, and it results in many very unpersonalized e-mail messages.

Cache A place to store something more or less temporarily. Web pages you request are stored in your browser's cache (pronounced "cash") directory on your hard disk. When you return to a page you've recently looked at, the browser can get most of the information from the cache rather than the original server. A cache saves you time and the network the burden of some additional traffic. You can usually vary the size of your cache, depending on your particular browser.

CGI—Common Gateway Interface Guidelines that define how a web server communicates with another piece of software on the same machine, and how the other piece of software, the CGI program, talks to the web server. Any piece of software can be a CGI program if it handles input and output according to the CGI standard.

Cgi-bin This is the most common name for the directory on a web server that holds a CGI program. Most programs located in the cgi-bin directory are text files, scripts that are executed by binaries located elsewhere on the same machine.

Chat   Real-time conversation between one or more individuals across a network. IRC and ICQ are common forums for such discussions, which are often held in topic-driven "chat rooms."

Clickstreams   The paths a user takes as he or she navigates a Web page or cyberspace in general. Advertisers and online media providers have developed software that can track users' clickstreams.

Click-Through   A hit generated from a banner advertisement when a user clicks on the banner ad.

Click-Through Rate   The percentage of banner ad views that resulted in a user clicking on it (a click-through).

Cookie   On the Internet, a cookie refers to a piece of information sent by a web server to a web browser. The browser software is expected to save the cookie and send the information back to the server whenever an additional request is made. Cookies may contain information such as user preferences, registration or login information, online shopping cart information, and so on.

Cost Per Click   The rate charged to an advertiser each time a user clicks on their banner ad. This is one method site owners can use to collect advertising revenue from banner ads.

Crawlers   Crawlers quietly comb through web sites and index the information they find.

CPM—Cost Per Thousand Page Views   Banner ad rates are typically measured in cost-per-thousand (page views)—shorthand for the cost of delivering a marketing message to 1000 people.

CPTM—Cost Per Thousand Targeted Ad Views   This implies that the audience you have targeted is of a particular demographic. (See *Demographics*.)

Cybermall   A collection of online storefronts, better known as an Internet shopping mall.

Cybernaut   A person who uses the Internet.

Cyberspace   Used to describe all areas of information resources available through computer networks and the Internet. William Gibson originated the term in his novel *Neuromancer.*

Data Mining   Obtaining specific information from a data warehouse by running queries. Marketers can determine how many people in a database file fit a certain demographic and then market to that particular group of individuals.

Data Warehouse   A place for storing, retrieving, and managing large amounts of any type of data. Data warehouse software often allows you to conduct fast searches, as well as advanced filtering.

Planners and researchers can use this database freely without worrying about slowing down day-to-day operations of the production database.

Database Marketing   Actively maintaining and updating a database of clients and potential clients (data warehousing), mining the data for specific demographic information (data mining), and focusing your advertising campaign on the target market. For instance, once you determine the people in your database that fit a particular demographic, you can then send a targeted e-mail marketing message to these people.

Demographics   Specific data about the size and characteristics of a population or audience that can be used for marketing purposes.

Domain Name   The unique name that identifies an Internet site. A domain name always has two or more parts, separated by dots. The part on the left is the more specific, and the part on the right is the more general. A given machine may have more than one domain name, but a given domain name points to only one machine. For example, the domain names *connexnetwork.com* and *yahoo.com* can all refer to the same machine.

Download   The transferring of data from one computer to another across the Internet.

DTD (Document Type Declaration)   Specifies the organization that issued the language specification and the exact version of the specification. This information is typically found at the beginning of an HTML document or other programming documents. In XML, a DTD specifies the meaning of every tag and tag attribute contained within a set of XML pages.

E-Commerce   The process of buying and selling goods and services on the Internet

E-mail—Electronic Mail   Mail messages, usually text, sent from one person to another via computer. Messages can also be sent automatically to a large number of addresses on a mailing list.

Effective Frequency   The optimum regularity with which you execute an e-mail marketing campaign

Emoticons   Symbols made from punctuation marks and letters that look like facial expressions. Commonly used in e-mail and in Internet chat rooms to convey expressions and additional meaning to written text.

Exposure   How broadly known you or your product is from Internet exposure.

Extranet A new buzzword that refers to an intranet that is partially accessible to authorized outsiders. Whereas an intranet resides behind a firewall and is accessible only to people who are members of the same company or organization, an extranet provides various levels of accessibility to outsiders. You can access an extranet only if you have a valid username and password, and your identity determines which parts of the extranet you can view.

Ezine, e-Zine—Electronic Magazine Used to describe an electronic magazine, including those of print magazines such as *National Geographic* and *Newsweek* that have electronic editions. Thus, an e-zine database includes both electronic-only magazines and electronic-edition magazines.

FAQ—Frequently Asked Questions The most common questions on a particular subject or problem area. There are hundreds of FAQ files on subjects as diverse as car repair and franchise advice.

Firewall A set of related programs located at a network gateway server to protect the resources of a private network from users of other networks.

Flame, Flaming Flaming usually involves the use of harsh language directed toward a group or individual for sending unwanted messages (marketing) on a newsgroup or mailing list.

Forum Another name for a newsgroup in which people are formed together in a group to chat and discuss.

FTP—File Transfer Protocol The common method of moving files between two computers through the Internet medium. FTP is a method for logging onto another computer or Internet site for the purpose of retrieving and/or sending files.

Hit A single request from a web browser for a single item from a web server; thus, for a web browser to display a page that contains three graphics, four "hits" would occur at the server: one for the HTML page, and one for each of the three graphics. Hits are often used as a rough measure of visits on a server.

Home Page, Homepage The main web page for a business, organization, person—or simply the main page of a collection of web pages.

Host Any computer on a network that can hold files available to other computers on the network. It is quite common to have one host machine provide several services to other machines, such as WWW and Usenet.

HTML—HyperText Markup Language, HTM The coding language used to create documents for use on the World Wide Web. These documents have a file extension of html or htm. HTML code looks a lot like old-fashioned typesetting code, where you surround a block of text with codes that indicate how it should appear. HTML or HTM files are meant to be viewed using a World Wide Web client program, such as Netscape or Internet Explorer.

HTTP—HyperText Transport Protocol The most important protocol used in the World Wide Web for moving hypertext files across the Internet. Requires an HTTP client program on one end and an HTTP server program on the other end.

Hypertext Clickable text that links to another document; that is, words or phrases in one document that can be clicked on by a reader, causing another document to be retrieved and displayed.

Image Map A single graphic that has multiple hot links to different pages or resources.

Impression Sometimes used as a synonym for view, as in ad view. Online publishers offer, and their customers buy, advertising measured in terms of ad views or impressions.

Interstitial Ad Meaning in between, an advertisement that appears in a separate browser window while you wait for a Web page to load. Interstitials are more likely to contain large graphics, streaming presentations, and applets than conventional banner ads, and some studies have found that more users click on interstitials than on banner ads. Some users, however, have complained that interstitials slow access to destination pages.

Intranet A private network inside a company or organization that uses the same kinds of software found on the public Internet, but that is only for internal use and cannot be viewed outside the network.

ISDN—Integrated Services Digital Network A faster way to move more data over existing regular phone lines. Rapidly becoming available around the world, it is priced comparably to standard analog phone circuits. It can provide speeds of roughly 128,000 bits per second over the regular phone lines.

ISP—Internet Service Provider A provider that allows access to the Internet. Usually there is a cost to the consumer, although there are still some free community networks.

Java Programming language that is specifically designed for writing programs. It can be safely downloaded to your computer through the Internet and immediately run without fear of viruses or other harm to your computer. Using small Java programs, called applets, web pages can include functions such as animations, calculators, and other fancy tricks that cannot be done by normal HTML.

LAN—Local Area Network   A network limited to the local area, usually the same building or floor of a company.

List Server Software   An application installed on a publicly accessible server that manages messages sent to and from a mailing list. This software is required if you intend to administer your own publicly accessible mailing list.

Login   The account name used to gain access to a computer system, not a password. Also can mean the act of entering onto a computer system.

Lurking   Reading Usenet newsgroups, consumer online service forums, or Internet mailing lists without posting anything, just reading. A lurker is a person who observes what everyone else is doing within that group.

Mailbots   Software programs that automatically respond to all incoming e-mail. A mailbot, or autoresponder, replies to them by sending the author a file or message.

Mailing List Manager   A software program that collects and distributes e-mail messages to a mailing list (see *list server software*).

Mailing List, Mail List   A system that allows people to send e-mail to one address, whereupon their message is copied and sent to all other subscribers to the list. This method allows people with different kinds of e-mail to participate in discussions together.

Meta-Index   A listing of Internet resources pertaining to a specific subject category, intended as a resource for those who have an interest in specific topic. A meta-index is simply a collection of URLs for related Internet resources, all arranged on a web page by their titles.

Net   The shorthand version for Internet.

Netiquette   Internet etiquette.

Netizen   From the term "citizen," referring to a citizen of the Internet, or someone who uses networked resources.

Netpreneur   An online entrepreneur.

Netscape   A web browser and the name of a company. The Netscape browser was based on the Mosaic program developed at the National Center for Supercomputing Applications (NCSA).

Newbie   A newcomer to the Internet

Newsgroups   Name given to discussion groups on Usenet.

Opt-in Mailing List People are given the choice to take part in a system that allows people to send e-mail to one address, whereupon their message is copied and sent to all other subscribers to the list. This method allows people with different kinds of e-mail to participate in discussions together.

Page View The number of times a page is viewed.

Password A code used to gain access to a locked system known only to one person or a specific group of individuals. Good passwords contain letters and nonletters and are not simple combinations such as john12.

Portal A new term, generally synonymous with gateway, for a World Wide Web site that is or proposes to be a major starting site for users when they get connected to the web or that users tend to visit as an anchor site.

Posting A message entered into a network communications system, such as a newsgroup submission.

Privacy Policy A policy for protecting the privacy of individually identifiable information. An organization engaged in online activities or electronic commerce has the responsibility to implement and post a privacy policy.

Registration You submit personal information to become part of a mailing list or newsgroup, in order to receive other information in return.

ROI (Return On Investment) The amount of profit you obtain from your original investment.

Secure Server A network-accessible (i.e., the Internet) computer that uses SSL (Secure Socket Layers) for encryption to allow for private online transactions. The encryption protects an online shopper's credit card and personal information from being compromised while conducting an e-commerce transaction.

Search Engine The most popular way to find resources on the Internet. There are numerous search engines, each with their own unique styles and capabilities.

Server A computer that stores information and makes these files available to other users on a network or the Internet.

Signature A block of information used at the end of every message or online document sent by that user.

Site A unique location on the Internet to post your information and get noticed.

Snail Mail A slang term for the regular postal service.

Spam, Spamming   An inappropriate attempt to use a mailing list, Usenet, or other networked communications facility as if it were a broadcast medium by sending the same message to a large number of people who didn't ask for it.

Spider   An automated program that indexes documents, titles, and/ or a portion of each document acquired by traversing the web.

SQL—Structured Query Language   A specialized programming language for sending queries to databases.

Store Front   A set location on the Web that stores and displays a collection of information about you and your business.

Streaming Media   The simultaneous transfer and display of the sound and images on the World Wide Web.

Subject   The subject line in an e-mail message stating the topic of the mail.

Subscribe   Submitting information to an e-zine or mailing list in order to receive information.

Superstitial   Nonbanner rich-media ads that can be any size on the screen and can be authored in most any creative format. Preloaded using a patent-pending "polite" delivery system that eliminates the latency problems often experienced with streaming online advertising solutions, superstitials only play on a user-initiated break in surfing, such as a mouse click.

Telnet   A program that allows people to log on to other computers or bulletin board systems on the Internet and run software remotely from their location.

Thread   A sequence of responses to an initial message posting. This enables you to follow or join an individual discussion in a newsgroup from among the many that may be there.

Unsolicited E-mail   Sending e-mail ads to people without their consent.

Upload   The transfer of a file from your computer to a server online.

URL—Uniform Resource Locator   The standard way to give an address of any resource on the Internet that is part of the World Wide Web (WWW). The most common way to use a URL is to enter into a WWW browser program, such as Internet Explorer, Netscape, or Lynx, and type the URL in the location bar.

Usenet   A discussion-groups system. Comments are passed among hundreds of thousands of machines, with over 10,000 discussion areas, called newsgroups.

User session   A user session is logged when a person with a unique address enters or reenters a web site each day (or some other specified period). A user session is sometimes determined by counting only those users that haven't reentered the site within the past 20 minutes or a similar period. User session figures are sometimes used to indicate the number of visitors per day.

Vaporlink   A link within a site on the Internet is supposed to lead to more information (hypertext). A vaporlink is one that has become nonexistent and does not lead anywhere, a dead link.

Virtual Community   A community of people sharing common interests, ideas, and feelings over the Internet or other collaborative networks.

Virus, Viruses   A program (or programs) that, when executed, contaminates a user's hard drive—often with unwanted results (erases files, sends unauthorized e-mail from your machine, contaminates other documents, etc.).

Visitors   People who have accessed or visited your site.

Web   The shorthand version of World Wide Web.

WWW—World Wide Web   The whole constellation of resources that can be accessed using Gopher, FTP, HTTP, Telnet, Usenet, WAIS, and some other tools. Also referred to as the universe of hypertext servers (HTTP servers), which are the servers that allow graphics, text, sound files, etc., to be mixed together.

Appendix B

Newsgroups

The following list of newsgroup categories is provided compliments of Lewis S. Eisen, Law and Technology Consultant, Ottawa, Ontario, Canada: *http://home.magmacom.com/~leisen/mlnh/mlnhtables.html.*

Each of these newsgroup categories has a number of subcategories. Each subcategory will have a number of sub-subcategories.

A

a2000.	Amsterdam 2000, Nederland (ISP)
ab.	Alberta, Canada
abingdon.	Abingdon, Oxon, UK
abq.	Albuquerque, New Mexico, USA
acadia.	Acadia University, Nova Scotia, Canada
acs.	University of Calgary computer science Alberta, Canada
acs.	Ohio State University, USA
adass.	Astronomical Data and Archiving Systems and Software
ahn.	Athens-Clarke County, Georgia, USA
ak.	Alaska, USA
akr.	Akron, Ohio, USA
alabama.	Alabama, USA
alc.	Newsgroups discussing alcohol
algebra.	Discussions about algebra
algonet.	Algonet, Sverige (ISP)

alt.	Usenet alternative newsgroups
aol.	America Online, ISP
apana.	Australian Public Access Network Association
apc.	Association for Progressive Communications
apk.	APK Net, Ohio, USA (ISP)
ar.	Grupos de Argentina
arc.	NASA Ames Research Center, California, USA
argh.	ARGH network, Deutschland
arkane.	Arkane Systems, UK
aston.	Aston University, Birmingham, England
asu.	Arizona State University
at.	Oesterreich (Austria)
athena.	M.I.T., Cambridge, Massachusetts, USA
atl.	Atlanta, Georgia, USA
aus.	Australian and Australasian newsgroups
austin.	Austin, Texas, USA
auth.	Aristotle University of Thessaloniki, Greece
autodesk.	Autodesk Inc. corporate newsgroups
av.	Antelope Valley, California, USA
az.	Arizona, USA

B

ba.	San Francisco bay area, California, USA
backbone.	Prima e.V., Dortmund, Deutschland (ISP)
balt.	Baltimore, Maryland, USA
baynet.	Bayerische Burgernetze, Deutschland
bburg.	Blacksburg, Virginia, USA
bc.	British Columbia, Canada
bcs.	Boston Computer Society, Massachusetts, USA
be.	Belgique/Belgie/Belgien(Belgium)
bend.	Bend, Oregon, USA
bermuda.	Bermuda
best.	Best Internet Communications, California, USA
bhm.	Birmingham, Alabama, USA
bionet.	Biology Network
birmingham.	Birmingham, England
bison.	Manitoba, Canada
bit.	Originating from BITNET (IBM mainframe)
biz.	Usenet business newsgroups
blgtn.	Bloomington, Indiana, USA

bln.	Berlin, Germany
bnr.	Bell-Northern Research
bocaraton.	Boca Raton, FL
bochum.	Bochum, Deutschland
boston.	Boston, Massachusetts, USA
boulder.	Boulder, Colorado, USA
br.	Brasil
brasil.	Brasil
bremen.	Bremen, Deutschland
bremnet.	Bremen und Umgebung, Deutschland
brocku.	Brock University, Ontario, Canada
byu.	Brigham Young University, Utah, USA

C

ca.	California, USA
cabot.	Cabot College, St. John's, Newfoundland, Canada
cais.	Capital Area, USA (ISP)
calgary.	Calgary, Alberta, Canada
calstate.	California State University, USA
caltech.	California Institute of Technology, USA
cam.	Cambridge area, England
can.	Canada
canb.	Canberra, Australia
capdist.	Albany (Capital District), New York, USA
carleton.	Carleton University, Ottawa, Ontario, Canada
cd-online.	CD-Online, Nederland (ISP)
central.	Internet Company of New Zealand (ISP)
centralor.	Central Oregon, USA
cern.	Cern, Geneva, Switzerland
ch.	Switzerland
chi.	Chicago, Illinois, USA
chile.	Chile
chinese.	China and Chinese-language newsgroups
christnet.	Christian Network
cid.	cid, Berlin, Deutschland (ISP)
cis.	Cyberhalk Internet Services, USA
cisnet.	University of Malta, Computer Info. Serv.,Malta
cityscp.	Cityscape Internet Services, UK (ISP)
cityweb.	Cityweb Network GmbH, Deutschland

cl.	CL-Netz (German-language newsgroups)
claranet.	Claranet, UK (ISP)
clari.	Clarinet News Service (commercial)
cle.	Cleveland, Ohio, USA
clinet.	Clinet, Finland (ISP)
cmc.	Chambers Multimedia Connection, Eugene, Oregon, USA (ISP)
cmh.	Columbus, Ohio, USA
cmu.	Carnegie Mellon University, USA
cna.	Chinese-language newsgroups
co.	Colorado, USA
comp.	Usenet computer newsgroups
compuserve.	CompuServe (ISP)
computer42.	Computer42, Deutschland (ISP)
concordia.	Concordia University, Quebec, Canada
conn.	Connecticut, USA
cor.	Corvallis, Oregon, USA
cornell.	Cornell University
courts.	U.S. court decisions
cov.	City of Coventry, West Midlands, UK
covuni.	Coventry University, West Midlands, UK
cs.	University of British Columbia computer science, Canada
csn.	Colorado SuperNet, USA
cth.	Chalmers Univ of Technology, Goteborg, Sverige
cu.	University of Colorado, USA
cville.	Charlottesville, Virginia and region, USA
cym.	Wales and Welsh newsgroups
cz.	Czech Republic newsgroups
D	
dal.	Dalhousie University, Halifax, Nova Scotia, Canada
dc.	Washington, DC, USA
ddn.	Defense Data Network, USA
dds.	Dutch Freenet language groups
de.	International German-language newsgroups
delaware.	Delaware, USA
demon.	Newsgroups from the Demon network, UK
denver.	Denver, Colorado, USA
det.	Detroit, Michigan, USA

dfw.	Dallas Ft. Worth, Texas, USA
dk.	Danmark (Denmark)
dod.	Department of Defense, USA
dortmund.	Dortmund, Deutschland
dsm.	Des Moines, Iowa, USA
dti.	Dream Train Internet Inc., Japan (ISP)
duke.	Duke University
dut.	Delft Institute of Technology, Nederland

E

easynet.	Easynet, UK (ISP)
ed.	Edinburgh, Scotland
edm.	Edmonton, Alberta, Canada
eduni.	Edinburgh University, Edinburgh, Scotland
ee.	Eesti (Estonia)
efn.	Eugene Free Computer Network, Eugene, Oregon, USA
es.	grupos de Espana
esp.	grupos en espanol
eug.	Eugene/Springfield, Oregon, USA
eunet.	European Networks
example.	Bogus hierarchy reserved for standards documents
execpc.	ExecPC Internet, New Berlin, Wisconsin, USA (ISP)
eye.	Eye WEEKLY Newspaper, Toronto, Ontario, Canada

F

ffo.	Frankfurt (Oder), Deutschland
fido.	Originating from Fidonet
fido7.	Russian-language Fidonet
finet.	Finland and Finnish-language alternative newsgroups
fj.	Japan and Japanese-language newsgroups
fl.	Florida, USA
flora.	FLORA Community Web, Ottawa, Ontario, Canada
fnal.	Fermi National Accelerator Laboratory, Illinois, USA
fnet.	Originating from Fnet (France)
fnord.	Fnord Discordian Network
fr.	International French-language newsgroups
francom.	Groupes de discussion en français
franken.	Franken, Deutschland
fras.	Freie Amiga Software (German Amiga binaries)

free.	Entirely unregulated newsgroups
freenet.	Groups originating from freenets
ftech.	Frontier Internet Services, UK (ISP)
furr.	Furrynet, USA

G

ga.	Georgia, USA
gay.	Gay and Lesbian newsgroups
gbg.	Goteborg, Sverige
geometry.	Discussions about geometry
ger.	GerNet, Deutschland (ISP)
git.	Georgia Institute of Technology, USA
gnu.	GNU operating system
gov.	Government information newsgroups
govonca.	Government of Ontario, Canada
greenend.	The Green End Organization, Cambridge, UK
grk.	Greece and Greek-language newsgroups
gruene.	Partei Die Grunen/Bundnis 90, Deutschland
gu.	University of Goteborg, Sverige
gwu.	George Washington University, Washington, DC, USA

H

hacktic.	Dutch/English hackers' newsgroups, Nederland
halcyon.	Halcyon Corporate newsgroups
hamburg.	Hamburg, Deutschland
hamilton.	Hamilton, Ontario, Canada
han.	Hangul-language newsgroups (Korean)
hannet.	Hannover, Deutschland
hannover.	Hannover, Deutschland
harvard.	Harvard University, Massachusetts, USA
hawaii-online.	Hawaii-Online (ISP)
hawaii.	Hawaii, USA
hebron.	Hebron, Israel
helsinki.	Helsinki, Finland
hepnet.	High-Energy Physics Network
hfx.	Halifax, Nova Scotia, Canada
hiv.	HIV-related issues
hk.	Hong Kong
hna.	Hunter Network Association, Australia (ISP)

hookup.	Hookup, Canada (ISP)
houston.	Houston, Texas, USA
hr.	Croatian newsgroups
hrnet.	Human Rights network
hsv.	Huntsville, Alabama, USA
hum.	Humber College, Etobicoke, Ontario, Canada
humanities.	Usenet discussions about humanities
hun.	Magyarorszag (Hungarian newsgroups)
hy.	University of Helsinki, Finland

I

ia.	Iowa, USA
iaf.	Internet Access Foundation, Nederland
ibm.	IBM-based newsgroups
ibmnet.	IBM Global Network
ic.	ICONSULT, Deutschland (ISP)
iconz.	Internet Company of New Zealand (ISP)
idirect.	I-Direct (ISP)
ie.	Ireland
ihug.	The Internet Group, New Zealand (ISP)
iij.	IIJ (ISP)
iijnet.	IIJ (ISP)
in.	Indiana, USA
infko.	Universitaet Koblenz, Deutschland
info.	Internet technical information
inforamp.	Inforamp, Canada (ISP)
intel.	Intel Corporation
interlog.	Interlog, Canada (ISP)
is.	Iceland and Icelandic newsgroups
israel.	Israel
it.	Italia
ithaca.	Ithaca, New York, USA
iu.	Indiana University, Indiana, USA
iupui.	Indiana UniversityPurdue Univ. at Indianapolis, USA
ivm.	IVM GmbH, Deutschland (ISP)

J

japan.	Japan and Japanese-language newsgroups
jaring.	Jaring network, Malaysia (ISP)
jerusalem.	Jerusalem/Y'rushalayim/al-Quds, Israel

jhu.	Johns Hopkins University, Baltimore MD, USA
jogu.	Johannes-Gutenberg-Universitaet Mainz, Deutschland
jusos.	JungsozialistInnen, Deutschland

K

k12.	International educational network
ka.	Karlsruhe, Deutschland
kanto.	Japanese-language newsgroups
kassel.	Region Kassel, Deutschland
kc.	Kansas City, Kansas/Missouri, USA
kennesaw.	Kennesaw State University, Georgia, USA
kiel.	Kiel, Deutschland
kingston.	Kingston, Ontario, Canada
knf.	Kommunikationsnetz Franken e.V., Deutschland
knox.	Knoxville and surrounding area, Tennessee, USA
koblenz.	Koblenz, Deutschland
ks.	Kansas, USA
ksu.	Kansas State University, USA
kth.	Royal Institute of Technology, Stockholm, Sverige
kun.	Katholieke Universiteit Nijmegen, Nederland
kw.	Kitchener-Waterloo, Ontario, Canada
ky.	Kentucky, USA

L

la.	Los Angeles, California, USA
laurentian.	Laurentian University, Sudbury, Ontario, Canada
leeds.	Leeds, England
li.	Long Island, New York, USA
life.	LifeNet Christian Network
lon.	London, England
lou.	Louisiana, USA
lspace.	Discussions about Terry Pratchett
lu.	Luxembourg newsgroups
luebeck.	Luebeck, Deutschland
lv.	Latvian newsgroups

M

malta.	Malta and Maltese newsgroups
man.	Manitoba, Canada
manawatu.	Manawatu district, New Zealand

maus.	Originating from MausNet (Deutschland)
mc.	Mississippi College, Clinton, Mississippi USA
mcgill.	McGill University, Montreal, Quebec, Canada
mcmaster.	McMaster University, Hamilton, Ontario, Canada
md.	Maryland, USA
me.	Maine, USA
medlux.	Russian-language medical newsgroups
melb.	Melbourne, Australia
melbpc.	Melbourne PC User Group, Australia
memphis.	Memphis, Tennessee, USA
mensa.	Discussions among members of Mensa
metocean.	Metocean, Japan (ISP)
metu.	Middle East Technical Univ., Ankara, Turkiye
mex.	Mexican newsgroups
mi.	Michigan, USA
miami.	Miami, Florida, USA
microsoft.	Microsoft newsgroups
midlands.	English midlands, UK
milw.	Milwaukee, Wisconsin, USA
misc.	Usenet miscellaneous newsgroups
mistral.	Brighton, England
mit.	Massachusetts Institute of Technology
mn.	Minnesota, USA
mo.	Missouri, USA
mod.	Moderated newsgroups
ms.	Mississippi, USA
mtl.	Montreal,Quebec,Canada
mu.	Marquette University, Milwaukee, Wisconson, USA
muc.	Munchen, Deutschland
muenster.	Muenster, Deutschland
mun.	Memorial University, Newfoundland, Canada
mv.	MV Communications, Inc. (ISP)
mx.	Mexico

N

nagasaki-u.	University of Nagasaki, Japan
nanaimo.	Nanaimo, British Columbia, Canada
nas.	NASA Numerical Aerospace Simulation Facility, USA
nasa.	National Aeronautics and Space Administration, USA

nashville.	Nashville, Tennessee, USA
nb.	New Brunswick, Canada
nbg.	Nuernberg, Deutschland
nc.	North Carolina, USA
ncar.	Nat. Center for Atmospheric Research, Colorado, USA
ncf.	National Capital Freenet, Ottawa, Ontario, Canada
ncle.	Newcastle (and Hunter Valley), Australia
ncsc.	North Carolina SuperComputing, USA
nctu.	National Chiao-Ting University, Taiwan
nd.	North Dakota, USA
ne.	New England area, USA
nebr.	Nebraska, USA
net.	Usenet II (usenet2.org)
netscape.	Netscape, Mountain View, California, USA
netz.	Originated by Netz e.V., Deutschland
nevada.	Nevada, USA
neworleans.	New Orleans, Louisiana, USA
news.	Usenet news
newsguy.	Newsguy News Service
nf.	Newfoundland, Canada
nh.	New Hampshire, USA
ni.	Northern Ireland
niagara.	Niagara Peninsula, Canada/USA
nj.	New Jersey, USA
nl.	Nederland
nlnet.	Nlnet (ISP)
nm.	New Mexico, USA
no.	Norge (Norway)
nord.	Norddeutschland
nordunet.	Nordic National Research Network
north.	Weser-Ems Region, Deutschland
northwest.	Northwest region of England, UK
nrw.	Nordrhein-Westfalen, Deutschland
ns.	Nova Scotia, Canada
ntua.	National Technical University of Athens, Greece
nu.	Newcastle University, Australia
nv.	Nevada, USA
nwt.	Northwest Territories, Canada
nwu.	Northwestern University, Illinois, USA

ny.	New York State, USA
nyc.	New York City, New York, USA
nyu.	New York University, USA
nz.	New Zealand

O
oau.	Orlando, Florida, USA
oc.	Orange County, California, USA
oecher.	Aachen, Deutschland
oerebro.	Orebro, Narke, Sverige
ogi.	Oregon Graduate Institute, USA
oh.	Ohio, USA
ok.	Oklahoma, USA
okinawa.	Okinawan newsgroups
oldenburg.	Oldenburg, Deutschland
olnet.	Oldenburg und Umgebung, Deutschland
on.	Offenes Netz Luebeck, Deutschland
online.	Telenor Online, Oslo, Norge (ISP)
ont.	Ontario, Canada
or.	Oregon, USA
osu.	Ohio State University, USA
ott.	Ottawa, Ontario, Canada
owl.	Ostwestfalen-Lippe, Deutschland
own.	One World Net
ox.	Oxford University, UK

P
pa.	Pennsylvania, USA
pb.	Der Fahrgastverband PRO BAHN, Deutschland
pdaxs.	Portland Metronet, Oregon, USA
pdx.	Portland, Oregon, USA
pei.	Prince Edward Island, Canada
peru.	Groupos del Peru
pgh.	Pittsburgh, Pennsylvania, USA
phil-priv.	The Philippines and Filipino newsgroups
phl.	Philadelphia, Pennsylvania, USA
phoenix.	Phoenix, Arizona, USA
phx.	Phoenix, Arizona, USA
pi.	Planet Internet, Nederland (ISP)
pinnacle.	Pinnacle, UK (ISP)

pipex.	Pipex (ISP)
pitt.	University of Pittsburgh, Pennsylvania, USA
pl.	Polska (Polish-language newsgroups)
planet.	PlaNet FreeNZ co-operative, New Zealand
pnw.	Pacific North-West (USA/Canada)
prima.	Prima e.V., Dortmund, Deutschland (ISP)
princeton.	Princeton area, New Jersey, USA
prodigy.	Prodigy (ISP)
ps.	People of Scandinavia (ISP)
psi.	PSINet (ISP)
psu.	Pennsylvania State University, USA
pt.	Portugal and Portuguese newsgroups
pu.	Princeton University, New Jersey, USA
purdue.	Purdue University

Q

qc.	Quebec, Canada
queens.	Queens University, Kingston, Ontario, Canada

R

rabbit.	Rabbit Network (ISP)
rain.	RAINnet (ISP)
realtynet.	Real estate network
rec.	Usenet recreational newsgroups
redhat.	Red Hat Software, North Carolina, USA
region.	Mittlehessen, Deutschland
relcom.	Relcom, Commonwealth of Ind. States (ISP) (Cyrillic)
rg.	Rio Grande Valley, New Mexico/Texas, USA
rhein.	Rhein area (Cologne and Bonn), Germany
ri.	Rhode Island, USA
rmii.	Rocky Mountain Internet (ISP)
roanoke.	Roanoke, Virginia, USA
ru.	Rutgers University, New Jersey, USA
ruhr.	Ruhrgebiet, Deutschland
rv.	Rogue Valley, Oregon, USA
rwth.	Rheinisch-Westf\'e4lische Tech. Hochschule, Deutschland
rye.	Ryerson University, Toronto, Ontario, Canada

S

saar.	Saarbruecken, Deutschland

sac.	Sacramento, California, USA
sackheads.	Sysadmins with too much time on their hands
sacramento.	Sacramento, California, USA
sae.	World Council of Hellenes Abroad, Greek language
salford.	University of Salford, UK
sanet.	SAnet (South Africa)
sat.	San Antonio, Texas, USA
sba.	Santa Barbara, California, USA
sbay.	South Bay region, San Francisco, California, USA
schl.	Newsgroup echo of KidLink mailing lists
schule.	German-language school newsgroups
sci.	Usenet science newsgroups
scot.	Scotland and Scottish newsgroups
scruz.	Santa Cruz, California, USA
sd.	South Dakota, USA
sdnet.	San Diego, California, USA
sdsu.	San Diego State University, California, USA
se.	Sverige (Sweden)
sea.	Seattle, Washington, USA
seattle.	Seattle, Washington, USA
sfnet.	Suomi-Finland, Finland and Finnish-language newsgroups
sfu.	Simon Fraser Univ., British Columbia, Canada
sg.	Singapore
sgi.	Silicon Graphics, Inc.
shamash.	Jewish newsgroups
si.	Slovenian newsgroups
simcoe.	Simcoe County, Ontario, Canada
sj.	Saint John's, Newfoundland, Canada
sk.	Saskatchewan, Canada
sk.	Slovakian newsgroups
slac.	Stanford Linear Accelerator Center, USA
slo.	San Luis Obispo, California, USA
slonet.	SLONET (ISP)
snafu.	Snafu, Deutschland (ISP)
soc.	Usenet social issues newsgroups
socs.	McGill Univ. Sch. of Comp. Sci., Quebec, Canada
sol.	Sol.net Network Services, Milwaukee, Wisconsin, USA
solent.	Solent, UK (ISP)
solinet.	Gewerkschaftliche Themen (German trade unions)
sonoma.	Sonoma County, California, USA

south-wales. Southern Wales and Welsh newsgroups, UK
spk.   Spokane, Washington, USA
spokane.   Spokane, Washington, USA
srg.   Swiss Broadcasting Corporation
srjc.   Santa Rosa Junior College, California, USA
stgt.   Stuttgart, Deutschland
stl.   St. Louis, Missouri, USA
stmarys.   St. Mary's Univ., Nova Scotia, Canada
su.   Stanford University
sudbury.   Sudbury, Ontario, Canada
sunet.   Swedish University Network, Sverige
surfnet.   Dutch university newsgroups, Nederland
swipnet.   Swipnet Tele/2, Sverige (ISP)
swnet.   Sverige (Sweden)
syd.   Sydney, New South Wales, Australia

T
t-online.   T-Online, Deutschland (ISP)
tacoma.   Tacoma, Washington, USA
talk.   Usenet talk newsgroups
tamu.   Texas A&M University, USA
taos.   Taos, New Mexico, USA
tba.   Tampa Bay, Florida, USA
tct.   Discussions about Therianthropy
tdw.   Tidewater, Virginia, USA
tele.   Tele Danmark Internet (ISP)
terranova.   Terra Nova Visuals, Finland
thur.   Thuringia, Deutschland
tin.   TIN, Italia (ISP)
tip.   The Internet Plaza, Nederland (ISP)
tipnet.   Telia, Sverige (ISP)
tn.   Tennessee, USA
tnn.   The Network News (Japanese)
tor.   Toronto, Ontario, Canada
torfree.   Toronto Freenet, Ontario, Canada
toulouse.   Toulouse, France
tp.   Toppoint, Kiel, Deutschland
tr.   Turkiye and Turkish-language groups
trentu.   Trent University, Ontario, Canada
triangle.   Research Triangle Park, North Carolina, USA

trumpet.	Discussions of Trumpet programs
tulsa.	Tulsa, Oklahoma, USA
tvontario.	TVOntario, Ontario, Canada
tw.	Taiwan
tx.	Texas, USA

U

u3b.	Discussions on AT&T 3B systems
ualberta.	University of Alberta, Canada
uark.	University of Arkansas, USA
ubc.	University of British Columbia, Canada
uc.	University of California, USA
ucalgary.	University of Calgary, Alberta, Canada
ucam.	University of Cambridge, UK
ucb.	University of California at Berkeley, USA
ucd.	University of California, Davis, USA
ucsb.	University of California at Santa Barbara, USA
ucsc.	University of California at Santa Cruz, USA
udes.	Universite de Sherbrooke, Quebec, Canada
uf.	University of Florida, USA
ufra.	Unterfranken, Deutschland
uiowa.	University of Iowa, USA
uiuc.	University of Illinois, Urbana-Champaign, USA
uk.	United Kingdom
ukc.	University of Kent at Canterbury, UK
ukr.	Ukraine and Ukranian language newsgroups
uky.	University of Kentucky, USA
ulaval.	Universite Laval, Quebec, Canada
um.	University of Maryland, USA
umiami.	University of Miami, Florida, USA
umich.	University of Michigan, USA
umn.	University of Minnesota, USA
umoncton.	University of Moncton, New Brunswick, Canada
umontreal.	Universite de Montreal, Quebec, Canada
unb.	University of New Brunswick, Canada
unc.	University of North Carolina at Chapel Hill, USA
unisa.	University of South Australia, Adelaide, Australia.
uo.	University of Oregon, USA
uoc.	University of Canterbury, Christchurch, New Zealand
upenn.	University of Pennsylvania, USA

uqam.	Universite de Quebec a Montreal, Canada
us.	United States
usask.	University of Saskatchewan, Canada
usf.	University of South Florida, USA
usu.	Utah State University, USA
usyd.	University of Sydney, New South Wales, Australia
ut.	University of Toronto, Ontario, Canada
utah.	Utah, USA
utcs.	University of Texas, Computer Science, USA
utk.	University of Tennessee, Knoxville, USA
utexas.	University of Texas, USA
uunet.	Originating from UUNet (UNIX)
uva.	University of Virgina, USA
uvic.	University of Victoria, British Columbia, Canada
uw.	University of Waterloo, Ontario, Canada
uwa.	University of Washington, USA
uwarwick.	University of Warwick, UK
uwash.	University of Washington, USA
uwindsor.	University of Windsor, Ontario, Canada
uwisc.	University of Wisconsin, Madison, USA
uwm.	University of Wisconsin, Milwaukee, USA
uwo.	University of Western Ontario, London, Canada

V

va.	Virginia, USA
van.	Vancouver, British Columbia, Canada
vatech.	Virginia Polytechnic Inst. and State University, USA
vechta.	Universitaet Vechta, Niedersachsen, Deutschland
vegas.	Las Vegas, Nevada, USA
vic.	Victoria, British Columbia, Canada
vmsnet.	Originating from Digital VAX network
vol.	Telecom Italia Video On Line (ISP)
vpro.	VPRO TV-station newsgroups, Nederland
vt.	Vermont, USA
vu.	Vanderbilt University

W

wa.	Western Australia
wales.	Wales
wash.	Washington, USA

west-virginia.	West Virginia, USA
westf.	Westfalen, Deutschland
wi.	Wisconsin, USA
wimsey.	Wimsey, British Columia, Canada (ISP)
witten.	Witten, Deutschland
wlu.	Wilfred Laurier University, Waterloo, Ontario, Canada
wny.	Western New York, USA
worldnet.	AT&T Worldnet
worldonline.	World Online, Nederland (ISP)
wpi.	Worcester Polytechnic Institute, Massachusetts, USA
wpg.	Winnipeg, Manitoba, Canada
wxs.	World Access/Planet Internet, Nederland (ISP)
wyo.	Wyoming, USA

X

xs4all.	Xs4all, Nederland (ISP)

Y

yakima.	Yakima, Washington, USA
yale.	Yale University, Connecticut, USA
yk.	Yellowknife, Northwest Territories, Canada
yfn.	Youngstown, Ohio Free-Net, USA
yolo.	Yolo County, California, USA
york.	York University, Ontario, Canada
ysu.	Youngstown State University, Ohio, USA

Z

z-netz.	Originating from Z-Netz (German newsgroups)
za.	South Africa and Afrikaans newsgroups
zipnews.	Zippos News Services (commercial)

©1999 Lewis S. Eisen. Reproduction in whole or in part is permitted so long as original author is duly credited.

Appendix C

Search Engines

The Most Popular Search Engines

The algorithms the major search engines use to determine your site's ranking and the information reference to index your site change quite often, so what may hold true today may not hold true tomorrow. I recommend visiting the respective search engines before you submit and reviewing any material available in regard to site submissions. Many search engines have information on their submission pages, on help pages, and sometimes on a submission tips page. You can also check out various sites on the Internet that offer submission tips and tricks for the major search engines, some of which are included within Chapters 3 and 4 of this book. Two of my favorites are Search Engine Watch *(http://www.searchenginewatch.com)* and Search Engine World *(http://www.searchengineworld.com)*.

AltaVista
Site Address: *http://www.altavista.com/*
Submission Address: *http://www.altavista.com/cgi-bin/query?pg =addurl* or click on "Add a URL" from AltaVista's home page.

AltaVista went live in December of 1995. In August 1999, CMGI, Inc. acquired 83% of AltaVista's outstanding stock from Compaq. As well, Shopping.com and Zip2 became wholly owned subsidiaries. AltaVista consists of multiple platforms: AltaVista Search, AltaVista Live, AltaVista's Shopping.com, and AltaVista Local Portal Services.

Pages (millions): 250
Meta tag support: Yes
Index body text: Yes
Frames support: Yes
Image maps: Yes
Alt text: Yes
Link popularity affects position: Yes
Keywords in title important: Yes
Higher rankings for reviewed sites: No
Case sensitive: Yes
Title: Page title, if none "No Title"
Description: Meta tag or first text on page
Time to index submissions: 24 to 48 hours
Type: Spider—Scooter
Tips: AltaVista likes keywords that are located near the top of your page, so use descriptive keywords where possible. Keywords used in the title of your page also seem to influence page rankings.

Excite

Site Address: *http://www.excite.com/*
Submission Address: *http://www.excite.com/info/add_url* or click on "Add URL" from Excite's home page.
Has been around since 1995. Excite bought out WebCrawler in 1996. These acquisitions are still independently operated.
Pages (millions): 150
Meta tag support: Yes
Index body text: Yes
Frames support: No
Image maps: No
Alt text: No
Link popularity affects position: Yes
Keywords in title important: Yes
Higher rankings for reviewed sites: No
Case sensitive: No

Title: Page title, if none "Untitled"
Description: The few most dominant sentences on your page
Time to index submissions: 2 to 3 weeks
Type: Spider—Architext
Tips: Make the first 100 characters of your page as descriptive as possible. Excite will try to make the description from the text at the start of your page but will keep going until it is satisfied that it has enough descriptive sentences. Your sentences must be complete for Excite to use them in forming your description. This does not necessarily mean that uncompleted sentences at the beginning of your page will not be used. Excite would just rather use complete sentences.

Go/Infoseek

Site Address: *http://infoseek.go.com/*
Submission Address: *http://www.go.com/AddUrl?pg=SubmitUrl.html* or click on "Add URL" from Infoseek's home page.
Infoseek has been online since 1995. It is a very well-known search engine. Infoseek also manages a directory separate from its search engine. Sites are listed categorically, and some are even reviewed and recommended by Infoseek.
Pages (millions): 75
Meta tag support: Yes
Index body text: Yes
Frames support: No
Image maps: Yes
Alt text: Yes
Link popularity affects position: Yes
Keywords in title important: Yes
Higher rankings for reviewed sites: Yes
Case sensitive: Yes
Title: Page title, if none lists the first line on page
Description: The Meta tag, if none first 200 characters in body of page
Time to index submissions: 1 to 7 days
Type: Spider—Sidewinder
Tips: Use the Alt attribute because Infoseek will include it in your description. This is especially helpful for sites that are mainly graphical in content. Never use keywords that do not relate to the content of your site. Infoseek punishes those who do with lower rankings.

Google

Site Address: *http://www.google.com/*

Submission Address: *http://www.google.com/addurl.html* or click on "Add your URL" from Google's About page.

Google was founded in 1998 by Larry Page and Sergey Brin, and has quickly become a very popular search tool on the web.

Pages (millions): 70 to 100

Meta tag support: No

Index body text: Yes

Frames support: Yes

Image maps: No

Alt text: No

Link popularity affects position: Yes

Keywords in title important: Yes

Higher rankings for reviewed sites: No

Case sensitive: No

Title: Page title, if none URL

Description: First text found on page, including hypertext links

Type: Spider—Googlebot

Tips: Keywords in your domain name and link popularity will really help you out with Google. To increase your link popularity and get other sites to link to you, perhaps you should consider reciprocal links to other sites.

HotBot

Site Address: *http://www.hotbot.com/*

Submission Address: *http://hotbot.lycos.com/addurl.asp* or click on "Add URL" from HotBot's home page.

HotBot was launched in 1996. HotBot uses Inktomi's search engine technology.

Pages (millions): 110

Meta tag support: Yes

Index body text: Yes

Frames support: No

Image maps: No

Alt text: No

Link popularity affects position: Yes, HotBot uses DirectHit

Keywords in title important: Yes

Higher rankings for reviewed sites: No

Case sensitive: Mixed

Title: Page title, if none lists URL
Description: Meta tag, if none uses approximately the first 240 to 250 characters in the body of your page
Time to index submissions: 48 hours
Type: Uses Inktomi's Spider
Tips: If you do a search and feel your site is not positioned correctly in the search results, then you can let the people at HotBot know about. Send all the relevant information to *bugs@hotbot.com*.

Lycos

Site Address: *http://www.lycos.com/*
Submission Address: *http://www.lycos.com/addasite.html* or click on "Add Your Site to Lycos" from their home page.
Lycos went online in 1994. Lycos is a well-recognized spider.
Pages (millions): 50
Meta tag support: No
Index body text: Yes
Frames support: Limited support
Image maps: No
Alt text: Yes
Link popularity affects position: No
Keywords in title important: Yes
Higher rankings for reviewed sites: No
Case sensitive: No
Title: Page title, if none lists URL
Description: A snippet of the page that as been determined to represent it
Time to index submissions: 2 weeks
Type: T-Rex
Tips: Don't have an image map at the beginning of your page because Lycos will be unable to interpret it.

NorthernLight

Site Address: *http://www.northernlight.com/*
Submission Address: *http://www.northernlight.com/docs/ regurl_help.html* or click on "Register URL" from NorthernLight's home page.
NorthernLight started in September of 1995. Their web results are combined with information from premium material, giving you access to books, magazines, databases, and newswires.

Pages (millions): 189
Meta tag support: No
Index body text: Yes
Frames support: Yes
Image maps: Yes
Alt text: No
Link popularity affects position: No
Keywords in title important: Yes
Higher rankings for reviewed sites: No
Case sensitive: Modified sensitivity
Title: Page title
Description: Approximately the first 25 words of the page body
Time to index submissions: 2 weeks
Type: Spider—Gulliver
Tips: Submit only *one* of your pages to NorthernLight; let their spider find the remaining pages on your site.

WebCrawler

Site Address: *http://www.webcrawler.com/*
Submission Address: *http://www.webcrawler.com/info/add_url/* or click on "Add your URL" from their home page.
WebCrawler has been around since 1994 and has since been purchased twice. It is now owned by Excite but is still operated independently.
Pages (millions): 2
Meta tag support: Yes
Index body text: Yes
Frames support: No
Image maps: Yes
Alt text: No
Link popularity affects position: Yes
Keywords in title important: Yes
Higher rankings for reviewed sites: Yes
Case sensitive: No
Title: Page title, if none lists URL
Description: Meta tag, if none looks at first textual information body of page
Time to index submissions: 2 to 3 weeks
Type: Uses Excite's Spider

Tips: Use of keywords in your page titles, descriptions Meta tag, keywords Meta tag, and in content near the top of your page influences your ranking with WebCrawler.

Yahoo!

Site Address: *http://www.yahoo.com/*

Submission Address: To submit to Yahoo you must visit their site, find an appropriate category that relates to your page, and then click on "Suggest a Site."

Established in 1994, Yahoo! is a well-recognized directory. It is the largest of its kind and is the most popular with Internet users. Yahoo! is a directory, but it does not read pages on the net like the other search engines discussed here. To have your site added to Yahoo!, you must fill out a submit form on the site. You must register your site in a category and your site is checked by employees to verify that it matches the category you have chosen. If your site is commercial in any way, you must register it in a subcategory of Business and Economy.

Pages (millions): 1.2+

Time to index submissions: 6 to 8 weeks

Tips: Yahoo gives higher rankings to sites that are reviewed. When submitting pages submit your base URL, (e.g., *http://www.yourdomain.com/*), as this stands a greater chanced of being indexed by Yahoo. Take your time to find the most appropriate subcategories for your site and be sure to fill out their submission form completely and accurately. Yahoo is very picky about who they add to their directory

Other Search Engines and Directories

555-1212.com

Site Address: *http://www.555-1212.com*

Submission Address: *http://www.infospace.com/info.go555/submit.htm*

In addition to area code lookup, you can shop online, find businesses near you, get your friends' telephone numbers and e-mail addresses, browse classified ads, and much more.

AOL.com Search

Site Address: *http://search.aol.com/*
Submission Address: *http://search.aol.com/add.adp*
This is AOL's search engine. It once ran off of the Excite engine but now uses the DMOZ.org directory. Submit to DMOZ.org, and AOL Netfind will also list your site.

Ask Jeeves!

Site Address: *http://www.askjeeves.com*
Submission Address: N/A
Ask Jeeves accepts fully worded questions and crawls through search directories, engines, and meta-directories until an answer is found. You cannot submit a site directly to Ask Jeeves.

BigStuff.com

Site Address: *http://www.bigstuff.com/*
Submission Address: *http://www.bigstuff.com/add.htm*

The Biz

Site Address: *http://www.thebiz.co.uk*
Submission Address: *http://www.thebiz.co.uk/default.asp? page=submit&listby=all*
The Business Information Zone has been developed for users seeking UK-relevant business information, products, and services on the Internet, whether users are in the UK or overseas.

BizWeb

Site Address: *http://www.bizweb.com*
Submission Address: *http://www.bizweb.com/InfoForm/*
BizWeb is a web business guide to 43,165 companies listed in 194 categories.

Cyber411

Site Address: *http://www.cyber411.com*
Submission Address: N/A
Cyber411 obtains its search results from multiple search engines. You cannot submit a site to it directly.

Direct Hit

Site Address: *http://www.directhit.com*

Submission Address: *http://www.directhit.com/util/addurl.html*
Direct Hit is a relatively new search engine that bases its search criteria on page popularity.

DMOZ Open Directory Project
Site Address: *http://www.dmoz.org*
Submission Address: *http://www.dmoz.org/add.html*
DMOZ is a directory in which actual humans review your site's content to determine whether or not it meets their standards. Many major search engines including AOL Netfind and AltaVista incorporate the DMOZ directory listings into their own search results.

Dogpile
Site Address: *http://www.dogpile.com*
Submission Address: N/A
Dogpile obtains its search results from multiple search engines. You cannot submit a site to it directly.

FAST Search
Site Address: *http://www.alltheweb.com*
Submission Address: *http://www.alltheweb.com/addurl.html*
FAST Search currently indexes more than 200 million web documents with the eventual goal of indexing 1 billion.

GoTo.com
Site Address: *http://www.goto.com*
Submission Address: *http://www.goto.com/d/about/advertisers/*
GoTo is the one of the fastest, easiest, most relevant search engine on the web, as well as the small advertiser's best friend. You select the search terms that are relevant to your site. Then you determine how much you are willing to pay on a per-click basis for each of those search terms. The higher your "bid," the higher in the search results your site appears. It's targeted, cost-per-click advertising and you set the cost per click.

iAtlas
Site Address: *http://www.iatlas.com*
Submission Address: *http://www.iatlas.com/ash/registry/*
A business-related search engine.

Internet Promotions MegaList
Site Address: *http://www.2020tech.com*
Submission Address: *http://www.2020tech.com/submit.html*
20/20 Technologies is a one-stop Internet advertising solution. Their services include web page design, Internet research, and Internet promotions. The submission URL lists dozens of useful search engine submission resources.

ICQ iT!
Site Address: *http://www.icqit.com*
Submission Address: *http://search.icq.com/default.asp?act.addurl=addurl*
Submit your site to one of the largest chat networks on the Internet.

Keyword.com
Site Address: *http://www.keyword.com*
Submission Address: Visit the site and enter a keyword.
This is a free service that allows you to "reserve" a keyword and have searches for a keyword directed immediately to your site. Only one keyword can be reserved per site. Your Internet keyword will remain active as long it is entered a minimum of six times every 60 days.

Linkcentre Directory
Site Address: *http://linkcentre.com*
Submission Address: *http://linkcentre.com/addurl.html*
Search the Linkcentre Directory or add your web page immediately for greater exposure on the Internet.

LinkMaster
Site Address: *http://www.linkmaster.com*
Submission Address: *http://www.linkmaster.com/register.html*

LookSmart
Site Address: *http://www.looksmart.com*
Submission Address: *http://www.looksmart.com/aboutus/partners/subsite2.html*
LookSmart is a large, selective Internet search directory. Many engines, including MSN Search, currently use it to determine their own search results.

Manufacturers Information Net
Site Address: *http://mfginfo.com*
Submission Address: *http://mfginfo.com/htm/infoform.htm*
This site provides a complete source of information for industry and those services related to manufacturing. Use the search engine to locate information on manufacturers, suppliers, professional services, and many more resources on and off the site.

MasterSite
Site Address: *http://mastersite.com*
Submission Address: *http://mastersite.com/addurl.htm*

McKinley's Internet Directory
Site Address: *http://www.mckinley.com*
Submission Address: *http://magellan.excite.com/info/add_url/*
Magellan's technology offers a unique way to search the web: by concept. Like most search engines, they've programmed this search engine to look for documents containing the exact words you entered into the query box. But Magellan goes further and looks for ideas closely linked to the words in your query. This feature broadens your search.

Metacrawler
Site Address: *http://www.metacrawler.com*
Submission Address: N/A
Metacrawler obtains its search results from multiple search engines. You cannot submit a site to it directly.

MSN Search
Site Address: *http://search.msn.com*
Submission Address: *http://search.msn.com/addurl.asp*
This is Microsoft's entry into the search engine fray. You can submit one URL per day to their engine.

NationalDirectory
Site Address: *http://www.nationaldirectory.com*
Submission Address: *http://www.nationaldirectory.com/addurl.html*
Claims to be the "least spammed" search directory on the World Wide Web.

Nerd World
Site Address: *http://www.nerdworld.com*
Submission Address: *http://www.nerdworld.com/nwadd.html*
Nerd World's most prominent feature is their search engine and subject index.

Netscape Search
Site Address: *http://search.netscape.com*
Submission Address: *http://home.netscape.com/netcenter/smallbusiness/onlineessentials/addsite.html*
Netscape, maker of one of the world's best-known browsers, also has its own search/portal site.

SavvySearch
Site Address: *http://www.savvysearch.com*
Submission Address: N/A
SavvySearch obtains its search results from multiple search engines. You cannot submit a site to it directly.

SiteExplorer
Site Address: *http://www.sitexplorer.com*
Submission Address: *http://www.sitexplorer.com/add.html*
Another search engine to add your site to.

Small Business
Site Address: *http://www.bizoffice.com*
Submission Address: *http://www.bizoffice.com/submit.html*
Small and home-based business links. Hundreds of links to quality sites.

Snap
Site Address: *http://www.snap.com*
Submission Address: *http://www.snap.com/LMOID/resource/0,566,-1077,00.html?st.sn.ld.0.1077*
A human-compiled directory that also supplements its results with Inktomi's database.

Trade Wave Galaxy
Site Address: *http://www.einet.net/galaxy.html*

Submission Address: *http://www.einet.net/cgi-bin/annotate?/galaxy*
Galaxy is known as the professional's guide to a world of information.

What-U-Seek
    Site Address: *http://whatuseek.com*
    Submission Address: *http://www.whatuseek.com/addurl-tableset.shtml*

Appendix D

Internet Marketing Resources

Internet Resources for each topic covered in the book are located at the end of each chapter. Here, additionally, we have included a number of great Internet marketing resource sites.

A1 WWW Promotion Sites
http://www.a1co.com
Excellent resource for locating hundreds of directories, indexes, and catalogs that will list your site for free. Also has a handy tool for locating large e-zine sites.

Al Czarnecki Communications
http://www.web.net/alcom
A communications site with tips and resources to help you build important relationships, public relations, social marketing, and fund raising.

Adbility.com: Adbility's Web Publishers' Advertising Guide
http://www.adbility.com/WPAG/
Adbility's Web Publishers' Advertising Guide contains hundreds of listings, with directory pages categorized into subsections and subpages related to web site promotion.

Advertising Age's Business Marketing Online
http://www.netb2b.com/
Offers business-to-business marketers educational information on creating and running a web site, including case studies and how-to articles.

Ad Resource: Internet Advertising and Web Site Promotion Resources
http://adres.internet.com/
Ad Resource features information on Internet advertising and web site promotion to help individuals understand the World Wide Web, e-mail advertising, and how attract visitors to their site.

BizGold
http://www.bizgold.com/
Resources for home-based businesses, small businesses, and entrepreneurs to help succeed on the Internet in making money and establishing an online presence.

ChannelSeven.com
http://www.channelseven.com/
Internet advertising and marketing campaign news. A great resource for builders, advertisers, and marketers of Internet businesses.

ClickZ Network
http://www.clickz.com/
All kinds of articles related to advertising and business.

CNET.com—Web Building
http://www.builder.com/
Just about everything you need to know surrounding web site design and construction.

Connex Network Incorporated
http://www.connexnetwork.com
Connex Network provides consulting services to companies interested in marketing on the Internet. Their Web Site Report Card reviews your site against 50 criteria and provides feedback to assist you in improving your site from a marketing perspective. Their Internet marketing strategies are prepared specifically for your company

with your objectives, your products and services, and your target customers in mind. Connex also delivers general and company-specific Internet Marketing Workshops. Connex Network Incorporated is owned by the author of this book.

CyberAtlas

http://cyberatlas.internet.com/
Internet statistics and market research for web marketers.

CyberPulse

http://www.cyberpulse.com
Bob and Varda Novick know their stuff when it comes to online marketing. Excellent resource area covering mailing lists, newsgroups, advertising, promotion, and so on. Don't let the plain graphics fool you.

Deadlock Dispatch

http://www.deadlock.com/promote
If you're really serious about your promotion campaign, there's a whole new world of in-depth articles and really clever online marketing strategies one mouse-click away.

Directory of Ezines

http://www.lifestylespub.com/cgi-bin/ezines.cgi?10166
Lifestyles is the presenter of The Directory of Ezines, a well-researched, up-to-date list of internet newsletters that accept classified advertising. Each listing within The Directory of Ezines tells you everything you need to know about advertising in a specific newsletter.

eBoz! Your Guide To Creating Successful Websites

http://www.eboz.com/
A resource for information pertaining to Internet marketing and direct marketing.

DrNunley.com

http://drnunley.com/
Tips on marketing, advertising, online marketing, and the Internet.

E Weekly

http://www.eweekly.com
An online newsletter that contains articles on small business and In-

ternet commerce and marketing. Back issues are also available. There are a number of connections to projects of the sponsor, Cyber Media.

Gator's Bite
http://www.gators-byte.com
A weekly column dedicated to helping your potential customers find your site, and keep coming back! You can join the Gator's mailing list that sends you the weekly information. Check out past articles as well.

InfoJump—The Magazine & Newspaper Article Search Engine
http://www.infojump.com/
Over 4000 online publications and over 5,000,000 articles from online magazines, newspapers, journals, newsletters, and e-zines. If you plan to publish an e-mail newsletter, be sure to get it listed here.

Information City: Web Tools and Internet Software
http://www.freereports.net/
Help for the new or experienced webmaster. Variety of free tools and resources, resell products, and information on search engines.

InfoScavenger
http://www.infoscavenger.com/engine.htm
This site provides an annotated hotlist of resources to help you get your web page to appear at the top of the list when someone uses AltaVista, Infoseek, or other engines to find you. This web site has a nice, specific mission.

Internet Business Webliography
http://www.lib.lsu.edu/bus/marketin.html#Internet
Links to information related to the Internet, business on the Internet, and marketing online. This site also contains many links to other sites containing marketing related information.

Internet Marketing Center
http://www.marketingtips.com/main.html
All kinds of tips, strategies, and secrets for Internet marketing, online advertising, and web site promotion. There is also a newsletter you can sign up for.

Internet World: The Voice of E-Business and Internet Technology
http://www.internetworld.com/
Magazine containing Internet news, marketing, management, infrastructure, ISP marketing, and e-commerce development.

Marketing SuperSite
http://www.ntu.edu.sg/library/int-mktg.htm and *http://www.ntu. edu.sg/library/ecomm.htm*
This resource list from the National Technology University in Singapore is almost too big. Contains links to a massive number of articles and web sites concerned with promotion, marketing, and commerce on the Internet.

Meta Tag Builder
http://www.MetaTagBuilder.com
This free area (provided by NetPromote) helps site owners create Meta tags in the correct format simply by inputting web site information and clicking a button.

NetPromote
http://www.NetPromote.com
This site provides a free web promotion service for companies and individuals. NetPromote also offers consulting services that guarantee top-20 placement on the major search engines, plus unlimited resubmissions to the best search engines for life, for free.

Promotion 101
http://www.Promotion101.com
This division of NetPromote provides a free online tutorial to help web site owners learn how to better their placement on search engines and increase traffic to their sites. Includes the Ultimate Top 20 Search Engine Placement Guide. Also articles on optimizing web pages.

Search Engine Showdown
http://www.notess.com/search/
Detailed analysis of Internet Search Engines, their features, databases, and strategies.

SelfPromotion.com

http://selfpromotion.com
Automatically add your URL for free to over 100 of the biggest and most important indexes and search engines! Apply for hundreds of awards and improve your ranking in the search engines.

Sitelaunch

http://www.sitelaunch.net/
Sitelaunch is a good source of free tools, guides, and resources to help you with your web site.

Site Promotion Resources

http://www.pageresource.com/promorec/index.html
Resources for web site promotion.

Smithfam's Internet Marketing Resources

http://www.smithfam.com/
All kinds of tips, tricks, ideas, concepts, and strategies that successful marketers are using to create wealth online.

StatMarket

http://www.statmarket.com/
Real-time source of Internet statistics and user trends including Internet demographics, market statistics, and market trends.

Submit It!

http://www.submit-it.com
You can use Submit It to register your URL with hundreds of search engines and directories.

The Internet Monitor

http://www.internet-monitor.com/
Tips, articles, and seminars on proven marketing strategies for trade publishers.

The Tenagra Corporation—Internet Marketing Resources

http://marketing.tenagra.com/imr.html
Links and information about Internet marketing.

VeryHot.com
http://www.veryhot.com
Links to many great Internet marketing tools.

Virtual Promote
http://www.virtualpromote.com/home.html
A great source of information and tools to get your site noticed.

Web Resources
http://www.webresource.net
Lots of good information on HTML and creating and maintaining a web site.

Website Promotion Tools
http://www.newapps.com/appstopics/Win_95_Web_Site_Promotion_Tools.html
A large list of programs of interest to webmasters to help in web site promotion.

WebStep 100
http://www.mmgco.com/top100.html
John Audette of Multimedia Marketing Group put together this list of the top 100 directories, indexes, and catalogs. The links are all annotated, and you can get to each site's registration page from the link on WebStep.

Webmaster Resources
http://www.webmaster-resources.com
A handy and useful site for helping you design your own web site. Good advice, lots of links, and plenty of useful information about web hosting companies, awards, tracking programs, mailing list servers, web site promotion, and sponsorships.

The WebMaster's Notebook
http://www.cio.com/WebMaster/wm_notebook_front.html
This comprehensive site contains information of value to anyone that runs, or wants to, a WWW site: tools and links, technology notes, online web seminars, web reports, and the WebMaster Magazine.

Webmasters' Guild

http://www.webmaster.org/

Not-for-profit, professional organization for webmasters—to disseminate information and discuss issues of concerns to web masters: network configuration, interface and graphical design, software development, business strategy, writing, marketing, and project management.

Webmaster Magazine

http://www.web-master.com

An electronic magazine that examines the use of the web by, and within, business. Topics include how companies are using the web to improve operations, reduce expenses, and connect to their customers.

Webmaster Reference Library

http://webreference.com

Hundreds of carefully selected and annotated web sites and articles of interest to webmasters.

WebPromote Weekly

http://www.webpromote.com/

The WebPromote Resource Center provides information, tools, and products for marketers to be more effective on the web, featuring WebPromote Weekly, FreeSubmit, and the META Tag Builder.

WebWorkers TOP 10 Web Business Directories

http://www.webworker.com

Resources for creating and promoting an online business. Outstanding web business opportunities and web business services that enable the prospective entrepreneur to be successful.

Wilson Internet Services

http://www.wilsonweb.com/webmarket

This site links to marketing information (more than 225 online articles primarily directed toward marketing small businesses on the web). Topics include how to design a web site, how to market on the web, and marketing theory.

Appendix E

Implementation and Maintenance

To accomplish the best results from your Internet marketing strategy, you should develop an Implementation and Maintenance Schedule.

Schedule

Every Implementation and Maintenance Schedule will be different since every company's Internet marketing strategy will be different. See Figure E-1 for a sample schedule. We have provided brief explanations in the following paragraphs to help further clarify the items included in this sample.

Search Engine Submissions

You should take your list of directory and search engine submissions and divide it into four groups. Weekly, you should take one group, go to each of the directories and search engines in that group and search for your company by name and also by several key words. If you appear in the first 10 to 20 search rankings and are happy with the

Name	Weekly	Biweekly	Monthly	Bimonthly	Quarterly	Yearly
Domain Name						✓
Search engine submissions	✓					
Press release				✓		
Banner advertising			✓			
Update/rename titles			✓			
Cool sites			✓			
Check competitors					✓	
Cybermalls					✓	
Newsletter			✓			
Newsgroups	✓					
Mailing list postings		✓				
Guest book	✓					
Signature files			✓			
Mailing lists			✓			
Links		✓				
What's new	✓					
Calendar of events	✓					
Employment opportunities	✓					
Offline promotion					✓	
Tune-up					✓	
Web browser testing			✓			

Figure E.1. Implementation and Maintenance Schedule.

description, you don't have to do anything with that search engine or directory.

If, however, you do not appear or are not satisfied with the description, you should resubmit all your pages to that directory or search engine. The search engines and directories purge their databases from time to time to ensure all entries are current. The next week take the next group and go through the same process. This way you check every directory and search engine at least monthly to ensure you are still there and easily accessible.

Press Releases

Press releases should be scheduled at least bi-monthly. If you have a major announcement the press releases may be more frequent.

Banner Advertising

Check banner advertising locations of your ads. Determine the effectiveness of these ads and look for new sites for more exposure. Check prices and traffic flow of these new sites to determine how relevant they may be in increasing the traffic to your site. Adjust your banner advertising strategy accordingly.

Title Pages

Update and retitle your pages monthly unless you add a new section that requires more frequent updates (for example, Tip of the Week). Retitling your pages and updating your site is useful for two main reasons. First, spiders, crawlers, and bots are continuously visiting sites to see if there have been changes (they update their information accordingly). Second, many of your site visitors use software that lets them know when their bookmarked sites have been updated. They will only revisit your site when they know there have been changes.

Cool Sites

Submit to Cool Sites, Site of the Day, or Top 5%. In order to better your chances of becoming one, you should check on how often to apply, usually monthly.

Check of Competitors

You should regularly review your competitors' sites.

Cybermalls

Cybermalls continually change, as does everything, so do a quick check to find new malls or changes to the ones that interest you.

Newsletter

A newsletter should be scheduled monthly so you are getting your name and information in front of clients and potential clients on a regular basis.

Newsgroups

Newsgroups that you participate in should be visited every couple of days and you should try to post messages. The more often you post, particularly providing answers to queries or assistance, the more recognized and valued you are (and is your expertise). Make sure you have the sig file attached for maximum marketing effect.

Mailing Lists

There are new mail lists appearing daily. Review (and update if appropriate) those that you participate in on a monthly basis.

Guest Book

Your guest book should be checked and monitored so you can see who is visiting and what they have to say. Weekly you should copy the new contact list to the appropriate databases (e-mail lists, newsletter, etc.).

Sig Files

Keep your sig files current. Review and change them on a regular basis with new information or achievements.

Links

The more reciprocal links you can get the better. You should constantly be looking for additional, appropriate sites from which to be linked. As a minimum, you should schedule time bi-weekly to actively seek appropriate link sites.

What's New

Your What's New Page should be updated regularly, weekly if possible.

Calendar of Events

If you choose to have a calendar of events on your site, ensure that it is kept current, at least updated weekly.

Employment Opportunities

This section should also be monitored and updated weekly, deleting positions that have been filled and adding new positions as they become available.

Offline Promotion

Make sure that your offline marketing materials and your online materials are consistent (message, logos, corporate colors, etc.). Also ensure that, where appropriate, you include your URL in your offline promotion materials. This should be checked at least quarterly.

Tune-Ups

Tune-ups should be done quarterly unless changes are made to the site. One location to check is Web Site Garage at *http://www. websitegarage.com.* Here you can check spelling, browser compatibility, HTML design, link popularity, load time, and much more.

WebBrowser Testing

Test your site with the major web browsers. This should be done whenever there is a new release of Netscape or Internet Explorer. You should check monthly to determine if there have been new releases.

Index

DTD (Document Type Declaration), 36–37
dynamic pages, 48–49
Dynamic Submission 2000 Version 4, 121

E
eBags.com, 324, 338, 354
ebay, 353
e-business cards. *See* signature files
ECNow, 352
Ecola Newsstand, 419
e-commerce, 331–355
    brands and trust, 351
    customer rules, 336–337, 345, 351–352
    cybermalls, 314
    database integration, 337–338
    defined, 314, 335–336
    expectations and, 336
    features of, 336–345
    firewalls, 351
    fraud, dollars lost to, 352
    gift-wrapping, 338–339
    growth of, 331–335
    privacy issues, 332–333, 345–352
    promotions codes, 340, 341–342
    proxies, 351
    reminder services, 342
    reservations online, 3, 342–344
    security, 350–351
    shipping options, 340–341
    shopping carts, 314, 322–323, 324, 337, 338
    tracking promotions, 340, 341–342
    Web seals of assurance, 347–350
    Web trust, 345–352
Ecotourism Web Ring, 427
editors and media relations, 392–393
EEF's Extended Guide to the Internet, 174
Egghead.com, 354
eGroups, 187, 188
Electronic Commerce Modeling Language, 352–353
Electronic Commerce Resource Center, 353
Electronic Newsstand, 419
Elizabeth Arneson's list of Bed and Breakfasts, 246
Elmed Targeted Email Software, 201
e-mail, 154–174. *See also* newsgroups
    ASCII text format, 171–172
    attachments use tips, 160–161
    autoresponders (mailbots), 155, 164–165
    benefits, 155
    blind carbon copy (BCC), 157
    brochures, electronic, 166
    bulk e-mail, 157, 181, 198

    call to action, 158–159
    caps, avoiding, 156
    cost savings with, 155
    customer service using, 169–171
    downloading, 159
    emoticons, 161–162
    e-zines, 407
    folders for, 167
    formatting tips, 157–159, 168
    Frequently Asked Questions (FAQ), 166
    From heading, 156
    HyperText Markup Language (HTML) format, 171–172
    lists, developing, 166, 181
    marketing tips, 165–168
    multiple accounts, 166–167
    netiquette, 168
    newsgroups, 136
    opt-in marketing campaigns, 167–168, 181
    personalizing, 156, 165, 166, 167
    press releases, 394–395
    push technology, 463
    reply tips, 159–160, 168
    responses library, 166
    shorthand, 162–164
    signature files in, 160
    snail mail versus, 155
    speed of, 155
    subject line importance, 156
    testing, 157, 161
    To heading, 156
    viruses, 161
EmailAddresses.com, 174
E-mail Netiquette, 172
E-mail Press Release Service Comparison, 400
E-mail—The Mining Company, 174
eMarketer, 353
Emblaze, 471
emoticons, 161–162
enews.com, 334
EntertainmentBlvd.com, 476
Entrepreneurial Trend, 224–225
Epicurus Awards, 230, 235
E-Releases, 399–400
Essential Links: Portal to the Internet, 258
EStats, 331–332
Esther's Massive Signature File Collection, 153
Etext Archives, The, 419
eToys.com, 334
E-Trade, 355
European Bed and Breakfast Ring, 431

Reader Feedback Sheet

Your comments and suggestions are very important in shaping future publications. Please email us at *moreinfo@maxpress.com* or photocopy this page, jot down your thoughts, and fax it to (850) 934-9981 or mail it to:

Maximum Press

Attn: Jim Hoskins

605 Silverthorn Road

Gulf Breeze, FL 32561

_____

_____

_____

_____

_____

_____

_____

_____

_____

_____

_____

_____

_____

_____

_____

_____

_____

_____

101 Ways to Promote Your Web Site Second Edition
by Susan Sweeney, C.A.
552 pages
$29.95
ISBN: 1-885068-45-X

Marketing With E-Mail
by Shannon Kinnard
320 pages
$24.95
ISBN: 1-885068-40-9

Business-to-Business Internet Marketing, Second Edition
by Barry Silverstein
528 pages
$29.95
ISBN: 1-885068-37-8

Marketing on the Internet, Fourth Edition
by Jan Zimmerman
480 pages
$34.95
ISBN: 1-885068-36-0

Internet Marketing for Information Technology Companies
by Barry Silverstein
464 pages
$39.95
ISBN: 1-885068-46-8

Internet Marketing for Your Tourism Business
by Susan Sweeney, C.A.
592 pages
$39.95
ISBN: 1-885068-47-6

Building Intranets with Lotus Notes & Domino, 5.0, Third Edition
by Steve Krantz
320 pages
$32.95
ISBN: 1-885068-41-7

Internet Marketing for Less than $500/Year
by Marsha Yudkin
$29.95
ISBN: 1-885068-52-2

To purchase a Maximum Press book, visit your local bookstore
or call 1-800-989-6733 (US) or 1-850-934-4583 (International)
online ordering available at *www.maxpress.com*

Exploring IBM RS/6000 Computers, Ninth Edition
by Jim Hoskins
and Doug Davies
444 pages
$39.95
ISBN: 1-885068-27-1

Exploring IBM AS/400 Computers, Ninth Edition
by Jim Hoskins and Roger Dimmick
576 pages
$39.95
ISBN: 1-885068-34-4

Exploring IBM S/390 Computers, Sixth Edition
by Jim Hoskins and George Coleman
472 pages
$39.95
ISBN: 1-885068-30-1

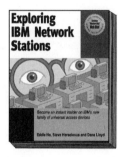

Exploring IBM Network Stations
by Eddie Ho, Dana Lloyd, and Stephanos Heracleous
223 pages
$39.95
ISBN: 1-885068-32-8

Exploring IBM Personal Computers, Tenth Edition
by Jim Hoskins and Bill Wilson
384 pages
$34.95
ISBN: 1-885068-25-5

Exploring IBM Technology, Products & Services, Third Edition
edited by Jim Hoskins
240 pages
$54.95
ISBN: 1-885068-44-1

To purchase a Maximum Press book, visit your local bookstore
or call 1-800-989-6733 (US/Canada) or 1-850-934-4583 (International)
online ordering available at *www.maxpress.com*